Procopius of Caesarea

Procopius of Caesarea

Tyranny, History, and Philosophy at the End of Antiquity

Anthony Kaldellis

PENN

University of Pennsylvania Press

Philadelphia

Published by
University of Pennsylvania Press
Philadelphia, Pennsylvania 19104–4011

Library of Congress Cataloging-in-Publication Data

Kaldellis, Anthony.
    Procopius of Caesarea : tyranny, history, and philosophy at the end of antiquity /
Anthony Kaldellis.
        p.   cm.
    ISBN: 0-8122-3787-0 (cloth : alk. paper)
    Includes bibliographical references and index.
    1. Procopius.   I. Title
DF505.7.P7 K35   2004
907.202—dc22   2003070518

For John V. A. Fine, Jr.

Contents

Acknowledgments

This book has been read at various stages by John Fine, Traianos Gagos, Ray Van Dam, Beate Dignas, Stephanos Efthymiadis, Dimitris Krallis, Kim Vogel, and Chris Lillington-Martin, all of whom I thank for their valuable suggestions. Dimitris was present at the creation on that gray day in November 1999 overlooking the Gulf of Corinth. Stephanos is probably the best philologist of Byzantine Greek I will ever know and has taught me much about the literary merits of Byzantine texts. Traianos and Ray I have thanked before and will no doubt do so again for the sound advice they have given me over the years on both personal and professional matters, as well as for sharing with me their expertise and insight. To John, who guided my first steps as a scholar, an overdue dedication. I could not have asked for an advisor more kind, generous with his time, or open-minded.

I am also grateful to Eric Halpern of the University of Pennsylvania Press for his interest in my work and for seeing it through all stages of the publication process. The anonymous reader of the Press offered a model of constructive criticism that improved especially organization and presentation. I am also grateful to my own Department of Greek and Latin and College of Humanities at the Ohio State University, which have provided for the past two years a friendly and intellectually diverse environment in which to work and funds to assist with publication.

My greatest debt always remains to my parents.

Introduction

Justinian was the last Roman emperor of ecumenical importance and the last to claim a place among the famous rulers of antiquity. After the late eleventh century, he was known to every educated man in the West as the arbiter of the Roman legal tradition. The *Corpus* was indeed the empire's last great contribution to the cultural heritage of Europe.

Yet the impact that Justinian had on his own world, from Spain to Iran, was more immediate and destructive as he sought to extend Roman authority once again to all the shores of the Mediterranean. His armies conquered North Africa and Italy, terminating the historical existence of their Vandal and Gothic overlords. Both lands, especially Italy, would lie in ruins for centuries as a result. Meanwhile, the war effort weakened imperial defenses at home. The Persians seized the opportunity to plunder Syria and destroy its metropolis Antioch, which never recovered from the combined assault of sacking, plague, and earthquake. The Arabs grew in power between the two warring empires, paving the way for their meteoric rise in the next century. The Slavs made their historical debut, plundering and settling across the Balkans, which began to slip from imperial control. Germanic federations, including the Saxons, Gepids, and Lombards, continued their restless westward trek, disrupting the fragile equilibrium established in the previous century during the great migrations. Justinian's agents and often his armies were in contact with all these peoples, influencing their movements in ways that imperial policy could not always predict. The 540s witnessed the outbreak of a plague that decimated the population of Europe and the Near East, especially along the coasts.

Important transformations were also taking place within the eastern empire. Beyond the legal compilation, Justinian issued a continuous stream of new and often contradictory laws on almost every topic, sometimes confusing even himself. He was eager to streamline the administration and impose doctrinal uniformity and did not allow tradition to get in his way. He dispensed with the aristocracy when it would not bend to his will and ruled through hand-picked agents, who were often rude, ruthless, unpopular, and, like himself, of lowly origin. The government became markedly autocratic, as was reflected in the ceremonies of the court and its ideology. A popular rebellion in the capital, backed by elements of the old order, was brutally suppressed, leaving 30,000 dead in the hippodrome. Justinian did not neglect culture either, though he did not promote it. At his imperial command, the 900-year saga of Platonic philosophy came to an end, though its high priests lingered under Persian protection. Justinian also persecuted pagans and other religious minorities. Purges purified the bureaucracy—or so it was thought. While some took their own lives, others learned dissimulation. Imperial culture became more orthodox and less classical. Book production declined. Heresy was also on Justinian's mind, too much so for the liking of many. His efforts to impose doctrinal unity finally led to the creation of an independent Monophysite Church, setting Constantinople against both Rome and the eastern provinces. At the same time there was a frenzy of imperial construction: dozens of churches and forts across the empire were ascribed to Justinian's initiative. He rebuilt Constantinople after the riots of 532, and the church that replaced Hagia Sophia still stands as the chief symbol of Byzantine Christianity.

History seemed to accelerate during Justinian's reign, and many believed that the result was chaos and upheaval. Few emperors had started so many wars or tried to enforce cultural and religious uniformity with such zeal. There had been despots before, but few, or none, had made despotism a matter of legal principle. This is important, for Justinian was anything but unprincipled. Few rulers had ever been as eager to provide ideological justification for their policies. In his edicts Justinian buttressed everything from his wars to his regulation of the price of vegetables with divine authority. He was constantly musing about how his reign fit into God's plan and expected total ideological conformity from all writers linked to the court. In the words of one legal historian, Justinian was "conscious of living in the age of Justinian."[1] Perhaps he hoped in this way to shape posterity's view of him.

It was not to be. Most of the history of the sixth century, and much of what is summarized above about the reign, we know chiefly through the words of another, the historian Procopius of Caesarea in Palestine. The age does not lack literary sources or dissidents critical of the regime, but the works of Procopius proved the most popular and influential, both at the time of their publication and afterward. In part this is because they present a comprehensive picture, treating wars, the ethnography of foreign nations, court scandal, economic and administrative reforms, and architectural innovations. The range of competence reflected here is impressive. Procopius' description of Hagia Sophia is technically precise, his account of the plague was composed with an eye for medical detail, and his narrative of the Nika riots is gripping from a literary point of view. By themselves these passages would testify to his versatility. But in his case, versatility has become an ambiguous virtue. As Edward Gibbon noted, Procopius "successively composed the *history*, the *panegyric*, and the *satire* of his own times."[2] This made him unique among ancient historians and notorious in the eyes of modern scholars.

The *Secret History*, finished around 551 but never published by its author, who feared for his life, contains a vicious attack on Justinian and every aspect of his regime. Its tendency to exaggerate rhetorically cannot be denied, but its basis in fact has not been successfully impugned. The *Secret History* shatters the façade of consensus and benevolence presented by Justinian and his spokesmen by confirming the worst that cynics can imagine about the motives and behavior of emperors and their officials. The image of the regime never recovered after the publication of this treatise in the early seventeenth century. The *Buildings*, on the other hand, written sometime in the 550s, endorses Justinian's ideology of Christian rule, paying special attention to the construction or repair of churches, fortifications, and other public works. It is difficult to avoid the conclusion that the author of the *Secret History* was insincere when he wrote the *Buildings*, and it is possible that he wrote it under pressure. If the first text offers a rare glimpse into a dissident mind of late antiquity, the second shows how that mind responded to the constraints of imperial orthodoxy. Tyrannies always require displays of conformity, with seemingly schizophrenic results.[3] These two works allow us to study the Janus-like relationship of dissent and orthodoxy in the sixth century.

Yet the fame of Procopius rests primarily and justly on his narrative of the wars of Justinian. Seven books described events to 551—the year in which the *Secret History* was finished—and a supplement written two years later covered the events of 552. The *Wars* ranks among the most expertly written histories to have survived from antiquity and Byzantium. Its author was an eyewitness to much that he described, for he traveled along the eastern frontier, to North Africa, Italy, and the capital, in the service of Belisarius, the most celebrated general of the age. His work had to narrate simultaneous warfare on at least four fronts and, to the degree that it was safe, relate those wars to events at court. Procopius was up to the challenge. His informants had traveled throughout the world, and he knew how to scrutinize sources carefully and organize his wide-ranging material coherently. If his narrative is sometimes sketchy when his sources were few or unreliable, it can be gripping when he had a front-row seat or was himself present on the stage of history. His prose is simple and direct and, if read aloud, its rhythm is often pleasing to the Greek ear. But there were moments when prudence cautioned obscurity or circumstance called for eloquence.

Procopius' cultural views were firmly rooted in the classics. He prized above all what he called "liberal education" and men of "liberal character" and watched with sadness as both were destroyed by a corrupt regime whose values did not stem from classical culture. He denounced Justinian's ideological persecution of dissidents and religious minorities and dismissed Christian theology as an "insanely stupid" attempt to investigate the nature of an unknowable entity.[4] Such skeptical attitudes were less rare among the educated classes of the sixth-century empire than is usually assumed. But more important for the purposes of the present study is Procopius' intimate familiarity with classical literature, especially with his models Herodotus and Thucydides. He was also a careful reader of Plato, whose political philosophy deeply affected how he wrote history. It is therefore no surprise to find that Procopius had close links to the non-Christian Neoplatonists of his time, though in contrast to them he was skeptical about the possibility of metaphysical knowledge and seems not to have believed in divine providence. All these claims will occasion controversy, and we will return to them again. Yet no one disputes that Procopius at least tried to write history in the classical style or that he is the single most important source for his age. He was among the first authors to offer contemporary evidence about Anglo-Saxon Britain and pre-Viking Norway, where he was eager to travel though never had the chance.[5] He preserves crucial information about many of the peoples who were changing the landscape of Europe and the Near East, from Frankish Gaul to Yemen and the steppes of central Asia.

And yet, despite the abundance of information in his work, Procopius was no mere compiler. Relying on the canons of historiography, he tried to make sense of his rapidly changing world, relating the behavior of groups to their underlying values. He was generally tolerant and inquisitive about the customs of foreign groups—more so than any of his contemporaries—and interpreted his material in such a way as to both instruct and entertain his readers. Though modern historians will find much with which to quarrel, on the whole the result is a success. No one who reads the *Wars* can dismiss it casually. It was acclaimed an instant classic in its author's lifetime, and soon writers could be found who aspired to imitate him; praised his learning, eloquence, and wisdom; and corrected him with diffidence.[6] "I neither have nor desire another guide than Procopius," wrote Gibbon, "whose eye contemplated the image, and whose ear collected the reports, of the memorable events of his own time."[7]

The existence of such a guide has had predictable effects on general surveys of the age of Justinian. Many paraphrase the *Wars* and *Secret History*, often failing to include information contained in other sources relevant to the same events. Even historical novels, written in many languages, have a distinctively Procopian feel. Yet among scholars esteem for Procopius has lessened of late. Studies issuing mostly from Britain have impugned his judgment, denied his learning and even his mental competence, and cast him as a proponent of state repression and Christian theocracy. His classicism, it is said, was only superficial affectation, for at heart he belonged to the surrounding culture of churches, holy men, and relics, however much he may have tried to hide that fact from himself and his readers. He was an average thinker—there being no other in those times—and had not yet come to grips with the implications of his Christian beliefs. In other words, in emulating the classics he was out of touch with his own self. If his testimony has not been convicted of serious error, his flaws are rather mediocrity in analysis, limited vocabulary, irrelevant anecdotes, and vapid speeches. This view is now dominant and is expressed in many recent publications.

The present study takes issue with the current consensus, though the uncritical use of Procopius as a factual source will also be questioned, even if not for the reasons alleged by his critics. What both approaches lack is sensitivity to the literary dimension of ancient historiography. There is a point to speeches, anecdotes, elevated language, and allusions, beyond the degree to which they can be reduced to facts. Both those who rely on Procopius' testimony uncritically and those who see him as out of touch with his world dismiss much of what he wrote as "rhetoric." But in doing so they tacitly admit that their aim is not to understand his work on its own terms. What does it tell us about his methods that whole passages of the *Wars* are lifted verbatim from Plato's *Republic*? Equally important, what does it tell us about current methods that this has not yet been seen? Academic specialization has played a role here. Procopius' modern readers are usually social, military, or art historians who seem to have limited familiarity with the literary side of ancient historiography and almost no knowledge of philosophy. But Procopius indicated his fundamental allegiance to those two traditions through both the form and the content of his works. To ignore this is like trying to read Augustine without knowing Scripture.

Procopius must be restored to his proper context. This means that we must understand classical historiography on its own terms by paying careful attention to precisely those literary aspects that make it so different from modern conceptions of how history should be written. For instance, it was for a good reason that so many ancient historians renounced poetic invention in their prefaces.[8] That could only have happened in the presence of temptation or precedent. Modern historians do not feel the need to make such disclaimers because their poetic impulses have been checked by long years of graduate training. When we pick up a modern monograph, we know exactly what to expect: an introduction, perhaps with a "theoretical" discussion, thematic chapters with footnotes citing sources, and a bibliography. Also, we know the kind of research that went into its making and the kinds of conclusions it aims to establish (generally factual, relating to historical causation or cultural analysis). Yet ancient texts reflect a different set of priorities, methods, and goals; in particular, a greater acceptance of techniques that today are regarded as more appropriate to literature than to history.

Considerable controversy surrounds the discussion of the rhetorical aspects of historical narratives. There is a widespread apprehension that such inquiries imply that those narratives are *nothing other* than works of literature, that they have no basis in fact and are essentially equivalent to fiction.[9] One might label this reaction hyperbolic were it not for the immense influence exerted during the past few decades by theories that assert just that. Hostile to the very concepts of truth and reality, postmodernist theorists have argued very polemically that history is fundamentally a form of fiction. By drawing attention to the many similarities between historical and literary texts, they have affirmed that historians, like novelists, essentially invent the content of their works, except that they labor under the illusion that they are also describing a truth that is independent of their creative efforts.

Though I do not believe that this epistemology has merit,[10] I also do not think that we are entitled to ignore the literary dimension of historiography. Granted, there is a difference between fact and fiction, and historians have a duty to seek the truth. Yet ancient historians knew that the truth can be presented in literary form and that different truths can be told about the same event. They also knew that facts by themselves are meaningless, even if they are true; what matters are the ideas and interpretations that are built on them, for these constitute historical insight. Thucydides used a variety of dramatic devices taken from tragedy to fuse fact and interpretation.[11] Other ancient historians actually invented material, or at least substantially recreated it, in order to reveal deeper or general truths. Livy and Tacitus shaped, possibly invented, but certainly tampered with the facts in order to make indirect points about the age in which they lived.[12] We need not discuss here the thorny issue of the degree to which Herodotus invented the stories that grace his *Histories*. Suffice it to say that general introductions now admit that his work can be read intelligently, his meanings discovered and deciphered, without any regard for factual veracity. This is merely to say that the *Histories* can be read as literature.[13] At the end of the ancient tradition, Procopius tells stories that he deems "not altogether unworthy of trust," though he admits they are factually unreliable.[14] It is incumbent on us to explain what he found worthwhile in fictional stories.

While postmodernists forget the difference between creating and recreating, positivist approaches miss the importance of literary creativity. Aristotle also took too narrow a view of history when he compared it unfavorably to poetry, arguing that "the one relates actual events, the other the kinds of things that might occur. Consequently, poetry is more philosophical and more elevated than history, because poetry relates more of the universal, while history relates particulars."[15] Though he was referring to Herodotus, possibly the most inventive ancient historian, Aristotle failed to recognize the degree to which history is also *poiesis* and thus the degree to which it can be philosophical. It is in any case naive for scholars to subject ancient authors to a positivist analysis that aims to do nothing more than separate fact from falsehood by identifying biases and removing distortions. This approach is quite inadequate for authors of the caliber of Thucydides, and even when applied to his imitators it yields only shallow misunderstandings. Too much Byzantine scholarship has taken this path.

A more fruitful approach is proposed by Socrates in the *Phaedrus*, a dialogue that subjects rhetoric to philosophical criticism and gives insight into the practices of reading and writing. Asking "in what way is it beautiful to speak and to write" (259e), Socrates sets out the principle of "logographic necessity," according to which "every speech, just like an animal, must be put together to have a certain body of its own, so as to be neither headless nor footless but to have middle parts and end parts, written suitably to each other and to the whole" (264c). In discourses of this kind nothing is redundant, not a single word. Everything exists for a reason and is so articulated as to serve specific functions within the whole. Speech thus acquires the organic unity of a living animal. To understand such a creature, one must grasp the "necessity" that calls it into being and determines the shape of each of its parts and then relate those parts to the activity of the whole. This principle formulates metaphorically modern notions about what it means to interpret literary texts,[16] and there is evidence to suggest that it became part of theorizing about history in antiquity and shaped the way in which historians actually wrote, though some undoubtedly did so better than others. Diodorus of Sicily, for instance, whose history was well known to Procopius and his contemporaries, stated that "the genre of history is simple and self-consistent and as a whole is like a living organism. If it is mangled, it is stripped of its living charm" (20.1.5). The same comparison had already been made by Polybius (1.4.7–8), another author who was read in late antiquity.

The discussion in the *Phaedrus* is meant to illustrate how Plato wrote his own "speeches," the dialogues, and how they ought to be understood.[17] Yet can a work of history be written in this way, constrained as it is to relate events that have already happened, that the historian cannot control, and that may not necessarily fit into an organic whole? Philosophers are usually not interested in specific historical facts and enjoy greater control over the shape and content of their writings. Plato never claimed to be writing a factual account of the life of Socrates and even deliberately flouted chronology to make philosophical points on occasion.[18] Yet, even granting the constraint imposed on historians by the nature of their subject, when we consider the range of interpretations that they may place upon their material through organization and arrangement, choice of language, selection and omission, implication and nuance, rhetorical strategies, or the indirect messages they may convey through speeches, anecdotes, and allusions, the principle of logographic necessity may justifiably be brought into play in interpreting their works as well. "Just as fictional objects and events owe their identity to the multiple aspects, descriptive and evaluative, through which they are presented, so too real objects make their appearance in works of fiction, not through a fully extensional presentation, but only under some set of aspects or other."[19]

The same holds true for real objects and events that appear in works of history. For example, no one doubts that the Sicilian expedition really happened, and only narrow specialists are interested in the military details for their own sake.[20] The important questions are why it occurred, what broader political developments it was linked to, why it failed, and whether it could have succeeded under the command of Alcibiades. Thucydides' suggestions about these issues structure his narrative and determine his choice of words at every point, but they are *nowhere* formulated explicitly. Procopius, it will be argued, was a careful reader of Thucydides and, contrary to what is commonly believed, copied more than just his vocabulary.

How might this approach work in practice? When reading ancient historians of proven intelligence and literary skill, certainly those who were first-rate thinkers, for example Thucydides and Xenophon, but also those who placed philosophy at the heart of their thought, for example Polybius and Procopius, we must not confine our analysis to the level of accuracy, bias, and ideology. Of each we must of course ask Is he accurate? and What were his sources?, but also Why does he tell this story here, especially when it is not obviously relevant to the sequence of events? Why does he tell it in this way, using these words? What purpose does it serve? What themes hold his work together so that it is not merely a chronological assemblage of bits of information? We must understand the general reasons behind specific choices, the dialectical relation between the parts and the whole.[21] Here, for example, are some questions about Procopius that will be asked for the first time in this study: Why does he sometimes refer to the Persian king Chosroes by his patronymic ("the son of Cavades") and sometimes not? Why does he use language taken from the liturgy or ecclesiastical architecture when discussing Justinian and Theodora? Why is his account of the trial of the Persian nobleman Seoses lifted almost entirely from accounts of the trial of Socrates?

These questions may at first sight seem trivial, and those who have failed to ask them may be tempted to dismiss them in this way. But closer inspection reveals that they are indeed perplexing. If we cannot answer these questions, we cannot claim to understand Procopius' authorial strategy, and this in turn undermines our use of the *Wars* as a historical source, for these details point toward the deeper concerns that unify his work and shape it on many levels.

It is worth looking more closely at Thucydides here, both because he was Procopius' model and because scholarship on him has provided models for my own research into Procopius. Discussion of Thucydides has traditionally been more focused on the history that he records, the rise and fall of the Athenian empire, and has treated the historian as a source of information who stands between us and those events. Thucydides himself used Homer in this way when he tried to reconstruct the distant past of Greece. Disregarding the poetic qualities of the *Iliad*, or suspecting them as sources of distortion, Thucydides counted the vessels and men in the Catalogue of

Ships (1.10); this was the extent of his Homeric exegesis. Likewise, modern historians study Thucydides' literary techniques, personality, possible biases, and limitations in order to understand how personal factors may have shaped his view of events. The goal here is to remove the man from the work. He is studied chiefly in order to be circumvented, however much he may be admired.

But what if this kind of investigation should prove inconclusive by revealing that the personality of Thucydides cannot be so easily extracted from his narrative? What if personal factors go well beyond a simple bias against an individual politician such as Cleon or a disregard for economic policies such as the Megarian Decree? Such particular distortions and limitations can in theory be identified, and the narrative can be corrected to reflect a less personal view of events. And much scholarship does proceed according to such optimistic and, in the case of Thucydides, at least, simplistic assumptions. It is in fact doubtful whether any such biases exist in Thucydides, and they are often postulated by scholars whose own ideological priorities are easier to discern. The problem posed by Thucydides does not concern particular, localized distortions but is rather the possibility that every aspect of his text, from the level of individual passages to its overall structure, is indelibly shaped by his pedagogical intentions and literary methods. The mind of Thucydides is reflected everywhere in his work. It is a grid that binds the whole together on every level, giving it shape and meaning. It affects decisions about what to include, about the language appropriate to each situation, and about the structure and aims of the narrative. And what if, to push the matter further, Thucydides' political analysis is ultimately so profound that it takes a philosopher of the first rank, such as, say, Thomas Hobbes, to fully understand it?

At this point, research into the Peloponnesian War itself may be put on hold, perhaps indefinitely, superseded by the study of its historian. The greatest of Thucydides' living interpreters, Jacqueline de Romilly, has labored for decades to expose the complexity of his narrative and the care with which it was composed. Tying her analysis initially to a traditional topic—*Thucydide et l'impérialisme athénien*—she soon abandoned historical questions altogether. *Histoire et raison chez Thucydide* is a close literary reading of the text that exposes the careful deployment of vocabulary, the deliberate omissions, the subtle correspondences between seemingly unrelated passages, the structure of individual episodes, and the purpose they serve within the overall context of the work; in short, how literary techniques create impressions and even convey the historian's main ideas, though only to the most careful readers. This point needs emphasis: Romilly insists that Thucydides, like virtually all other classical authors, never presents his deepest ideas directly and explicitly. He "hides" them everywhere in his work yet nowhere in particular. They are known only to those who can detect hidden thoughts behind the language. The "history" of the Peloponnesian War recedes further and further. There is not a single phrase in Thucydides that is not complicit in his interpretive design. There is no pure, uncontaminated factual reporting, just as there are no biases, prejudices, or ideology. This conclusion is not a trivial one. It cannot be applied to just any author. According to Nietzsche, Thucydides unconditionally refused to deceive himself about anything. Yet "one must follow him line by line and read no less clearly between the lines: there are few thinkers who say so much between the lines."[22]

Where does this leave the study of the Peloponnesian War? Well, perhaps that topic no longer seems as interesting as it did at the outset. It is possible to fall so completely in love with the mind of Thucydides—as seems to have happened to Romilly—that it now becomes the chief object of inquiry. Put bluntly, Thucydides is more interesting than the Peloponnesian War. From this point of view, the war is studied only insofar as it casts light on its historian. The hierarchy of objectives has been reversed. Here everything external to the text, even the history it describes, is subordinated to the understanding of the author's intentions and strategies.

Historical inquiry thus leads to literary analysis. Scholars have examined how Thucydides manipulates his readers' reactions and expectations through the use of sharp breaks, shifts in perspective, gradual reversals of roles, withholding crucial information until moments of greatest impact, and the use of paradigmatic instances in place of constant repetition.[23] These are not "merely literary" aspects of the text that the modern historian can set aside in producing a "purified" narrative. It is only through this approach that Thucydides' main themes emerge, around which he has structured every aspect of his text. We see the Athenians become a naval people to defeat the Persians, then establish an empire and threaten the freedom of Syracuse, which in turn becomes a naval city to repel the new Persians. We witness the growth of imperial ambition, the exposition of its internal logic, and its downfall as it turns in on itself. What is more important, we learn about two views of justice, that of Athens and that of Sparta, and their consequences for political communities and their neighbors.

Much of this can also be found in Procopius, who, as we will see, had studied Thucydides as carefully as any of the scholars discussed above and applied what he had learned to the composition of his own work. Procopius actually reproduced what we are only now beginning to understand in Thucydides. This indicates a careful study of his classical models. Procopius' alleged "limited vocabulary" is also a Thucydidean strategy: it enables readers to track the distribution of key concepts and appreciate subtle connections and changes.

Procopius learned from many others who wrote in the millennium that lay between him and ancient Athens. From Herodotus he learned how to use anecdotes to make general points and how ethnography can be used to discuss one's own culture indirectly. Anecdotes are of special interest precisely because they are foreign to modern historical methods. Ancient authors, including Procopius, are criticized for them. This reaction misses their purpose, in large part because it applies modern notions of factual truth to ancient texts, which often subordinate the facts to a broader conception of "truth," one that can paradoxically be truer than the facts. Consider the following example. At no point in history did Pontius Pilatus allow the Jews to choose between Jesus and the armed "robber" known as Barabbas. The story was made up, probably by the evangelist known as Mark. From his standpoint after the great Jewish revolt, it was entirely true to say that the Jews chose the armed resistance of Barabbas over Jesus' way of peace, but this "choice" was made on a far larger scale than could be captured by any single episode. A false story contains a deeper truth, one moreover that historians cannot dispute.[24] To worry about its lack of historicity is to miss its underlying point. There are many such stories in Procopius. As has been noted, sometimes "historiography is concerned with a larger, typical truth that overrides the facts in specific cases."[25]

An additional device used by many ancient writers is the literary allusion. As will be argued throughout this book, this was not "affectation" but a central aspect of the way many authors constructed and presented their meanings. These cannot be deciphered unless the reader establishes a dialogue between the two texts. I will give an example from Plato's *Republic*. The reason for this choice (and for the choice of the New Testament above) is that in these texts we observe how literary devices can serve broader religious or philosophical aims, such as I believe that Procopius also had. To be sure, his aims were not as profound as those of Plato or Mark, but he took certain liberties with history that are not altogether different from those taken by the authors of the deeds and sayings of Socrates and Jesus, who were, after all, historical individuals. Plato's Socrates is traditionally considered a foe of democracy, and a passage always adduced in support of this position is his sequence of regimes in Book 8 of the *Republic*, which places democracy fourth, only one step above tyranny. Yet few have noted that Socrates explicitly bases his sequence on that of the ages of man in Hesiod: golden, silver, bronze, heroic, and iron.[26] Democracy corresponds to the age of heroes, a startling conclusion. This does not of course mean that Plato's heroes were the same as those of Athens, but his hero was a product of Athens and Plato knew it. It is therefore not a coincidence that he makes Socrates say that all philosophical politics must begin in a democracy. This suggests a more nuanced view than the traditional view would allow (to say the least), though we have to follow a literary allusion to see it. There are very many such allusions in Procopius, chosen carefully and not merely for literary pretension.

Rarely have the strategies discussed above been applied to the historians of late antiquity, and the approach proposed here may strike some scholars as counterintuitive and misguided. Byzantinists in particular tend to treat historical narratives as nothing more than "sources" and subordinate them to the imperatives of social, military, or political history. The purpose of "source-studies" is to pave the way for additional historical research. This attitude stems in no small part from the very low opinion Byzantinists have of the works they study, a problem that will be confronted below. The literary ambitions of Byzantine authors are often treated with contempt and regarded as little more than distortions that only hinder the search for historical truth. Such attitudes essentially preclude the very possibility of intellectual history and result in profound misunderstandings of the sources on which modern, allegedly purified, reconstructions are based. Yet there are signs that attitudes are slowly changing.[27] One scholar has even gone so far as to wonder whether Procopius has been read at all in modern times, by this referring not to the text itself but to its comprehension.[28]

We come then to the basic questions that will be asked in this study. What was Procopius' relation to his classical models? Chapter 1 reexamines the problem of classicism. The dominant consensus holds that it was largely a matter of vocabulary, an artificial affectation that ultimately blinded Procopius to the realities of his own age. In contrast, it will be argued here that Procopius learned far more from his models than has been suspected, including the sequence of exposition and the characterization of protagonists through the contrast between speech and action. More important, it will be shown that through literary allusions Procopius makes his classical sources complicit in his own strategies of meaning and that unless we examine them in tandem we will miss the point of his own work. Also, it is in part through a network of carefully chosen and locally varied allusions that Procopius establishes a relationship among his three works.

Why does the main narrative of the *Wars* begin with a series of anecdotes of almost no historical value? Chapter 2 seeks to rehabilitate the use of anecdotes by looking at the most notorious sequence of them in the *Wars*. It will be argued that they are not merely silly and entertaining digressions (from a narrative that has not yet begun!) but actually lay out the fundamental parameters of the history that follows. Reports of omens also work in the same way later in the narrative.

Why are whole chapters of the *Wars* lifted from Plato's *Republic*? Chapter 3 will restore the centrality of Platonic political philosophy to the historical thought of Procopius by exposing the many passages of the *Wars* that are directly modeled on Plato's dialogues, often through extensive quotation. Connections will be discovered between Procopius and the non-Christian Platonists of his own day. Their fear of the regime of Justinian is reflected in the *Wars*, as is their strategy for avoiding its grasp, a strategy that Procopius both followed and recommended when he wrote the *Secret History*. This Platonic mimesis will add an entirely new level to the classicism of late-antique authors, taking the problem to the most fundamental level of their thought.

How did Procopius represent the regime of Justinian? Chapter 4 will argue that there is considerable continuity between the *Wars* and the *Secret History* and that the negative portrayal of the regime in the latter text "seeps" into the former. The Persian king Chosroes is something of a surrogate for Justinian in the *Wars*, in accordance with the general parallel that Procopius establishes between the later Roman empire and classical ideas of oriental despotism. This chapter also takes a close look at the *Secret History* itself, which is not a random collection of accusations. It is instead a carefully written literary work, and part of it contains the first extant commentary on the laws of Justinian. It also argues that Procopius' classical education did not sufficiently prepare him (though nothing could) for the kind of tyranny represented by Justinian, which was rooted in metaphysics, ascetic in practice, and bureaucratic in logic. This explains the shrill tone of the *Secret History* and its ultimate failure to understand the regime.

Why does Procopius talk about *tyche*, that is, amoral chance, on some occasions and about God on others? Chapter 5 will take a fresh look at one of the most controversial questions about Procopius: what are we to make of his baffling view of divine things? Contrary to the consensus that holds that he was a conventional Christian who became confused by reading too many classical authors, it will be argued here that Procopius makes many statements that cannot reasonably be ascribed to a Christian, if due allowance is made for the fact that he lived in an age of persecution, which he more than any of his contemporaries abhorred and decried. The main flaw with prior treatments of his views about God and *tyche* is that they have never examined those passages in the context of his narrative as a whole. When this is done, it emerges that Procopius modulates his vocabulary carefully with an eye to the particular situation and the overall impression he wants to convey in each of the *Wars*. It will be shown that he did not believe in a providential deity, but rather in a battle between human virtue and amoral chance in which the latter tended to prevail.

This study does not offer a history of Justinian's wars or even a historical commentary on the *Wars*. Rather, it asks a question prior to both of those tasks: how should Procopius be read? This is emphatically a historiographical study. Yet his works fill many hundreds of pages, and a general study covering most major themes would inevitably result in superficiality. It is the details that interest us here, and I have chosen to focus on details that are dismissed with impatience, such as anecdotes, or never discussed, such as philosophy. Military, social, and cultural historians will be cautioned and admonished and given new guidelines for the use of these texts. I have tried to identify Procopius' classical models and examine his use of them while taking into account recent studies of those models. Much has no doubt escaped my attention on both counts, as I lack the depth of his classical learning and my academic specialization has taken its toll. Also, given the recent growth of interest in the sixth century and the fact that Procopius is a major source for almost every aspect of it, it has proven impossible to cover all the bibliography. I have made an effort to identify the most insightful and up-to-date discussions (and it has been gratifying to see how often those two coincide). I have tried to be as thorough as possible with scholarship dealing with Procopius as a historian, though no doubt much has escaped me.

This study will situate Procopius in his immediate historical context as well as in his transhistorical literary context. Classicism was, after all, a way of talking about the present by using ancient paradigms whose store of accumulated meaning could be modulated to respond to new circumstances. A new evaluation of intellectual life in the age of Justinian is in order. Writing before the very end of antiquity, Procopius and his fellow travelers represented the last flowering of classical thought in an empire that was abandoning classical models. At least we can say that in following those models Procopius left behind some of his own. This brings us back to Thucydides, his ancient imitators, and his modern students.

Thomas Hobbes was not primarily interested in the Peloponnesian War when he decided to translate Thucydides, "the most politic historiographer that ever writ." Hobbes believed that "a man of understanding . . . may from the narrations draw out lessons to himself, and of himself be able to trace the drifts and counsels of the actors to their seat."[29] Conversely, "the narration itself doth secretly instruct the reader, and more effectually than can possibly be done by precept."[30] Those lessons were timeless, as Thucydides himself had predicted, because they were based on the constancy of human nature. In this way, he rose above the particular event that he chose to narrate. Hobbes and others, for example Romilly, studied Greek history in order to understand Thucydides. From this point of view, the only reality reflected in the text worthy of study is the clarity, dignity, and humanity of Thucydides himself.

Chapter 1
Classicism and Its Discontents

The Preface of the *Wars*

"Procopius of Caesarea composed a record of the wars which Justinian, the emperor of the Romans, waged against the barbarians of the east and of the west." The first sentence of the *Wars* announces its author and his theme and does so by imitating the first sentences of Thucydides and, to a lesser degree, of Herodotus. This form of mimicry was by no means original. In the second century A.D., the satirist Lucian of Samosata had complained that many historians of his time tried to imitate the great founders of classical historiography in this very way, hoping to appropriate for themselves the hallowed prestige of the classics. An acerbic and unforgiving critic, Lucian castigated them for superficial affectation. "Crepereius Calpurnianus the Pompeiopolitan composed the history of the war between the Parthians and the Romans." Such introductions constituted crimes against good taste. Yet we must also admit that they were the inevitable product of the undisputed and stifling authority of classical texts. There simply were no alternative models. In the end, even Lucian could only encourage future historians to model themselves on Thucydides, albeit in a more thoughtful and tasteful manner. His response to bad imitation was better imitation.[1] But the dearth of grand themes made the imitation of great historians as shallow as it was inevitable.

In the age of Justinian, four centuries later, those models no longer held sway unchallenged. Competing conceptions of historiography had developed and even gained popularity. The universal chronicle evolved to meet the needs of those who desired concise summaries of world history that highlighted the importance of Christianity within the course of creation. By the time Procopius finished the *Wars*, John Malalas had released the first edition of his chronicle, covering events from creation to the reign of Justinian. Marcellinus, who had worked on that emperor's staff, had twice updated the chronicle of Jerome, itself a translation and continuation of that of Eusebius.² The triumph of the Church was likewise accompanied by the rise of ecclesiastical history. Its founder Eusebius conceived it explicitly in opposition to the themes of politics and war. Others, he says derisively, have written of victories and trophies and endless slaughter; he will instead commemorate the peaceful wars of the spirit and document the triumph of universal piety over local chauvinism.³ His successors knew that they belonged to a tradition that did not trace back directly to Herodotus and Thucydides, though they admitted that they had to deal increasingly with secular events.⁴

So the first line of the *Wars* does more than simply announce its author's name and theme. It acts as a declaration of allegiance to a specific cultural tradition amid viable competing alternatives. Procopius intends to adhere to the canons of classical historiography and compose a narrative in the high style that tackles the eternal themes of politics and warfare. Just as modern historians use introductions to explain their subject matter and method and situate themselves within broader philosophical debates, their ancient counterparts used prefaces to create a niche for themselves within the broader tradition of classical historiography and reveal their political and pedagogic aims.⁵ The entirety of the preface to the *Wars* is riddled with allusions to Thucydides, Herodotus, and other classical texts, notably Homer. This places constraints upon us, his modern interpreters. Before we attempt to situate him within his specific historical context, we must first make an effort to view him as he viewed himself, namely within the transhistorical context of classical historiography. His dialogue with Thucydides takes priority over his possible links to John Malalas. In this chapter, therefore, I will discuss Procopius' complex relationship to his classical models. As we will see, it was not a straightforward relationship of imitation, for circumstances forced Procopius to adopt an ironic stance toward both his models and his subject matter.

We should note first that Procopius' laconic introduction elegantly captures a crucial difference between his theme and those of his models. Whereas Herodotus declared his intention to record the great deeds of both the Greeks and the Persians, who are presented in his first sentence as equal contenders for fame; and Thucydides chose to write about the war between the Peloponnesians and the Athenians, who were equally guilty for the war, Procopius' theme lacks balance. It concerns the wars waged by one man, Justinian, against the barbarians of both the east and the west.⁶ Justinian is situated at the center of events, both geographically and in terms of the logic of the narrative. He gets all the praise or blame, as the case may be.

He is the equivalent of a nation in Herodotus and a *polis* in Thucydides. Procopius has formatted the standard prologue-form to the unique requirements of his own narrative. We are reminded of the way Thucydides' own first sentence both recalls and distances itself from that of Herodotus.[7]

Alluding next to Herodotus, Procopius states that his purpose is to rescue momentous events from the oblivion of time,[8] for memory of them may be useful both to his own contemporaries and to future generations, who may find themselves in similar circumstances (1.1.1). His narrative will benefit those who are at war as well as those "who are engaged in any kind of contest" by showing what the outcome was for those who planned their actions well (1.1.2).[9] The *Wars* therefore was written for posterity. It was designed to be both comprehensible and useful to future generations. This means that Procopius based his narrative and lessons on the fundamental nature of man, which, at least according to Thucydides, transcends the particulars of time and place. It also requires that his text be comprehensible to future readers. That is why it was written in a language that had survived the test of time in the past and could therefore be relied upon to do so in the future. This is, of course, the language of classical literature. In other words, the very purpose of the *Wars* depends upon the timelessness of human nature and the continuity of language. These might be taken at first sight to be the two pillars of Procopius' "classicism." And human nature is perhaps best understood through a study of classical literature, linking the two together. It is therefore not surprising to discover that throughout his work he is fascinated, and irked, by the changes that are constantly occurring in the names of places and things and in the meaning of words. The psychological explanations that he offers for these changes again draw upon his classical models, notably Thucydides.[10]

It is also worth forming a preliminary notion of the pedagogical aims of the *Wars*. Procopius' claim that the work will benefit those who are at war seems to associate him with Polybius, who filled his *History* with tactical advice for generals and statesmen, and distance him somewhat from Thucydides, whose primary aim was to improve his readers' "understanding."[11] But war, as we will see, was not the only arena in which Procopius intended the *Wars* to be useful. And he does refer vaguely to those "who are engaged in any kind of contest."

Be that as it may, Procopius next states his qualifications as a historian (firsthand witness, advisor to the most important general of the age);[12] draws the customary distinction among rhetoric, poetry, and history (only the last aims at truth);[13] and asserts that his own testimony will be impartial

(1.1.3–5). Yet he emphasizes that this impartiality will chiefly involve the blame of close associates, perhaps of the general whom he has just now mentioned. He will not disguise their "wretched" deeds (μοχθηρά). The truth expounded in the *Wars* by the man who also wrote the *Secret History* of the reign of Justinian will consist mainly of blame. This contrasts strongly to his most moralistic predecessor, Polybius, and his immediate successor, Agathias, who emphasized that the praise of virtue can inspire future generations to emulate great deeds. In their view, truth was not primarily about blameworthy actions.[14] Perhaps Procopius could find no models of virtue in contemporary history, and perhaps Belisarius was not the primary target of criticism in the *Wars*. Let us note that at the beginning of the *Secret History*, a work that he wrote at the same time, Procopius declares that he will reveal first the wretched deeds (μοχθηρά) of Belisarius and then the wretched deeds of Justinian and Theodora (1.10). It is no accident that this word is used in the programmatic statements that introduce both works.[15] This establishes a pattern of resonance that recurs throughout the two works. We must also remember that both Justinian and Belisarius were still alive when the *Wars* was completed. In contrast to Procopius, for instance, Agathias deliberately wrote about those who were dead. He could criticize Justinian with relative freedom.[16]

Alluding now again to Thucydides, Procopius makes the bold claim that the events recounted in the *Wars* are the greatest and mightiest in all of history. They are more "amazing" than anything else of which we have knowledge. This boast, however, is subsequently qualified and potentially deflated: "assuming that the reader of this work does not give the prize to ancient times, in the belief that current events are unworthy of amazement" (1.1.6–7). Most Greek historians, especially those to whom Procopius alludes in his preface, unequivocally asserted the greatness of their own themes in a deliberate attempt to surpass their predecessors.[17] Procopius is following in this tradition, although, as we will see, with an ironic intention. He was the first to even suggest the possibility that ancient wars were greater and modern ones "unworthy of amazement." Herodotus, for instance, deliberately presented the army of Xerxes in such a way as to make it surpass the Achaean expedition against Troy, whose forces are listed in the second book of the *Iliad*. Thucydides, Procopius' chief model in this section of the preface, was the first to produce a rigorous comparison between the ancients and the moderns in order to support his contention that the Peloponnesian War was greater than all wars of the past, both in the heroic age (i.e., Homer) and in recent history (i.e., Herodotus). Thucydides gave ample justification for his bold claim, by tracing and explaining the growth of power in Greece from pre-Homeric times to his own day. Polybius also made a cogent argument for assigning an even greater importance to the conquest of the world by the Roman republic, an event that had no equal in scale, swiftness, novelty, or duration.[18]

Let us pause and consider the many legitimate points that Procopius could have made in defense of the importance of the wars of Justinian: warfare on all three continents against warlike enemies;[19] the reconquest of extensive territory, perhaps more than was ever taken by the Romans in the same amount of time; spectacular victories; the capture of enemy kings; tens of thousands of men mobilized and killed by war and plague; and many cities captured and destroyed. In his legislation, Justinian exulted in the military accomplishments of his reign and expected writers close to the court to broadcast his triumphal boasts. John Lydus, a civil servant and antiquarian, wrote that the emperor had asked him to deliver a panegyric on his reign and "write the history of the war that he had successfully conducted against the Persians."[20] In the *Buildings*, a panegyrical work catering to similar needs, Procopius praised the conquest of new territories and the subjugation of barbarians.[21] In the *Secret History*, he likewise expanded upon the momentous effects of Justinian's wars, though from a negative point of view, by stressing the destruction they caused to both the conquered regions and to the Roman empire itself. Justinian "caused calamities for the Romans, so great and so numerous as had never been heard of previously by anyone in the entire history of the world."[22] Despite its pessimism, this statement still affirms the greatness of the historian's theme in the traditional agonistic manner. Obviously, Procopius could not express those views openly in the preface to the *Wars*. Yet he offers there no serious justification for his Thucydidean boast, whether panegyrical, vituperative, or just plain descriptive. Not one of the emperor's boasts is confirmed in the preface.[23] The historian seems to be rejecting imperial propaganda passively, through silence. He even suggests, through some imaginary naysayers, whom he seems to have invented for this purpose, that antiquity was greater after all.

Procopius fails to defend the greatness of his theme in any way comparable to Thucydides and Polybius, who argued the point with the utmost seriousness and methodological rigor. Instead, he reduces the comparison between ancients and moderns to a bizarre contest between Homeric archers and the cavalry of the sixth century. This contest, incidentally, aims to defend the latter from ridicule rather than establish its greatness. The levity of the comparison trivializes the alleged greatness of Justinian's wars. In addition, the defense of modern archery contains fatal logical flaws, which one might label obvious were it not for the fact that they have not yet been noticed.

There are some, Procopius claims (1.1.8), who assert that modern soldiers are mere archers, whereas ancient soldiers were true hand-to-hand warriors whose valor no longer survives. These devotees of antiquity, who in this respect followed classical Greek models,[24] apparently did not think very highly of archers. To refute their position properly, Procopius must either defend archery itself or argue that modern soldiers, whether archers or not, are equal to the hand-to-hand fighters of antiquity. But he does neither, and this is to say nothing about whether a contest of archers can by itself establish the greatness of Justinian's wars. Procopius begins by denigrating Homeric archery (1.1.9–11), which only strengthens the position of his imaginary opponents. He then contrasts the weakness of Homeric archers to the mounted and armored archers of the sixth century, to the latter's obvious advantage (1.1.12–15). The argument is, of course, inconclusive, as he almost admits afterward. For in order to counter the position of the defenders of antiquity, he must show not only that modern soldiers are better than the most despised element of the Homeric armies but that they are equal or comparable to its highest glories, namely to Achilles and the other heroes. This he does not even attempt to do. The Homeric age was great because of its heroes, but heroes are absent from Procopius' preface. This is why he admits, at the end of his comparison, that despite his arguments and the greatness of Justinian's wars, some will still revere antiquity and think poorly of modern times (1.1.16). This is more a tacit admission of the weakness of his claim than resignation in the face of the irrational tenacity of the reverence for antiquity. By restating the view that favors the ancients as completely unaffected by his arguments, he hints that he has done little to diminish its credibility. Nothing in the age of Justinian can match the glory of the Homeric heroes. An age may be redeemed or ennobled by a great leader, as Plutarch thought of the democracy led by Pericles, but this possibility is also not even hinted at by Procopius. In the *Buildings*, he would describe a statue erected in the capital depicting Justinian in the "heroic" guise of Achilles.[25] Again, such flights of imperial fancy find no support in the preface to the *Wars*.

Unfortunately, many scholars have been deceived by the hollow fanfare of the preface into thinking that Procopius genuinely admired mounted archers. They fail to appreciate the inconclusive and ironic nature of the preface, and they also fail to compare what he says there to what actually happens in the remainder of his narrative. This is not unrelated to the refusal to read historical texts in any but the most literal ways. I will argue in a separate study that far from admiring mounted archers, Procopius was highly troubled by their prominence in sixth-century warfare and expressed nostalgic admiration for the infantry armies of ancient Rome. Mounted archers represented to him yet another aspect of the empire's gradual barbarization. But only a critical examination of his entire text can reveal the rhetorical purpose that is served by their presence in the preface.

As for the archers of the *Iliad*, Procopius has unfairly underestimated their effectiveness in order to lower the standard that modern soldiers must meet for his argument to have prima facie plausibility. Given that he cites many specific passages of the *Iliad* as evidence and that he probably knew that work as well as anyone else, we are entitled to scrutinize his representation of Homeric archers. He claims that the word "archer" was an insult but does not mention that it was used in such a way by Diomedes, whose wounding by Paris had just removed him from the fight. Frustrated, Diomedes expresses the view neither of the other warriors nor of the poet himself, and his abuse is aimed specifically against the effeminate Paris, not archers in general.[26] Procopius unfairly ascribes Paris' cowardly attributes to all archers.[27] Hand-to-hand fighters were honored more, yet "archery was a crucial factor in the Trojan War."[28] At least two gods and a number of lesser heroes are presented as archers.[29] Procopius wrongly claims that they played no role on the battlefield and could not inflict serious injuries. In reality, bows were used in battle by whole contingents as well as by individual heroes and could kill or incapacitate individual warriors just as they could turn the tide of battle. Procopius fails to mention these events and hides the fact that many heroes survived arrow wounds only through direct divine intervention.[30]

To summarize. Procopius mentions none of the factors that could validate his claim for the greatness of Justinian's wars. He compares them only to the Trojan War and even then avoids comparing modern archers to the heroes of Homer. Moreover, he fails to convince us that the archers of Justinian were unquestionably superior to those depicted in the *Iliad*. It has been suggested, with justice, that this is a mockery of the classical tradition, and the "proof" that Procopius adduces for the importance of his theme has been viewed as woefully inadequate even by those who do not perceive its levity.[31] The contest of archers satirizes Thucydides' rigorous *Archaiologia* and Polybius' grand arguments for universal history. The mockery, however, is probably aimed not at the tradition itself but at the pretentious ideology that surrounded Justinian's wars. Procopius was no fool. When he offers us palpably bad arguments for the claim that those wars were the greatest in history, we may suspect that he is directing our attention to the very weakness of that position, a position, moreover, that he could not very well refute openly. It was through pointed omissions that ancient authors tended to "emphasize" their ideas, however counterintuitive that may seem to us.[32] Procopius' fatuous contest of archers subtly exploits the literary devices of the tradition to deflate the emperor's achievements and deprive them of the glory that only a work of classical historiography could bestow.

A Typology of Classicism

Yet perhaps the foregoing analysis is premature. We have initiated a dialogue between Procopius and his classical models without first determining their precise relationship. Procopius was a subject of the later Roman empire and a product of its intellectual trends, yet by constructing his preface around classical allusions he seems to position himself within the broader context of classical historiography. His theme is contemporary, yet as a historian he intends to stand above or to the side of his age, reporting on it as would another Thucydides. But can we take this stance at face value? How deep was his knowledge of classical literature? Varying degrees of engagement can be imagined. Perhaps he was an attentive student of classical texts, especially of Thucydides, which would have granted him a critical perspective on the postclassical realities of the sixth century. On the other hand, it is possible that his classicism was merely literary affectation and that he knew classical texts only from anthologies and his rhetorical training. His classicism would then be a mask of high culture beneath which hid a typical man of his age, that is, Christian, superstitious, and theocratic, according to the prevailing view of this period. This second alternative is the one that scholars now overwhelmingly favor. Upon this question hinges our entire understanding of Procopius as a historian and, by extension, of the sixth century in the transition between antiquity and Byzantium. The problem of Procopius *is* the problem of classicism.

It is customary, when discussing the classicizing historians of the later empire, to cite Lucian's famous treatise on *How History Should Be Written*. The only one of its kind surviving from antiquity, this level-headed and amusing little book laments the general decline in standards among historians. Written toward the end of the century that began with Tacitus and Plutarch, it stands midway between them and Herodian. It already condemns the classical affectation, shallow pomp, and corrupt Greek style for which scholars continue to blame Byzantine literature.

At the very end of his treatise, Lucian alludes to certain aspects of ancient historiography that are in danger of being forgotten today. These we may call artistic, in the sense that Lucian intends when he compares historians to architects. Like architects, historians can craft works that contain multiple and overlapping levels of meaning, give false initial impressions, and conceal their secrets from casual observers. The following story that he tells about the lighthouse of Alexandria, the ignored conclusion of his otherwise often-cited text, proves that despite the banalities proffered elsewhere in his treatise, Lucian had an eye for the subtlety and esoteric qualities of ancient writing.

Do you know what the Cnidian architect did? He built the tower on the Pharus, the greatest and most beautiful of all works, that a beacon might shine out from it to sailors far out at sea, lest they be driven on to Paraetonia, which they say is an extremely difficult coast and impossible to get away from once you have hit upon the reefs. So, having built this work, he inscribed his own name on the masonry inside, and, having plastered it over with gypsum and hidden it, inscribed upon it the name of the reigning king, knowing, as indeed happened, that a short time afterwards the letters would fall away with the plaster and the following would be revealed: "Sostratus of Cnidus, the son of Dexiphanes, to the Savior Gods on behalf of those who sail at sea." Thus, he too did not have his eye on the immediate moment or his own brief life-span, but rather on our time and on eternity, for as long as the tower shall stand and his art (*techne*) shall abide.[33]

The lighthouse of Alexandria was one of the wonders of the ancient world, but Lucian does not explain exactly how this story is relevant to the writing of history. Clearly, historians should write for posterity and eschew the allure of immediate celebrity. But this does not account for Sostratus' deceit or for the multilayered nature of his work. Perhaps authors too can hide things in their texts, away from the gaze of kings. In time, these hidden truths can be safely discovered by future readers or by those who know how to look past the "plaster" that lies on the surface. Like the lighthouse of Alexandria, a work of history may be designed with two different audiences in mind.

It is interesting that Lucian rounds off his discussion of Sostratus' esotericism by combining two famous classical allusions that few of his readers would have missed. By joining the famous Hippocratic saying that "life is short, but art (*techne*) is long" to Thucydides' ambition to produce "a possession for eternity," Lucian suggests that historians can confer immortality upon their works if they treat their practice as an "art" or "science" like medicine. This involves adhering to certain rules, like those laid down in his own treatise or exemplified by canonical authors such as Thucydides.

No one went farther in pursuit of this goal than Procopius of Caesarea, though there is considerable room for disagreement about the extent to which even he succeeded. Procopius and his successor Agathias exemplify what is today called classicizing historiography. This term designates a class of historical texts produced during the later Roman empire that share certain literary features. It also implies that their authors were not fully classical but only attempted or pretended to be so. Their goal was imitation, not the development of a new kind of historical narrative, one perhaps more suited to the changed realities of their own times. They recognized a higher standard that was created in the past and aspired to recreate it in a postclassical world. Procopius and Agathias lived in a Christian empire full of churches, monks, and theological disputes but wrote as though they lived in classical Athens. They used the language of Thucydides and Demosthenes, not the spoken Greek of their own time, and often copied phrases verbatim into their narratives from their classical models. They avoided nonclassical words as though they were foreign and strange, particularly Christian ones. And, like most ancient historians, they focused on wars and politics. Ethnographic digressions such as those in Herodotus and grand speeches such as those in Thucydides were also standard features of classicizing historiography.

This style of writing has elicited little but disapproval and apprehension from modern scholars. The first reaction was one of suspicion. In the nineteenth century, German philologists realized that classicizing historians such as Procopius lifted words and phrases directly from their classical models, thereby possibly distorting or even inventing the history they were describing. Procopius clearly modeled contemporary events on passages in Thucydides. For example, an extensive network of verbal correspondences makes his account of the sixth-century plague suspiciously similar to Thucydides' account of the plague in Athens. By the late nineteenth century, it seemed as though the details of that event, along with the details of certain sieges, which Procopius modeled on the siege of Plataea in Thucydides, might vanish from the history books in a puff of Teutonic source-criticism.

Classicism was not just a matter of style; the factual content itself was perceived to have been contaminated. As Lucian said of shallow imitators of Thucydides, one could leave them "and still know exactly what they were going to say next," because they were more interested in literary affectation than factual reporting.[34] Yet these fears proved to be misplaced. The historicity of the events in question has been confirmed through the independent testimony of nonclassicizing sources. Procopius' accounts have also been shown to differ in crucial ways from those of his classical models, despite the undeniable verbal borrowings. It is now common practice to defend the accuracy of his account of the plague and the sieges and even to assert the compatibility of verbal imitation with factual reliability.[35]

Since then the interpretive problems associated with classicism have tended to become increasingly more trivial, focusing exclusively on matters of vocabulary. In the mid to late 1960s, scholarly attention focused on the peculiar circumlocutions by which Procopius and Agathias referred to Christian subjects and Roman administrative terms. For example, Procopius referred awkwardly to monks as "the most temperate among the Christians, whom they usually call monks." And, when describing the church of Hagia Sophia, Agathias wrote not "dome" but "that circle or hemisphere or whatever else they call it that projects on top in the middle."[36] Previously scholars believed that this "objective" way of referring to Christianity indicated that these authors were probably unbelievers, but recent examinations have shown that this form of expression was an integral part of the imitation of classical literature and does not necessarily have any bearing on religious belief. Classicizing authors pretended that nothing had changed since the days of Thucydides and so had to explain neologisms to their readers. Even Christian authors wrote in this way, for example the seventh-century historian Theophylact. Classicism is now seen as mere "affectation." It was "just a stylistic device."[37]

Since classicism no longer poses interesting challenges, whether historical or religious, it has become a dead issue. It is generally assumed that the problem has been laid to rest simply because a few odd circumlocutions have been assigned from the sphere of religion to that of style.[38] Classicism is now treated as merely a matter of style, and bad style at that, as an affected attempt to reproduce a "high" form of literature. One commonly reads statements such as "Procopius' classical mask is purely literary," and these are always made in connection with his vocabulary and awkward circumlocutions.[39] In fact, many recent discussions imply that classicism was a matter only of words and phrases.[40] This view, as we will see, barely scratches the surface of the problem, but the consensus that has developed around it has had a stifling effect on discussion. Furthermore, relegating the whole matter to the realm of style has made it easier for Byzantine scholars to indulge the bizarre contempt they feel for Byzantine literature. Classicizing historians, we are told, were "undoubtedly more interested in artistic packaging than factual content," and that packaging is invariably "distasteful to modern readers."[41]

A more promising approach was suggested by Averil Cameron in her study of Procopius, a lucid and influential monograph that is, sadly, fraught with fundamental contradictions. Cameron correctly notes that classicism "goes much deeper than the superficial adoption of vocabulary," all the way down to the author's very "modes of thought." Consequently "there is no separation between his thought and its expression. . . . The understanding of the classicism of Procopius is not a simple matter of peeling off an external layer." And because classicism is not merely a stylistic device, it must be part of any discussion of the historian's opinions.[42] Unfortunately, these laudable programmatic statements prove to be a false start. The book's actual thesis is that Procopius was a typical "product of his age" whose fundamental beliefs owed nothing to classical thought.[43] His classicism was a "superstructure," whereas his "underlying approach" was thoroughly Christian.[44] So thought and expression are radically separated after all. The "seductively classical appearance" constitutes only "the surface of Procopius' work," a mere "classical tinge."[45] And as for classicism shaping "modes of thought," that seems to mean nothing more than that Procopius followed Thucydides in writing a narrative with speeches and battles. Imitation gave the "external characteristics" of his work merely a "Thucydidean look."[46] This is only a modern restatement of Lucian's complaint of superficial imitation.

Cameron's insight that content cannot be understood apart from form must be preserved, even if she did not follow through with it. *What* Procopius has to say is inseparable from *how* he says it. Classicism goes well beyond the level of words and phrases, of "tinges" and "external characteristics." Opportunities for new discoveries are being missed here through sheer prejudice. One could, for instance, examine the narrative structure of these texts. I am referring to the way in which writers such as Procopius shaped factual information and the techniques by which they interpreted it without crudely interjecting their own personal opinions. It is these devices that give narratives a literary dimension by creating expectations, manipulating reactions, and leading readers to a deeper understanding of events.

Consider, for example, speech-and-battle sequences, a staple of both classical and classicizing historiography. Jacqueline de Romilly has carefully dissected the structure of such episodes in Thucydides, demonstrating that speeches delivered before battles debate the same points in perfect correspondence and use the same language, only from opposite points of view. The ensuing battle is then narrated in such a way as to reveal which of the two commanders had a better grasp of the situation prior to the engagement. It is only through the speeches that the reader can actually understand what happens during the battle and why. This includes the motivation, planning, and tactics of both sides as well as the outcome. Ideally, not a single word is wasted—recall Plato's principle of "logographic necessity." Romilly chose as her principal example the naval battle of 429 near Naupactus.[47] The commanders on both sides had to address dispirited soldiers in need of encouragement, and Thucydides mentions this fact before each of their speeches. However, we need not discuss this specific passage, because a passage of Procopius' *Wars* shows exactly the same narratological features.

In 534, the Roman general Solomon brought his troops against the Moors at a place called Mammes (4.11). The commanders on both sides had to address soldiers who were dispirited and in need of encouragement, and Procopius mentions this fact before each of their speeches. He uses the same words on each occasion, and they are also exactly the same words with which Thucydides describes the low morale of both sides before Naupactus.[48] This allusion serves to establish a correspondence between his text and that of Thucydides, a correspondence on which Procopius will follow through. He did not choose to quote the Athenian historian here for reasons of "affectation" or because he allegedly found the phrase in some putative anthology of Thucydidean clichés. As we will see, the entire structure of his account of the battle is Thucydidean through and through.

In his speech, Solomon reminds his troops of their victory over the Vandals, who, in turn, had defeated the Moors in the past (23–24). He disparages the enemy's equipment: their armor is shabby and they flee after throwing their spears (25–27). So if the Romans withstand the first attack, they will easily rout the enemy (28), for they are better trained and more experienced, whereas the Moors trust in numbers, and preparation almost always prevails over numbers (30–32). The camels should not be feared, because missiles will drive them back (33). And the Moors' resolve will collapse, because it is based on a false sense of victory that does not reflect their actual strength (34–35). Finally, Solomon urges his troops to observe silence and good order (36), repeating exactly the orders issued by the Athenian Phormio before the battle at Naupactus in Thucydides.[49]

The Moorish leaders rebut Solomon's speech point by point in reverse order. They strengthen their soldiers' resolve by mentioning their recent victories and greater numbers (38–39). They point out what Solomon had omitted, that they are fighting for freedom because "necessity" impels them to resist "slavery" (40–41). They disparage Roman equipment and tactics: if the Romans advance on foot, they will be defeated by Moorish speed, whereas their horses will be terrified by the camels (42). The Roman defeat of the Vandals proves nothing: not only had the Moors also defeated the Vandals in the past, but the outcome of war depends on either chance (*tyche*) or the general's virtue, and Belisarius, the general who defeated the Vandals, is absent (43–45).

The account of the ensuing battle consists largely of phrases taken from the speeches, as the latter are proven alternately prescient or mistaken by the actual course of events. The Roman horses were thrown into disorder (*akosmia*) by the camels (48), just as the Moors had predicted (42), frustrating Solomon's call for an orderly deployment (*kosmos*: 36). The Moors advanced and threw their spears (49), just as Solomon had predicted they would (27). Thinking quickly, Solomon bid his troops to dismount and hold their ground behind their shields (50–51). He knew, of course, that Roman arms could withstand Moorish weapons (29). Taking some of his men on foot, he killed the camels and routed the Moors (51–53). Just as he had predicted, the Romans could defeat the Moors easily if they could just withstand the initial assault (27–28).

The predictions and strategies formulated by the commanders on either side are put to the test during the course of the battle. The Moors were correct that the camels would throw the Roman cavalry into confusion, and Solomon's claim that missiles would drive them back came to nothing. But ultimately the Roman had the better grasp on the situation, knowing that arms and discipline would prevail if only the Romans could stand their ground during the initial confusion. What no one could predict was that the Romans would win by dismounting and fighting on foot, but this strategy is attributable to the same general's genius. In the thick of battle, he devised a way to counter the disadvantages of his army (the horses) and stake the outcome on its advantages. So the Moors were correct that the battle would be won by either chance (*tyche*) or the general's virtue. *Tyche* is accordingly never mentioned during the battle.

It is only because of the speeches that the reader can understand the course of the battle. The narrative by itself is a bare factual summary that proves nothing. We can learn from it what happened but not why. For this we need plans, intentions, and analysis. That analysis is not offered by the historian in his own voice. He allows the protagonists to debate all the important factors, inviting readers to draw their own conclusions from the interplay between speeches and event. This authorial strategy is entirely Thucydidean.[50] Again, hardly a word is wasted in the close correspondence between the two speeches. They examine in turn the same factors and even debate the significance of previous battles, only from opposite points of view. This gives us a global perspective on the whole event, "for the issue of battles is usually decided in the minds of the opposing commanders, not in the bodies of their men."[51]

Furthermore, it would make little sense to imagine this rhetorical debate as historical. The Moors must have known what Solomon had said in order to reply to his arguments, but how could they have? Should we imagine them nearby, listening and replying? But given that they do in fact *reply* to Solomon, they must be addressing the same audience. That (implied) audience is of course Procopius' readers, not either (or both) of the armies. The two speakers, qua speakers, are not historical persons. They are literary vehicles of military analysis, antithetical and therefore dynamic. No such speeches were delivered before the battle of Mammes. They are only texts, and they are intended for our benefit. To dismiss them as nothing more than "lengthy set speeches" that merely "expand" the encounter is unfair and misses the point.[52] Such dismissals *take for granted* the effect produced on the reader by the subtle interplay of speech and action and therefore never make it into an object of conscious reflection.

There is a close correspondence in the *Wars* between speech and action. As in so many passages of Thucydides, military instructions are executed in exactly the same language in which they are issued. The more foresighted the plan, the closer the verbal resemblance between conception and execution.[53] This tight correspondence, manufactured at the level of the text by the historian, reveals the natural connection between plan and action. It contains implicit verdicts about prescience and efficiency, which may well be negative: events may not go according to plan. To grasp these verdicts, however, we must read the text carefully, comparing speeches with deeds, and not only on the level of individual passages. Themes may recur and develop across whole books of the *Wars*. Like Thucydides, Procopius says relatively little in his own voice.

The Gothic king Vittigis delivers two long and striking speeches at the beginning of his reign, after the capture of Naples by Belisarius in late 536. In the first speech (5.11.12–25), he claims that victory depends on planning and not on rash action. He emphasizes patience and preparation and even urges the Goths to accept the shameful label of cowards should a prudent retreat secure victory in the long run. "For the virtue of a man is not revealed by his actions at their beginning, but rather at their very end." The Goths accordingly marched from Rome to Ravenna, where they began preparing for war (5.11.26–28). In his second speech (5.13.17–25), Vittigis gives more advice that is "necessary," if not "pleasant." The Goths must make peace with the Franks in order to free up the troops stationed on their northern frontier. To do so, they must surrender southern Gaul and pay the Franks for an alliance. Vittigis calculates that this small sacrifice will preserve the Gothic realm in the long run; without it, the whole might be lost forever.

Just as Vittigis invites us to compare the beginning of his reign to its end, Procopius invites us to compare the king's speeches to his actions. The two grow increasingly divergent, as this seemingly cautious and far-sighted Periclean strategist gradually loses his control over the war.[54] He begins to waver and change his mind in anger (5.16.19–21). He fails to take adequate precautions, causing severe losses to his side (5.27). By the end of his reign, he has become indecisive and very ineffective at making the necessary preparations. Patience has turned into inaction. Unable to deal with the situation, he barricades himself in Ravenna, callously abandoning his followers in other cities to starve in false expectation of imminent assistance.[55] Procopius does not directly comment on the king's failure. His authorial stance is ostensibly neutral. But Vittigis' speeches present a program of action and an implicit standard by which we must judge him. The speeches are invented by Procopius and are designed to capture the king's *intention*. It is up to us to follow through on the expectations they create and come to a better understanding of his reign. We may therefore not dismiss the speeches in the *Wars* as "pure rhetoric," as so many of Procopius' critics have done.

The influence of Thucydidean techniques on the narrative goes well beyond the use of speeches. Consider choices regarding the distribution of information. In general, the narrative proceeds chronologically, but the historian is not constrained to relate events at precisely the moment they occur. That would prove quite unworkable and would defeat the guiding logic, resulting in incoherence or triviality. Each part of the text is structured around a certain theater of operations and is told from a certain point of view. External developments that affect the main story or necessary background information are introduced at the point of highest relevance, not in chronological order. Chronology is subordinated to the internal logic of the text, sometimes even to the author's dramatic goals. This makes it easier for us to follow the narrative without having to remember odd bits of information that do not become operative until much later. It also relieves the author from having to repeat himself and enables him to clarify causal relationships as directly as possible.

For example, Procopius does not tell us that Belisarius had fortified the Milvian bridge outside Rome until the Gothic army reached it (5.17.14). Belisarius fortified the bridge precisely because he expected the Goths to attempt to cross it. Procopius reports this not when the strategy was conceived and implemented but when it became operative in the conflict. Had the Goths taken a different route, we might never have heard about this garrison. Procopius then explains that the general did not hope to prevent the Goths from reaching Rome but rather wanted to buy time for the reinforcements that had been sent by the emperor. This is the first that we hear of these troops. Belisarius apparently already knew about them, but we do not until it impinges on the narrative. We hear about the garrison only because the Goths reached the bridge, and we hear about the reinforcements only because Procopius must explain the garrison.

The fact that the Byzantines controlled the seas during the first siege of Rome is mentioned only toward the end, when Procopius must explain why the Gothic garrison at Portus had exhausted its provisions and was forced to abandon it along with other coastal cities (6.7.16–20). The information is mentioned only when it acquires explanatory value, otherwise it would not have contributed to the story and would have been, strictly speaking, irrelevant. Conversely, we do not learn that the Goths had a navy (or had built one) until it blockaded Rome and caused a famine while Totila was besieging the city in 546 (7.13.5–7).

This strategy of delayed information is also used by Thucydides, usually to create contrasts or cause readers to reconsider the significance of earlier events.[56] These same literary devices are used extensively in the *Wars*, as we will have occasion to note in the subsequent thematic analysis. The point to observe here is that the entire structure of the text may be classicizing in ways that have so far remained invisible and that go beyond the imitation of classical vocabulary. Procopius picked up from Thucydides narrative strategies that engage the reader's active participation in the unfolding of events. He was not a shallow classicizer but a classical writer of the first order. This requires emphasis. Whereas we are now only *discovering* the literary techniques of classical historians, Procopius actually *reproduced* them, and, we might add, with considerable success. Far from the affectation dismissed by so many, we find here an element of genuine style, something that is "intuitively appreciated, a performance that, if done well, need not be talked about."[57] But we must talk about it if we are ever to get beyond the surface, for any account of the heart of things must account for their appearance on the surface, the starting point of every inquiry.

So far we have considered the formal imitation of classical texts, focusing on literary devices that Procopius may indeed have learned from Thucydides but whose efficacy is ultimately not based on classical provenance and that do not require the reader to directly compare the two texts. Recent scholarship, however, has begun to consider the possibility that the relationship between them runs deeper, that it is perhaps impossible to grasp the central political and historical theses of a classicizing work of history unless one is equally well versed in its classical models. What is being proposed here is an artful strategy of indirect reference that relates contemporary individuals and events to classical paradigms through the use of subtle allusions. Verbal imitations may serve a deeper purpose after all: they alert careful readers to specific passages in classical texts that contain missing premises, suggest unflattering parallels, or supply an entire framework of analysis for the events being described.

This contrived interplay between narrative and classical model can provide anything from a benign or heuristic comparison to an allusion that actually subverts the claims made on the surface. Examples can be offered from all points on this spectrum. For instance, extensive verbal and structural correspondences link Procopius' account of the first siege of Rome to Thucydides' account of the siege of Syracuse. Again, this case of imitation does not invalidate the factual basis of the narrative. More interesting, however, is the implied invitation to the reader to contrast the two accounts and draw conclusions about the importance of various aspects of the siege and the role of specific individuals. Belisarius, for instance, is compared favorably, though indirectly, to Nicias: his proud letter to the emperor is a "conscious reversal" of Nicias' pathetic letter to the Athenians.[58] Likewise, the recall of Belisarius from Italy in 540 and the disastrous policies of his replacements are linked to Thucydides' eulogy of Pericles and condemnation of his successors, who brought defeat and ruin to Athens. This passage is not without serious, albeit implicit, criticism of Justinian.[59] The same is true of the beginning of the *Vandal War*, where the emperor's decision to attack the Vandals is carefully modeled in structure and language on Xerxes' decision to attack Greece in Herodotus. This is a damning comparison, though visible only to readers who know the source.[60] As we will see, the comparison of Justinian to various barbarian despots is a central aspect of Procopius' political thought. Later in the same text, as Belisarius marches across Libya preaching liberation to the inhabitants and justice to his soldiers, Procopius contrives a parallel to Brasidas' campaigns in northern Greece, which reveals the cynicism and opportunism of imperial policy and the plight of the locals, who were forcibly involved in a struggle that strained their loyalties. Procopius intended that the motives and actions of his own characters be evaluated against the Thucydidean backdrop, to which he alludes through carefully chosen quotations.[61]

Individual cases of allusive intertextuality in Procopius have been detected and analyzed with clarity and insight, especially by Italian scholars, whose works have been somewhat excluded from the discussion, though, to be fair, they are not the most accessible. More important, such individual discussions have not become part of a systematized discourse about classicism. There is no doubt that the Byzantines enjoyed crafting and detecting allusions to classical authors, and "as a rule the author was not designated by name, for this was at best inferred from the allusion."[62] Yet Byzantine authors rarely commented on each other's books, which makes it very difficult for us to know how they read each other and hence how they could expect to be read themselves.[63] A recent book has demonstrated the great extent to which they shaped their own works around classical allusions, a practice insufficiently appreciated by modern textual editors. This work demolishes the naive notion that Byzantine texts can somehow be read "on their own terms" without constant reference to their classical models.[64] Other fields in classical studies, for example Latin poetry, have focused on the problem of intertextuality, for which they have developed sophisticated analytical tools.[65] But the study of Byzantine literature, which is still trapped within nineteenth-century paradigms, has barely recognized the nature of the problem. Few are willing to engage in the dialogue that allusions establish between classicizing authors and their models, possibly because such sustained comparisons can potentially challenge entrenched notions about the limitations of intellectual life in Byzantium. Though the same practices are freely ascribed to ecclesiastical authors using biblical texts, they are rarely subversive in those cases, tending in fact to reinforce the conservative assumptions of scholarly interpretation. Yet recent work has demonstrated that authors such as Procopius made esoteric allusions to works of classical literature and even used them to disguise, dissemble, or add nuance to their own positions.

Classical allusions could be used to completely subvert the surface of a text whenever authors wanted to express opinions that for various reasons could not be stated openly. Procopius' successor Agathias, a lawyer, was particularly adept at manipulating classical quotations in order to refute Christian doctrines about the soul and bolster his praise for the Platonists persecuted by Justinian.[66] Such devices could endow a narrative with two overlapping levels of meaning, as was suggested by Lucian's anecdote about the lighthouse of Alexandria. Only a few readers would see past the outer layer to the inner message that was carefully hidden from the gaze of kings. It is possible that virtually all ancient literature worth reading was written in this way. Witness how Isocrates, a master of oratory and one of the founders of the rhetorical tradition that stood at the heart of Byzantine education, describes one of his own compositions:

> those who read it casually will find it to be simple and easy to understand, but those who go through it carefully, attempting to discover what the others failed to see, will find it difficult and hard to understand, full of history and philosophy, and filled with every kind of device and falsehood, though not such as is customarily used to harm one's fellow citizens, but rather such as may playfully benefit or delight an audience.[67]

In the course of our analysis, we will find that Procopius practiced this form of esoteric rhetoric. A striking example that has already been exposed by J. A. S. Evans should suffice for now. In 532 the Nika riots in the capital nearly toppled Justinian's regime. The emperor, barricaded in the palace, was about to flee when the empress Theodora delivered a rousing oration, boldly encouraging him to fight back. According to Procopius, at the end of her speech she quoted "an old saying, that kingship (*basileia*) is a good burial shroud." Curiously, Procopius has made Theodora slightly misquote the original saying, which is reported by Isocrates, Diodorus, and Plutarch. It runs as follows: "*tyranny* is a good burial shroud." It was said by one of the companions of Dionysius, the notorious tyrant of Syracuse, when he was barricaded in his palace by a popular rebellion. Dionysius was about to flee, but in the end, like Justinian, he used mercenaries to massacre the rebels. The parallels are too close to be coincidental. Procopius has given

Theodora's speech two levels of meaning. On a superficial level, it seems as though her bold speech saved the regime. Readers who know their classical history, however, in particular the narrative of Diodorus, are treated to an implicit comparison of Justinian to one of the most brutal tyrants in history. Even though Procopius painted Justinian as a murderous tyrant in his *Secret History*, he could not make that comparison in a public work such as the *Wars*. But he could still mine the latter with ambiguous allusions. The fact that the esoteric message of Theodora's speech tallies perfectly with the way in which Procopius presents the empress in the *Secret History* supports the validity of Evans' interpretation.[68] It is inconceivable that he was trying to present a positive picture of Theodora, whom he despised more than any other person.

There is considerable resistance among some scholars to the idea of double-edged remarks, for what is at stake is the presumed transparency of ancient sources and their susceptibility to traditional philological techniques, which prefer the safety of the surface to risky esoteric readings.[69] It is important to understand exactly what Procopius has done here, by reconstructing his strategy. In recounting the Nika riots, he was stuck by their similarity to the mass revolt of the Syracusans against the tyrant Dionysius. The opportunity to make a comparison was too good to pass up and there were a number of ways to do it. But quoting verbatim from Diodorus' account would probably not do the trick. Though in the sixth century Diodorus' preface was well known and copied by many, including Procopius and Agathias, it is unlikely that even readers with a solid classical education would easily recognize an allusion to Book 14 of his history. But Procopius was blessed in that the event had generated a famous saying that had been reported by a number of ancient authors and could easily be linked to its original context. All he had to do was work that saying into his account of the riots, but the problem was that it included a reference to tyranny and could not be used in its original form. This, however, was more of an opportunity than a drawback, because changing a well-known saying could quietly draw attention to the sleight of hand. That is why he makes Theodora very pointedly declare that the last line of her speech was "an old saying."

Literary classicism involves far more than just style and narrative structure and goes to the heart of Procopius' historical and political thought. As stated earlier, the problem of Procopius *is* the problem of classicism. Our aim, however, should not be to compile lists of verbal borrowings. We must try to understand the complex and playful relationship that exists between the historian and his models, to "consider what use the thinker in question had actually made of his sources."[70] Sensitivity to those classical models will enable us to perceive the humor and nuances that hide behind even some of the smallest details of his text.[71] Through the system of indirect reference that this relationship establishes, Procopius may be saying more—or less—than is explicitly stated on the surface of his text.

In general, an allusion may be deemed to be significant when the passage to which it refers has an obvious bearing on the subject matter being discussed. Skeptics may deny that such allusions were ever intended by Procopius, arguing that he used a common stock of phrases and sayings lifted from anthologies. In this case, resonance would have to be attributed to coincidence. Though I have trouble believing that this can happen more than once in a single text, my argument is in the end accumulative. Coincidence can be invoked only so many times. It is one thing if the original context of an allusion implies an esoteric interpretation of Procopius' text once or twice; it is another thing if this happens *virtually all the time*. This indicates that the quotations were not chosen at random; say, on the basis of stylistic qualities. A large number of Procopius' allusions are significant in this sense, if not almost all of them. We must decode them and translate them into modern forms of discourse, because we have lost the ability to read those texts in the direct way intended by their author. As it happens, when these allusions are brought together and studied as a group, they fall into meaningful and coherent patterns that cannot but reflect deliberate strategies. This study will focus on those strategies. One of its surprising conclusions will be that a considerable number of Procopius' allusions refer us to the dialogues of Plato, and the *Republic* in particular. The historian of Justinian's wars turns out to be a student of philosophy, and one of the inner stories of his narrative revolves around the fate of philosophy under that most Christian of imperial tyrants.

A Distorting Mirror?

One of the paradoxes of Byzantine studies is that first-rate historians and philologists spend their lives studying a body of literature they detest. This is particularly true of scholars in the British tradition, who have always valued clarity of expression and denounced obfuscation and "rhetoric." Rhetoric has always been regarded as a central aspect of Byzantine literature, which, as so many books and articles imply or directly state, was devoid of literary merit. Edward Gibbon initiated this tirade, which has by no means been put to rest.

Not a single composition of history, philosophy, or literature, has been saved from oblivion by the intrinsic beauties of style or sentiment, of original fancy, or even of successful imitation. . . . In every page our taste and reason are wounded by the choice of gigantic and obsolete words, a stiff and intricate phraseology . . . and the painful attempt to elevate themselves, to astonish the reader, and to involve a trivial meaning in the smoke of obscurity and exaggeration. Their prose is soaring to the vicious affectation of poetry: their poetry is sinking below the flatness and insipidity of prose.[72]

Though Gibbon's attack was directed against the literature produced after the mid-ninth century, his modern successors, for example R. Jenkins, have extended the charge to cover the entire Byzantine period and all forms of its literary expression.

Byzantine civilization must be characterized, from first to last, as wanting in that great gift which nature reserves for her favorites, poetic feeling and expression. . . . Byzantine letters are deficient in every single thing which, ordinarily speaking, characterizes a letter. . . . The direct influence of Herodotus and Thucydides, though avowed in all ages was superficial. . . . The paralyzing grip of Hellenistic rhetoric was a straight-jacket which held its prisoners in a state of mental retardation.[73]

These views contain implied comparisons to classical antiquity. R. Browning proposed that whereas "the classical scholar's texts are usually worth reading from some point of view, what the Byzantinist finds is so often empty rhetorical verbiage."[74]

It would be easy to dismiss such opinions by setting them down to arbitrary differences in taste. Yet the problem is more serious, for aesthetic judgments can be legitimate only after the attempt has been made to understand the works in question. The opinions quoted above are based on false beliefs; that is, they are factually wrong in ways that should not apply to informed aesthetic views. In fact, they only posture as literary criticism, because they are not based on close readings of the texts. They are really little more than impatient and superficial dismissals, based on prejudice and a distorting lack of perspective. Byzantine rhetoric was deliberately allusive, indirect, playful, and obscure, and hyperbole was often intentionally ironic. Most Byzantine authors would probably have considered it too vulgar—or too dangerous—to state the truth simply and directly. The more redundant and obscure their words, the more they were probably trying to say indirectly. At some point, differences of taste may naturally prove to be irreconcilable. But until then our goal should be to understand what our sources are trying to tell us, with sympathy and a mind open to ways of writing other than our own. D. Afinogenov's harsh rule might also be appropriate: "nobody should devote himself to serious literary analysis of Byzantine texts unless he enjoys them as pieces of art."[75] Moreover, this analysis should preferably be done without the help of modern literary theory, which actually does exemplify, if any body of writings ever did, the qualities decried by Gibbon and Jenkins.[76] When all is said and done, we may find that Byzantine authors were more intelligent and profound than their modern detractors and had better taste to boot.

Scorn for what is perceived to be "affectation" has marred the discussion of Procopius in recent decades. C. Mango has formulated two theses regarding classicizing authors that have shaped all subsequent discussion. Let us note that he has also endorsed Jenkins' harsh verdict on Byzantine literature and admitted to deriving no pleasure from reading it: in his view, Byzantine historians are read solely for the sake of the "information" they may contain. Using Procopius and Agathias as examples of "highbrow" literature, Mango compares their works to "distorting mirrors" and "antique masks" that fail to give a "true reflection" of their own age. They lack "flavor" and omit "the business of everyday life." Their circumlocutions for Christian terms are again touted as a central component, if not the essence, of their classicism.[77] In addition, their classical mask was only a disguise, a "mock façade" for a reality that was merely "dressed in theatrical costume." If we remove the disguise, we find typical Byzantine mentalities, what Mango calls "the average Byzantine's intellectual horizons." And these "can most fully be appreciated only on the basis of lowbrow literature."[78] In other words, highbrow literature is lowbrow literature in disguise. Both reflect the outlook of the "average" Byzantine, leaving no room for anything above average. So the Byzantines were either average or illiterate. The unstated assumption behind this view of their literature is that for about a millennium, learned men read and studied Homer, Demosthenes, Herodotus, and other classical authors, and were even educated on the basis of those texts, but managed not to absorb any of their ideas or values. The influence of ancient texts was confined to rhetorical forms and matters of phraseology. They smoked but never inhaled.

So classicism both distorts contemporary reality and is superficial in having nothing to do with an author's fundamental beliefs about the world. As we will see when we turn to Procopius, a tension exists between these two positions, because one can only know that an author was an "average" Byzantine if the realities of his time are somehow reflected in his work, but if they are reflected clearly one cannot make the case for distorting classicism. The stronger the former argument, the weaker the latter, and vice versa. A delicate balance must be maintained for this approach to work, but such caution is far from the realities of Byzantine scholarship. Mango provides no proof whatsoever for either of his theses regarding Procopius. His position rests on an arbitrary view of the "flavor" of the sixth century, and he makes no attempt to demonstrate the degree to which it is reflected in Procopius' works. Yet scholars have accepted his position uncritically.[79]

Both horns of the dilemma have been directed against Procopius. Again they lack mutual coherence and, in the case of the alleged distortion, supporting evidence. Averil Cameron, as we saw, has argued that beneath the classical "superstructure" of Procopius' work lay a typical Christian mind of the sixth century. At the same time, she has asserted that his entire conception of history, based as it was on classical models, prevented him from making sense of the world around him. Specifically, his "self-imposed limitations" led him

to omit altogether many of the major religious and social issues that actually determined governmental action, and to disregard, most of the time, the day-to-day impact of Christianity on the lives of the majority. . . . These limitations were not conducive to a high level of political and historical analysis. . . . Secular historiography in the classical manner could no longer be adequate for a world in which the very issues had changed.[80]

Such sweeping accusations should be supported by numerous specific examples. We expect to be told exactly *what* Procopius neglected to discuss and exactly *how* it calls his interpretation of events into question. But this never happens. The charge is merely asserted over and over again, usually on the most general level, as though it had somewhere else been proven in detail. As in the passage quoted above, we hear of Procopius' failure to "handle the Christianization of the state" and his exclusion of "ecclesiastical history." But these are very vague categories. What specific aspects of the Christianization of the state did he neglect that were relevant to his subject matter? Of course, the assertion that Procopius excludes religion from his narrative is simply false, which undermines the "distortion" argument. Anyone can see that the *Wars* is full of bishops, churches, reported miracles, and holy men. This undeniable fact leads critics such as Cameron to make concessions, for instance that Procopius excludes religion "unless it impinges on the military narrative."[81] Yet if Procopius was primarily a military historian and discussed religious issues to the degree required by his subject matter, then we must conclude that the charge of ignoring crucial evidence is unfair. Other scholars who have scrutinized specific portions of his narrative have concluded that Procopius did full justice to the importance of religious issues, for instance the role of Arianism in the wars and revolts in Libya.[82]

Procopius' critics want to have it both ways. On the one hand, they claim that his adherence to the classical tradition led him to neglect important aspects of his age, and so he failed as a historian; on the other hand, those aspects are supposedly so pervasive in his works that he can be classified as a typical (Christian) product of his own age. Thus, when it suits the first argument, the cult of the Virgin is called a "noticeable gap" in Procopius' works: it is merely "implied" in the *Buildings* and receives "no emphasis" in the other works. To support the second argument, the opinion is cited with approval *in the same book* that the cult of the Virgin is "a notable feature" of the *Buildings*.[83] Either way, a lack of emphasis on the cult of the Virgin is no more a "gap" in Procopius' works than the absence of cavalry tactics is a gap in the works of Augustine. Yet the tangle of contradictions is compounded further: the same scholar had argued previously that the cult of the Virgin did not become prominent until the *late* sixth century and had traced its popularity to developments that postdated the reign of Justinian.[84] All bases are therefore covered: the Virgin was prominent in the works of Procopius; she was not prominent; and she could not have been prominent.

Despite the frequent repetition of the accusation in general terms, only one other specific "gap" is cited, but its relevance to Procopius' work is never established and even its general significance is questionable. Cameron accuses Procopius of failing to discuss Justinian's condemnation of the Three Chapters, which she confidently places among "the real issues of the day . . . the issues that were predominant."[85] The importance of the issue is doubtful, and the claim is akin to Mango's vague reference to the "flavor" of the age. The dispute over the Three Chapters was a very marginal matter, relevant and comprehensible only to Justinian and a small group of contentious bishops, mostly Libyans. Malalas, supposed by Cameron and others to have been more in touch with "what mattered" in the sixth century, says nothing about it. The major ecclesiastical historian of the century, Evagrius, whose work reflects an Antiochene point of view, devoted a mere two pages to it (in 4.38). By contrast, Evagrius' summary of Procopian material (mostly military) runs to almost twenty chapters (4.12–29). This yields a very different view of what the "real issues" were, at least for contemporaries, who did not view wars and plagues as mere "discourse."

Cameron fails to justify her assertion about the supreme importance of the Three Chapters, nor does she prove its relevance to Procopius' narrative. She does not mention that the *Vandal War* effectively ends with the events of 546, whereas the dispute over the Three Chapters really picked up in the late 540s (and feelings ran high in the early 550s). Curiously, in a previously published article, she herself had asked: "In all the reaction to the Three Chapters controversy it is the voices of the bishops that we hear; but what about their flocks? What were their reactions?" The answer, as she admits, is that we do not know, and at least according to one religious historian, whom she cites, the majority of the Libyan population felt alienated from the leadership of their Church.[86] Yet two pages earlier she had made the claim against Procopius that the wars in Libya "were as nothing to the majority of Roman Africans compared with the threat which Justinian's policy was presenting to the integrity of their faith." Again, the reader is left uncertain about which side of this baffling logic to accept.

So, we wonder, did Procopius distort the realities of the sixth century or did he faithfully reflect them? Was he a classical historian who missed the importance of Christianity or was he only superficially classical and in all important respects a typical product of his age? Recent critics such as Cameron have argued in favor of both alternatives, which is a safe procedure, because the contradictions that result can then be laid at Procopius' doorstep. However, that leaves us in the dark. The present study will argue that *neither* alternative is correct, for they both misrepresent what it meant to be a historian writing in the classical tradition. To accuse Procopius of "disregarding the day-to-day impact of Christianity on the lives of the majority" is to miss the point entirely. Daily life was never the primary concern of classical historiography, far less that of the majority. If Procopius fails to satisfy the modern fascination with trivial information about the common man, or woman, then the same charge should be leveled against all classical historians.[87] Even so, it remains a fact that no other author gives us a better sense of the flavor of life in the sixth century. If only we look past the gripping accounts of battles and sieges, we will find that he described human life in all its variety and, unlike the theologians, did not do so in order to condemn or reform it.[88] Ecclesiastical authors, whom his critics claim were more "in touch" with the realities of the period, were rarely interested in this life at all, and the notion that abstract theological disputes "mattered more" to contemporaries than war, plague, and famine is a modern conceit. In fact, one of the most authoritative scholars of Byzantium argued in a little-read book that the average Byzantine neither knew nor cared about the teachings of the Church Fathers, who in turn cared very little for the actual existential situation of their flocks.[89] As far as the sixth century is concerned, no text offers us the variety of information that we find in the *Wars* and *Secret History*, though it must be repeated that it was not Procopius' primary aim as a historian to offer us that kind of information.

This defense too is insufficient, because it takes a very narrow view of Procopius' aims and does a terrific injustice to the profundity of classical history, which was never just "military history." As students of cultural diversity, few modern philosophers surpass Herodotus; as analysts of power and ambition, only one or two rival Thucydides. As we will see, in his mentality, Procopius was a thoroughly classical historian, and the proliferation of Christian themes in his work is part of an attempt to make sense of the way in which politics and religion intersected in the sixth century. The subject matter of a classical historian may be far broader and his techniques more subtle than Procopius' critics have imagined. John Matthews' fair and sympathetic assessment of Ammianus Marcellinus is equally applicable to the great historian of the sixth century:

Here was a writer prepared to make sense of this age in the relatively familiar terms of the classical historian, with the repertoire one was used to—high politics, conspiracies and civil war, battles and sieges, social satire and moral judgments, learned digressions, vivid portrayals of character, a multiplicity of names and places—together with much that one was not—eunuchs in politics, Germans in the high command, bishops in the cities, frank despotism and religious bigotry. Criticize as one may Ammianus' opinions and choice of emphasis, it is hard to imagine a writer more responsive to the issues and personalities of his time, and hard to think of a topic on which, however peripheral to his own preoccupations, he does not make some contribution to our understanding.[90]

The view of classicism offered here reverses the polarity of "superstructure" and "underlying mentality." As this study will argue, it was classical culture that gave shape to Procopius' fundamental objectives, outlook, and modes of expression, whereas his occasional conformity to Christian beliefs was little more than window-dressing for authorities that he could not resist otherwise, though this is not to say that religion was not an important category of his historical thought. Through careful allusions, which begin as early as the first sentence of his work, Procopius points to the tradition against which he wants to be read. But Herodotus and Thucydides, to say nothing of Plato, are entirely absent from Cameron's analysis. Instead of engaging with the classical tradition, she and many other Byzantinists anxiously downplay the importance of the classics for understanding Byzantine texts and regularly assert, against all the evidence, that the Byzantines had only a superficial knowledge of them.[91] Ignoring his fairly explicit cultural allegiances, Procopius' critics have deliberately tried to make him "less classical" by reading him against his contemporaries, regardless of whether they shared his interests and intellectual values. In other words, they integrate him into his historical context by detaching him from his transhistorical intellectual context. Not only does this prevent us from seeing him on his own terms, we run the risk of greatly misunderstanding his work.

Introducing the *Secret History* and the *Buildings*

At first glance, the most peculiar feature of Procopius' corpus is its division into three parts that reflect different outlooks on the reign of Justinian. Perhaps no other ancient author wrote a history, an invective, and a panegyric, all for the same ruler. How are we to understand the relationship between them? This must be done before any attempt is made to decipher Procopius' larger meanings, for example his political thought. Has he given any hints that might help us clarify the relationship between his works? Unfortunately, discussions of this question have paid too little attention to his own directions and have placed too much faith in modern tools of analysis such as dating, biography, and genre.

In truth there is only one Procopius, but few scholars have been willing to trust him on this. His authorial testimony, particularly regarding the *Secret History*, has too often been circumvented. This testimony is both explicit and implicit. The former consists of his direct statements on the content and purpose of each work. The latter involves a tight network of classical allusions deployed and skillfully varied to deepen the relationship among the three texts that is implied in the direct statements. The remainder of this chapter will therefore examine the following related problems: how the *Secret History* complements the *Wars* through secret "passages" that lead from one text to the other; how the *Buildings* reverses the language of the *Secret History* in such a way as to leave little doubt about their author's true views; and, finally, whether the *Buildings* is a sincere work at all. The focus here will be on the use of classical allusions and paradigms, as it has been throughout this chapter. But first it is necessary to deal with attempts to circumvent the testimony of Procopius.

Efforts to date the texts with greater precision, for instance, have led to no insight regarding how they should be read. The *Secret History* and the first edition of the *Wars* seem to have been completed around 551, shortly after the last events they describe; the supplementary Book 8 of the *Wars* was finished a few years afterward, probably in 554; and the *Buildings* was composed probably in the middle years of that decade. So far, attempts to date the texts with greater precision have yielded no facts of any relevance to their interpretation, so it does not matter for our purposes whether any of these dates are shifted by a few years. The works of Procopius, with the possible exception of the *Buildings*, do not reflect the influence of events that they themselves do not discuss. No changes in his views can be linked to specific events, though scholars have looked there for the "key" to solving this problem.[92]

Biography is equally futile. We know nothing about Procopius' life beyond what he tell us, and he tells us nothing directly about his family, upbringing, education, or close friends.[93] He does not even give us a complete account of his travels around the Mediterranean with Belisarius. As if by chance, he appears in the narrative here and there. Clearly he traveled more and knew more people than he tells us.[94] In short, what we know about his life explains nothing crucial about his political and historical thought. Attempts to trace his views to his social class are problematic, because we know little about that either. Granted, his social views were generally conservative, and he tended to side with the land-owning classes against the encroachments of the imperial bureaucracy. But the same was true of almost all ancient authors, especially of the imperial age, and it tells us nothing interesting about Procopius in particular. His social rank is unclear. It is unlikely that he was a senator, and the little that we know about his career does not require him to have come from an especially wealthy background. What can be inferred about his career does not really answer the questions posed by his works, for any attempt to explain a unique particular by referring it to a general circumstance is bound to fail. To quote Hegel, "a great deal is often said about the mild Ionic sky which supposedly produced Homer, and it did undoubtedly contribute much to the charm of the Homeric poems. But the coast of Asia Minor has always been the same, and is still the same today; nevertheless, only *one* Homer has arisen among the Ionic people."[95]

Many have regarded the *Secret History* as a manifesto for senatorial circles hostile to Justinian's fiscal policies.[96] Yet, although Procopius did condemn measures that hurt the landowning classes, there is no proof that he was acting as the spokesman for any particular group or social class. As we will see, the work is too closely connected to the *Wars* to be considered in isolation, it is too idiosyncratic to be a manifesto, and it targets far more than just economic policies. Procopius complains on behalf of almost every group in the empire, including bureaucrats, soldiers, peasant farmers, merchants, skilled craftsmen, and prostitutes. It is impossible to link him to any opposition group, and besides, the very existence of such groups, apart from the pagan intellectuals, has never been proven.[97] It is usually inferred on the basis of the *Secret History*, making the argument perfectly circular. Therefore, the social determinism that has been applied to Procopius' works by one of his critics with the aim of laying bare his alleged "class prejudices" should be rejected.[98] To the degree that he can be assigned to any group, the present study will argue that Procopius was linked to the Platonists, whose hostility to Justinian was fundamentally intellectual. Ancient philosophers did of course prefer conservative social orders, though not for reasons that had to do with economic privilege. Procopius' allegiances in this case were philosophical, not social.[99]

Genre is another modern chimera. The same scholars who offer a class-based interpretation of Procopius' criticism of Justinian also argue that the *Secret History* was constrained to operate within a particular genre of anti-imperial invective, or *Kaiserkritik*, of which it happens to be the best extant example, one actually followed by later dissidents.[100] However, it does not appear that there ever was such genre. A moment's reflection reveals that Roman authors attacked emperors in a wide variety of literary formats, including poems, plays, orations, histories, satires, and epigrams, that targeted an equally wide variety of failings, abuses, and vices. Those texts are certainly worthy of parallel study, but "emperor criticism" was not a formal genre. The contents and structure of the *Secret History* are what they are because Procopius decided that they best suited the ideas he wanted to convey, not because he was constrained to write within a predetermined literary format. It is those decisions that we must try to understand.

So let us turn to what Procopius says himself. The first sentence of the *Wars* declares his intention to narrate "the wars which Justinian, the emperor of the Romans, waged against the barbarians of the east and of the west." We noted above in our discussion of the preface that in comparison to the balanced introductions of his classical predecessors, Herodotus and Thucydides, who declared that they would recount the wars of the Greeks and the barbarians or of the Peloponnesians and the Athenians, Procopius treats Justinian as the equivalent of whole nations and assigns him a more active role in the wars of the sixth century than he does his barbaric opponents. This imbalance in the introductory sentence, however, points toward, or rather aggravates, an even greater imbalance in the text as a whole. For despite the prominence accorded to Justinian in the first sentence, the remainder of the *Wars* discusses the barbarians far more than it does Justinian, to say the least. One could even say that Justinian is relatively absent from the work, despite being its alleged protagonist. He never speaks in direct discourse, even in critical situations. This gap is highly unusual for a work of classical history, in which important men and women were supposed to speak in order to reveal their personalities and minds.[101] Theodora, for instance, is granted a speech in the most critical of circumstances, wherein she reveals herself more fully than in any of her actions (1.24.33–37).[102]

The *Secret History*, by contrast, is primarily about "the lives of Justinian and Theodora" (1.4); that is, it redresses the imbalance between the introductory sentence of the *Wars* and its content by discussing events that happened everywhere within the Roman empire (1.1). And Procopius goes on to make this link between the two texts explicit. The deeds of Justinian and Theodora could not be revealed in the *Wars* due to the fear inspired by the cruelty of the regime and the ubiquity of its spies (1.2–3). The *Wars*, then, focuses on the barbarians beyond the frontiers; the *Secret History* on the tyrants within (cf. 14.2). The degree to which Justinian and his opponents, or tyranny and barbarism, differ can be determined only through a careful comparison of the two texts. And yet we must note that Justinian does not speak in the *Secret History* either. There is something peculiar about Procopius' depiction of Justinian, to say the least. The emperor seems to be other than fully human.

In short, the *Secret History* is an esoteric supplement to the *Wars*. Had Justinian's life been shorter, its contents may have been incorporated into the *Wars*.[103] Contrary to what Cameron has claimed, the *Wars* is the "basis" against which the unpublished work should be read, as Procopius specifies when he says in the preface of the *Secret History* that he will tell there what he could not include in the *Wars* out of fear.[104] This does not mean, however, that it is nothing more than a series of isolated corrections and subversive revelations, lacking structure and internal aims of its own. Fear may have compelled Procopius to express his dissidence in secret; genius led him to express it in an artful, purposeful, and intelligent way. The *Secret History* is by no means a straightforward confession of its author's beliefs, political or religious. It is a literary work like the *Wars* and fully classicizing in all the senses discussed earlier in this chapter. The *Secret History* has its own secrets.

The composition and fortuitous survival of a dissident treatise such as the *Secret History* should cause us to read works such as the *Wars* written by other authors with greater caution that we would otherwise. Many ancient historians may have lacked the courage to set their true thoughts down and limited themselves to carefully guarded statements in their published works. Even so, some of the accusations of the *Secret History* are reflected in the *Wars*, a work that manages to present the reign as unfavorably as possible under the circumstances. Notably, Procopius establishes an interplay between his two texts through the use of classical allusions. We will uncover a number of these correspondences in the course of our discussion; one example should suffice here. At the beginning of the *Vandal War*, Procopius calls Justinian, who was contemplating the invasion of Libya, "sharp at formulating plans and resolute in implementing his decisions (ἦν γὰρ ἐπινοῆσαί τε ὀξὺς καὶ ἄοκνος τὰ βεβουλευμένα ἐπιτελέσαι)" (3.9.25). This alludes to a phrase in an important speech in Thucydides, which, when read in context, discloses an implicit criticism of the emperor, one moreover that Procopius himself makes openly in the *Secret History*. At the assembly in Sparta, at the beginning of the Peloponnesian War, the Corinthians condemned the Athenians as "innovators, sharp at formulating plans and implementing in deed whatever they decide (νεωτεροποιοὶ καὶ ἐπινοῆσαι ὀξεῖς καὶ ἐπιτελέσαι ἔργῳ ἃ ἂν γνῶσιν)" (1.70.2). Procopius has carefully omitted the damning word "innovation," knowing that classically educated readers would catch the allusion to the Corinthians' famous speech and supply it for themselves. As it happens, "innovation," or the disruption of the established order, is the main charge against Justinian in the *Secret History*. In precisely one of the passages where the emperor is accused of being an innovator (νεωτεροποιός), Procopius deploys a variant of the Thucydidean phrase, calling him in the same sentence "sharp at formulating and implementing base designs (ἐπινοῆσαι μὲν τὰ φαῦλα καὶ ἐπιτελέσαι ὀξύς)" (8.26).[105] The correspondence is not due to coincidence and reveals how carefully Procopius chose the context from which he culled his allusions. The esoteric reading of the *Wars* tallies with what is said openly in the *Secret History*. Another way by which he managed to accuse Justinian of innovation in the *Wars* was by placing the charge in the mouth of a Gothic envoy to Persia (2.2.6).

The relationship between these texts is complex and yet internally structured and self-contained; it has nothing to do with dates, biography, or genres. A single author stands behind them, and he speaks consistently in the same language. The problem of Procopius is the problem of classicism, and the *Secret History* is an esoteric commentary on the *Wars*, not an independent work in its own right. Let us note in this connection that the author plays the same games in the *Buildings* as well. The Thucydidean phrase used in the *Wars* and *Secret History* to refer to Justinian (6.5.4) is applied there to the emperor's barbarian opponents! Again classicism turns out to be not an affected imitation of "vocabulary" but a careful choice of textual parallel, varied with omissions required by context but tending toward the same purpose. Procopius reveals in the *Secret History* what he could not in the *Wars*, but he also gives those fortunate enough to possess the secret work many hints about how to read the public work. As we will see again and again, the allusions in the *Wars* and the *Buildings* point to what Procopius says in the *Secret History*, which is exactly what we would predict if we took at face value his claim that it is the latter work that reveals his true view of the regime.

Still, precisely because it is an esoteric work, the *Secret History* differs in crucial respects from the *Wars*. These differences are best indicated by, although by no means limited to, the fact that in the *Wars*, "tyrant" refers almost exclusively to "illegitimate" usurpers—that is, the word accords with the usage of imperial propaganda—whereas in the *Secret History* tyranny is used in the classical sense of oppressive despotism and is only marginally concerned with a regime's legitimacy.[106] Still, even on this matter, there are "passages" leading from the *Wars* to the *Secret History*; for example, the famous speech by Theodora which, unbeknownst to the empress herself, compares the "kingship" of her husband to the "tyranny" of Dionysius of Syracuse. In addition, some sections of the *Wars* are designed to undermine the imperial usage of "tyranny" and "kingship" by praising the beneficial rule of men branded as tyrants in imperial propaganda. Procopius does not even require us to do much work here: he says that they were officially labeled tyrants and, in the same breath, praises their just and benevolent rule.[107] I can think of few historians of the imperial age who dared to express themselves with such frankness, and certainly none who did so under a ruler such as Justinian.

The *Buildings*, on the other hand, is not a work of history, although one of its many deceptions is that it begins by pretending to be one. In the first sentence of its preface, Procopius calls it a "history" and lifts some arguments from the preface of Diodorus of Sicily for the moral utility of history (1.1.1–5).[108] As opposed to the preface of the *Wars*, which adduces the blame of close associates as a sign of its own impartiality (1.1.5), the preface to the *Buildings* emphasizes that the praise of virtuous deeds will benefit emulous future generations. This too sets the *Buildings* apart from the *Wars* and the *Secret History*, whose emphasis is also on blame. Yet despite its claim to be a history, the work's true nature is revealed when it begins to praise Justinian, mentioning his glorious wars, purification of religion, and mercy toward conspirators. The author announces that his theme will be the emperor's buildings (1.1.12, 17). This is a panegyric, not an impartial history, and the language used in the preface and throughout reveals the influence of rhetorical conventions ("I lack confidence in the power of my speech to do justice to the magnitude of these accomplishments," "my lisping and thin-voiced speech," etc.).[109]

Therefore, considerations of genre apply to the *Buildings* in a way that they do not to the *Secret History*. We are entitled, indeed required, to interpret this work within the context of the panegyrical literature of the later Roman empire. The theme of this particular work may be more narrow than others of its kind, but there was always room for variation, and the glorification of a ruler's buildings certainly accorded with the conventions of the genre.[110] Considerations of biography also apply. Many have wondered what induced a man who risked so much by writing the *Secret History* to compose a work that extols Justinian as a virtuous Christian monarch and directly reverses the accusations of the unpublished work. The majority of scholars who have examined this question have assumed—rightly, in my view—that the *Buildings* was an insincere work of flattery prompted by interest or danger.[111] The hope for personal advantage is suggested openly by Procopius in the preface, where he states that subjects are most grateful to rulers who benefit them and bestow praises upon them that far outlast the benefits they themselves have received (1.1.4). It is also easy to see how the author of the *Wars* and the *Secret History* could in some way or another have incurred Justinian's anger and was compelled to prove his loyalty by publicly endorsing the regime's ideology of beneficent Christian rule. It has even been proposed that Procopius was involved in an attempt to assassinate the emperor that failed or was exposed, for twice in the preface he pointedly praises Justinian for showing mercy toward conspirators (1.1.10, 16).[112] It is unknown whether the work was actually presented before the court. In some respects it appears to be unfinished, although that view has been contested.[113]

Some of the differences between the *Buildings* and the *Secret History* concern the moral or theological interpretation of the reign. Whereas in the *Buildings* he praises the enforcement of religious uniformity (1.1.9), in the *Secret History* he states—using the same words—that the emperor's zealous belief in Christ led him to commit untold crimes against his subjects, giving priests free rein to oppress minorities and himself killing heretics in order to obtain religious uniformity, "for he did not consider it to be murder if his victims were of a different faith" (13.4–7). Other times, ambiguous statements in the *Buildings* seem to be clarified ironically by what Procopius had written in the *Secret History*. For example, in the *Buildings*, he castigates "the insolence and boundless luxury" of certain unnamed persons who built villas in the suburbs outside the capital (4.9.3–5);[114] in the *Secret History*, he reveals that it was Justinian who had filled the suburbs with pointless buildings, "as if the palaces in which all the previous emperors had preferred to live were not enough for him and his household" (26.23). Finally, there are factual discrepancies between the two texts. These are so strikingly antithetical that they are certainly deliberate. For example, in the *Buildings*, he praises the emperor for restoring the defenses of Thermopylae and stationing soldiers there in place of the farmers who defended the pass against enemies (4.2.1–15); in the *Secret History*, he reveals that it was the venal *logothetes* Alexander, who, with the emperor's approval, replaced the farmers with soldiers as a pretext for appropriating local funds to the imperial treasury (26.31–34). Recent attempts to date the archaeological remains suggest that Procopius exaggerated the scale of Justinian's repairs to the walls of Thermopylae. There are many more parallels of these kinds between the two works.[115]

There is no question which is the real Procopius. When reading him, as well as many other Byzantine writers, we would do well to heed an observation made in 1720 by John Toland, a disciple of John Locke:

Considering how dangerous it is made to tell the truth, tis difficult to know when any man declares his real sentiments of things. . . . There is nevertheless one observation left us, whereby to make a probable judgment of the sincerity of others in declaring their opinions. Tis this. When a man maintains what's commonly believ'd, or professes what's publicly injoin'd, it is not always a sure rule that he speaks what he thinks: but when he seriously maintains the contrary of what's by law established, and openly declares for what most others oppose, then there's a strong presumption that he utters his mind.[116]

Procopius certainly "utters his mind" more freely in the *Secret History* than in the *Buildings*. Yet that does not necessarily mean that the former text is an immaculate confession of his beliefs while the latter is a purely rhetorical encomium that could have been written by anyone in the same circumstances. We will examine the *Secret History* in a later chapter. For now let us look at the *Buildings*, which also reflects Procopius' hostility to the regime, though for obvious reasons it is far more veiled than in the *Wars*. Scholars have detected many instances of possible sarcasm. For example, Procopius seems to mock Chalcedonian theology when he unnecessarily digresses to ridicule the ancient "myths" about centaurs, which "childishly say that there was a strange race of men in times past compounded of the nature of two creatures" (4.3.12). Let us note in this connection that his successor Agathias was also highly adept at intruding implicit criticisms of the Church into denunciations of pagan rites and beliefs.[117] As an astute study of techniques of dissimulation cautions, "a remark slipped in surreptitiously can be more important than the conventional development around it."[118] Procopius also describes an equestrian statue depicting the emperor in the guise of Achilles. He mentions the brilliant radiance that flashed forth from its helmet and adds that "one could say poetically that here is that Star of Autumn" (1.2.9–10). When classicizing authors say things "poetically," they are usually alluding to Homer, and the allusion here has been duly detected: in the *Iliad*, Achilles is compared to the Autumn Star, "which is brightest among the stars, and yet is wrought as a sign of evil and brings on the great fever for unfortunate mortals" (22.26–31). It would not have been at all unreasonable for Procopius to expect some of his readers to know the *Iliad* by heart and recognize the implications of the pointed comparison of Justinian to both Achilles and the Autumn Star, the bringer of evil. Procopius emphatically directs our attention to his source by referring to "that" Autumn Star. He introduces another curious Homeric allusion in 1.1.15, where he calls Justinian "gentle as a father." The lines spoken right after this in the *Odyssey* by Telemachus are: "and there is now this greater evil still: my home and all I have are being ruined" (2.47–49). It was a common literary device in antiquity to quote a line from Homer or another famous poet and allow the audience to supply the following lines, which turn out to be surprisingly relevant. We even have amusing examples of men able to recognize the context and sinister implications of a line of poetry even when they were half asleep or drunk.[119]

Again, in the preface of the *Buildings*, the emperor is compared to two great leaders, Themistocles and the Persian king Cyrus. Both are ambiguous, particularly Themistocles, who is rarely, if ever, invoked in panegyrics. Procopius cites one of his boasts, that he knew how to make small states large (1.1.7). Let us look at the original context of that statement. Plutarch begins his *Life* of Themistocles by saying that his origins were obscure, his father Neocles undistinguished, and his mother a barbarian from Thrace or Caria. On the next page, he reports that later in life the Athenian statesman would rudely boast that he could make small states great when others ridiculed his complete lack of cultural refinement and social skills. That is why Procopius pointedly calls Themistocles "the son of Neocles," though there was only one Themistocles known to the tradition.[120] In the *Secret History*, he targets the lowly origins of Justinian's family: his uncle, the emperor Justin, used to be a poor Illyrian farmer and remained illiterate throughout his reign, a fact that is attested in other sources; while Justin's wife was a barbarian slave who used to be his concubine.[121] Later in the *Buildings*, he mentions the Illyrian "village" from which Justinian hailed before discussing his foundation of Justiniana Prima nearby (4.1.17).[122] As with Theodora's speech in the Nika riots, Procopius has selected an exact parallel from a classical text that suggests an unflattering truth. Themistocles' feelings of social inferiority may provide psychological insight into the imperialist ambitions of the Roman monarch.

As for Cyrus, Procopius compares him to Justinian because "he was the most excellent king of whom we have ever heard and most responsible for creating an empire for his people" (1.1.12). Be that as it may, he was also a Persian king—that is, a barbarian—and, as we will see, one of Procopius' objectives in his other works is to portray Justinian as a barbarian despot, an alter ego to his nemesis, the Persian king Chosroes. The Roman emperor in the *Secret History* and his Persian counterpart in the *Persian War* are shown to possess the same wicked character and are denounced for the same vices. Through a variety of literary devices, the historian postulates a moral and political equivalence between them.[123] There were many other virtuous rulers besides Cyrus to whom Justinian could have been compared,[124] but he was the only barbarian king who could be invoked in a panegyrical work. That is why here the historian pointedly calls Cyrus "the Persian," though there were only two men with that name in the tradition, and both were Persians. Naturally Justinian was superior to Cyrus. Compared to his reign, the rule of Cyrus "may be regarded as a kind of child's play (*paidia*)," a pun on the title of Xenophon's famous treatise, the *Cyropaedia*, or "Education of Cyrus" (1.1.15). But the phrase also recalls a striking passage in the *Secret History* that attacks Justinian's administration for making "the state seem like the game of 'King' played by children (παί-ζοντα παιδία)" (14.14). This correspondence is unlikely to be coincidental, but what does the passage in the *Secret History* have to do with Cyrus? Well, it just happens to be based on a passage in Herodotus that describes a game played by the young Cyrus and his playmates in which they pretended that Cyrus was their king (1.114: παῖδες παίζοντες, εἷς . . . τῶν παίδων συμπαίζων).

Whoever denies that centaurs, *that* Autumn Star, a gentle father, Themistocles "the son of Neocles," Cyrus "the Persian," and the games of children are intended ironically must explain why they are present at all. There is too much coincidence here and too great a correspondence between the original context of the allusions in the *Buildings* and the accusations in the *Secret History*. It is our task to understand Procopius' choices, particularly when they seem odd, and to maintain the coherence of his stance toward the regime without invoking subconscious motives. Like many other panegyrics, the *Buildings* is an insincere and possibly coerced work of flattery, full of subversive allusions and grievous factual distortions. Some of its lies have been exposed by archaeological research and by the comparison of the author's panegyrical boasts to the often contradictory narrative in the *Wars*.[125] As a panegyrist Procopius lacks enthusiasm for his subject and, as has aptly been said, "often seems bored."[126] He mentions the bare minimum of imperial virtues required to give his work a passing grade, and his descriptions are rhetorical in the worst sense. In fact, he hints at this possibility in his comparison of Justinian to Cyrus. It is entirely possible, he says in passing and quite unnecessarily, that Xenophon exaggerated Cyrus' deeds through the "power of his speech (δύναμις τοῦ λόγου)" (1.1.13–14). Such skepticism only suggests the possibility that Procopius' own praise may be exaggerated, and, as it happens, in the very first line of the *Buildings* he refers modestly to his own "power of speech (λόγου δύναμις)," using exactly the words that he applies later to Xenophon (1.1.1). The number of coincidences continues to mount. What Procopius cannot say explicitly about his own mendacious rhetoric he attributes to a panegyrist of the past, one moreover who could be shown by any competent historian to have engaged in fiction. It is for that reason all the more an interesting choice for comparison.[127]

But is the *Buildings* thoroughly insincere? Procopius' most influential recent interpreter has attempted to salvage certain aspects of the text as truly indicative of his worldview. Averil Cameron has questioned whether concepts such as "sincerity" are really applicable to the *Buildings* and has suggested that regardless of what the panegyrist may have thought about Justinian, he still accepted the basic premise that Christian emperors ruled by the grace of God. The *Buildings* therefore confirms the thesis that Procopius was a conventional Christian of his age. Though this view is supported by more assertion than proof, it merits discussion as it is symptomatic of a general misunderstanding of Byzantine intellectual life that has come to constitute a scholarly orthodoxy. Panegyrical texts stand at the heart of this orthodoxy, for they most clearly expound the ideology out of which scholars have constructed an imaginary metaphysical entity called the Byzantine Mind, which they ascribe without much variation to all individual Byzantine writers. Those texts furnish virtually all the generalizations that underlie the modern belief in a uniform Byzantine worldview and enable scholars to circumvent the thorny hermeneutical problems posed by highly idiosyncratic authors such as Procopius.

Cameron fails to offer analytical arguments in support of her thesis about the *Buildings*. Instead she merely places words such as "insincerity," "real," and "true" within quotation marks, thereby suggesting that they are inappropriate or misguided and that scholars who use them are somehow naive. Yet she fails to provide the rigorous conceptual proof required by that stance. Placing words within quotation marks may achieve a certain rhetorical effect, but it does not qualify as an argument. It is only a posture and impossible to maintain consistently: she calls other scholars' views about what Procopius believed the supposedly "true" or "real" beliefs of Procopius, but her own conclusions about what was true or real do not receive skeptical punctuation marks.[128]

The question of sincerity lies at the heart of panegyrical discourse. Contrary to what Cameron states at one point without explanation, there is no difference between modern and ancient notions of sincerity.[129] Witness Augustine, who confessed "how unhappy I was . . . on that day when I was preparing to deliver a panegyric on the emperor! In the course of it I would tell numerous lies and for my mendacity would win the good opinion of people who knew it to be untrue."[130] Augustine's testimony alone refutes the assertion that "panegyric certainly did not evoke the problem of 'sincerity' ascribed to it by modern scholars."[131] Many ancient and Byzantine sources attest explicitly that it did exactly that.[132] It was a commonplace of ancient political thought that tyrants could not endure equality and demanded abject flattery.[133] As a modern philosopher asked, "Is any speech addressed to a tyrant by a man who is in the tyrant's power likely to be a sincere speech?"[134] Any dictionary will define flattery as insincere praise, and Cameron gives no reason why we should reject this perfectly good word. We possess abundant evidence about flattery at Justinian's court from Procopius and others. The deacon Agapetus composed a series of edifying aphorisms for the emperor that repeatedly warned against "the deceitful words of flatterers" who have no regard for truth.[135] Procopius realized that Justinian was highly susceptible to flattery (see below), and another contemporary, John Lydus, who was asked by the emperor to write a panegyric on the reign and then a history of the war against Persia, knew that "it was not safe to refuse the requests of an emperor such as he."[136]

Cameron dismisses out of hand the notion that there may be irony in the *Buildings*, claiming at one point that it would make its author's "knowledge of Homer very sophisticated,"[137] and we presumably know that the Byzantines are not supposed to have had a sophisticated knowledge of the classics. An essential aspect of allusions is thereby adduced as an argument against their existence! Cameron is, however, fully aware that the text contains many misrepresentations, distortions, and deliberate falsehoods, especially on the archaeological side, which even she ascribes to "panegyrical considerations." Her warning that certain "panegyrical devices" in the work cannot be trusted, "even when there is no direct evidence to the contrary," strongly implies that even she views this kind of rhetoric as mendacious.[138] So why should we accept that Procopius was "sincere" when he praised the emperor as ruling by the grace of Christ? Cameron gives no arguments for this view, saying only that the *Buildings* is not insincere in this regard because it offers a "sustained Christian interpretation of the reign."[139] But Procopius could hardly have written any other kind of panegyric for Justinian, especially if he were in dire need of his favor or pardon. Cameron also knows that sixth-century authors were under severe political constraints, and she even suggests that "conformism was essential" in those parts of their works where they endorsed "the general theory of imperial rule that was now standard." Yet on the next page, she simply asserts that "there is no reason to think that they failed to subscribe to it," despite the fact that "much" of what they say "can be attributed to panegyrical convention."[140] But how much? Cameron wants to save the *Buildings* only insofar as it can help her make its author into a conventional Christian; otherwise, she is prepared to jettison its factual claims as "panegyrical" and even to deny that Procopius was sincere when he applied the theory of Christian kingship to Justinian in particular.[141] It seems as though Procopius could lie about everything but his religion, a limitation that is fortunate for modern scholars preoccupied with the religious beliefs of men in late antiquity.

Procopius, as we will see, was no Christian and therefore did not subscribe to any Christian theory of kingship. In any case, his views on this important matter cannot be determined on the basis of a work as treacherous and insincere as the *Buildings*. In the *Secret History*, he explains that Justinian was highly susceptible to flattery, particularly when it elevated him to the level of God. "His flatterers would persuade him with no difficulty that he was raised up to the heavens and walked upon air (μετέωρος ἀρθείη καὶ ἀεροβατοίη)" (13.11; cf. 14.16–17, 22.29). This allusion to the portrayal of Socrates in Aristophanes' *Clouds*—hoisted up in a basket searching the heavens for gods[142]—makes a mockery of the emperor's piety, but it also strengthens the point that Justinian was more likely to be influenced by pious flattery. Well, in the *Buildings*, Procopius happens to use the very same words to describe how the mind of anyone who enters Justinian's great church of Hagia Sophia "is raised up to God and walks upon air (πρὸς τὸν θεὸν ἐπαιρόμενος ἀεροβατεῖ)" (1.1.61). Surely this is not another coincidence! The entire purpose of the discussion in which the words occur in the *Secret History* is to explain how they might be used to flatter Justinian's religious accomplishments, exactly what Procopius does in the *Buildings* and with exactly the same language. The one text again explains the other.

The allusion to the *Clouds* leads us to a deeper, more sinister conclusion. Socrates' comic claim to be walking on air occurs most famously at the beginning of the play but is repeated sarcastically and ominously at the very end by Strepsiades, who burns down the philosopher's house and accuses him of having insulted the gods and prying into the dwelling of the Moon (1503–1509). Both passages refer to Socrates' "contemplation" or "contempt" of the Sun (περιφρονῶ is ambiguous), which Strepsiades correctly views as Socrates' contempt for the gods. What might this suggest about Procopius' attitude toward the god of Hagia Sophia if his viewpoint was Socratic? Be that as it may, in the *Secret History*, Procopius again alludes to both phrases when he accuses Justinian of "prying into celestial things, and developing an undue curiosity about the nature of God" instead of dealing with pressing matters of state. "The entire earth," he says, "was drenched in blood" (18.29–30). The relationship between the *Buildings*, the *Secret History*, and their classical sources are again complex and not merely verbal.[143] But to understand how the allusions that bind them together function in practice, the reader must know Homer, Plutarch, Xenophon, Herodotus, and Aristophanes. Classical scholars are perhaps better prepared to understand Procopius in this respect than social or art historians of the sixth century.

Procopius even tells an anecdote about the emperor's inability to detect false and ambiguous praise. Tribonian, the famous legal scholar, once told him that "he was afraid lest the emperor be snatched up to heaven one day because of his piety." Justinian was so confident of his own greatness and, we might add, so devoid of humor, that he took this "joke" quite seriously (13.12). Curiously enough, the tenth-century lexicon *Souda* links this episode to Tribonian's presumed Hellenic atheism and opposition to Christianity.[144] Be that as it may, the ancient rhetorical tradition offered much practical advice on tyranny and flattery. In an important article on the art of safe criticism in ancient Greece and Rome, F. Ahl adduces Seneca: "the more open flattery is, the more outrageous, the straighter it keeps its own face . . . the more quickly it takes its victim by storm."[145] Those with power *want* to believe that they are admired; they need little persuasion. Procopius knew that with Justinian the most effective flattery was that which prayed upon his religious vanity, for the discussion of flattery in the *Secret History* focuses exclusively on its religious side. Therefore, if we go by what Procopius himself tells us, the religious aspect of the *Buildings* is the one we are *least* authorized to accept as sincere. That he offers in that work a "sustained Christian interpretation of the reign" proves only that he knew what he had to say given his circumstances. The work elevates Justinian very close to God, suggesting at one point that he had earned "honors equal to those of God" (1.10.19). This phrase has been ascribed to irony when viewed from the historian's point of view and to uncommon vanity when viewed from that of the emperor.[146]

Procopius' mention of the emperor's divine honors merits further discussion, because it too has a curious parallel in the *Secret History*. The historian mentions this honor in a description of a famous, albeit now lost, mosaic in the palace. In the center were depicted Justinian and Theodora, surrounded by scenes of conquest and war. And "around them *stands* the Senate of the Romans, all in a festal mood. This is indicated by the cubes of the mosaic (ψηφῖδες) which brighten their faces with merry colors. They exult and smile as they bestow on the emperor honors equal to those of God on account of the magnitude of his achievements." Contrast the passage from the *Secret History* that laments the Senate's fate under Justinian: "The Senate *sat* as though in a picture (ὥσπερ ἐν εἰκόνι), having no control over its vote (ψῆφος) and no ability to do good, given that it assembled on account of an ancient law and an empty form (σχῆμα)" (14.8).

The discussion of flattery in the *Secret History* clarifies both the aim and the techniques of the *Buildings*. The emphasis in both texts on religion indicates only that Procopius understood the ideological dimension of Justinian's tyranny, not that he accepted it. But the historian never ceased to ponder the problem of coercion in societies such as his own in which power was distributed very unequally. In Book 8 of the *Wars*, written perhaps at the same time as the *Buildings*, Procopius placed some very interesting social observations in a letter sent in late 551 by the Persian general Mermeroes to Goubazes, the king of the Lazi, who was at the time an ally of Rome and at war with Persia.[147] We will later have occasion to notice how the historian exploited the speeches and letters of his characters to interject his own thoughts into the narrative. For the moment let us observe the wise words of this general, which have less to do with the immediate context of the military narrative and more to do with the struggles of Procopius himself, their true author. Note how toward the end of the letter he explicitly signals to the reader the universal applicability of his thoughts to all human societies.

There are two things that regulate the lives of men, power and prudence. Some, who are more powerful than their neighbors, live according to their own will and always lead those who are inferior in whatever way they please, while others, who are enslaved to their superiors on account of their weakness, compensate for their impotence through discretion, approaching the powerful through flattery, and are no less able to live amidst their own possessions, enjoying by their flattery all those things of which they would have been deprived by their weakness. And these things do not hold true among some nations, while it is differently among others; rather, one can say that it holds true for all human beings everywhere in the inhabited world, no differently from any other natural characteristic. (8.16.23–24; cf. 2.6.3 with 2.6.7)

To conclude: students of late antiquity have imbued the word classicism with a negative connotation. It denotes lack of originality, sterile imitation, derivation. The possibility has not been considered that it may instead have been a source of strength, that writers such as Procopius actually learned from their classical models and used them as a mirror on which to reflect their own meanings through a closely knit network of allusions and structural parallels. As Seneca put it, "he who writes last has the best of the bargain, for he finds already at hand words which, when marshaled in a different way, show a new face. And he is not pilfering them, as if they belonged to someone else, when he uses them, for they are common property."[148] But Procopius was hardly the first to write in this way. Classicism began immediately with the birth of the classical, in the eighth century B.C.. The first known verse inscription, the famous Cup of Nestor, contains an allusion to Homer. The joke on the cup cannot be fully understood unless one knows the text of the *Iliad* to which it refers. It is "nearly the oldest example of alphabetic writing and, at the same time, Europe's first literary allusion, an extraordinary fact."[149] The Greeks wrote like this throughout all periods of antiquity, and that Procopius did so should in no way be correlated with the fact that he happened to live in what is now called the "later" Roman empire. Plato himself was "late" compared to Homer and Hesiod, to whom he constantly alludes. Already by the fifth century B.C. the epic poet Choerilus could pen verses complaining, with allusions to Homer, that everything had already been apportioned, the arts had reached their limits, there was nowhere to go and nothing left to say.[150] The classical tradition classicized from the very beginning, in the very ways in which we observe in Procopius. We should not hesitate to enroll him among the ranks of the classical historians, and among the best. There is no category of analysis that has been brought to bear on his models that cannot be applied with profit to his own text. The following chapters will explore his anecdotes, Platonic mimesis, political thought, and belief in *tyche* and will argue that the philosophy of Procopius was as indebted to his classical models as was his way of writing.

Chapter 2

Tales Not Unworthy of Trust: Anecdotes and the Persian War

Ancient and Byzantine historical narratives represent a nexus of scholarship and literature. To describe real events, they utilize techniques of empirical verification in conjunction with a broad range of literary devices. Also, they have moral or philosophical goals that seem inappropriate to factual reporting today. This has long been known, though its implications have not been absorbed into the mainstream of scholarship, at least not with regard to Byzantine writers. Narratives are still evaluated primarily in terms of factual reliability, while anything that may distort that is set down to "bias" or, at best, "worldview" (a more charitable, if nebulous category). Still, there are passages that do not make even that cut and are ascribed to incompetence or bad judgment. This is the fate of many anecdotes found in the works of all but a very few ancient historians such as Thucydides. Along with omens, they are among those aspects of ancient historiography that make modern readers most uncomfortable. They seem to be little more than unsubstantiated rumor and are furthermore not susceptible to quantification, which frustrates social historians.

But this is to miss their purpose and function. A man's personality, for instance, was not always simply described in so many words. Often a story was told about him from which it could be inferred. So too the character and history of nations. Whereas modern studies of wars introduce the two sides by analyzing their social and political structures, foreign interests, and geography, many ancient historians conveyed the essential points through anecdotes. Readers have to think hard about these stories to appreciate their significance, for serious authors would never include them merely to entertain. The function of anecdotes is intimately linked to the main themes of the work in which they appear. That is why so many of them lack historical context: it is easier that way to structure them around key ideas. Detecting and appreciating those concepts, that is, *reading,* should be an intellectual challenge and not a passive reception of information. Readers are required to draw their own conclusions. Procopius' successor Agathias, for instance, suggests in his preface that anecdotes were central to the moral purpose of his history: they made the harsh teachings of political philosophy more palatable.[1] Plutarch more or less admitted that the material contained in his lives of Theseus and Romulus was legendary but not for that reason devoid of merit.[2] "Legends can often cut to simple truths that the fastidious accuracy of the historical record obscures."[3]

Discussion of the anecdotes in Procopius has not gone beyond the question of factual validity. This approach is preferred, I suppose, because it is safe: it precludes literary judgments, which may be faulted as subjective. There is no danger in comparing different versions of the same story found in separate sources, and analyses on the grounds of coherence and plausibility almost always have skeptical conclusions—again, safe for scholarly reputations. This approach, however, runs a greater risk than literary subjectivity, for it may entirely misrepresent the purpose of specific passages. Anecdotal "truth" functions on a different level than factual reliability. Some authors even explicitly warn that some of their stories are not strictly true. It is precisely here, in this paradox, where the historian is least constrained by and least interested in factual reliability, that we must seek the key to his intentions and "truth."

I have chosen to focus on the series of anecdotes that constitute the introduction to the *Persian War*, though my approach applies equally to those in the introductions of the *Vandal* and *Gothic War*. Even if my specific interpretation of these stories is wrong, I still believe that we must engage them in a similar way. They should no longer be dismissed as stupid and pointless.

Procopius' account of the war between Rome and Persia essentially begins with the invasion of Roman territory by the Persian king Cavades and the fall of Amida in 502–503 (1.7). Before launching into that narrative, however, he outlines, as promised at the end of the preface (1.1.17), a brief history of the relations between the two states in the century following the death of Arcadius in 408. This section of the work, which I will call the introduction of the *Persian War* (1.2–6), has been regarded as one of his weakest passages. It consists of a series of unconnected episodes, some of which are highly anecdotal, impressionistic, or outright fictitious while others retain a measure of credibility but are so vague as to give no concrete information about the relations between the two states. Among other stories, we are treated to what one scholar has called a "ludicrous anecdote about a 'swimming' oyster that was pursued by a shark."⁴ Scholars have agonized over these tales, doubting their credibility and vainly searching for their sources. Yet in the end they remain at a complete loss as to why a historian of Procopius' caliber would include such fanciful material in his work. One scholar interested here only in factual reliability passes over the introduction with little discussion: "it does not amount to much real history—rather to a mixture of anecdote and notices taken from a variety of sources, mixed in with a fair amount of literary dressing."⁵ Another has concluded that it must be a light hearted joke on Herodotus after all: Procopius is "poking fun at his classical models" and "is not meant to be taken too seriously."⁶ Another proposed that "the purpose of the introductory chapters was to entertain the reader, rather than to examine earlier events."⁷ But even in the modern world of short attention spans, digressions and entertainment are reserved for later on, when the audience is fatigued. Why would Procopius *begin* a serious narrative with entertainment?

I contend that we must read these stories with the utmost seriousness. This is not to deny the presence of playfulness. Yet their primary purpose is to establish the fundamental parameters of the remainder of the narrative. They also point toward the heart of Procopius' political thought, which, as we will see, was in many ways indebted to the teaching of Plato's *Republic*. That Procopius expounds his political thought in a series of largely unhistorical vignettes and not, as with scholars today, in a theoretical introduction rich in technical jargon and abstract theory indicates the difference in the ways that ancient and modern historians grapple with the problems of historical truth.

The following investigation of the introduction to the *Persian War* will focus on four interrelated problems: (a) What function does each story serve within the context of the *Persian War* as a whole? In other words, why did Procopius choose to include a particular story in his introduction and why does it take the particular form it does? (b) Is historical accuracy the guiding principle of his exposition, or did he occasionally bend the truth to convey a message of his own? (c) Are the stories in the introduction independent of each other, as has been assumed so far, or do they form a greater whole? In other words, does the introduction as a whole tell a story that cannot be found in any of its constituent parts? and (d) How do the stories of the introduction tie in with other passages where Procopius divulges his political thought, notably in the *Secret History*? I will argue that there is a close correspondence of expression between the two texts, which indicates that Procopius' political thought was not only coherent but actually shaped his view of recent history.

Arcadius and Isdigerdes (1.2.1–10)

We begin with the dilemma of the dying emperor Arcadius (395–408), who realized that his seven-year-old son Theodosius could not rule independently yet feared that an ambitious regent would overthrow him.[8] To forestall a Persian war and simultaneously prevent court factions from toppling the dynasty, Arcadius ingeniously designated as regent the Persian king Isdigerdes (Yazgird I, 399–420), entreating him to safeguard the succession. Isdigerdes, distinguished by "nobility of mind and virtue," faithfully carried out this charge. The peace was maintained because no Roman dared provoke the Persian king by overthrowing the young Theodosius.

Scholars are divided about the historicity of this peculiar event.[9] The first to doubt it was Procopius' continuator Agathias, who admitted it was widely known, though he had never seen a written version of it prior to Procopius. Agathias did not reject it outright but thought it implausible, primarily because a Christian emperor would not have entrusted a pagan with something so important (4.26.3–8). There does not seem to be any way to resolve this dispute today. It is clear, however, that Procopius presents the episode out of its historical context, for he fails to consider the religious and economic relations between the two states at that time. We know that serious discussions were under way in 408–409 regarding trade and the status of Persia's Christians that resulted in substantive agreements.[10] Furthermore, the episode seems irrelevant to the course of the wars of the sixth century. One scholar could explain its presence only by claiming that it "appealed" to Procopius "as a colorful tale."[11] But let us take a closer look. What is the significance of this tale to the wars of the sixth century?

We must first wonder why Procopius chose to begin his introduction with the reign of Arcadius. Given the long peace of the fifth century, the reign of Cavades, who resumed hostilities against Rome, presents a more logical starting point. In this connection we must note that the "regency" episode, unlike those that follow it in the introduction, is exceptional in that it focuses more on the Roman ruler than on his Persian counterpart. It is therefore to Arcadius that we must turn. He was the first of the later emperors who did not campaign in person and preferred to reside perma-

nently in the capital. This policy, which decisively shaped the Roman response to Persian attacks for over two centuries, constitutes a major factor
in the narrative of the *Wars*.[12] To give just one example, Belisarius is made
to say at one point that Justinian "is so far removed from events that he
cannot adjust his actions to the changing circumstances" (2.16.10). Interestingly, Procopius also begins the *Vandal War* with the reign of Arcadius'
brother, Honorius, who followed the same policy in the west. Honorius is
presented as especially pusillanimous, and the two brothers are contrasted
to their father Theodosius I, who, Procopius notes, was "a very capable
military leader" (3.1.2). Despite being a dynastic founder, therefore, Theodosius was really the last of a kind, for his sons inaugurated a new model
of Roman kingship, to which Justinian, mutatis mutandis, conformed. We
know too that the propaganda of Arcadius' court downplayed the value of
military glory, emphasizing the king's piety instead. One modern historian
has even referred to "the demilitarization of imperial ideology."[13]

Procopius initially presents this new model of demilitarized kingship
in a positive light. Arcadius himself was an imbecile, as the historian openly
admits,[14] but he made a wise decision that secured internal stability and
peace on the frontier. In accordance with the actual ideology of Arcadius'
regime, Procopius attributes that decision either to divine inspiration or to
learned advisors, though he does not divulge their names.[15] His account
lacks circumstantial detail, probably because it represents a schematic ideal
rather than an accurate historical narrative. The two factors that contributed to Arcadius' decision represent the two political ideals of antiquity:
rule by the wise, even if only indirect, and rule that is divinely inspired.
Only these factors could redeem a ruler such as Arcadius, who was distinguished by neither wisdom nor military skill. In this context, is it worth
noting that these same factors recur at the end of Book 1 of the *Wars*, only
in reverse form: Justinian's advisors were corrupt and evil and God opposed
his regime (1.25).

The Persian king Isdigerdes possessed precisely those virtues that his
Roman counterpart lacked. Like all Persian kings depicted after him in the
Persian War, he was a soldier, and his only action in the episode is to
"threaten war" upon those who would conspire against his charge.[16] He
was noble and virtuous, qualities manifested not only in his fidelity to Arcadius' will but also in the "strength and foresight" that ensured the successful discharge of his promise.[17] Whereas Arcadius had need of divine
inspiration or wise advisors to conceive his plan, Isdigerdes required neither
in order to carry it out. The success of Arcadius' plan depended upon Per-

sian virtue and a degree of mutual trust. Yet it was precisely the decline of Persian virtue that led to wars between the two nations in the sixth century and the absence of mutual trust that led to the unnecessary prolongation of those wars. The regency episode represents an ideal situation on both sides, from which all elements of discord and hostility have been removed. The Roman and Persian kings here possess their respective virtues to the highest degree. Agathias' criticism was astute but misplaced, because he did not appreciate the overall dynamic of Procopius' introduction. The theme of religious tension is introduced gradually in the narrative of the *Persian War*, as are all the factors that made tyrants more common than virtuous kings on both the Roman and the Persian side and made hostility between them inevitable. The peace hinged upon fragile moral qualities.

Far from being a colorful, albeit irrelevant, anecdote of dubious historicity, the regency episode captures the essential parameters of the relationship between Rome and Persia, setting them on an ideal plane that foreshadows the downward course of the ensuing narrative. It sows the seeds of Roman weakness and Persian aggression. What happens to Rome when its rulers remain sedentary but lose their wise advisors and divine assistance (as under Justinian), and what happens to Persia when its rulers remain warlike but lose their nobility and virtue (as under Chosroes)? In a sense, the *Persian War* is nothing other than the chronicle of that decline. The first tale related in the introduction is as profound from a historical point of view as it is effective from a literary one. From this point of view, it has little to do with the facts about Arcadius.

Anatolius and Vararanes (1.2.11–15)

After Theodosius II attained maturity and Isdigerdes died, the Persian king Vararanes (Bahram V, 420–438) invaded Roman territory. Procopius offers no explanation for this hostile action. In response, Theodosius sent as his sole envoy the commander of the eastern army, appropriately named Anatolius, who approached the Persians without escort and dismounted before the king, an action which by itself convinced Vararanes to return to his own country and settle the dispute peacefully.

If we evaluate this story as a factual narrative we must find Procopius guilty of gross error or, at best, naive credulity. The war with Vararanes occurred in 420–422, but some believe that Anatolius was *magister militum per Orientem* during the war of 440–441 against Yazgird II (438–457).[18] If this is true, his account is hopelessly confused and useless. Even if an Anatolius did hold that office during the earlier war of 420–422, which does indeed seem to have been the case after all, we are still faced with an utterly implausible account of the conflict, not to mention a conflation of the events of the two wars.[19] According to the detailed information found in contemporary sources, in 420–422 there was heavy fighting on two fronts and the negotiations were probably concluded by Anatolius' successor, a man named Procopius.[20] More important, can we really believe that a Persian king called off an offensive merely because a Roman general dismounted before him?

Procopius had first hand experience of too many wars to believe a story like that. He almost certainly had more information about the war of 420–422 but chose to produce this stylized episode instead. Its "truth" resides not in the facts that it relates but in what it tells us about the framework of the military encounters between Rome and Persia. First of all, it moves us from the Constantinopolitan court to the Roman border. This is where most of the action of the *Persian War* will take place. The emperor is now distant; he must act through delegates. This will remain the only method of response to the Persians for the remainder of the narrative. The Persian king, on the other hand, is present at the head of a substantial army, as will be all of his successors. He commands its unquestioned obedience: when he turns his horse around, "the entire Persian host" follows him without a word. Let us note here that Procopius never depicts Persian kings holding court. Always on the move, they seem never to reside for any length of time in cities. When the king speaks with advisors, Procopius never specifies where; when envoys seek him out, they "overtake him" or "happen upon him," never in a city or palace but at locations such as "in Assyria, near the two towns Seleuceia and Ctesiphon" (2.28.4–6). Persia has no fixed center.

The Roman general Anatolius, on the other hand, does not have an army. No Roman army is mentioned in the entirety of the introduction to the *Persian War*. This is disconcerting and probably foreshadows the dismal state of Roman defenses when the Persians invade in earnest. When Chosroes decided to violate the Eternal Peace, he encountered minimal resistance. The only thing the Romans could do was send their bishops to beg him for mercy. At one point Chosroes even suggested to the Roman envoys that the Persians would be happy to "guard" the empire for a small price (2.10.21–23). Thus, the behavior of Anatolius foreshadows the Roman response to the aggression of Chosroes. Anatolius' humility before Vararanes is the first occurrence of a recurring pattern. In the *Persian War*, Romans will repeatedly prostrate themselves before a foreign tyrant, unable to resist him with arms.

Like his predecessor, Vararanes is warlike; he invades Roman territory with neither cause nor pretext. His successors will repeatedly do the same. Vararanes has lost something of the virtue of Isdigerdes, though he has retained his warlike nature, and foreshadows the open aggression of Cavades and Chosroes. Yet he still has a degree of honor: it is precisely "the sheer magnitude of the honor" shown to him by Anatolius that persuades him to turn back. Perhaps his invasion was simply inspired by a desire for glory and honor. And he treats Anatolius "with great courtesy," a trait that will also decline. The Persian kings will ultimately break free of these ethical qualities, which for the moment restrain the tyrannical and arbitrary nature of their position.

With superb economy of language, this episode prepares us for what is to come by initiating the gradual decline of Persian virtue, illustrating the parameters of the wars on the frontier and suggesting that the Roman modes of defense were woefully inadequate.

Ephthalites, Persians, and Romans (1.3.1–1.4.13)

The next episode begins with yet another Persian king, Perozes (459–484), attacking his neighbors with a large army. These were the so-called White Huns, or Ephthalites, whose territory bordered on the Sasanid realm to the northeast.[21] Procopius describes two expeditions, both of which ended in disaster. The Roman emperor (Zeno) is again represented by a delegate; an ambassador named Eusebius accompanied the first expedition.[22] Perozes was led by the Ephthalites into a trap, but the Persian officers who realized this were too timid to speak up. Instead they entreated Eusebius to intervene. Kings, it seems, do not look kindly on the bearers of bad news, and sometimes only foreigners may tell the truth safely. Even Eusebius could not speak openly to Perozes: he devised a fable about a lion lured by a bound goat into a trap set by hunters. Fables are a safe way of speaking the truth before kings.[23] We may consider the possibility that the fable of Eusebius is to the situation of the Persian army what the stories in Procopius' introduction are to the wars of the sixth century, and soon Procopius too will treat us to an animal fable.

Perozes understood the purport of the fable, but too late: his army was surrounded, and the king of the Ephthalites demanded that Perozes prostrate himself (*proskynein*) as to his master (*despotes*) and swear an oath that he would never again attack the Ephthalites. Perozes gave pledges of peace, but, having consulted his magi, resorted to the following stratagem to avoid the humiliation of prostration: he bowed before his victorious enemy at dawn, when the Persians were accustomed to bowing before the rising sun. So although technically he complied with the demands of his enemy, his action carried a twofold significance, for it could be viewed as either submission to a stranger or reverence for native customs. Whereas Eusebius' fable had two related meanings, an outer one of no interest that pointed toward an inner one of critical importance, the prostration of Perozes had two completely different meanings. However that may be, "not long after this Perozes disregarded his oath" and again attacked the Ephthalites, who again pretended to flee, leading him into a concealed trench, where he perished along with his entire army and all of his sons.[24]

Procopius prefaces his account of Perozes' two expeditions with an interesting ethnographic digression on the Ephthalites (1.3.2–7). This passage repays close study as it reveals some interesting truths about the relations between Persians and Romans, the chief subject of the introduction of the *Persian War*. We will return later to the place of Perozes in the sequence of Persian kings.

Procopius claims that the White Huns, or Ephthalites, are unlike their relatives the other Huns in appearance because they are white and their faces are not disfigured. "Nor are they nomads," for they possess a city, Gorgo, and a settled land. "They do not live in a savage manner, as the Huns do, for they are ruled by one king, possess a lawful political system (*politeia ennomos*), and always deal with each other and their neighbors in an upright and just way; in these respects they are not inferior to the Romans and the Persians." This is high praise indeed for the barbarian Ephthalites. Yet the effect is marred by their only custom (*nomos*) that Procopius recounts: each of their prosperous citizens selects twenty or more companions, with whom he shares his wealth and influence. When he dies, they are buried alive with him.[25] The Ephthalites may indeed have *nomoi*, or customs, but they are utterly alien, even repelling. We wonder how justice and civility can coexist with such *nomoi*.

Procopius' excursus is disturbing, for it calmly equates the most atrocious customs with the civilized life of his Roman readers. How is it possible for just and upright people to bury their citizens alive? The apposition magnifies the foreignness of the Ephthalites by forcing the reader to conjoin

such discordant elements as lawful society and ritual mass murder. This
reminds us of passages in Herodotus that also describe quite abominable
customs "in an altogether neutral fashion, even using technical vocabulary,
as if they were the simplest and most common practices in the world."[26]
This has the effect of forcing his readers to compare their own customs to
those of the barbarians. Like Procopius, Herodotus often likens a foreign
nation to the Greeks but then subverts the comparison by ascribing barbaric customs to them. The Medes and the Lydians, for example, swear
oaths just like the Greeks, only they cut their arms and lick each other's
blood (1.74). The Lydians have the same *nomoi* as the Greeks, except that
they prostitute their daughters (1.94).

Why does Procopius, a Roman, speak so highly of the Ephthalites?
Who are the Ephthalites? He claims that they are not nomads, but his narrative is inconclusive. They have but a single "city," on the border with
Persia (1.3.2, 1.4.10), but never try to defend it against attack, as Romans
would.[27] When they hear of Perozes' second invasion, they are nowhere
near it; they and their king are somewhere in the interior, thinking only of
"their land, their weapons, and other possessions" (1.4.3–4). Perozes by-
passes Gorgo as though it were of no importance (1.4.10). The city's name
means "grim, fierce, terrible," whence the homonymous monster of classical mythology. In Procopius, as in Byzantine Greek, the word can also mean
"swift."[28] We now wonder what the Ephthalites do in peacetime. We know
that they are horsemen (1.4.7) and that they are always on the move, at least
when they are at war.

There are interesting parallels between this part of the *Wars* and the
account in Herodotus of Darius' disastrous expedition against the Scythians
(4.118–142). The Scythians were the archetypal nomads of the ancient world;
they also obeyed a single king and had terrible *nomoi* of their own (4.59,
4.76, 4.80). In the accounts of both Procopius and Herodotus, Persian kings
lead large armies against elusive horsemen of the north; both campaigns
end ignominiously. Both enemies pretend to flee before the invading force
while remaining effectively invisible and in full control of events. The
Scythians and the Ephthalites both defeat the Persians without ever fighting
a battle by leading them astray and into traps.[29] It is worth noting here a
curious similarity in their burial customs: according to Herodotus, when a
Scythian king died, more than fifty of his attendants, whom he had chosen
from among his own people, were strangled to adorn his tomb (4.71–72).

Thus, despite Procopius' explicit claim that the Ephthalites are not
nomads, that they have a city and laws and a just society, there is still

something ineluctably Scythian about them. This quality remains in the margins of the text, on the periphery of our vision. Whereas the digression elevates the Ephthalites from the "beastly" level of the Huns, who were often called Scythians by contemporaries,[30] their actual behavior indicates that they have not entirely shed their nomadic qualities. Modern research, drawing on eastern sources and archaeological reports, casts the Ephthalites as nomadic in conscious defiance of Procopius' claim that they were not.[31] Yet these are the people whom he presents as equals in civilization to the Romans and the Persians. The comparison is undeniably peculiar; the Roman reader would probably find it utterly preposterous. I believe that it is entirely an invention of Procopius. None of the information available to him would have justified it.

But perhaps we are missing the point, just as the king of the Ephthalites did not realize that Perozes' homage was directed not at him but at the sun rising behind him. The primary goal of the excursus may after all be not to praise the Ephthalites, who are incidental at most to the narrative of the *Persian War*. Perhaps its purpose is accomplished in that unobtrusive and unnoticed secondary clause that states that they were not inferior to either Romans or Persians; that is, the clause that postulates an equality between Rome and Persia with regard to the highest things. Recall that "a remark slipped in surreptitiously" may be "more important than the conventional development around it."[32] Let us consider what it might mean.

On the strictly diplomatic level, in the official correspondence between rulers and the speeches and treatment of ambassadors, the legal fiction of the equality of the two empires was proclaimed and even scrupulously observed by both sides.[33] Procopius often has Roman envoys call Chosroes the "brother" of Justinian, and we find analogous metaphors for the two rulers in other sources, for example the two eyes of the human race, the two shoulders or the two mountains of the world, and so forth.[34] The empires were, after all, roughly matched in military strength, a fact that naturally generated respect. And continuous contact on the individual and mercantile level no doubt led to a degree of mutual appreciation and understanding. Yet chauvinistic attitudes were probably bound to prevail in the long run.[35] Outside the tactful world of diplomatic exchanges, Greek and Roman writers inevitably looked down on the Persians, who were, after all, barbarians, and therefore enemies of civilization. In this respect, they closely adhered to the view of Persia that they had inherited from the classical Greeks, who depicted its state as fundamentally tyrannical, its ruler as above the law, its subjects as offensively servile. The Persian king was the archetype of the oppressive despot.[36] Given the centrality of classical sources in the education of literate Greeks during the empire, it was inevitable that they should view first the Parthians and then the Sasanids through the lens of Herodotus' Achaemenids.[37] Some historians modeled their narratives directly upon Herodotean stories (which, as we saw, does not necessarily falsify them),[38] while others erroneously depicted the Sasanids as self-conscious heirs of the Achaemenids who grandiosely demanded the return of all lands conquered by Cyrus and Darius. Interestingly, the Achaemenid connection was more obvious to the Greeks than to the Sasanids, who do not seem to have known much about the empire of Darius.[39] Agathias, for instance, dealt with Persia extensively, and, though he seems not to have relied heavily upon Herodotus, he followed classical sources in depicting the Great King as a despot and his people as irredeemably barbaric.[40] The *Strategikon* of the emperor Maurice (ca. 600) calls them "wicked, dissembling, and servile . . . they obey their rulers out of fear" (11.1). Procopius also instinctively calls the Persians barbarians and deftly employs classical concepts and images to present their kings, especially Chosroes, as ambitious despots who ruled above the law and their subjects as slaves who obeyed out of fear.[41]

And yet it is this same Procopius who claims that the Persians were equal to the Romans in obeying "one king, possessing a lawful political system (*politeia ennomos*), and always dealing with each other and their neighbors in an upright and just way." What is the meaning of this equation? Roman diplomats did maintain the fiction that of all the nations in the world only Rome and Persia had a legitimate political system, a *politeia*,[42] but none of them went so far as to claim that the Persians were just and upright. Not only does Procopius make this unconventional claim in the context of two unjust Persian invasions of Ephthalite territory, he stands alone in extending the privileged status of *politeia* to the Ephthalites. It is important to realize that he is speaking here in his own voice and not from an official diplomatic standpoint. And yet in the *Persian War* he consistently depicts Persia as a despotic state that treated its neighbors and subjects in an unjust and lawless manner. How are we to understand the equation of Romans, Persians, and Ephthalites? Perhaps we are looking at the wrong side of the equation. Instead of seeing it as a compliment to the barbarians, we should see it as an indirect indictment of the Romans. For the Ephthalites to attain parity with the Persians and the Romans, the Romans must be lowered to the level of the archetypically barbaric Persians and the vaguely Scythian Ephthalites.⁴³ If it is ludicrous to say that the Persian state behaved in a lawful and just manner to its neighbors, in the midst, no less, of a narrative that highlights its aggression, it is then sarcastic to equate Persia with "the upright and just" Roman empire. We may be satisfied that this passage is intended ironically if Procopius elsewhere depicts the Roman empire of the sixth century as a lawless despotism in which tyranny has displaced *politeia*. That is exactly the main argument of the *Secret History*, and it is also reflected in many passages of the *Wars*.

The theme of the barbarization of the Roman empire follows multiple paths of exposition in the *Wars*. Procopius naturally treats the barbarization of the army, in terms of both recruitment and tactics, and traces its effects on the empire's ability to wage war. This theme will be examined in a separate discussion. His interest in barbarization also focuses on the two kings, the two most powerful individuals in the world, who came to resemble each other in strange ways. For instance, during the great invasion of 540, Chosroes briefly becomes a Roman emperor, whereas at the beginning of the *Vandal War*, Justinian is cast as a new Xerxes, contemplating the conquest of western lands.⁴⁴ In the *Secret History*, Procopius calls Justinian "a barbarian in his speech and dress and manner of thinking" (14.2), and the main theme of the work is the total subversion of law and justice by that avaricious tyrant and his murderous consort. Justinian "managed to demolish the entire political structure (*politeia*) of the Romans" (13.32),⁴⁵ "he unscrupulously abolished the laws" whenever there was money to be made (27.33), and "the scales of justice were set up in the marketplace" (14.10). In addition, like his Persian counterparts, he insisted on being called "despot" and demanded that magistrates be called "slaves" and perform *proskynesis* to him (30.21–26). So now we know what it means to say that the Romans were equal to the Persians in "possessing a lawful political system." It was tyranny that united Romans and Persians in a common fate, for "tyranny is essentially rule without laws, or, more precisely, monarchic rule without laws."⁴⁶

As it happens, a fifth-century source tell us of a Greek who believed that life was actually *worse* in the Roman empire than among the Scythians, which is what he and Priscus, the historian who met him at Attila's court, called the Huns. Although he believed that the Roman laws (*nomoi*) and polity (*politeia*) were good, he lamented their ruin by corrupt and incompetent authorities. Priscus' reply does not really address the Greek's charges. In fact, it seems that "the speech . . . acts as a vehicle for Priscus to attack current abuses."⁴⁷ Complaints such as this were common in the later empire, though few perhaps would have preferred life with Attila.[48] Procopius was probably unique among his contemporaries in depicting the empire as barbarized on a multiplicity of levels, the throne being only the most prominent and consequential. The excursus on the Ephthalites takes us as far from Byzantium as the *Persian War* ever goes, but it is only there that we learn something fundamentally important about the Roman empire of the sixth century. Other ancient writers had also used this technique, going as far as Sri Lanka to disguise political dissidence behind the seemingly neutral language of ethnography.[49]

Whereas the first two episodes of the introduction illuminate some of the essential differences between the two empires, the third begins by pointing to their important similarities. When tyranny is factored into the equation of Rome and Persia, the irony of the discourse on lawfulness and justice is made apparent. The naive confidence of the Roman reader in the superiority of his own culture may begin to falter. As we will often have occasion to see, the stories about the Persian kings in the introduction to the *Persian War* tell us as much about Roman tyranny as they do about Sasanid despotism. These stories may not be strictly true, but they prepare us for the gradual unfolding of Procopius' political thought.

The Pearl of Perozes (1.4.14–31)

We may now turn to the story in the introduction that has most perplexed commentators, who vainly search for sources and dismiss in frustration the whole passage as "anecdotal."[50] Where has Procopius' good sense gone? Why does he relate fanciful tales at such length?

It is said, Procopius reports, that as Perozes was about to fall into the ditch of the Ephthalites, he cast away an extraordinarily large and beautiful pearl to prevent another from possessing it after him. Though Procopius doubts that such a thought would occur to Perozes under those circumstances, he proceeds to relate at length the tale of the pearl, which he has learned from the Persians. "Perhaps this story will not seem altogether unworthy of trust," he says, but in any case it is "worth telling." In other words, like so much else in the introduction, its function is independent of its historical validity. According to the tale, a monstrously large shark fell deeply in love with a pearl oyster swimming in the Persian Gulf and could not bear to leave it, even when forced by necessity to hunt for food. A fisherman reported this fact to Perozes, who was seized with a great longing to possess the extraordinary item and induced the fisherman to obtain it for him. In a long speech, the latter asked in return that the king provide for his children should he be devoured by the shark in the attempt, which is in fact what happened.[51]

The story of Perozes' pearl was cherished by later Byzantine authors,[52] though for reasons that probably had little to do with its function in the *Wars*. Procopius questions its validity and openly doubts that the king would bother to discard the pearl in the face of imminent death. He emphasizes repeatedly that it is the Persians who tell the tale about the shark. And yet he still deems it worthy of inclusion, hinting that its value is independent of whether or not it is true. The rhetorician Aphthonius (ca. 400) had defined fables as "false sayings that mirror the truth."[53] What counts, as with so many of Herodotus' equally quaint stories, is the purpose that it serves in the narrative.[54] Procopius presents us with a blend of animal fable and royal anecdote; the two are bridged by the fisherman, who is devoured by the shark and callously sacrificed by the king. In fact, the king and the shark are contenders for possession of the pearl. The shark is called a "lover" of the pearl no less than three times and exhibits all the aggression and indifference for basic needs that characterize human lovers.[55] Perozes is likewise seized by a powerful "longing" (*pothos*) to own the pearl, a longing that consumes itself at his death, when he tries to destroy it so that no one else may own it after him.

The fundamental contrast in the story is between king and subject. To the fisherman, money is dear, life dearer, and children most valuable (1.4.22 ff.). He faces danger partly from greed but mostly from concern for his offspring. His worries are humble, all too human compared to the immoderate longing of his master (*despotes*) for beautiful and rare items. The fisherman hopes that Perozes will seek a reputation for "virtue" and provide for his children if he should be devoured by the shark. But the fisherman is sorely mistaken; such virtue has passed from Persia since the days of Isdigerdes, who cared for the son of the foreign Arcadius. Perozes neither acknowledges his request (1.4.27; was he even listening?) nor, for all we know, grants it once the pearl is in his hands. The magnitude of his *pothos* deafens him to the words and needs of his subjects. The reader's expectations, built up by the pathetic speech of the homely fisherman, are shattered by Procopius' silence about whether the king provided for his children once he had acquired the pearl.

This fable, which takes the decline of Persia, and not only of Persia, one step farther, reveals an important truth about the nature of royal power and desire, just as Eusebius' fable of the lion and the hunters revealed Perozes' rashness and imminent defeat. *Pothos*, or immoderate longing, was a term used repeatedly by Arrian for Alexander the Great's passion "to see" new lands and unique relics and associate himself, like Perozes, with extraordinary objects and achievements.[56] The connection extends beyond this concept. Procopius' claim that the story of the pearl is worth telling and may not seem altogether incredible directly echoes the preface of Arrian's *Anabasis*. As it happens, Arrian was widely read in the sixth century, and his prefaces would have been the most well-known parts of his works, so an allusion seems probable.[57] With respect to their *pothos* and longing, Perozes and Alexander were also similar to Xerxes, the archetypal barbarian despot, who was repeatedly seized by "the desire to see" remarkable sights while leading his army into Greece.[58] Likewise, when he invaded the Roman empire in 540, Chosroes was also seized by "a desire to see" famous cities and attractions, or so Procopius claims (2.11.2). Note that Perozes valued his pearl chiefly because no other king had ever possessed its equal, a fact that is stated at the outset of the tale (1.4.14). There is something quite immoderate about his *pothos*, which leads him to sacrifice a loyal subject in order to obtain a valuable object. In a passage that, as we will see, shaped Procopius' political thought, Plato argued in the *Republic* that *pothos* was central to the emergence of the tyrant (573a). And Perozes stands exactly midway between the virtue of Isdigerdes and the tyranny of Chosroes.

Yet for all his fierceness (1.3.12), dishonor (1.3.21), faithlessness (1.4.1), and callous selfishness, Perozes is not a complete tyrant. He is neither entirely savage nor erotically motivated; those qualities belong to the shark. Perozes is instead characterized by an immoderate desire for valuable objects. His fundamental urge is to acquire. He wants the land of the Ephthalites and longs for the pearl, which symbolizes his grasping nature, just as it does that of Justinian and Theodora in the *Secret History*, interestingly enough (11.41–12.4).

The shark, on the other hand, is "dreadfully savage" and a fervent "lover." We must not overlook the political dimension of Procopius' insistence in this passage on cognates of *eros*. In Greek thought, *eros* could designate any "desire destructively excessive . . . for something other than sex."[59] Nietzsche would later call it the Will to Power. According to Thucydides, the greatest event in the Peloponnesian War, the Sicilian expedition, was undertaken by the Athenians in a frenzy of imperialistic passion, which the historian attributes to *eros*. And the empire of the Athenians was acknowledged by them and others to be a tyranny.[60] It is interesting that in

Herodotus, *eros* refers only to illicit sexual desire or desire for tyranny, a deliberate combination.⁶¹ This association of ideas was actually common in Greek thought. Not only was sexual lust often referred to as tyrannical⁶² but, conversely, Plato argued in the *Republic* that the roots of political tyranny lay in the untamed erotic drives of the tyrant. And eroticism in the *Republic* is by no means restricted to sex.⁶³

As an erotic predator, the shark has few rivals in Procopius; all are tyrants. We will examine Cavades and Chosroes in due course.⁶⁴ For now we should note the prominent, albeit careful, use of *eros* in the *Secret History*, a work devoted to the condemnation of the tyrannical regime of Justinian and Theodora. The latter's sordid background is too well known to need discussion.⁶⁵ Even after her elevation to the throne, it was rumored that *eros* could captivate her heart, causing her to lash out with bitter savagery against an unfortunate young man, who was made to "disappear."⁶⁶ She is also made to refer to paramours as "pearls" (3.16–17). Yet the greatest concentration of cognates of *eros* in Procopius' work (no less than six in about as many lines) is deployed precisely when Justinian falls in love with Theodora. It is no coincidence that *eros* completely dominates the narrative at this point, for it was erotic drives that formed the union that ultimately ruined the Roman empire.⁶⁷ Initially, the marriage was opposed by the old-fashioned empress Euphemia, but after her death Justinian compelled Justin, a doddering old man, to abrogate the ancient law prohibiting marriages between senators and courtesans (*hetairai*) and issue a more accommodating regulation, which Procopius amusingly calls *nomos heteros*. Thus does *eros* overturn the natural order, inducing sharks to neglect their hunger, husbands to forgive the adultery of their wives,⁶⁸ and ambitious men to abolish ancient laws.

It has not yet been noticed that Procopius' account of the marriage between Justinian and Theodora, albeit unquestionably historical,⁶⁹ is modeled on the marriage of the mad Persian king Cambyses to his sister, as told in Herodotus. Cambyses knew that ancestral custom opposed his desire to marry her, so he cowed the royal jurists into circumventing the ancient law and "discovering" a new one that better suited his interests: "he who was King of Persia could do anything he wished" (3.31). Herodotus' tongue-in-cheek comment that the shifty jurists had thereby saved the ancient law from annulment does not quite hide the fact that the new law represented the subversion of all law. And this is precisely what Procopius states, by echoing the language of Herodotus: Justinian's marriage was made possible by the annulment of the ancient law.⁷⁰ Thucydides had also alluded to this very passage in Herodotos to highlight the tyrannical nature of the Athenian empire,[71] and the *Secret History*, as we have seen, revolves around the subversion of law by the tyrant Justinian.

The two marriages stand at critical junctures in the narratives of the two historians. Herodotus flouts proper chronology by placing Cambyses' realization that he could do whatever he pleased in the middle of his account of the mad king's attacks on the customs of the Egyptians and the Persians, even though in reality the incestuous marriage must have occurred much earlier. The new law enunciated by the Persian jurists reveals the fundamental principle of despotism, and it is no accident that Herodotus derives it from Cambyses' erotic passion for his sister and then uses it to interpret his autocratic and brutal behavior in Egypt. Similarly, it is only after recounting Justinian's illegal marriage to Theodora that Procopius calls him a tyrant for the first time in the *Secret History*: "he straightaway mounted the imperial dignity as a tyrant" (9.51; note the pun). Thus Procopius follows Herodotus in deriving despotism from the ruler's *eros*, consolidated by the public ratification of a forbidden marriage (cf. 10.1–5). This is exactly what Plato called "a tyranny established by love."[72] The parallel between the two despots extends to the religious sphere. Like Cambyses, Justinian attacked the religions of his subjects. And the first complaint that Procopius makes against his coronation is that it took place three days before Easter, when such ceremonies were prohibited by religious custom (9.53; the date is correct).[73] Soon afterward he condemns Justinian's attacks on Christian heretics, Samaritans, and Hellenes (11.14 ff.).

Themes from classical treatments of despotism and *eros* are tightly woven into Procopius' narrative at this point. Readers familiar with the *Republic* will recall that the erotic attachment to courtesans (*hetairai*) plays an important role in the early formation of a tyrant's soul; for their sake he will even squander the resources of his parents (573d–574c). Note that immediately after mentioning Justinian's extravagant *eros* for Theodora, Procopius accuses him of consuming the resources of the state to augment her fortune and win her favor. And the phrase that he uses to make this point contains a poignant quotation from Xenophon's *Symposium*, a dialogue on *eros*.[74]

We must not lose sight of the fact that *eros* represents more than just sexual desire, that it can designate traits that we do not normally associate with sexuality. Though "erotic" in the sense we have discussed, Justinian was by no means a sensual man. Procopius does not pillory his sex life as he does that of Antonina or the young Theodora. There is even a disconcertingly asexual quality about him, compared, that is, to other ancient or Byzantine tyrants. Justinian may have been an "ardent lover," but it was only "of murder and money" (8.26, 22.29). We can hardly imagine what went through Procopius' mind when the emperor issued an edict in 538 declaring that "we know, though we are lovers of chastity . . . that nothing is more vehement than the fury of love."[75] A comparable case from classical literature is the grim protagonist of Xenophon's *Cyropaedia*, whose only erotic impulse is for the hunt, though he falls short of outright tyranny.[76]

Our analysis of what is arguably the most peculiar episode in the introduction to the *Persian War* has yielded some partial answers to the questions posed at the beginning of this chapter. Like other stories in the introduction, the tale of the shark is obviously not literally true. We must evaluate it by a different standard, which is what Procopius himself advises us to do. Like the fable told by the Roman ambassador Eusebius, it reveals basic truths about the political world of the sixth century. It would be otiose to name here the people prefigured by the savage and erotic shark.[77] The Persian tale introduces us to categories of historical analysis, for example the concept of *eros*, that Procopius intends to use later in his work. It foreshadows, and is thereby linked to, some of the central themes of the *Wars* and the *Secret History*.

The Tyranny of Cavades (1.5–7)

Do these old legends, blurry accounts of wars, and Persian fables have any overall point? So far we have examined individual episodes of the introduction and uncovered part of a network of terms and images that unifies Procopius' works. An undeniable consistency of thought underlies his idiosyncratic treatment of seemingly unrelated topics. Yet we still lack a clear idea of the introduction as a whole. Does it have an overall design that is greater than the sum of its parts?

Before we tackle this question, we must examine the two final episodes, the first of which offers an account of the first ten years of the reign of Cavades (488–531). The problem of Procopius' sources here becomes acute but no less insoluble. His outline roughly corresponds to the Persian sources, as do some of the anecdotes, but he makes mistakes and misrepresents the significance of events. Some scholars are content merely to note a few of the errors and move on to discuss Cavades' invasion of Roman territory in 502, when the *Persian War* properly begins.[78] In doing so they overlook the aim of Procopius' account, which, however unhistorical, describes the rise to power of a strong-willed and effective tyrant. Unfortunately, there is no way to know whether Procopius merely shaped the material he had in order to produce this picture or whether he greatly distorted it. Be that as it may, his portrait of Cavades completes the representation of Persian kingship built up in the introduction, whose purpose is to set the stage for Chosroes, a complex personality that dominates the bulk of the *Persian War*. It has not yet been noticed that Chosroes is the only ruler in Procopius' works who is frequently designated by his patronymic, "Chosroes the son of Cavades," and, what is more, that this occurs only when he invades Roman territory, behaves like a despot, or commits an atrocity.[79] This device subtly signifies the continuity between father and son in despotism and aggression. It is worth noting that the strategic use of patronymics to reveal the changing qualities of individuals is also a feature of Homeric poetry.[80]

The historical Cavades seems to have been a hostage of the Ephthalites when the latter killed his father Perozes, and not, as Procopius says, safely back in Persia (1.4.2).[81] Perozes' brother Balash succeeded to the throne (484–488) but was deposed in favor of his nephew Cavades, who had him blinded. Cavades initially supported the radical religious movement of the Mazdakites, who championed social and economic reform in favor of the poor. It seems that the Mazdakites preached the sharing of women and property; the sources, however, attribute only the former measure to Cavades, and it has been argued that the movement did not acquire its economic impetus or even its eponymous leader until the beginning of the reign of Chosroes.[82] In any case, the nobility deposed and imprisoned Cavades for trying to pry open their harems and replaced him with his brother Zamasp (496–498). Procopius is therefore wrong in saying that Cavades was the only son of Perozes to survive the battle against the Ephthalites (1.4.34). Also, he knows or says nothing about the Mazdakites (whom other Byzantine sources called Manichaeans) and attributes the law on the sharing of women solely to Cavades, transforming it into a measure resented by "the multitude" (1.5.1). On the other hand, he generally agrees with Persian accounts of Cavades' escape from prison,[83] marriage to a daughter of the king of the Ephthalites, and return to Persia at the head of a powerful army. The fate of his brother Zamasp is unclear;[84] Procopius has, in any case, confused Cavades' earlier struggle against his uncle Balash ("Blases") with his later one against Zamasp, about whom Procopius knows or says nothing. He is also wrong in saying that the Persians paid tribute to the

Ephthalites for only two years after the death of Perozes (1.4.35). It seems that they did so down to the reign of Chosroes.⁸⁵

Given that we are primarily interested in the way Procopius presents these events, we need not contribute to the futile search for his sources. For in spite of its factual errors, his account has an internal logic of its own, based on the use of concepts and images that only the educated Greek reader would have recognized. We discover once more the presence and subtle exploitation of polysemic terms that recur in strategically placed passages.

In Procopius' version, Cavades, the youngest (νεώτατος) son of Perozes, bursts onto the stage of history by ruling "in a more violent manner" and introducing innovations (νεώτερα) into the political system (πολιτεία). Let us note incidentally that when Chosroes later consolidates his hold on the throne, Procopius introduces him as "Chosroes, the son of Cavades . . . an immoderate lover of innovations" (1.23.1: νεωτέρων ἐραστής).⁸⁶ It is interesting that Chosroes was also the youngest of the three sons of Cavades who competed for the throne (1.11.3–5). And when Procopius tells us in the *Secret History* that Justinian was "a lover of murder and money," he immediately adds that the quarrelsome emperor was also an "excessive innovator" (νεωτεροποιὸς μάλιστα).⁸⁷ In dozens of passages in the *Wars*, as in the works of most ancient historians, "innovation" is synonymous with sedition, rebellion, treason, and murderous plots. This usage suggests a highly conservative mind-set and was typical among ancient writers: change is almost always for the worse.

Let us return to Cavades. Though he introduced many innovations, Procopius mentions only one, which, we are not surprised to learn, deals with sexual matters. His law aimed at establishing the sharing of women among the Persians but was resented by the people, probably because they realized that it would enable Cavades to enjoy their women rather than the opposite. Innovations that overturn hallowed customs are intrinsically unpopular, especially when they are introduced by violent men and concern family life. As the cynical and vehement Thrasymachus says in Plato's *Republic*, "tyranny, by stealth and violence, takes away what belongs to others, both what is sacred and profane, private and public" (344a).⁸⁸ Thus at the very outset of his reign, Cavades is associated with violence and radical sexual politics. Nevertheless, it is still odd that Procopius attributes to him the measure of holding women in common, which was famously associated with Plato's ideal regime of the philosopher-kings in the *Republic* (457c ff.). One could argue that despite the Platonic terminology, no such allusion is intended; Procopius is simply reporting what his sources correctly told him about Cavades' reforms. Salutary though such caution may be, we will see in the next chapter that Procopius' entire introduction is structured around the teachings of the *Republic*. In such a context, any mention of holding women in common can only refer to Plato's peculiar idea, which was so notorious and firmly tied to his name that some called it a "Platonic" practice even when it was ascribed to the Scythians by Herodotus.[89]

We are very fortunate to possess the reaction of a clever and educated contemporary to Procopius' portrayal of Cavades, which demonstrates that in the sixth century one could still depend on readers to catch such allusions. Though it may be true that "Agathias was not much of scholar,"[90] he knew his classics well. With Procopius' account before his eyes, he wrote of Cavades:

In his dealings with his subjects he was harsh and cruel, showing no respect for the social order, introducing revolutionary innovations into the body politic and subverting their age-old customs. He is even reputed to have made a law that wives should be held in common, not, I imagine, in accordance with the reasons of Socrates and Plato and the hidden benefit discussed in the dialogue, but merely in order to facilitate concubinage and allow any man who felt so inclined to sleep with any woman of his choosing. (4.27.7)[91]

Agathias' comments strengthen the probability of a Platonic allusion, for Cavades' measure immediately made him think of Socrates and the *Republic*, even though Procopius mentions neither. It is interesting that Agathias believed that the sharing of women in the *Republic* had a hidden meaning and that its straightforward and literal application by Cavades was consistent with the actions of a tyrant, not a philosopher. There is then a difference between the "benefit" sought by Plato and Cavades' desire for concubines, but that difference is "hidden."[92] Agathias also confirms our view of Procopius' Cavades as a tyrant, as does the seventh-century historian Theophylact, who, also based entirely on the *Wars*, called the father of Chosroes "a murderous man who exercised power violently and converted monarchy into tyranny" (4.6.6–11). This is a fairly accurate reading of the introduction of the *Persian War*.

Cavades' first attempt at tyranny failed. The Persians refused to share their wives with him and imprisoned him in the famous Castle of Oblivion, elevating his uncle Blases to the throne (1.5.1–9). To escape, Cavades ordered his beautiful wife to have sex with the jailer, who, as it happened, "conceived an exceedingly passionate love for her (ἠράσθη αὐτῆς ἔρωτα ἐξαίσιον)" (1.6.1–2). This is an ironic sequel to his proposed legislation, but it is consistent with the continued association of tyranny and *eros*. With the outside help of the loyal Seoses, Cavades escaped disguised in his wife's clothing. But now the little comedy comes to an end and Procopius confronts us with the cruel implications of Cavades' escape. The deposed king callously abandoned his wife to suffer punishments over which Procopius draws a discreet silence, ostensibly because he had conflicting versions. Cavades married a daughter of the king of the Ephthalites, raised a powerful army, and marched back to Persia to reclaim his throne (1.6.1–11). He cruelly blinded his uncle (even though he knows two conflicting versions of this event, Procopius records them both) and executed the general Gousanastades,[93] who had previously advocated Cavades' execution. Cavades is the first Persian to kill other Persians in the introduction.

Cavades then had to replace Gousanastades. This event is the first in a series of episodes that pointedly illustrate the king's ambiguous relationship to the law during his second reign. To make the point, and draw our attention to its significance, Procopius again invents historical material and probably distorts the reality of Sasanid institutions. The first of these episodes occurs right before Cavades reclaims the throne from his uncle Blases; the last is not resolved until after his death. Thus one could say that the second reign of Cavades is defined by events that emphasize the tension between tyranny and law. By examining them in detail, we will come to a better understanding of Cavades' position in the sequence of Persian kings from Isdigerdes to Chosroes. The events we will look at here are the replacement of Gousanastades, Chosroes' succession to the throne, and the trial of Seoses.

(a) Gousanastades had commanded the province that adjoined the land of the Ephthalites. Upon his return, Cavades declared that he would give that position to the first Persian who swore allegiance to him (1.6.12). But "having said that, Cavades immediately repented his words, for he remembered that a law (*nomos*) did not allow certain offices to be bestowed upon any Persians other than those to whom the honor was granted by right of birth." And he feared that he would be compelled to break the law should the applicant not qualify properly for the office (1.6.13–14). As it turned out, however, the man who offered to serve him, Adergoudounbades, was a relative of Gousanastades and thus the king was not forced to decide between the law and his promise. But we must question Procopius' narrative, which has rightly been greeted with skepticism by at least one scholar familiar with Persian customs.[94] Is it likely that Cavades would forget such a law? And how did Procopius know the king's mind? Even if the account is accurate, we must still ask why Procopius chose to divulge Cavades' thoughts in such a dramatic fashion at this point. Good historians never pry into the minds of kings without reason. In this passage "law" is mentioned three times in three consecutive sentences. Cavades understood that it opposed his will, but he also knew that breaking it would not be in his interest. Procopius reveals his thoughts in order to make explicit the tension between the royal will and the law. Ultimately, the sole reason that Cavades did not "disgrace the law" was "chance," or *tyche* (1.6.15). It was pure chance that the law was upheld when it fell into the hands of Cavades.

Let us also note that when Adergoudounbades first approached Cavades, he "bowed" before him (προσεκύνησε), called him "master" (δεσπότης), and begged him to "use him as a slave in whatever way he pleased" (1.6.16). Perozes had earlier been called "master" by the humble fisherman (1.4.22), and Adergoudounbades' conduct was probably typical for the Persian court. Still, it is significant that Procopius depicts the tyrannical Cavades as the first king in the *Wars* before whom noble Persians bow like slaves. There is little question of law between masters and slaves. Recall that the king of the Ephthalites punished the defeated Perozes by demanding that he bow before him and call him "master," which the Persian naturally deemed a great dishonor (1.3.17, 22). This, then, is an important development in the gradual rise of Persian despotism in the introduction of the *Persian War*.

(b) The eleventh chapter of Book 1 begins and ends with statements on the relationship between Cavades and Persian law that involve his plans for the succession of his son Chosroes and the trial and execution of his loyal supporter Seoses. But in accordance with the linkage of Roman and Persian affairs that governs so much of the *Persian War*, Procopius links the first of these two events to the death of the emperor Anastasius and the rise of Justin and the second to the deposition of Anastasius' nephew Hypatius from office and the torture of Hypatius' friends by Justin. Procopius thus moves from the accession of a Roman emperor to the succession plans of the Persian king and from the trial of a Persian official who frustrated those plans to the trial of Hypatius, the most conspicuous remnant of the previous regime.[95] Also, the heart of the chapter depicts the reversal of the trusting relationship between Arcadius and Isdigerdes, as Cavades' request that Justin adopt and safeguard the succession of his son Chosroes is refused by the Roman court.[96] The interweaving of these events exhibits considerable literary skill. The themes of the introduction have come full circle.

Procopius tells us that Cavades had three sons: Caoses, who was entitled to reign "by law" because of his age; Zames, who was barred from the succession because he had lost an eye but loved by the Persians for his courage, military skill, and undeniable "virtue"; and Chosroes, about whom are told only that he was "exceedingly loved" by his father (1.11.3–5, 1.23.4). Naturally, it was he who prevailed in the end. In Procopius' account, each son represents a different claim to political power: the whole passage rather schematically depicts the triumph of royal will over law and virtue. Procopius underlines this point by saying that Cavades' dislike for Caoses "violated both nature and law." The arbitrariness of his actions is further emphasized by the parallelism between his "completely unjustified" (ἐξ αἰτίας οὐδεμιᾶς) attack on Rome (1.7.3) and his "inexplicable" (οὐδενὶ λόγῳ) preference for Chosroes over his other sons, both of whom had stronger claims to rule (2.9.12). Procopius links this royal preference to a digression on the power of *tyche* in human affairs (2.9.13).[97] However that may be, it is worth noting that the same phrases that designate the arbitrariness of Cavades in the *Persian War* are used throughout the *Secret History* to characterize Justinian. Procopius will often pair on a single page "completely unjustified" murders with "inexplicable" diplomacy.[98] Thus, once again the essential features of Persian despotism, as presented in the introduction to the *Persian War*, resonate in the attack on Roman tyranny in the *Secret History*. The fortunes of Rome and Persia are again subtly linked by the economy of Procopius' prose.

When Cavades died, Caoses claimed the throne "by right of law," but his father had specifically designated Chosroes as his heir. The Persian nobles, asserting that their vote alone could decide the issue, "recalled the virtue of Cavades and straightaway declared Chosroes king" (1.21.17–22). The reader might wonder at the nature of Cavades' "virtue," a term that here seems to be used in an amoral sense. At the end of the introduction, Procopius praises the shrewdness and energy with which he "strengthened the kingdom and guarded it securely" (1.6.19), a claim that has been taken to reflect his admiration for Cavades.[99] Yet a Persian could say with justice that it was precisely because of his virtue that Cavades subverted Persian law, for it is mentioned by Procopius only when it overrides the "law" of succession.[100] A Roman, on the other hand, would not be wrong in thinking that the unprovoked attacks of Cavades reflected the opposite of the "virtue" of Isdigerdes (cf. 1.2.8–10), just as his diplomatic dealings with Justin reversed the trusting relationship that had once existed between Isdigerdes and Arcadius. Cavades' virtue is independent of any ethical qualities[101] and bodes ill for both Rome and Persia.

We may again suspect that this narrative, however historical in outline, is not intended to reflect faithfully the realities of the Persian empire. Procopius set out to describe and delineate for his audience the rise of a particular kind of tyranny, and to that end he drew upon the concepts used in his classical sources. There was in fact no law of succession that favored eldest sons in Sasanid Persia, though that was certainly what Herodotus and Xenophon had implied about the Achaemenid empire.[102] And the schematic conflict between law, virtue, and royal favor is ultimately derived from the conceptual world of ancient political thought.[103] Procopius is writing more *for* classically educated Greeks than *about* Sasanid Persians.[104]

(c) The Persian noble Seoses had loyally helped Cavades escape from prison and regain his throne (1.6). He then held the highest office in Persia for over twenty years. In 522, he participated in and probably undermined the abortive negotiations on the adoption of Chosroes by Justin, the details of which need not concern us here. Suffice it to say that Cavades had hoped the adoption would guarantee the smooth succession of his favorite son, as Arcadius had once requested of Isdigerdes.[105] When Seoses returned from the conference, he was tried and executed. Procopius is our only source for this event, which is significant in many ways, although here we will discuss only its implications for the administration of justice in Persia and Rome. According to Procopius, Seoses was "slandered" by an enemy to Cavades for having exceeded the commands of his "master." His trial was carried out in a spirit of "envy rather than concern for the law" (1.11.31–32). Cavades feigned grief at the downfall of his old friend "but had no desire to save him." Concealing his anger behind words of gratitude, the king justified his inaction by saying that he did not wish to undermine the laws (1.11.36–37)! Procopius exposes his dual deceit: while publicly proclaiming friendship and gratitude, he secretly longed for Seoses' destruction; while posturing as the champion of law, he presided over legal proceedings that showed no "concern for the law." In addition, Seoses was on trial for frustrating the king's own attempt to "violate both nature and law" by securing the illegal succession of Chosroes. Looking ahead, we note that this kind of dissimulation was one of the chief characteristics of both Chosroes and Justinian.[106]

In accordance with the linkage of Persian and Roman affairs that governs the narrative, the trial of Seoses is followed by a parallel event in Byzantium. Hypatius was "slandered" to the emperor Justin, he was deposed from his command, and his closest associates were "bitterly tortured" (1.11.38–39). This conjunction of events prepares us for another parallelism of Roman and Persian affairs in Book 1, namely the artful coincidence of the rebellion against Chosroes and the Nika riots in Constantinople, to which Procopius devotes two sequential, and obviously linked, chapters (1.23–24). Let us note in this connection that, according to Procopius, "slander" was one of the chief mechanisms of the Roman administrative and judicial system and impels much of his narrative. The reason for this is stated unambiguously in the *Secret History*: Justinian "was extremely receptive to slander, and severe in inflicting punishment. For he would never judge a case by investigating it, but would make his decision just by listening to the opinion of the slanderer" (8.28). Once again important elements of Procopius' analysis of Roman tyranny in the *Secret History* are mirrored in his account of Persian despotism in the introduction to the *Persian War*.

The "History of the Armenians" (1.5.7–40)

Very little in the introduction to the *Persian War*, and possibly even nothing, is ultimately superfluous or merely trivial. Procopius did not place any information there simply because he had it. He certainly knew more about the relations between Rome and Persia in the fifth century than he lets on. The primary aim of our analysis should be to understand his criteria for selection.

The introduction may be disappointing as a history of international relations, yet all of its anecdotes and digressions prepare the reader for, and thus partly reveal, the broader themes that structure the *Persian War*. Of course, we cannot adequately grasp those themes until after we have read the whole text carefully and repeatedly; that is, we are not aware of them when we read the introduction for the first time. Nevertheless, with proper sensitivity to patterns and points of emphasis, even a first reading of the introduction can offer a view of what is to come. One may notice, for instance, the schematic decline in the virtue of the Persian kings or the ambiguous relationship between the will of Cavades and Persian law.

Before we tackle the question of the overall structure of the introduction, we must examine another one of its peculiar components, a long digression (cf. 1.5.40) on the relations between the Persians and the Armenians in the fourth century. It is interpolated very awkwardly between Cavades' imprisonment and his escape from the Castle of Oblivion. It interrupts the narrative of his career, splitting apart his two reigns with seemingly irrelevant material from the fourth century. We will of course resist the facile option of dismissing it as a clumsy attempt by Procopius to flaunt his knowledge of foreign customs and histories.

The clue for understanding the function of this digression is given twice by Procopius in two strategic locations, at its very beginning and its very end. We must take our bearings from what he says, although the significance of the digression may not be immediately clear. Procopius tells us that its purpose is to prove that the Persian law of total silence regarding occupants of the Castle of Oblivion was broken on at least one occasion, which is related in what he first calls "the history of the Armenians" (1.5.9) and later "the composition (συγγραφή) of the Armenians" (1.5.40).[107] Procopius is referring to a text written by Armenians about their own history and not merely to the events of Armenian history as such, which could have been recorded in a Greek or a Persian source. This is significant because Procopius rarely divulges his sources. The Armenian provenance of the digression, to which he twice draws our attention, must be a central aspect of our interpretation of its purpose. It is important that we learn about the breaking of a Persian law from an Armenian source.

As it happens, we possess the source that Procopius used, in one form or another. Previously considered a *History of Armenia*, written by a certain Faustus of Byzantium, it has recently been shown to be the *Epic Histories* written by an anonymous Armenian in the second half of the fifth century. All the information in Procopius' digression can be found in the Armenian text, and, except for the order of events, there are no major discrepancies. Some minor differences are owed to Procopius' reworking of the material, which, as we will see, produced some interesting results.[108]

The Castle of Oblivion (literally "of Forgetfulness") derived its name from a law that made it a capital crime ever to mention those who were confined there.[109] The law was broken in the 360s, when the Persian king, whom Procopius strangely calls Pacurius, possibly a corruption of Shapur II (309–379),[110] offered to grant any favor to an Armenian who had led Persian forces to victory. Such magnanimous offers made by absolute rulers or gods in ancient literature rarely end happily.[111] True to form, the Armenian requested that he spend a day with his former ruler Arsaces, who was imprisoned in the Castle of Oblivion.[112] "This of course greatly annoyed the king, that he should be so forced to abrogate an ancient law, yet in order to be perfectly true to his word, he allowed the request" (1.5.33). The similarity with the predicament of Cavades, who, upon his return to Persia, also made an offer that could have violated an ancient law (1.6.12–17), is unmistakable. The two events are in fact parallel: the Armenian digression is inserted between the two reigns of Cavades, its explicit purpose is to show how an ancient law was abrogated, and Pacurius' decision, which demonstrates the superiority of royal will over law, literally introduces the account of Cavades' second reign, which, as we have seen, revolves around that very theme.

So, right before his account of Cavades' second reign, Procopius presents a fourth-century instance of the conflict between the law and the royal will. Why the duplication? Why did Procopius interrupt his narrative so awkwardly in order to give us Cavades before Cavades? There is, let us note, a crucial difference between the two kings that has nothing to do with their actions or character but rather involves their historical context. The conspicuous intrusiveness of the fourth-century material highlights the fact that, unlike Cavades, Pacurius does not belong to the sequence of Persian rulers in the introduction. That sequence, as we will see in the following chapter, presents a schematized and essentially unhistorical view of the decline of Persia into tyranny. Yet Procopius did not literally believe that during the course of the fifth century Persia lapsed from the virtue of Isdigerdes into the violence of Cavades. The aim of the introduction is theoretical. It treats the virtues and vices of kings, and Persian kings in particular, from the viewpoint of political theory. Because they stand outside that schematic sequence, the actions of Pacurius suggest that the tension between law and will was an essential feature of Persian kingship. It was not a historical innovation of Cavades, who is more of a symbolic than a historical figure. The Armenian digression prevents the reader from taking the political message of the sequence of kings too literally from a historical point of view. The actions of Pacurius remind us that actual Persian monarchs resembled Cavades far more than they did Isdigerdes.

This interpretation, however, does not account for the Armenian provenance of the digression, which Procopius so uncharacteristically emphasizes. We must, therefore, begin anew and follow a different line of reasoning. The law that Pacurius broke forbade Persians to say anything about prisoners in the Castle of Oblivion and, by extension, about any instances when the law was broken. There are events in Persian history that Persians cannot or will not talk about. To learn about them we must turn to their neighbors, who are not necessarily bound by the laws and customs of Persia and who are not intimidated by its power, so long as they stand freely on their own soil. This qualification is suggested by the magical inter-rogation of Arsaces by Pacurius, which is narrated within the Armenian digression. So long as Arsaces stood upon Persian soil, he behaved as a "slave" and "suppliant" before the Persian king, but when he walked upon the Armenian soil strewn about the other half of the king's tent, he boldly threatened the Persians and "concealed none of his secret intentions."[113]

The truth can sometimes be spoken only by foreigners,[114] though they too must be mindful of circumstances. As we saw earlier, the Persian offi-cers in Perozes' army "held their tongue out of fear" and had to beg the Roman Eusebius to intercede and reveal their plight to the king. Eusebius cautiously spun a fable that indirectly alerted Perozes to the danger (1.3.12–13). So too only an anonymous and hostile Armenian text can reveal how a Persian king broke an ancient law of Persia regarding matters that could never be mentioned by any Persian.[115] A truth that only foreigners can reveal is of course a hostile one, for there is little danger in praising one's own country or king. We are reminded of Procopius' suggestion in the preface that his own impartiality will result primarily in a fair distribution of blame.[116]

The implications of this conclusion naturally extend to the Roman empire and its historian. Ugly or secret truths about Rome can sometimes be spoken only by its enemies. That is why Procopius often places them in the mouth of foreign speakers, especially victims of the Roman emperor. The use of this technique in the *Wars* has been noted and discussed, espe-cially with regard to Justinian's foreign and military policy.[117] It was em-ployed by many ancient historians[118] and by some modern ones as well. According to Machiavelli, whose admission is succinct and elegant, those who would understand his depiction of Cosimo de' Medici in the *Florentine Histories* should "note very well what I will make his adversaries say, be-cause that which I will not want to say myself, as from me, I will make his adversaries say."[119] Machiavelli claimed to have learned this trick from Livy.

We will have occasion to discuss how Procopius used the mouths of his characters to say things that he could not say in his own voice, whether for political or literary reasons. Yet there is no reason to assume that he exploited the speeches of foreigners to reveal the truth only about political and military issues. It is possible that he presented many other aspects of the Roman world through their eyes. Let us look at a minor example from the Armenian digression, which is actually an inside joke, but which nicely complements Procopius' quiet equation of Romans and barbarians. Ac-cording to the Armenian text, the Armenians and the Persians established an alliance when the former attacked and slaughtered "the Greeks" (i.e., the Romans), with whom the Persians were at war.[120] Although his source must have been perfectly clear on this matter, Procopius chose not to designate "the Greeks" by name in his version of the story but referred to them cryptically as "certain other barbarians who lived not far from the Armenians" (1.5.11).

Procopius could not have expected many of his readers to detect the small substitution and appreciate the irony. The Armenian *Epic Histories* was not, after all, an accessible text, and the fictive nature of the war it relates would have prevented a meaningful comparison of Procopius' digression to other histories of fourth-century Armenia. The joke was probably meant for himself and a few friends; we are very fortunate to be able to detect it today. Though highly esoteric, it still indicates that Procopius' view of his fellow Romans was not much more favorable than his view of Justinian, whom he also considered a "barbarian."[121] We will see this thesis confirmed repeatedly in the *Wars* and with regard to many aspects of late Roman civilization. Procopius was the conscience of his age, not the Roman chauvinist who emerges from recent discussions.[122] He may have despised barbarians, yet his view of the Romans was far from rosy. To his stance we may with only slight exaggeration compare that of Arthur Schopenhauer: "every nation ridicules the rest and all are right."[123]

The most skilled manipulator of the foreigner's perspective in antiquity was undoubtedly Herodotus, a major influence behind Procopius' *Persian War*. We have reviewed sufficient evidence to substantiate the claim of a "spiritual affinity" between the two historians.[124] In the first book of his *Histories*, Herodotus continually induces his readers, through the subtle charm of his stories, to view foreign things through the eyes of foreigners and to turn that outside perspective back onto Greece itself.[125] We have already noted a few of Procopius' stories that seem to have that goal. Another interesting example occurs in the trial of the Persian official Seoses, which we discussed in the previous section with regard to Cavades' attitude toward Persian law. One of the charges brought against Seoses was that "he revered strange new divinities, and had buried his recently deceased wife, though it was forbidden by the laws for Persians to place the bodies of the dead within the earth" (1.11.35). Procopius does not tell us what divinities Seoses worshipped, nor does he explain why he buried his wife. Yet in this behavior, which was so abhorrent to the Persians that they condemned Seoses to death, the Roman reader could easily see a reflection of his own practices. As though to underscore the point, on the next page Procopius relates how Cavades tried to force the Caucasian Iberians, tendentiously presented here as zealous Christians, to adopt Persian customs. Procopius specifies only one of Cavades' demands, namely that the Iberians cease burying their dead (1.12.3–4). The language here is identical to that used in the accusations against Seoses on the previous page. Seoses' capital offense is revealed as an ordinary Christian practice.

The late sixth-century historian Menander the Protector reports that the treaty of 561 specified that Christians in Persia would be allowed to bury their dead, "as is our custom."[126] Other contemporary writers, for example Agathias, viewed the exposure of the dead as the most irreconcilable difference between Persians and Romans and condemned it as barbaric.[127] Yet regardless of his own opinion, in his account of Seoses' trial, Procopius refrains from editorializing, allowing the trial to proceed as though its premises were self-evident and natural. He thereby allows the Roman reader to see his culture from a foreign point of view, as potentially sacrilegious and punishable by death. Things that one takes for granted appear questionable when seen through the eyes of foreigners. This mode of presentation owes much to Herodotean pedagogy.

Let us be fair to Agathias, however, whose patriotism was in some respects affected. He knew that every society, including his own, functioned and persevered on the basis of cherished myths that could not be openly questioned. According to his *Histories*, only philosophers were exempt from the power of this opinion, though politically they were subject to its dominion in both Christian Rome and Zoroastrian Persia.[128] For true philosophers, the customs and beliefs of both states were equally false. Agathias believed that the wisdom of the sixth-century Platonists represented "the unrivaled peak" of his age.[129] The view from that peak flouts local patriotism and cultural pride. And so we may wonder what standpoint Procopius occupies when he calls the inhabitants of the eastern Roman empire "barbarians who live not far from the Armenians." Agathias barely disguised his philosophical sympathies, but he wrote after the death of Justinian. It is now time to expose the secret politics of Procopius of Caesarea.

Chapter 3
The Secret History of Philosophy

The Sequence of Regimes Ends in Tyranny

We have examined the individual stories that constitute the introduction to the *Persian War* and have shown how each story foreshadows some of the main themes that Procopius intends to develop in the main body of the narrative as well as in the *Secret History*. Those stories are not offered as factual reporting, that is, history understood in modern sense; rather, they establish the broad framework of the ensuing conflict. The introduction to the *Persian War* thus reflects the fusion of literature and history that we find in all classical historiography. The difference between these two spheres, which modern historians try to keep rigidly separate, is best indicated by the need to set aside questions of source and accuracy and inquire instead about the literary function of each story, that is, to pose questions now reserved for works of fiction. Procopius' pointed anecdotes and nuanced vocabulary, however implausible they may be from a historical point of view, frequently reveal a deeper aspect of his thought. A common grid of language binds together the *Secret History* and the *Wars*, reflecting their conceptual unity.

But what about the introduction as a whole? Does it amount to more than the sum of its parts? As we saw, it sketches the gradual decline of the Persian kings, from the virtuous Isdigerdes and the honor-loving Vararanes to the acquisitive Perozes and the violent Cavades. It consists of discreet episodes that focus on the character of each king, which they illustrate through legends, anecdotes, and, possibly, distortions of actual events. The individuals that emerge are distinctive, if not always believable from a historical point of view. But perhaps they are less important than the overall picture into which they have been integrated. This thesis has been stated well with respect to the *Histories* of Herodotus: "These stories begin to look as if they form part of a reasoned whole, a whole that is only presented in partial stories. They begin to reveal how Herodotus has marshaled particulars, and even a false particular, into a coherent whole that compels us to reflect on a universal question."[1]

Procopius presents us with a series of consecutive regimes, each of which is a step on the road from virtue to tyranny, although perhaps perfect tyranny does not emerge until the reign of Chosroes, the main protagonist of the *Persian War*. The schema to which Procopius has adapted his material was not without precedent. For instance, Cassiodorus' panegyric of the Gothic queen Amalasuntha lists her (legendary) ancestors, each of whom corresponds to a specific virtue. Amalasuntha is praised for combining them in herself. The technique is more crudely executed than in Procopius, to be sure, but Cassiodorus may have used this device in his (lost) *Gothic History*.[2] There were more serious antecedents in classical historiography. It was by devising a theoretical model of the sequence of regimes that Polybius had tried to explain the nature of the Roman state to his Greek audience. He related the cycle of political transformations allegedly experienced by Greek cities, from the origin of just kingship to the rise of violent despotism, in order to explain the stability of Rome's mixed constitution.[3] Although there are general similarities between the two sequences, and Chosroes does in a sense represent the summation of all the virtues and vices of his predecessors, the comparison with Polybius does not help us understand the focus of Procopius' introduction, which is concerned with the individual character of rulers and not the form of different regimes.

Polybius claimed that his sequence of regimes was only a summary of what had been said "by Plato and certain other philosophers" (6.5.1–2). He even suggested that a comparison between Rome and the *Republic* would have been in order, had Plato's ideal state ever existed (6.47.7–10). Book 8 of the *Republic* happens to contain the first sequence of political regimes in Greek political thought, and that sequence is, mutatis mutandis, strikingly similar to the one in the introduction of the *Persian War*. In addition, a Platonic template can help explain the peculiar form Procopius has given to individual episodes in his introduction.

Socrates begins his sequence with the ideal regime of aristocracy or kingship (543a, 544e), where virtuous guardians loyally protect the state against both internal and external enemies. Their description as fierce guard dogs who threaten strangers while behaving gently toward their charges exactly matches the portrayal of the virtuous Isdigerdes in the first episode of Procopius' introduction.[4] Like Socrates' guardians (414b), the first Persian king in the introduction kept watch over outside enemies and inside "friends." There is a double irony here. First, Arcadius, an idiot, could not be cast as a philosopher-king, although Procopius saves the comparison by granting him wise sages and divine inspiration, ideals that he never attributes to any other ruler. Second, the guardians who preserve the state in Procopius' introduction are themselves outsiders and ultimately become its prime enemies. Rome does not seem to have guardians of its own; indeed, no Roman army is mentioned in the introduction. This silence foreshadows the dismal performance of the Roman forces in the *Persian War*, in particular their complete absence during the great invasion of Chosroes in 540.

As we saw in our analysis of the episode, the regency of Isdigerdes gives rise to the very question asked by Socrates: what happens when the guardians, "given that they are stronger than the citizens, become like savage masters (δεσπόται ἄγριοι) instead of well-meaning allies?" (416b). Procopius' introduction offers an account of exactly such a transformation, and the remainder of the *Persian War* describes its consequences. It is precisely at the nadir of Roman fortunes, after the destruction of Antioch by the Persians, that he relates a fascinating discussion between Justinian's envoys and Chosroes (2.10.21–23). Chosroes demanded money so that the Persians could "guard" (φυλάσσοντες) the Caspian Gates; when the envoys asked whether this meant that they would forever pay tribute to the Persians, Chosroes responded by saying that they would instead be paying in order to use the Persians as soldiers, who would "guard" (φυλάξωσιν) Roman land in perpetuity. As in the introduction, no mention is made here of a Roman army.

Procopius was not the first to cast the military relationship between Rome and her barbarian enemies in a Platonic mold. In 398, Synesius of Cyrene, drawing an explicit comparison between the Roman empire and Plato's *Republic*, argued before a faction of courtiers that the empire should rely on native "guardians" and "guard-dogs" and eschew barbarian "wolves," for "the moment that the latter notice any weakness or slackness in the dogs, they will attack these and the flock and the shepherds likewise."[5]

Socrates' sequence of regimes runs through timocracy, oligarchy, democracy, and tyranny, "each successive regime representing a further decline in the rulers' concern for virtue."[6] Socrates is less interested in the regime as such than in the dominant characteristics of the men who most exemplify it. This enables Procopius to apply the philosopher's descriptions to a series of kings; that is, to consecutive rulers within a single political system (a *politeia*, as he calls it, in the case of both Rome and Persia). Socrates' timocratic man, like Procopius' Vararanes, is warlike and loves honor (545b, 549a). The oligarchic man, like Perozes, quickly loses the honor of his predecessor (cf. 551a with 1.3.22) and is fundamentally acquisitive in nature. During his rule, a sharp distinction emerges between poor and rich (551d), and the ugliness of his character is revealed whenever "the guardianship of orphans is entrusted to him," which reminds us of the fisherman's request in Procopius' introduction (cf. 554c with 1.4.25). Let us note that Justinian also "faced widespread and frequent censure" regarding the implementation of wills and guardianship of orphans.[7] Democracy is a special case in Socrates' schema, as it offers opportunities not found in other regimes. Plato seems to have viewed it as the best of all possible states in his time, so it partly stands outside the schema of decline.[8] But the nature of a democratic man is an unlikely type for a Persian king because it lacks specific character (557b–e: it "contains all species of regimes"). Procopius skips past him, moving straight to Socrates' tyrant, who, like Cavades, is violent and "if he's exiled and comes back in spite of his enemies, plainly comes back a complete tyrant" (565e–566a). Ruling despotically, he virtually enslaves the city (cf. 577c with 1.6.16). This exactly matches the account of Cavades' reign in the *Persian War*.

There are too many parallels here for this to be a coincidence. The chance that four types of personality will be arranged in one particular sequence by accident is only one in twenty-four. But once the full extent of Procopius' indebtedness to Plato is revealed below, there should be no reason to doubt that he constructed the introduction to the *Persian War* on a Platonic framework. Persian history in the fifth century did not just happen to follow the sequence outlined in Book 8 of the *Republic*. On the other hand, it is unlikely that Procopius invented everything; we have seen that his account agrees in some respects with the testimony of independent sources. It seems that he shaped his material subtly to yield a Platonic schema of decline or, perhaps, not so subtly: Cavades, we are told by historians of Persia, "was a mild man who tried to deal leniently with his subjects and enemies alike."[9] The overall message of the introduction in any case seems to be independent of the factual truth of the discrete stories that constitute it; sometimes the deeper issues so dominate the text that the surface narrative seems almost absurd.

Furthermore, the schema of decline does not apply to Persia alone. If we pull together Procopius' scattered statements, we see that the Roman emperors also deteriorated in virtue, albeit in a different manner, owing to the fact that, unlike their Persian counterparts, they were not soldiers. Not surprisingly, this process is documented primarily in the *Secret History*. The emperor Anastasius was neither a hero nor a philosopher nor a saint, but still he "was the most provident and prudent administrator of all the emperors." He left the treasury full of money, remitted the taxes on cities that had been attacked by barbarians, and never did anything without careful planning.[10] Yet his reign was not altogether perfect. In Book 7, Procopius has the Gothic king Totila praise both Anastasius and Theoderic for creating peace and prosperity (7.21.23: εἰρήνης δὲ καὶ ἀγαθῶν πραγμάτων . . . ἐνεπλήσαντο), yet in Book 1 the historian notes in his own voice that the inhabitants of Amida were not prepared for the invasion of Cavades precisely because of the prevailing peace and prosperity (1.7.4: ἐν εἰρήνῃ καὶ ἀγαθοῖς πράγμασιν). By carefully using the same words in different contexts, a technique that reveals not his "limited vocabulary" but the unity of his thought and the Thucydidean economy of his prose,[11] Procopius leads us to reflect upon the equivocal nature of Anastasius' reign. He may have been a good man and a conscientious administrator, but he was ultimately responsible for the disastrous lack of organization exhibited by the Roman army in its response to Cavades' invasion (cf. 1.8–9).[12]

Anastasius' successor, Justin, was old, weak, stupid, and illiterate, "a thing that had indeed never before occurred among the Romans." Yet overall "he did his subjects neither harm nor good."[13] As for Justinian, suffice it to say that "he caused calamities for the Romans, so great and so numerous as had never been heard of previously by anyone in the entire history of the world."[14] It was his disastrous reign that inspired the *Secret History*, possibly the most compelling and damaging invective from antiquity.

The historical fact that decisively shaped the political thought of Procopius was the nearly contemporary accession to the thrones of Persia and Rome of two of the most despicable autocrats in all of history. On its surface, the introduction to the *Persian War* takes us down the path that led to one of them, though readers who compare it to the *Secret History* will realize that Persian despotism is parallel to the Roman tyranny of Justinian. Moreover, Procopius' account of that decline is modeled on a Platonic template. The international relations of the fifth century are a stage on which the teachings of Platonic political philosophy are played out. For example, the relationship between Rome and Persia under Arcadius and Isdigerdes in the early fifth century is presented as a variation on the relationship between the ordinary citizens and the guardians of Plato's *Republic*. Procopius was not the first to view the virtues and faults of the later empire in Platonic terms. Priscus of Panium had done so in the previous century, and Procopius almost certainly knew his work.[15] Whereas they used Plato to interpret history, the converse was also possible; namely, the use of history, even barbarian history, to illustrate philosophical ideas. Whoever wrote the sixth-century dialogue *On Politics* adduced an anecdote about the Persian king Perozes to explain the ideal relationship between the ordinary citizens and the "guardians" of a state (4.60 ff.). The entire conception is naturally taken directly from the *Republic*.[16]

We are therefore faced with a kind of Platonic mimesis. The question is, what is its purpose in the *Wars*? By itself, the comparison of Persian kings to Platonic regimes is intriguing, but it can only be significant if it is part of a broader network of Platonic allusions that forms patterns visible to readers familiar with Plato's works. As it happens, that is exactly what we find in the *Wars*. The last great work of classical historiography is shaped at its most basic level by philosophical concerns.

Tyranny and the Politics of Philosophy

Tyranny, the culmination of Socrates' sequence of regimes, is a prominent feature of Procopius' works. One can even say that it is his chief historical and political concern. It is possible, however, that this places too much stress on the most apparent aspects of his work. Tyrants, after all, cut unmistakable figures. According to Socrates, the sequence that leads to them begins with the ideal regime of the philosophers. Are there any philosophers in the *Wars*? As it happens, there are, but they are not always easy to spot. The first to appear is so disguised that he is virtually unrecognizable, except, that is, to readers who have met his kind before. This fact, in turn, raises interesting questions about the intended audience of the *Wars*; not the one most likely to read the book but the one most likely to understand it. Like the introduction to the *Persian War* as a whole, the passages we are about to examine have received no attention in the scholarly literature. We can speculate on the reasons for this, but for now let us note only that their subtext is invisible to readers unfamiliar with the works of Plato and the other students of Socrates. Once identified, however, the allusions are obvious, indeed so glaring that one begins to wonder just how many Platonic echoes reverberate within Procopius' text.

Let us return once more to the trial of Seoses, which we looked at previously in connection with Cavades' subversion of Persian law and Procopius' attempt to present Roman customs, for example burial, from a foreign point of view. This trial actually forms a densely interwoven nexus for a number of the broader themes of the *Wars*. Procopius' account of it, the only one we have, is plausible on the surface, but its details are rather strange and the grounds for the accusation against Seoses are overdetermined. One enemy "slandered" him for sabotaging the negotiations with Justin. Others made additional accusations and brought him to trial. His enemies were motivated by "envy" rather than concern for law. They objected to the high office he held and did not like his "arrogance," though Procopius tells us that he was incorruptible and extremely just. This was not all. His "accusers" (κατήγοροι) added that he "was entirely unwilling to live according to the established manner (ἐν τῷ καθεστῶτι τρόπῳ) or uphold the laws of the Persians." Students of Plato should begin to find all this vaguely familiar. The explanation given for Seoses' peculiar behavior gives the game away: "for he revered strange new divinities (καινὰ δαιμόνια)." The "judges"—or should δικασταὶ be jurors?—in the end "condemned the man to death (θάνατον τοῦ ἀνθρώπου κατέγνωσαν)."

This trial narrative is little more than a cento of terms and phrases taken from accounts of the trial of Socrates, to which have been added a few circumstantial details from the (presumably) historical trial of Seoses. Socrates himself claimed that the charges against him were only "slander" motivated by "envy."[17] His friends praised his unrivaled devotion to justice but also hinted that arrogance may have gotten him into trouble to begin with.[18] In accordance with Athenian legal usage, Socrates' accusers were κατήγοροι and the "jurors" who "condemned him to death" (θάνατον αὐτοῦ κατέγνωσαν) were δικασταί. Two of the main charges brought against him were that he did not believe in the gods of the city and the infamous accusation that he introduced "strange new divinities" (καινὰ δαιμόνια).[19] Some of his accusers added that he taught others to have contempt for the "established laws (τῶν καθεστώτων νόμων)."[20] All these words and phrases recur in the trial of Seoses.

What is going on here? One conclusion, at least, is certain. This passage does not contain a straightforward account of a Persian trial. It simply cannot be used as a source of information on, for instance, judicial procedures in Sasanid Persia or the "heresy" to which Seoses supposedly belonged.[21] By dressing Seoses to look like Socrates, Procopius transposes legal terms and institutions from democratic Athens to sixth-century Iran.[22] But his purpose is not to suggest indirectly that the historical Seoses was really a philosopher. If that were true, he would simply have said so, as he does elsewhere of real philosophers who were slandered and executed. Rather, it seems that history did not give him exactly what he wanted so he tampered with it, though in a subtle way that would be obvious to only a few of his readers. The fact of his tampering, however, offers us a valuable clue about his intention, for the allusions convey a message that transcends its particular historical situation.

The problems posed by the trial of Seoses to the interpreter of Procopius cannot but be related to one of the most striking omissions of important information in the *Wars*, namely the total silence that he maintains regarding the seven Platonic philosophers attacked by Justinian. According to Agathias, after the emperor closed their schools, the philosophers "would not conform to the establishment (τὸ καθεστώς)," that is, Christianity, and traveled to Persia hoping that its new ruler Chosroes lived up to his reputation as a Platonic philosopher-king. But they soon realized that Persia was as barbarous as its king's devotion to philosophy was superficial. Yet they still managed to gain Chosroes' favor, thanks to which "a clause was inserted in the treaty, which at that time was being concluded between the Romans and the Persians, to the effect that the philosophers should be allowed to return to their homes and to live out their lives in peace without being compelled to alter their traditional religious beliefs. . . . Chosroes insisted on the inclusion of the point and made the ratification and continued observance of the truce conditional on its implementation." Agathias emphasizes that "the beliefs about God that held sway in the Roman empire were not to their liking."[23] His source for these events may have been one of those very same philosophers, probably Damascius or Simplicius. There is no good reason to reject the story, which has been scrutinized often but never seriously doubted and which also conforms well to what we know of Chosroes' character and the diplomatic relations between Rome and Persia in the sixth century.[24] What requires explanation is the complete silence that Procopius maintains about those events.

The negotiations leading up to the treaty mentioned by Agathias, the so-called Eternal Peace of 532, are covered extensively in the *Persian War* (1.16, 1.21–22). Procopius narrates in detail the protracted debate over the various terms but mentions neither the philosophers nor the clause protecting them upon which Chosroes insisted. Procopius has omitted all reference to what must have been an essential point in the negotiations. His influence in this matter, and the degree to which modern accounts paraphrase the *Wars* rather than synthesize all available sources, is revealed by the persistent exclusion of Agathias' information from discussions of the treaty, even though he provides what may be a verbatim quotation from it.

Scholars do not doubt the authenticity of his account, but they relegate it to discussions of culture and religion.[25] It is precisely because Procopius has been followed uncritically by all modern historians that his omission of the information provided by Agathias does not seem suspicious. Nor did Procopius include it in the *Secret History*, where the philosophers could have been cast as Justinian's victims.[26] We thus face the following paradox: Procopius has suppressed the politically significant actions of real philosophers, yet he has interpolated into his account of the trial of Seoses the shadowy, albeit unmistakable, outline of a philosopher who never existed.

The contours of this problem are brought into focus by other passages of the *Wars* whose protagonists are philosophers, specifically by two episodes from the introduction to the *Gothic War*, which takes us as far to the west of Byzantium as the introduction to the *Persian War* takes us to the east. These two passages illustrate the permanent tension between philosophy and kingship by depicting it first from the point of view of philosophy's private nature and then from the point of view of its potential for political rule.

The first passage concerns the Roman senators Symmachus and Boethius, who were executed by the Gothic king Theoderic (5.1.32–34). Procopius openly calls them philosophers, no doubt because they really were.[27] And even though they are ominously linked to Seoses by definite verbal and narrative parallels (see below), a number of factors lead us to believe that they should not have suffered his fate. First, the prince under whom they lived was Theoderic, "an extremely vigilant guardian of justice, who preserved the laws on a sure basis . . . attaining the highest degree of sagacity and courage. And he committed virtually no acts of injustice against his subjects, nor allowed anyone else to commit them who was inclined to do so" (5.1.27–28). Through a number of carefully chosen allusions, Procopius compares the Gothic king to Thucydides' portrait of Pericles, a vigilant guardian and true statesman.[28] This is high praise indeed.

Second, unlike Seoses, Symmachus and Boethius were not known to despise the established customs of their society and did not revere "strange new divinities," although they were, like Seoses, "second to none in their concern for justice." And just as he had excelled in arrogance, a quality that Procopius says was inbred in all Persian officials,[29] Symmachus and Boethius had no rivals in the virtues appropriate to cultivated Roman aristocrats, using their great wealth to help those in need.[30] But to no avail. Their magnanimity and practice of philosophy caused "envy" to rise up against them, just as it had against Seoses; they too were "slandered" to Theoderic, accused of plotting revolution, and put to death without a proper trial.[31] The Gothic king repented, even died of grief. Yet despite his undeniable virtues, he too sinned against philosophy, no less than his contemporary in the east, the tyrant Cavades. At this point the comparisons to Pericles cease; amid the horrid images and fatal visions of Theoderic's death, Procopius inserts an allusion to the death of the mad Persian king Cambyses, who repented of killing his brother before he accidentally and fatally wounded himself.[32] Procopius even manages to preserve Herodotus' dramatic symbolism of retribution: just as Cambyses "was wounded at just that point of his body at which he had struck the Egyptian god Apis," so too Theoderic died, after imagining the face of the recently butchered Symmachus upon the head of a fish served to him for dinner. This comparison is unfavorable to Theoderic and suggests that even the most benign monarchy may lapse into murderous despotism, especially against philosophers. Nevertheless, the text is not without sympathy for the Gothic ruler, for it draws our attention to the most pathetic moment of Cambyses' reign, highlighting his sincere remorse. Thus it differs greatly from the comparison of Justinian to Cambyses in the *Secret History*, the purpose of which is to emphasize the Roman ruler's despotic character and contempt for law.[33]

Thus, in the introductions to two books of the *Wars*, Procopius presents us with the virtually simultaneous executions of philosophers in kingdoms bordering on either side of the Roman empire. These passages do not by themselves constitute a political philosophy. Yet they are consistent with an implied politics of philosophy, for they reveal the precarious state of intellectual life in a dawning age of tyranny. "Seoses" was executed in 522 because his behavior was vaguely Socratic and his rank offensive to the envious. Symmachus and Boethius were executed ca. 525[34] because they practiced philosophy and were envied for their virtue and preeminence. And, though Procopius is silent about them, the Platonists of Athens were targeted by Justinian at the end of that decade precisely because they formed an "overtly anti-Christian" center.[35] Yet unlike some of their coreligionists later in the reign, they were not executed and continued to practice philosophy within the empire while Procopius was writing his histories.[36] Their political stance at that time is worth discussing, for it sheds light on both the omissions and the allusions in the *Wars*.

Before leading his students to refuge in Persia, Damascius had documented in his *Philosophical History* the bold and courageous efforts of philosophers in the late fifth and early sixth centuries to influence civic and imperial authorities in a direction favorable to polytheism. It seems that they did not "leave unexploited any channel through which power might trickle."[37] Damascius himself argued strongly in favor of political activism and dismissed "those who sit in a corner and philosophize at length about justice."[38] The ambitious interference with the treaty of 532 marked the high point, but also the end, of the Platonists' political struggles. The accession of Justinian inaugurated an era of unparalleled repression, which pagan intellectuals did not dare oppose openly and from which they never recovered.[39] Procopius commented on the brutality of the persecutions in the *Secret History* (11.31, 13.4–7). Given the climate of repression, philosophers understandably decided to lie low. In a commentary on Epictetus written after 532, Damascius' successor Simplicius discussed the public stance appropriate to a philosopher living in what he called "an age of tyranny."[40] In chapter 14 of that treatise, he composed a litany on the misfortunes that had afflicted mankind in his own lifetime, including

the common misfortunes, such as earthquakes and floods and conflagrations,[41] plagues and famines and the death of every kind of animal and produce, or those things that are done in an unholy manner by human beings to one another, such as the capture of cities and imprisonments and unjust murders and robberies and plunder and licentiousness and tyrannical violence that forces one to commit even impieties, not to mention the destruction of education and philosophy, of all virtue and friendship and trust in one another; and of all the arts and sciences, discovered and established over the course of many years, some have gone completely extinct, so that only their names are known, whereas of the majority of them, given by god for the improvement of our lives, such as medicine and architecture and carpentry and others of that kind, only shadows and images remain. (14.20–32)

Before discussing the significance of "the destruction of education and philosophy," we should note that there is an uncanny similarity between this woeful paragraph and Procopius' *Secret History*. Nearly all the misfortunes listed abstractly by the philosopher are documented in circumstantial detail by the historian. Like Simplicius, Procopius lists the natural disasters of the reign—earthquakes, plagues, floods, and famine—and twice mirrors Simplicius' schema of nature conspiring with human depravity to destroy mankind.[42] The conjunction of natural and manmade disasters was, of course, a common rhetorical theme, but there are verbal parallels between the two texts.[43] A close correspondence of language can also be observed in the accusations of murder and robbery.[44] The "licentiousness" mentioned by Simplicius is invoked four times in a single chapter of the *Secret History*, regarding the past life of Theodora, of course.[45] One wonders what Simplicius meant by it. The philosopher also refers to the "unholy" manner in which people treated each other; Procopius constantly refers to the "unholy deeds" encouraged by the regime.[46] More interesting is Simplicius' account of the destruction of education and the arts and sciences, including medicine and architecture (οἰκοδομική). Procopius levels an identical accusation, and it is ironic that an author who would write a panegyric on Justinian's *Buildings*, who complains even in the *Secret History* of the ceaseless construction of useless buildings, should also lament the neglect of public construction (οἰκοδομία) along with the decline of medicine.[47]

It is certainly possible that we are dealing with two independent observers, in which case the main thesis of the *Secret History* gains unexpected and independent confirmation. Yet the undeniable parallelism of content and language suggests the possibility that one text influenced the composition of the other. Either Procopius elaborated the philosopher's lament or, what seems more likely, Simplicius summarized Procopius' text when he turned to list the woes of his age. The conclusion is in either case inescapable that Procopius' outlook on the sixth century was identical to that of the most important Platonic philosopher of the age, an anti-Christian enemy of Justinian's regime.

There are even more parallels between the two. Near the middle of his commentary, Simplicius turns to the behavior that is appropriate to philosophers "in corrupt states (ἐν ταῖς μοχθηραῖς πολιτείαις)." His discussion takes its place in a long tradition of philosophical treatments of that issue. The passage from which all thinkers drew inspiration, including Simplicius and later even Thomas More in his *Utopia*, was in Plato's *Republic*. According to Socrates, "a human being who has fallen in with wild beasts . . . keeps quiet and minds his own business" (496d–e; cf. 620c–d). Comparing the Christian authorities to "sleeping beasts" liable to burst into murderous rampages, Simplicius advised his readers to shun public life and avoid controversy, or—and this is surely an autobiographical reference—"move to a better state."[48] Simplicius understood that under Justinian the survival of philosophy depended upon inconspicuousness and dissimulation, and, like Procopius, he knew that one of the dangers facing philosophers was "envy."[49] The historian's references to envy in this connection are important. In his works, envy appears in a variety of contexts, but the idea that others would envy philosophers is perhaps one that only philosophers can entertain.

Simplicius was not alone among contemporaries in stressing the precarious state of philosophy. In his lectures, the Alexandrian Platonist

Olympiodorus drew upon the same passage of the *Republic* to argue that a philosopher ought to flee a city if his fellow citizens were unworthy.[50] His own circumspection in dealing with thorny religious questions has been noted.[51] As for Procopius, in the preface of the *Secret History* (1.10), he declares that his purpose is to expose the regime's μοχθηρά. Equally curious is the fact that he uses the same term in the preface to the *Wars*, where he states that his history will not conceal the μοχθηρά of his own close acquaintances (1.1.5).[52] It is unlikely that this word was chosen at random, for it resonated with the audience for which Procopius composed this "inner" history. And even though he was not specifically discussing philosophers, in the *Secret History* he advocated prudent dissimulation as the correct response to the violent tendencies of Justinian's official faith. The only people who escaped persecution, he notes, were those who falsely pretended to be Christian. He advises his readers to do the same, calling it "stupid" to suffer for what he actually labels "some idiotic doctrine" (e.g., 11.24–32, 27.7). So much for the ideal of martyrdom. It is reasonable to assume that he followed his own advice, thus lulling the "sleeping beasts" that terrified Simplicius.[53]

It is curious that we do not know where the Platonists settled after Persia.[54] Procopius, of course, says nothing. In his voluminous writings, Simplicius says nothing explicit, practicing what he preached in his commentary on Epictetus. More curiously, forty years after 532, Agathias still refused to specify where the philosophers had gone, even though his cryptic (and slightly envious) remark that "they lived out the remainder of their days in pleasant contentment" indicates that he knew more than he was willing to tell.[55] Agathias was writing in the late 570s,[56] while the narrative of his *Histories* covers the years 552–559. His digression on the Platonists takes him back to 532, to a generation before the period covered by his work. He tells us what Procopius should have told us but did not, and yet he still tells us less than we would like to know. It is perhaps here that he reveals himself as the most perceptive interpreter of Procopius' intentions. Let us note in this connection that Agathias, referring to the account of the two reigns of Cavades in the *Wars*, enrolls Procopius among "the wise men of the past," which his modern interpreters have rightly called "a curious phrase."[57] It is also curious that the only individuals whom he designates as unequivocally wise are Plato, Procopius, and the Neoplatonists.[58]

Plato's Nightmare

Like the introduction to the *Persian War*, the first chapters of the *Gothic War* are a blend of fact and philosophical interpretation, the latter again including Platonic mimesis. Procopius here audaciously introduces a philosophical dialogue into his narrative that delivers a verdict on the Platonic teaching about justice, philosophy, and political rule. Procopius' choice of the dialogue form to satirize the exoteric tenets of Platonism is not without irony. Yet that invented dialogue, with its grim mixture of seriousness and play, indicates that he was one of the most insightful students of Plato's political philosophy, certainly in his own century. We will see that he had thoroughly mastered at least two dialogues, the *Gorgias* and the *Republic*, and fully understood the dramatic elements of the Platonic art of writing.

The sequence of Gothic kings presented in the introduction to the *Gothic War* is just as schematic as the sequence of Persian kings in the introduction to the *Persian War*. Procopius again distorts history to produce a contrast between Theoderic and his nephew Theodahad. In brief, we observe the following chiastic transformation. Whereas Theoderic (d. 526) was an excellent statesman who was illiterate, Theodahad (r. 534–536) was a learned philosopher who was utterly incompetent as a ruler. The young Athalaric (r. 526–534), Theoderic's grandson, is caught between the two not only chronologically but also in terms of his education, which was half Roman and half Gothic. We will first examine the schematic sequence that contrasts learning to statesmanship and then the Platonic themes that emerge in the dialogue between Theodahad and the Roman ambassador Peter.

As we saw previously, Procopius' view of Theoderic as a statesman is very positive and has never been doubted by modern scholars. It is important to note that his praise is not based solely on the Gothic king's success, for it emphasizes his justice and the love he engendered in his subjects (5.1.26–31). Procopius' allegations of illiteracy, however, have not gained credit with modern historians, and rightly so. As a youth, Theoderic spent a decade in Constantinople, where he no doubt received a literary education, and examinations of his reign have invalidated the additional claim that he forbade Gothic children from attending school.[59] Yet that claim, as well as the assertion that the king himself "had never even heard of letters," are not made directly by Procopius. He attributes them to Gothic nobles who opposed the efforts of his daughter Amalasuntha to educate her son Athalaric in the Roman manner (5.2.11–17). Still, Procopius neither refutes those allegations nor allows Amalasuntha to do so, thereby leaving the reader with the definite impression that Theoderic was illiterate and hostile to learning. Procopius has it both ways. He avoids speaking a great untruth in his own voice while insinuating the impressions required to create the contrast with the would-be philosopher-king.[60] Theodahad is introduced as very learned but inexperienced in warfare and the active life (5.3.1).

Athalaric is caught between those two extremes but fails to reconcile them. His mother placed him under a grammarian to make a proper Roman of him (5.2.6), but hostile Gothic nobles forcibly removed him from her care, insisting that he be raised "according to the customs of the barbarians," that is, as a warrior (5.2.8–17). The young man ultimately became neither and wasted away in debauchery. According to the underlying premises of the introduction, he was a living contradiction, a logical impossibility, as even his mother realized (5.3.11: εἰς τοῦτο ἀτοπίας). Finally he just "withered away" and died (5.3.10, 5.4.4–5).

In order to produce this stylized episode, Procopius has somewhat distorted events. First, he has made the reign of Athalaric, a period of eight years (526–534), seem like a few months, though he does give the correct dates.[61] This compression serves to dramatize the conflict over his education and bring the deeper issues of the introduction into sharper focus. Second, Procopius centers the narrative on that very conflict, even though he knows that it was only part of a broader struggle between two factions in Gothic Italy. However, it is not difficult for careful readers of the *Wars* to reconstruct the correct chronology as well as the political context from the information that Procopius provides, and historians have done so.[62]

The young king may have suffered from diabetes, but Athalaric's life and death are used by Procopius to signify the impossibility, or *atopia*, of uniting barbarian manliness and Roman learning in a Gothic ruler.[63] The same tension was found, in conjunction with other factors, in the regency of his mother, Amalasuntha. Procopius introduces her as sagacious, just, and respectful of Roman culture and notes in her obituary that she ruled with great virtue.[64] Yet her admiration for classical education incurred the enmity of the military nobility, and it is not entirely coincidental that both she and Theodahad, who also respected higher learning, were keen to surrender Italy to Justinian in exchange for estates and honor in the empire.[65] The introduction to the *Gothic War* posits a seemingly irreconcilable tension between the "manly" virtues of Theoderic, by which Gothic Italy was made strong, and the concern for literary culture, which is associated with a sickly child, a failed queen, and a perfidious coward.[66] Theodahad was learned to the degree that he was incompetent as a leader.

The failure of Amalasuntha was ultimately due to her main difference from her father, which Procopius appropriately reveals by exploiting the language of gender. The fundamental paradox of her position consisted simply in the fact that she was a woman, though her nature was "nearer to the masculine" and not soft like that of most women.[67] On one occasion (5.2.20) Procopius highlights the incongruity by conjoining a feminine article with the masculine word for "human being (ἡ ἄνθρωπος)," a rare usage.[68] Yet the Gothic warriors would never accept a female ruler, however masculine or virtuous. Accordingly, Procopius' high praise of Amalasuntha differs from his praise of her father in one subtle but decisive respect. Whereas Theoderic was "sagacious, just, and manly (ἀνδρία)," she was "sagacious, just, and nearer to the masculine (ἀρρενωπόν)."[69] Genuine "manliness" was what her regime could never attain. Her very position as regent depended upon the life and youth of her son (cf. 5.3.11), she was constrained to act through loyal and energetic men (5.2.25), her enemies feared that she would marry and elevate another man to the throne (5.2.10), and when her son died, she was compelled to share dominion with a man, Theodahad, who swiftly destroyed her (5.4.4–13). The idea that an able and even masculine woman can aspire to rule a state founded upon military virtue is revealed as unrealistic, if not downright utopian. Procopius thus seems to opt for the more qualified alternative in the question posed by Socrates in the *Republic* (453a), "whether female human nature can share in common with the nature of the male class in all deeds or in none at all, or in some things yes and in others no, *particularly with respect to war?*"[70]

The failure of Amalasuntha is therefore linked to the failure of Theodahad, the only philosopher-king depicted in the *Wars* and a man whom Procopius calls "by nature unmanly (ἄνανδρος: 5.9.1)." Women and philosophers may have much in common when examined as potential rulers, though both may prove to be failures, as Socrates and his interlocutors suspect in Book 5 of the *Republic*. Theodahad was also "well versed in Latin literature and the teachings of Plato" (5.3.1). His learning was noted by other contemporaries, and official spokesmen cast him as a philosopher-king.[71] But the figure that emerges from the *Wars* is in all other respects an antithesis of the philosopher-king depicted in the *Republic*; indeed, he is a direct caricature of that famous ideal. Once again the *Wars* mirrors the text of the *Republic*. For instance, Theodahad's chief vice was "love of money (φιλοχρηματία)," in direct contrast to Plato's philosopher-kings, who have no private property and are "in no way lovers of money (οὐδαμῆ φιλοχρήματος)."[72] Whereas Theodahad "had no experience of warfare" and "did not partake of the active life," Plato's kings, springing from the class of the guardians, must be "champions in war when they are young" and be "proven best both in philosophy and with respect to war."[73] Theodahad was a coward, easily seized by terror in the face of war. His character, wavering between dread and elation, was distrustful and unsteady (βέβαιον τὴν διάνοιαν οὐδαμῆ εἶχεν). The philosophers of the *Republic*, however, cannot be cowardly and must have a steady disposition (τὰς διανοίας . . . μετὰ βεβαιότητος), especially when facing "the fears of war."[74] These parallels constitute another mimesis of Platonic concepts and themes. Procopius wanted his philosophical readers to view Theodahad as the reversal of a philosopher-king. To add a final insult, he even had a wife (5.6.12).

The character and reign of Theodahad in the *Gothic War* are directly modeled on the doctrines of Plato's *Republic*. It is therefore not surprising that this caricature of a philosopher-king should participate in a dialogue that revolves around Socrates' teachings on justice and the role of philosophers in the state. Procopius' perspective in this dialogue corresponds with what we have seen of the fate of philosophers elsewhere in the *Wars*. In order to understand it we must first, as with any Platonic dialogue, know something about the character of the interlocutors and the historical circumstances of their discussion. Procopius fails us in neither respect, characterizing Peter with Thucydidean terseness: "he was one of the orators in Byzantium, sagacious, gentle, and well fitted by nature to persuade others."[75] This information, as we will see, suffices to explain his philosophical role in the dialogue with Theodahad. The revelations in the *Secret History*, which we will examine later, only deepen and elaborate the Platonic mold in which his character and speeches have been cast.

Terrified by Roman military offenses, Theodahad met secretly with Peter, offering to surrender Sicily and accept the emperor as his overlord (5.6.1–5).[76]

But shortly afterward, terror seized hold of the man's soul, giving him over to boundless fears, twisting his mind this way and that, and causing him to tremble at the very name of war, since, if the emperor was not pleased with the agreement he had made with Peter, war would swiftly be upon him. Immediately, therefore, he recalled Peter, who had already reached Albani, and took counsel with him in secret, asking him whether he thought that the agreement would be pleasing (πρὸς ἡδονῆς) to the emperor. And Peter said that he suspected that it would.

"But what if it pleases him in no way," he said, "what will happen then?"

And Peter replied, "Then you will have to wage war, most noble sir."

"But what are you saying? Are these things just, dear ambassador?" he said.

And Peter answered him immediately, taking up the argument, "And how can it not be just, my good man," he said, "for the pursuits (ἐπιτηδεύματα) appropriate to the soul of each to be guarded (φυλάσσεσθαι)?"

"What does that mean?" asked Theodahad.

"It means that your greatest pursuit is to philosophize," he said, "but for Justinian it is to be an excellent emperor of the Romans. And here is the difference, that for one practicing philosophy it would never be decent to cause the deaths of men, especially in such great numbers, and this is in accordance with the teaching of Plato, which you have manifestly embraced, making it unholy for you not to be free from all murder. But it is not at all unreasonable for him to lay claim to lands that once belonged to the realm which is properly his own."

Persuaded by this warning, Theodahad pledged to abdicate his throne in favor of the emperor Justinian. (5.6.6–11)

The speakers are a would-be philosopher-king and an orator in the employ of a tyrant.[77] Their dialogue is directly modeled on the conversations in the *Republic* and the *Gorgias* between Socrates, a political philosopher who abstained from actual politics, and various orators who wished to become or to serve tyrants. War is at the forefront of the discussion in the *Republic*.[78] "War" is also the first word of the *Gorgias*, and forms an "unspoken theme" underlying the entire dialogue.[79] Likewise, the dialogue between Theodahad and Peter occurs in the tense context of impending war, which Procopius manages to mention twice in the first sentence of the passage quoted above and once in the dialogue itself. The grim possibility of violence looms over the conversation between the two men.

Theodahad speaks as a philosopher by asking whether it is just for Justinian to declare war. Peter does not answer the question directly but finesses it as befits an orator. It is interesting that he deflects the accusation of injustice by appropriating and mocking the famous definition of justice expounded in the *Republic*. According to Socrates, whose language Peter mimics, justice consists of the performance by each soul of the task most suited to its nature.[80] Peter claims that the proper role of a philosopher is to philosophize and not to shed blood, whereas Justinian, who is presumably an utterly unphilosophical ruler, may wage war with justice. The Roman orator is throwing Socrates' definition back in the face of the Gothic philosopher-king. Is it not proper for men with murderous souls to behave as murderers? This struggle between justice and power in the context of impending war also reminds us of the horrific dialogue in Thucydides between the pious Melians and the Athenians, for whom might makes right (5.84–111). Like the Melians, Theodahad invokes justice precisely because he is powerless. Peter's threats are likewise a thinly veiled version of the harsh ultimatum delivered to the Melians by the Athenian generals.[81]

Peter's rhetorical tricks are not without interest, for through them Procopius manages to introduce some of his own dissident political views into the *Wars*. The ambassador's description of the proper tasks of the two men is not entirely straightforward, for he has cleverly shifted some of the essential attributes of Justinian over to the description of Theodahad, only in the form of negatives. Thus, instead of saying openly that it would be appropriate for Justinian's soul to kill multitudes of men and stain itself with murder, Peter says instead that those actions are not appropriate to a Platonic philosopher. The reader can easily read between these lines, as Justinian is about to embark on those very actions.[82] We are left with no doubts about the nature of the Roman emperor's soul, even though Peter employs various euphemisms in his direct description of its proper tasks to avoid stating the obvious. This tactic, of course, is consistent with Peter's soul, which is that of an orator. We wonder then about the soul of Procopius, who has managed in the *Wars* to make a spokesman of Justinian utter in a veiled manner the criticisms that he himself levels against that emperor in the *Secret History* (e.g., 6.20; 8.30).

Compared to Theoderic, Theodahad is a petty criminal and a worthless ruler. But compared to Justinian he is a Platonic holy man. Justinian emerges from this passage as a bloodthirsty warmonger, embodying the antithesis of philosophy. His agent Peter attacks the political claims of philosophy and subsequently compels Theodahad to acknowledge in a letter to Justinian the private nature of philosophy and its incompatibility with kingship (5.6.15–21). Peter twists Socrates' definition of justice to reaffirm the truth stated by his colleague, the orator Thrasymachus, in Book 1 of the *Republic*; namely, that justice is the advantage of the stronger.[83] Like Seoses, Symmachus, Boethius, and the sixth-century Platonists, Theodahad gave way to the power of tyranny.

The view of philosophy as a private pursuit that cannot defend itself against political power is famously expounded by Callicles in Plato's *Gorgias*. According to Callicles, philosophers—such as Theodahad—are inexperienced in all aspects of public life (484c–e), and when they are accused by wicked enemies they are unable to resist the charges and are put to death (486a–b). Callicles refers to such men as "unmanly (ἄνανδρος)" on many occasions (485c–d; 492b). As we have seen, this is precisely what Procopius calls Theodahad (5.9.1). Interestingly, Socrates does not openly challenge Callicles' position in the *Gorgias*. In fact, he later admits that philosophers' fates may be exactly as his interlocutor claims (508c–e), and, indeed, that is how he met his own end. Socrates even suggests that philosophers should mind their own business and not become busybodies (526c), which also tends to rule out political activity, just as do Peter's arguments in the dialogue with Theodahad and Theodahad's subsequent letter to Justinian.[84] This takes us back to his statement in the *Republic*, which was quoted by Simplicius and Olympiodorus, that "a human being who has fallen in with wild beasts . . . keeps quiet and minds his own business" (496d–e).

Peter's rhetorical abilities have a more sinister aspect. In the *Secret History*, Procopius says that it was Peter, instigated by Theodora, who persuaded Theodahad to kill Amalasuntha (16.1–5). The king perhaps required little encouragement, but independent evidence suggests that the accusation is plausible.[85] In fact, Procopius hints at Peter's complicity even in the *Wars* by closely conjoining, in one terse sentence, his arrival in Italy with the death of Amalasuntha.[86] This was probably as far as he could go in a public work, but it still constitutes a testament to his courage as a historian; scholars who have not lived in fear of murderous rulers can perhaps appreciate this only with difficulty.[87] In the *Secret History* (16.5), Procopius draws our attention to Peter's rhetorical skill by claiming not to know by what exhortations the ambassador persuaded the king to murder Amalasuntha. The same verb is used there for Peter's power of persuasion (ἀνέπεισε) as is used in the *Wars* for Theodahad's decision to abdicate his throne after his conversation with the Roman ambassador (ἀναπεισθείς). Peter can apparently persuade kings to commit murder as well as to abdicate. The belief in the omnipotence of rhetoric is propounded powerfully by Gorgias' vicious student Polus in Plato's dialogue: orators, through their skill, "just like tyrants, kill whomever they wish, confiscate possessions, and expel from the cities whomever it seems good to them."[88] Procopius lived to see Plato's worst nightmare: an alliance of rhetoric and tyranny against philosophy.

The *Wars* contains a story within a story. Procopius modeled numerous episodes recounted in his history on the teachings of Plato, sometimes even distorting the facts in order to do so. The dialogue between Peter and Theodahad is an invention, and what has been said about the source of that invention can be said about the historian himself: he "offers a fictional dialogue to explain the war. . . . [This] suggests the necessity to diverge from what we would today call the facts of history to that truth which lies more fully in the fictions of Platonic dialogues."[89]

The introduction to the *Persian War*, which stands at the beginning of the *Wars* as a whole, situates the events of the sixth century within the context of the tyranny described in Book 8 of the *Republic*. Lifted from Plato are not only the sequence of regimes itself but also the contours of the tyranny to which it ultimately led. The *Persian War* presents the Sasanid side of this equation, the *Secret History* the Roman side. The executions of

Seoses, Symmachus, and Boethius stress the anti-philosophical nature of the political context. Philosophers, whether private citizens or highly placed officials, are revealed as unable to withstand the violence of tyranny and rhetoric. Using the language of Callicles, Procopius caricatures a philosopher-king for the hollowness of his political ambitions. Despite his great debt to Plato, the historian depicts a world that utterly failed to live up to the ideals expounded in Book 5 of the *Republic*; indeed, he seems to depict it in explicit opposition to those ideals. A violent tyrant institutes the sharing of women; an able, virtuous, and "masculine" woman fails to lead a warlike people; and a philosopher-king is shown as ludicrously passive and incompetent as a ruler.

And yet this pessimism is offered not as hostile criticism of the ideals of the *Republic* but rather as a frustrated realization of their inherently unrealistic nature. Such a view may be closer to Socrates' own position than that of those who believe that the *Republic* contains a blueprint for an ideal state that can be realized in the world, even if only under rare circumstances or incompletely. Socrates himself grants that the law on women seems unlikely to work in practice and never offers arguments in favor of its possibility (457c–e, 472d); as for the ideal city, at the end of the discussion he reveals that it simply does not matter whether it can exist, given that it can only come about through "some divine chance" and does not exist "anywhere on earth" (592a–b). Only philosophers who have already been raised in just cities are in a position to benefit them (519c–520d; cf. 5.6.15–21 for Theodahad). According to Cicero, Plato "has created a state of a kind that is to be desired rather than hoped for . . . not such as to be possible, but in which it might be possible to see the workings of his theory of the state."[90] Examining the two radical doctrines of the dialogue, the equality of women and the rule of philosophers, some scholars have also "doubted the seriousness of these proposals. . . . The absurdity of a naked old woman practicing gymnastics is matched by the absurdity of a philosopher ruling over a city."[91] These ideas are "intended to suggest the impossibility of political justice and the absurd extremes to which politics must go in its search for an impossible perfection."[92]

Nevertheless, many of Procopius' contemporaries interpreted at least one of Plato's ideals as attainable, making the sixth century an age of philosopher-kings. In 533, Theoderic was called a "a purple-clad philosopher" by his successor.[93] Boethius prided himself on implementing, while in office, Plato's directive to join philosophy and secular power.[94] Theodahad naturally portrayed himself as a philosopher-king.[95] The deacon Agapetus claimed that the reign of Justinian finally brought to pass the prediction of Plato that happiness would be impossible if philosophers did not assume power or rulers did not philosophize, albeit in a Christian manner, of course.[96] A political theorist who wrote a dialogue *On Politics*, whose outlook was fundamentally Platonic, also endorsed the union of philosophy and kingship (5.123, 5.210).[97] Even Chosroes cultivated an aura of philosophy, propaganda that found expression in contemporary Syriac literature and was well known within the Roman empire, where the king was duly cast as a Platonist by his admirers.[98] It is against this backdrop of effusive pseudo-philosophical rhetoric that we must view Procopius' stance. The dialogue between Theodahad and Peter caricatures the pretensions of philosopher-kings and reveals the truth about Justinian, casting him as the antithesis of philosophy. Procopius' *Wars* marks the abandonment by serious students of Plato of the impossible ideal of philosophical rule. It would not be revived again until the eleventh century.

Platonic Texts, Platonic Readers

The *Wars* became an instant classic. When he came to write the preface to the supplementary Book 8 two years later, Procopius noted with pride that his work was already known throughout the Roman empire. By century's end, the *Wars* had inspired a host of imitators who referred to Procopius by name and deferred to his authority. Nor was his influence confined to other classicizing historians. The ecclesiastical historian Evagrius copied long passages of the *Wars* into his own book, as did later Byzantine chroniclers, for example Theophanes the Confessor. Procopius was consulted by the Renaissance humanists, who were interested in the early medieval history of Italy, and he has provided the basis for all modern reconstructions of the reign of Justinian. There is no question that he has found a readership, among both his own contemporaries and posterity.

Yet Procopius surely did not expect that all those readers would detect the Platonic allusions with which he laced his text. He knew that most would be fascinated by the political, military, and ethnographic parts and would not realize that more is going on beneath the surface. And that is exactly what has happened. To whom then was the Platonic mimesis addressed? Perhaps we can work back from the knowledge required to detect and make sense of the allusions to the more select group of readers that Procopius had in mind. This is a general and necessary feature of classicizing writing: readers will reach the deeper levels of a text to the degree that they are themselves classically educated.[99] Some may not grasp any of the allusions, while others will note only, say, poetic vocabulary. Those with a rhetorical training will appreciate aspects of the speeches and surely identify some of the Thucydidean allusions, though only those who have carefully studied the entirety of Thucydides and Herodotus will be able to understand the structural parallels that link their works to Procopius. At every level the readership becomes increasingly more select. Finally we reach those who knew the *Republic* more or less by heart and were concerned about the fate of philosophy under tyrants such as Justinian. We have come far from the classicism censured in recent studies, the affected and tasteless imitation of outdated language. As has been said of Thomas More and the humanists to whom he addressed the Platonic fable of the *Utopia*: "For such men the profound relation to the *Republic* was obvious and the explicit references almost too loud. On the other hand, as he was writing for a much wider audience who would not know the *Republic* as did the first group, or even at all, he had to take care not to make his message dependent on an understanding which they neither had nor could easily get."[100] The first group belonged to "those few" about whom the Platonic *Seventh Letter* (341e) says that "through a small indication they are capable of grasping the truth on their own." This must have been a small group. Who were they?

One of them, I propose, can be identified. John Lydus, the bureaucrat and antiquarian, seems to have been a close friend of Procopius. He too hated Justinian and had close connections to the Platonists and other pagans of the sixth century.[101] Another candidate is Simplicius, whose commentary on Epictetus may reflect a reading of the *Secret History* but whose outlook on the reign of Justinian was in any case identical to that of Procopius. Beyond them, we can only speculate on the *kind* of reader Procopius had in mind, because we are not so fortunate as to know everyone who read Plato carefully in the sixth century. For example, there is the jurist Tribonian, suspected by some of being a Hellenic "atheist," who structured the edicts that he wrote on behalf of his master Justinian around Plato's concepts and even included "crypto-quotations" to his dialogues, which Justinian most likely did not detect and would certainly not have condoned.[102] Platonic allusions embedded in Justinian's legislation probably constitute the greatest irony of the reign, matched only by the use of Aristophanic verses in Procopius' description of Hagia Sophia. Then there is the poet, lawyer, and future historian Agathias, a man of about twenty when the *Wars* was published, who revered the Platonists, praised Procopius' wisdom, and grasped at least some of the Platonic allusions in the *Wars*. By using the noble lie of providence in his *Histories*, he revealed his own Platonic outlook.[103] To this group we should add the anonymous author of the dialogue *On Politics*, whose ideas, as noted above, were fundamentally indebted to Plato's *Republic*. Unfortunately, our information is too limited to establish personal relationships among these men. But the textual and philosophical links that bind them together are undeniable and raise questions about the company Procopius kept when he was not on campaign with Belisarius. We must remember that we know little about his life and nothing that he does not tell us himself.

So much for Procopius' contemporaries. When we turn to modern readers, we find not only that his Platonic experiments have gone unnoticed, they have been positively denied: "There is little to suggest serious study of philosophy," he was "not a philosophical historian," and he had "no particular interest in Platonic doctrine."[104] Yet these prematurely definitive statements have been issued by scholars who have not detected any of the Platonic allusions in the *Secret History* and the *Wars*. Again we witness the distorting effects of academic specialization. Procopius has been studied mainly by social, military, and art historians, whose professional training does not recreate the *paideia* of any ancient author. This inevitably leads to divergent interests and misunderstandings. For example, only someone who knows ancient philosophy from handbooks can think that it consisted chiefly of "doctrine"; that is, metaphysics. The formal separation of texts into historiography and philosophy, along with the fact that these are studied as separate disciplines, has obscured the fact that most ancient historians were fully developed political theorists, or, as was true of many historians in late antiquity and Byzantium, that they drew their inspiration from philosophy and chiefly from Plato.[105] Whether we like it or not, philosophy stands at the heart of classical historiography and unless we are able to distinguish between factual reporting and Platonic mimesis we risk speaking at cross-purposes with our sources. Procopius' *Wars*, our main source for the history of the sixth century, turns out to be in many respects Platonic philosophy in disguise.

Chapter 4

The Representation of Tyranny

The first sentence of the *Wars* declares the work to be about the wars waged by Justinian against the barbarians. The narrative takes place mostly on the frontiers and in lands being conquered, paradoxically relegating the capital to the margins. Yet though he never left the capital, Justinian determined the course of those events more than any other person. The first sentence of the *Secret History* declares the work to be about what happened within the Roman empire, or about "the lives of Justinian and Theodora" (1.4). Justinian was at the heart of Procopius' concerns.

The *Secret History* is the most virulent invective from antiquity, and nothing can explain it except sheer loathing for Justinian and his regime. It is impossible to believe that this hostility did not also shape the *Wars*, which was written at the same time. Naturally, criticism of the regime in a public work had to be veiled or indirect, and we have found many instances of this. In a separate reading of the *Wars*, I intend to demonstrate that Procopius opposed Justinian's wars—not just the means by which they were waged, but entirely.

The focus of this chapter is not on the wars but on the way in which Procopius conceptualized and represented the tyranny of Justinian, first in the *Wars*, where it emerges indirectly, albeit with curious nuances that merit discussion, and second, in the *Secret History*, where its manifold elaboration calls for a comprehensive study. These are problems in literary representation, not historical analysis, though we are dealing here with the most important source on the most consequential reign of the later Roman period. In particular, I intend to discuss the parallels that Procopius establishes between Justinian and various Persian kings, especially Chosroes, and the way in which Roman and Persian rulers are made to converge. This will lead to a discussion of Justinian's demand for *proskynesis* and the title *despotes*. I will then examine Procopius' attempt in the *Secret History* to come to grips with the ideology of the regime and the possible limitations of his effort. The shrillness of the work reflects his frustration with the inadequacy of classical paradigms to represent a regime that was in some ways closer to modern than to ancient forms of tyranny. The last section will discuss the alternatives Procopius upheld in attacking Justinian. These were entirely secular and uninfluenced by the notions of divine kingship that are now routinely ascribed to all Byzantines. The chapter will conclude with Procopius' fascination with assassination, which he viewed as the only likely solution to the problem of tyranny.

Chosroes and Justinian, "Emperors of East and West"

Though the Roman emperors sometimes postured as the rulers of the entire world, especially when addressing their own subjects, their correspondence with their Persian counterparts reveals that the two monarchs had agreed to treat each other as equals, at least officially. As from Rome, a hierarchy radiated out from Persia to all peoples who acknowledged the Great King as their titular overlord. There was always tension between the two empires, especially concerning the fealty of those unfortunate enough to live between them, though nominally their equality was not in doubt, at least before the early seventh century. Ambassadors for both sides devised colorful metaphors to express this relationship. The kings were called the two eyes illuminating the world or the two shoulders or mountains of the world.[1] In the *Persian Wars*, Roman ambassadors address the Persian king as the emperor's "brother," which seems to have been conventional practice.[2] We should not forget that when the Persian king Cavades asked the Roman emperor Justin to adopt his son Chosroes, Chosroes and Justinian came close to becoming brothers in more than just a diplomatic sense. Notably, it is precisely when he recounts this episode that Procopius formally introduces the two future despots to his readers (1.11.5–10). In other words, they are first mentioned just when their relationship was the closest it would ever be.

Despite the many destructive wars the two autocrats would wage against each other in the decades to come, Procopius' hostile portrayal of Chosroes in the *Persian Wars* bears striking similarities to his invective against Justinian in the *Secret History*. The "eyes of the world" may have been bitter enemies, but they were still two of a kind. Common vices included a love for innovation, unsteady intentions, lies and dissimulation, broken oaths, feigned piety, and avarice.[3] These parallels have been noted by the historian's modern detractors, who typically ascribe them to a lack of insight and imagination: "he was applying a standardized vocabulary of abuse to both rulers."[4] As usual, the lack of insight belongs to those who make these charges. The counterpoint between Chosroes and Justinian goes much farther than a stock set of moralizing accusations: it extends to the historian's conceptualization of imperial rule in both Rome and Persia. Further, the parallelism between the two rulers is not limited to their characters but operates on a structural level as well: whole chapters of the *Wars* are designed to highlight the gradual assimilation of Roman and Persian sovereignty. At one point, Chosroes assumes the persona of a Roman emperor, while Justinian is constantly compared, through carefully chosen classical allusions, to a number of Persian despots. Naturally, Procopius is less interested in the Persian side of this equation; to this degree, Chosroes is a surrogate for his Roman "brother." The assimilation of the two autocrats is designed to expose the degree to which the Roman empire under Justinian had become indistinguishable from an oriental and barbaric despotism. This is a theme that we have already encountered in our analysis of the *Wars*. Moreover, we will see in this chapter that it emerges largely from the *Wars* itself. There is no need to invoke the *Secret History*, though accusations made in that work deepen the comparison.

Much as Xerxes dominates Herodotus' account of the Persian Wars of the classical period,[5] Chosroes gradually emerges as the dominant personality of the *Persian Wars*, a position he attains by the beginning of Book 2. Besides determining the shape of the war during most of its years, he is the only military leader whose personality merits an entire section of analysis (2.9) and whose actions elicit digressions on the workings of fortune.[6] Compared to Chosroes, Justinian is absent, speaking only through ambassadors and letters. Belisarius is even made to say at one point that the emperor "is so far removed from events that he cannot adjust his actions to the changing circumstances" (2.16.10). Exactly the same charge is made in Procopius' own voice in the *Secret History* (18.29), another instance of the artful counterpoint between the two texts. Consequently, the narrative ostensibly devoted to the wars of Justinian against the barbarians is in reality dominated by the personality and deeds of his Persian counterpart.

Before we examine the Persian attributes of Justinian, we should look first at the Roman attributes of Chosroes, for, as was noted above, the parallels between them go both ways. Whereas the most exciting narrative in the *Persian Wars* must be the account of the Nika riots in 532 and the most moving the description of the plague ten years later, the highlight of the military narrative is surely the invasion of Roman territory by Chosroes in 540, an act that broke the Eternal Peace eight years after it had been signed. It also led to the destruction of Antioch, a catastrophe from which the city never recovered. Without encountering any resistance worth the name, Chosroes marched up the Euphrates, extorting money from cities on the way or sacking them if they refused. Procopius describes this invasion and the plight of the helpless provincials in some detail (2.5–13).

Once Chosroes destroyed Antioch, he realized that there would be no serious Roman response to his movements. This gave him leisure to indulge his fancies. First, he went down to Seleuceia on the coast, for no other reason than to swim in the ocean, "sacrifice to the sun and whatever other divinities he wanted, and call upon the gods many times" (2.11.1). We will never know whether he was imitating past Near Eastern conquerors, for example Iahdun-Lim of Mari in the nineteenth century B.C. and the Assyrian Ashurnasirpal in the ninth, both of whom also waded into the waters of the Mediterranean and performed sacrifices on the coast to symbolize the ultimate success of their conquests.[7] Be that as it may, it is at this point of symbolic victory that the persona projected by the king in Procopius' narrative gradually loses the qualities of a foreign conqueror and assumes first those of the tourist and, finally, those of a Roman emperor.

Chosroes began to visit various sites that piqued his interest. He expressed "a desire to see" the city of Apamea (2.11.2), an urge that surely harks back to Xerxes' "desire to see" various sites in Greece during his expedition and possibly to Alexander the Great's famous "longing" to make new discoveries.[8] It is unlikely that the Sasanid king intended the allusion, though he knew his Greek literature.[9] It has probably been crafted by his historian, who also notes that everyone knew that the king merely wanted to plunder the city. On the way to Apamea he stopped to admire Daphne, the sylvan suburb of Antioch, where he sacrificed to the nymphs and burned a church of St. Michael (2.11.4–6).[10] He then put Apamea under military occupation. It is at this point that the king's behavior, which had so far been bizarre, became surreal. Chosroes was seized with the desire to attend the games at the hippodrome and commanded the populace to attend. Hearing that Justinian favored the Blues, he arranged for the Greens to win the chariot races, "desiring to go against him in this matter too" (2.11.31–32). Afterward, when a man came up to him and complained that a Persian soldier had raped his daughter, Chosroes ordered that the soldier be impaled. The populace cried out loudly that he should be spared. The king promised to release him to them but then impaled him secretly (2.11.36–38).

In a story told about that day of races in Apamea, the ecclesiastical historian Evagrius, a younger contemporary of Procopius, emphasized the fact that Chosroes was a foreign invader who had no business in the hippodrome or the city (4.25). But the narrative of the *Wars* moves in a different direction. At the apogee of the invasion, after the capture and destruction of Antioch, Chosroes is transformed by degrees into a kind of Roman emperor, albeit an anti-emperor. He presides over the games, in however farcical a manner, which was an imperial prerogative, and even dispenses justice before the crowd. In favoring the Greens, he competes directly with Justinian, thus placing himself on the same level. Procopius explicitly presents his actions as attempts to rival Justinian at his own game. Even his rigging of the races might have been perceived by contemporary readers as a parallel to Justinian, who was, as a study of the circus factions reminds us, "the only Byzantine emperor on record as showing *unfair* favors to his own color."[11] Procopius' narrative reveals that the Persian king understood the mechanisms of public opinion in the empire and the symbolic forms that governed the interaction between subject and ruler. For instance, Procopius' account of the Nika riots reveals that emperors were literally made and unmade in the hippodrome (cf. 1.24.42). And in a digression a few pages after the events at Apamea, Procopius projects the hippodrome's importance back to the days of Augustus (2.12.12; cf. also 5.6.4). We also know of incidents from the fifth and sixth centuries when rebels "staged chariot races to emphasize their claim to sovereignty."[12]

For the space of a few pages we are almost allowed to forget that Chosroes was a barbaric conqueror and witness his profoundly disturbing transformation into a rival Roman emperor. Even the people of Apamea forgot the difference after a day of games. They treated him as a legitimate political authority, not only attending his games but fearlessly addressing their grievances to him. Chosroes responded by ordering the execution of his own soldier and then acceding to the popular demand for mercy (though he secretly carried out the punishment). A similar conclusion can probably be drawn about the king's conspicuous sacrifices to pagan gods. This too can be interpreted as an attempt to become the reverse image of his "brother," pagan instead of Christian, just as he was Green instead of Blue. At the end of his tour of the Roman cities, Chosroes was approached by a delegation from Carrhae (Harran), who were bearing ransom for their city. Yet he let them go "because most of them were not Christians, but still happened to belong to the ancient faith" (2.13.7).[13] And, noting that the empire lacked defenses—how else could he have reached Antioch?—he suggested to Justinian's representatives that his own army could henceforth protect the Romans—for a fee, of course (2.10.23).[14] So during the course of his invasion, Chosroes managed to present himself as the patron of the Greens in the hippodrome, a source of justice against military abuses, the champion of neglected Roman gods, and the restorer of the empire's defenses. Naturally, it is impossible to take all this seriously. Procopius takes pains to demolish the king's sincerity and credibility. But it remains highly disturbing that the forms of Roman imperial rule could be mimicked so comprehensively by a barbarian invader. We begin to suspect that despite their differences, the two brothers were far closer than propaganda on both sides claimed, perhaps even that they were more or less interchangeable.

Chosroes' behavior at Apamea inevitably calls for comparison to Justinian's treatment of the crowd in the hippodrome of Constantinople, especially during the Nika riots of 532. That was the moment when his regime was in greatest danger of being overthrown. As it happens, Procopius has linked those riots to a rebellion instigated around the same time by the Persian nobility against Chosroes (1.23.1).[15] It is here that the parallelism between events in Rome and Persia is most explicit in the *Wars*.

The Nika riots have been exhaustively analyzed in modern scholarship, but primarily from the historical point of view. I do not want to add to that discussion here. Instead, I will examine two aspects of Procopius' account that have gone unnoticed or whose significance has not been grasped. These are, first, the subtle depiction of Justinian as a Persian despot, one of the main esoteric themes of the *Wars*, and, second, the idea that political assassination, or tyrannicide, is the only way to rid the world of such men. As it happens, tyrannicide is a topic that Procopius discusses extensively in the *Vandal* and *Gothic Wars* in passages we will discuss later.

The themes of oriental despotism and tyrannicide in the account of the Nika riots emerge from the speeches that Procopius records, or more likely invents, which contain allusions to relevant classical precedents. Also, specific events that are alleged to have occurred during the Nika riots are linked to other highly suggestive passages elsewhere in the *Persian Wars* itself. Procopius' hostility to the regime in its hour of crisis continues to be total and uncompromising.

In the middle of his account of the Nika riots, Procopius recounts a meeting of the Senate that occurred right after the proclamation by the people of Hypatius, the nephew of the emperor Anastasius (1.24.25–31). The account of this meeting consists almost entirely of a speech by a certain Origenes who is otherwise unknown. Modern accounts of the riots either omit the alleged meeting altogether or devote much less space to it than does Procopius.[16] The speech of Origenes is rarely if ever quoted, unlike the famous speech of Theodora with which it is paired. Geoffrey Greatrex put his finger exactly on the problem when he said to me that "it smacks more of historiography than of history." Yet it is precisely for that reason that we must look carefully at both speeches if we are to understand Procopius' representation of the event. The riots themselves need not be reassessed, only our view of their historian.

Procopius introduces the session of the Senate with an ambiguous comment. "Many expressed the opinion that they should go to the palace and join the fight" (1.24.25). *But on which side?* To defend Justinian or destroy him? The Senate seems to have been of one mind on this issue, only we do not know which it was. It is only at the end of his speech that Origenes reveals that the common goal was to remove Justinian from power; up to that point he refers only vaguely to "the enemy." This, I believe, is another of Procopius' attempts to subtly manipulate our reactions. Our justifiable uncertainty about the loyalties of the Senate runs up against the revelation that its members took each other's implacable hostility to Justinian for granted. Our initial uncertainty turns out to have been naive, for opposition to the regime seems to be natural. We may assume it, unless we are told otherwise. Only at the end of the account do we learn that Hypatius was also present, at which point he encourages the Senate to follow him to the hippodrome (1.23.31). This piece of information is crucial for understanding the climate of the meeting, but Procopius postpones it to the end. This is another way in which he dramatically manipulates our response to his narrative.

The meeting of the Senate during the Nika riots mirrors an event described earlier in the *Persian Wars*, the assembly of the Persian nobles after the deposition and imprisonment of Cavades and the elevation of his uncle Blases (1.5.1–8).[17] There are many striking parallels between the two assemblies, not least of which is that both were probably invented by Procopius, or transformed by him into literary dramas bearing little relation to what actually happened. Both depict assemblies of the nobility in the presence of a ruler elected to replace a hated tyrant. Yet neither Blases nor Hypatius take part in the deliberations. Each meeting consists almost entirely of the advice of one man, Gousanastades among the Persians and Origenes among the Romans, though the nobility follows their advice in neither case, to its ruin. Cavades' "confinement" in prison as his nobles assembled is mirrored by the voluntary "confinement" of Justinian and his court inside the palace as the senators made plans (καθείρξαντες σφᾶς αὐτούς: 1.24.10). I argued in an earlier chapter that the episodes with which Procopius begins each of the *Wars* almost always prefigure events or themes that occur later in the text, in the reign of Justinian. This establishes an ongoing dialogue and counterpoint between different parts of the text. Careful readers will notice the many similarities that link the account of the Nika riots to the deposition of Cavades and the debate that occurred afterward about his fate. What will especially come to mind is the Machiavellian advice of Gousanastades: kill the tyrant now while you have the chance. But the Persians decided against killing a man of royal blood.[18] The harsh truth of this advice was revealed when Cavades escaped from prison and killed his enemies with the help of a hired foreign army.

The paired speeches of Origenes and Theodora also raise intriguing parallels from Herodotus. J. A. S. Evans noted that Origenes lifts a phrase from a speech delivered by Dionysius of Phocaea at an Ionian assembly during the revolt against Persia.[19] The context of the allusion is appropriate and not chosen at random: Dionysius poses a stark choice between freedom and slavery (6.11). That the enemy here is a Persian king (Darius) makes his speech all the more appropriate as a source for an allusion set in a speech against Justinian. Evans also suggests that the "literary ancestor" of Theodora's speech—a woman boldly giving advice to a council of war—is the famous speech of Artemisia to Xerxes' council before the battle of Salamis. Though lacking verbal parallels, the allusion would again cast Justinian in the guise of a Persian monarch. We have already discussed Theodora's quotation of a proverb that links her husband to the infamous Dionysius, tyrant of Syracuse, with many parallels to the Nika riots and damning implications for his regime.[20] Whether we admit the allusion to Artemisia or not, it should be clear that Procopius sets up an unrelenting linkage between Justinian and many Persian kings: to Chosroes in the *Secret History* and *Wars*; to Cavades, Darius, and possibly Xerxes in the account of the Nika riots; to Cambyses in the *Secret History*; to Xerxes' decision to march against Greece at the beginning of the *Vandal Wars*; and to Cyrus in the *Buildings*. In the *Gothic Wars*, Justinian's letter to Theodahad is based on the letter of Xerxes to Pausanias in Thucydides, an appropriate choice for both correspondents considering their relationship at that moment.[21]

Procopius viewed the Nika riots as a terrible and unmitigated misfortune for both the people of Constantinople and the Senate, and this is what he declares in the very first sentence of his account (1.24.1). He then proceeds to give a hostile account of the factions who instigated the riots and seems to lay most of the blame on them (1.24.2–6). But he then goes on to present an equally negative picture of two of Justinian's chief officials, the prefect John the Cappadocian and the jurist Tribonian, whose abuses led to the popular unrest (1.24.11–18).[22] This is an instance of a device employed repeatedly in the *Wars*, whereby the ruler is criticized indirectly through his officials—what the Chinese call killing the horse to get to the horseman.[23] But then one of the main grounds of hostility toward this particular horseman was that he rode so many wild horses. Naturally, no criticism of Justinian's reaction to the riots could be made openly in the *Wars*. Procopius' account is studiously neutral; everything is said between the lines or through obscure allusions. It has been said that he "leaves out no point essential for the comprehension of the general course of the revolt and its political significance."[24] To see how far his stance was from that of the regime, we can turn to other writers such as Marcellinus Comes and Malalas, who made themselves its spokesmen by endorsing Justinian's distorted version of events, quite possibly by copying the official proclamation in which he announced his victory over his own people.[25]

Having seen Chosroes' Roman pretensions and Justinian's Persian guises, let us turn back to the events of 540, where many passages testify to the equivalence of the two in the eyes of their victims. After leaving Apamea, Chosroes moved on the city of Chalcis, demanding ransom and the surrender of the garrison. Procopius now makes an amazing statement: "the people of Chalcis were terrified of both kings" (2.12.2). To protect themselves from Justinian, they hid the garrison and denied its existence; to placate Chosroes, they collected with difficulty a sum of gold to satisfy his greed. This episode implies a comprehensive interpretation of the eastern wars. We are invited to consider the possibility that the wars were not between Rome and Persia, but between the two kings on the one hand and the inhabitants of the eastern cities on the other. The real victims of the wars were those who were caught between the two tyrants. In a separate study of the wars of Justinian, I intend to argue that Procopius insinuates in the *Persian Wars* what he says openly in the *Secret History*; namely, that the responsibility for the invasion of 540 lay as much with Justinian as with Chosroes. Both men contributed to the devastation.[26] Procopius sympathizes with all those who suffered at the hands of the kings, regardless of whether they lived in Africa, Italy, the Balkans, or the east, or whether they were subject to Rome or to its official enemies. Procopius does not value the suffering of Romans more than that of others. Modern interpreters have unfortunately never made much of the fact that each of the *Wars* has an unhappy ending. Procopius' guiding principle would then be something akin to what we call humanity.

Be that as it may, the equivalence of the two kings is also suggested by two omens that occurred before the fall of Antioch. Contrary to what is usually assumed, omens in classical historiography often have nothing to do with superstition.[27] Like anecdotes, they are vehicles of literary and political analysis. For example, Procopius tells us that shortly before the fall of Antioch, the standards of the units stationed there turned suddenly to face east and then again returned to face west. He views this as a sign "that the dominion over the place would pass from the western emperor to the one of the east" (2.10.1–3). Any Roman with a knowledge of history would take this as a reference to the rulers of the western and eastern portions of the Roman empire in the fifth century, after its division by Theodosius I. That is what they were called in other historical texts of the period and that is how Procopius refers to them in the introduction to the *Vandal War*. But here Justinian is the emperor of the *west* and *Chosroes* is the emperor of the east. The world is no longer divided between two Roman emperors, but rather between two imperial "brothers" of east and west. We could translate the word *basileus* as "king," but the ambiguity remains in the original: Chosroes has taken Justinian's place as emperor of the east. And, as we have seen, he does this in a very literal sense during the invasion of 540.

In his account of the warfare of the early 550s, which was published in the supplementary Book 8 of the *Wars*, Procopius interrupts his account of a siege of Edessa to relate another omen that occurred there before the end of the Eternal Peace in 540. "A woman gave birth to an infant which in all other respects was a normally fashioned human being, but had two heads. The significance of this was made clear by what happened later. For both Edessa and virtually the entire east and even most of the Roman empire to the north was contested by two sovereigns" (8.14.39–40). I have used the neutral word "sovereign," but *basileus* can mean both emperor and king. This ambiguous word suited Procopius' purposes beautifully, for it occluded any titular differences that may have existed between Chosroes and Justinian. In postulating an equivalence between the two, this omen signifies the same as the turning of the standards.

When Chosroes finally returned to Ctesiphon, he built a city nearby where he settled all the captives he had brought from Antioch. He called it "the Antioch of Chosroes" and provided it with all the amenities of a Roman city (2.14.1–4). The circle was now complete. Having become a Roman emperor in Roman lands, the king literally transported one of the greatest Roman cities into the heart of his own realm, thus symbolically extending his claim to be an emperor into his own sphere of authority. "He called the inhabitants of this city royal subjects, so that they were subordinate to no royal official, but only to the *basileus.*" Both empires now possessed a city called Antioch that was settled by Romans, one for Justinian and another for his eastern brother Chosroes. Historians have claimed that this new city was one of the many ways in which Persian kings imitated their Roman brothers; for his foundation of Antioch, Chosroes has been called a "Byzantinizer."[28] As far as Procopius was concerned, New Antioch was the culmination of a series of events that thoroughly undermined the uniqueness of the Roman imperial title, along with any cardinal differences that may have existed between civilized Roman government and its supposed opposite.

"Vanity of Vanities": Despotism and Imperial Ceremony

Oriental despotism, as conceptualized by classical writers, exalted monarchs to a near-divine level and reduced subjects to the symbolic—or real—status of slaves. No form of equality could exist between the two: the Persian king, whether Achaemenid or Sasanid, was the absolute master of a nation of slaves. This aspect of Persian despotism emerges forcefully in the *Persian Wars* with the return from exile of the tyrant Cavades. He was greeted by the young nobleman Adergoudounbades, who "called him master (δεσπότης) and was the first to bow before him (προσεκύνησε) as a king, and beseeched him to make use of him as a slave (δοῦλος) for whatever purpose he desired" (1.6.16). In these few lines Procopius sums up the nature of the relationship.

In Persian society, *proskynesis* was no mere token of respect. Herodotus had explained it as a sign of profound inferiority (1.134), and that was how Procopius viewed it. When Cavades' father Perozes was defeated by the king of the Ephthalites, the latter demanded *proskynesis* "because he had become Perozes' master (δεσπότης)" (1.3.17–22). Perozes considered this a great "dishonor" and contrived to perform it at dawn, when Persians "performed *proskynesis* before the rising sun" (1.3.21). He hoped in this way to salvage his pride. This episode brings out nicely the religious overtones of the practice: kings received *proskynesis* from their subjects as gods received it from kings. The Byzantine chronicle of Theophanes the Confessor reports that when the emperor Heraclius made overtures for peace to Chosroes II in 615, he was told that he had to renounce Christ and perform *proskynesis* to the sun.[29]

Chosroes made no changes to this system. He considered his highest-ranking general to be his "slave" (1.23.14). Even foreign kings who sought his friendship had to prostrate themselves to him. In 541, Goubazes, the king of the Lazi, renounced his Roman alliance by "performing *proskynesis* to Chosroes as to a master (δεσπότης)" (2.17.2). Ten years later, after he had again switched sides, Goubazes was instructed by a Persian general to seek forgiveness by "prostrating yourself before Chosroes your master, as your king and victor and lord" (8.16.27).[30]

To these practices we may compare the following account of Justinian and Theodora from the very end of the *Secret History*.

The innovations made by Justinian and Theodora in the governance of the state included the following. In the past the Senate, when it came before the emperor, was accustomed to perform *proskynesis* in the following way. Men of patrician rank would salute him (προσεκύνει) on the right breast.[31] The emperor would then kiss them upon the head and send them out. All the rest bent their right knee to the emperor and then departed. There was no custom of any kind regarding *proskynesis* to the empress. But under Justinian and Theodora, all who entered upon their presence, both those who held patrician rank and all the others, would fall upon the ground, with their chin pressed down, and, stretching their hands and legs as far away from themselves as possible, would touch with their lips one foot of each, and then rise again. . . . In the past those who attended upon the emperor called him "emperor" and his wife "queen," and each of the other magistrates by whatever office he happened to hold at the time; but if anyone should converse with either of these two and refer to them as "emperor" or "empress," and not as "master" or "mistress" (δεσπότης, δέσποινα), or if he should attempt to avoid calling any of the magistrates "slaves," he would be regarded as both stupid and profane and sent away as though he had sinned most terribly and insulted those who least deserved it. . . . So these two were always taking everything into their own hands to the ultimate ruin of their subjects, and compelled everyone to dance attendance upon them in the most servile (δουλοπρεπέστατα) manner. (30.21–30)

Earlier in the same work, Procopius says that Justinian was easygoing and accessible; anyone could approach "that tyrant" and discuss confidential matters with him (15.11–12; also 13.1–2). But this statement does not necessarily contradict the passage quoted above because it says nothing about courtly ceremony, while the former refers to senators and involves the presence of Theodora. Procopius is unrelenting in his attack against her in the *Secret History*. She made magistrates wait on her like "slaves" and insisted on the most humiliating form of *proskynesis*. "To such a state of servility (δουλοπρέπεια) had the state been reduced, with her as its instructor in slavery (δουλοδιδάσκαλος)" (15.13–16; cf. 15.27–35). Only against this background can her famous speech during the Nika riots be fully appreciated: "May I never be separated from this purple, and may I never live to see the day when I am not addressed by anyone I meet as mistress (δέσποινα)" (1.24.36). This speech is a masterpiece of characterization, one of Procopius' best. It is completely devoid of sound advice, strategy, or argument; indeed, the empress says nothing that is even remotely rational. Her speech consists entirely of a massive assertion of will. She cares only about what she will be called by others and whether she will still wear the trappings of power. Her speech in no way empowers women, as previously believed. It is instead a brilliant reflection of the character portrait of the empress contained in the *Secret History*: irrational, vindictive, and vain. The speech expresses the raw ambition of a woman who had no conception of the dignity of political life. To have lived under her power must have been unbearably degrading.

Incidentally, Procopius' portrait of Theodora is still the most psychologically compelling, and one of the most vivid, to survive from antiquity. Attempts to refute it invariably rely on psychological speculation, for the accusations in the *Secret History* have not been convicted of error and have been confirmed by other sources dealing with the same events: the "facts underlying Procopius' account are confirmed by incontrovertible evidence elsewhere."[32] It is easy to dismiss his "rhetoric," and many have done so, but it has also been shown beyond a doubt that other sources are far *less* reliable on Theodora than is the *Secret History*. Accusations of misogyny, furthermore, are circular and founder on Procopius' admiration for Amalasuntha. A dispassionate analysis of the evidence points to the conclusion that Theodora was in fact petty, arrogant, wrathful, unforgiving, ruthless, and willing to sacrifice everything to her personal feuds and avarice. Such people do exist, and we should not dismiss the testimony of historians who try to tell us about them at great personal risk.[33] Her patronage of a few holy men and her token charities were nothing to Procopius compared to the damage that she caused to a frayed political system. He was not the only contemporary who feared her, but he was more concerned about her role in the rise of despotism than about her theological views.

Classical authors regarded the despotic treatment of free men to be a basic feature of Persian kingship, and the evidence of the *Persian Wars* demonstrates that Procopius knew and accepted that association. Justinian's innovations with respect to courtly protocol can therefore be seen as yet another link to Persian despotism and certainly contributed to the historian's belief that the emperor was "a barbarian in his speech and dress and manner of thinking" (14.2; cf. 23.8). That is certainly how classically educated readers of the *Secret History* would have reacted to Justinian's demand for *proskynesis* and insistence on being called *despotes*. For a master is by definition someone who owns slaves: *dominus est, cui est servus*, wrote Isidore of Seville in the early seventh century,[34] and Greek usage in late antiquity was well defined in a dictionary of Attic words attributed to Manuel Moschopoulos (ca. 1300): δεσπότης λέγεται πρὸς δοῦλον, κύριος δὲ πρὸς ἐλεύθερον. *Despotes*, however, entailed radical subservience and could not be used as a polite form of address, unlike Latin *dominus*.[35] Did Justinian, like a Persian king, conceptualize his position to be one of dominion over slaves? The evidence from the *Secret History* is unequivocal. The same conclusion can be drawn from the *Wars*, though the evidence there is presented discreetly, often through the speeches of the emperor's foreign victims.

The nations conquered by, or even allied to, Justinian certainly thought of him as an oppressive slave-owner. Far from suppressing their grievances and resentment, Procopius allows them to vent freely. The Lazi complained to the Persians about their alliance with the Romans, saying that "in theory we are their friends, but in reality we have become their dutiful slaves, having suffered unholy treatment at the hands of those who tyrannize over us" (2.15.19). The Armenians likewise complained to the Persians that Justinian had enslaved their neighbors the Tzani (2.3.39). The Abasgi also revolted from Roman rule because they had good reasons to "fear that they would become slaves of the Romans" (8.9.10–12). Likewise, the Goths feared that Justinian had sent his armies to Italy to enslave them (2.2.9, 5.29.8, 6.29.17, 6.30.11). Procopius indeed says that when groups of them surrendered to Roman generals they became "slaves of the emperor" (e.g., 6.11.19, 6.29.33).

Some Goths even reproached Belisarius for preferring to be Justinian's slave rather than a king in his own right (6.30.25), and if Belisarius was a slave then surely so were all the empire's subjects. Chosroes was advised by his secretary Abandanes not to give battle to Belisarius because if he prevailed it would be over only "the slave of Caesar," yet if he were defeated he would be disgraced (2.21.14). Procopius has correctly made the secretary call Justinian "Caesar," which was in accordance with official Persian usage.[36] But is the characterization of Belisarius as a slave of Caesar also a projection of Persian values? Other evidence in the *Wars*, which we will examine below, indicates that Abandanes' words accurately reflected sixth-century Roman usage. Let us note here that his advice is based directly on the advice given to Xerxes by his vassal Artemisia regarding Mardonius' request to remain in Greece and continue the war after Salamis: if he wins, Xerxes, his "master," can take credit for the achievements of his "slave," but if he loses, he is, after all, only an expendable slave.[37] Procopius has inverted this advice to make it apply to a Roman "slave" fighting *against* the Persian king.

The theme of slavery to the emperor is most developed in the *Vandal Wars*. It is invoked with reference to Moors allied to Rome as well as to the defeated Vandals (e.g., 3.25.3, 4.5.12–13, 4.6.14, 4.22.7). Mirroring developments in the east, some Moors complained that they had been promised that they would be "subjects of the emperor" (4.11.9) but were now fighting to avoid "enslavement" to him (4.11.40). The most interesting exchange occurred between Pharas, himself a barbarian in the emperor's service, and the defeated Vandal king Gelimer, who was under siege in the fort of Papua during the winter of 533–534. Pharas reproached Gelimer for seeking to preserve a worthless "liberty" and encouraged him to become, like himself, the emperor's slave. "Would it not be entirely better to be poor and a slave among the Romans, than to lord it over the Moors at Papua? But to you it seems that being a fellow-slave of Belisarius is the peak of disgrace" (4.6.18–21). The argument disturbingly anticipates John Locke's *Second Treatise of Government*: "And a king of a large and fruitful Territory there [namely, America] feeds, lodges and is clad worse than a day Labourer in England" (5.41). Locke was trying to make his readers forget that there are reasons for being a king beyond how one "feeds, lodges and is clad." Pharas—that is, Procopius—is more candid.[38]

That Belisarius was a slave of the emperor no less than Gelimer (who eventually did surrender) was demonstrated later that year in the capital at the celebrations of victory that culminated in the hippodrome. "When Gelimer came before the imperial seat, they removed his purple cloak and forced him down to the ground to perform *proskynesis* to Justinian. This Belisarius also performed, becoming a suppliant of the emperor along with Gelimer" (4.9.12). It has been noted that this ceremony effectively "removed the distinction between the subjects of the emperor and his enemies."[39] Belisarius' *proskynesis*, along with the many references to him in the *Wars* as a slave, should be taken in conjunction with the attack in the *Secret History* on Justinian's "despotic" court protocol. No less than any

Persian king, he imposed on his magistrates and generals the status of slaves.

A careful recent analysis of Justinian's own views of imperial rule, conquest, and subjugation, as expressed in his laws and official pronouncements, concludes that he tended to blur the difference between Romans who had been "liberated" from barbarian dominion and barbarians who had been "enslaved" and reduced to the status of "subjects" by imperial armies. It seems that "Justinian was the first emperor to refer to Roman citizens consistently in legislation as his subjects."[40] The difference between subjects and slaves referred ultimately only to the manner in which they had been brought under his authority. This was precisely the ideological background of Procopius' protest. While the emperor boasted that he had liberated the Roman world from barbarian slavery, his historian was allowing all the nations to express their hatred of the slavery he had imposed upon them. And Procopius made similar complaints in his own voice. In the *Secret History*, he says that the emperor imposed severe financial demands on populations ravaged by constant war, showing himself "more oppressive than all the barbarians" (23.8). In the *Wars*, the blame is placed discreetly on the emperor's subordinates. In Italy, for instance, the Roman armies were at one point so lawless and oppressive "that they made the local population long for the barbarians" (7.9.1–6). So much for the ideology of liberation.

Just like every other age, the sixth century had its share of intellectuals who for ideological or opportunistic reasons endorsed the imposition of totalitarian systems of control, particularly regarding religious belief and social order.[41] The extremes to which Justinian carried this program was perhaps only an aspect of a more widespread development in social attitudes. Naturally, it sparked opposition. Procopius was not the only contemporary to protest against the emperor's illiberal conception of political life. Drawing on Plato's *Republic* and Cicero, the anonymous author of a dialogue *On Politics* called for a sharing of power between the emperor and other classes, in effect a limited constitutional monarchy.[42] And what are we to make of the quaestor Tribonian, who, in the constitutions that he wrote for Justinian, frequently refers to Marcus Aurelius, the paragon of republican rule, as "the most philosophical of emperors"?[43] An intriguing recent study has demonstrated that the jurist was profoundly influenced by Platonic philosophy and cleverly laced the legal texts that he wrote on behalf of his Christian master with Platonic concepts and allusions.[44] But the most startling and untimely criticism was produced by the civil official John

Lydus, who had studied under the philosopher Agapius, a disciple of the great Proclus. I intend to argue elsewhere that Lydus' politics were republican; in other words, he recognized no essential difference between Roman imperial rule and tyranny. But for now we need quote only one passage of his antiquarian work *On the Magistracies of the Roman State*. Writing at the same time as Procopius, Lydus states that Justinian "tolerates" being called a "master" (*despotes*), though "not only does he not delight in it, he is embarrassed."[45] This is a relatively transparent attempt to sugarcoat a serious criticism: Lydus has just spent the last two chapters arguing that it is "tyrants who like to be called 'lords' and 'masters' rather than 'kings'," an exact parallel to what Procopius tells us about Justinian. Lydus was probably a close friend of Procopius and one of the intended readers of the *Secret History*.[46]

The claims made by Procopius and Lydus require explanation, for the former accuses Justinian of breaking from tradition in demanding abject *proskynesis*, while both testify to the new prominence given to the title *despotes*. In the passage of the *Secret History* quoted above, the account of court protocol "in the past" presumably refers to any time before Justinian. It is true that during the early empire, what is today called the Principate, emperors did not demand to be called *despotai* (or *domini*), though some of their subjects did address them that way. Domitian was a notorious exception, and he swiftly came to a bad end. His successors were warned against making that mistake again.[47] Curiously, the only other emperor to whom Procopius compares Justinian in the *Secret History* is Domitian, in what must be one of the most macabre passages in ancient literature. Procopius compares the physical appearance of Justinian to a statue of the reassembled bits of Domitian after he had been dismembered (8.12–21).[48] The comparison is introduced by the statement that the Romans so hated Domitian that "not even when they had butchered his entire body into little bits did they feel that their rage against him had been exhausted." Certainly there is an element of wishful thinking here. In any case, Procopius chose Domitian as a model not because he too had insisted on being called *dominus* but probably because his reputation as a tyrant approximated that which he wanted to confer upon Justinian. Insane youths such as Caligula or Nero would simply not do. Interestingly, Procopius' friend John Lydus twice refers to Domitian as a tyrant in connection with administrative innovations, which Lydos also viewed as a sign of despotism.[49]

But are Procopius' charges about *proskynesis* and forms of address correct? At some point in the fourth century it became conventional wisdom that the emperor who had first required *adoratio* and allowed himself to be addressed as *dominus* was Diocletian and that this reform, including more resplendent imperial regalia, was knowingly modeled on Persian customs. These changes inaugurated the period of imperial rule known today as the Dominate. There has been considerable debate on the question of Persian influence. Some scholars prefer to see the reforms as a development internal to Roman forms of subject-ruler interaction, while others do not preclude a Persian model. Be that as it may, it is still important that contemporaries viewed these new protocols as inspired by Persia and hence believed that their own government was moving in a direction that had always been identified with Persian despotism, in which displays of power replaced civility and equality.[50]

At first glance we might conclude that Procopius and Lydus have simply revived, or independently reproduced, the schema propounded by the fourth-century authors, only they have ascribed the innovations to Justinian rather than Diocletian. If that is true, and if Justinian was following centuries-old customs after all, then the argument of his two critics fails because he was not an innovator.[51] Possibly they were opposed to the ideological tenor of the Dominate in general and wanted to blame Justinian for its most offensive elements by projecting the practices of the more moderate Principate onto the recent reign of Anastasius. But even if we grant a measure of exaggeration, this solution will not do. It requires us to accept that two authors lied about something that would have been patently false to most of their readers. We cannot just dismiss the circumstantial description of the different ceremonies given at the end of the *Secret History*.

If we read that passage closely, we see that Procopius is not accusing Justinian of introducing the title of *despotes*, but of requiring it to the exclusion of *basileus*. Also, Justinian did not introduce *proskynesis* but rather changed it drastically: instead of kissing the emperor's right breast and receiving a kiss on the head, senators now had to fall on the ground and kiss one of his feet. A further innovation was that they now had to treat the empress likewise. Procopius is explicit about the fact that the older ceremony was also a form of *proskynesis*, only it was far less degrading than what Justinian and Theodora required. Studies of *adoratio* have shown that the practice supposedly instituted by Diocletian was similar to that ascribed by Procopius to times prior to Justinian. An illuminating parallel is found in Eusebius' account of the funeral of the emperor Constantine: magistrates performed *proskynesis* to the late emperor by dropping to one knee and embracing him.[52] For Justinian's time we are fortunate to possess the transcripts and guidelines for imperial ceremonies prepared by Peter the Patrician, the emperor's long-serving *magister officiorum*. These were subsequently incorporated into the *Book of Ceremonies* edited by the emperor Constantine VII in the tenth century. We find in Peter's descriptions many high officials and foreign ambassadors "throwing themselves upon the ground" and "kissing the emperor's feet" on many occasions.[53] Similar acts of obeisance to Justinian are described in the Latin epic of Corippus on the Libyan campaigns of John Troglita as well as in the same poet's panegyric on the accession of Justin II.[54] These texts clarify as well as vindicate the testimony of the *Secret History*.

No word in English exactly translates *proskynesis*. In addition, as we have seen, the term signified different practices from time to time, though ancient authors were generally not aware of this fact. Procopius is an exception because he happened to witness a moment of transition. A similar uncertainty about the exact meaning of the term affects the study of Achaemenid Persia and, consequently, of its adoption by Alexander the Great. It will be recalled that after defeating Darius, Alexander began to adopt the customs of the Persian court, perhaps in an effort to conciliate the Persian nobility. But this put him in the awkward position of receiving homage from his Persian courtiers and not the Macedonians. The latter resented their king's transformation into a Persian despot, and their refusal to perform *proskynesis* left a powerful mark on all accounts of his final years. *Proskynesis* took many forms in Achaemenid society. Most commonly it probably involved no more than a bow, but before the Great King, full prostration was often in order.[55] It is not clear which form Alexander demanded. One Latin source implies that his courtiers touched their heads to the ground.[56] I mention this episode because it represents the most sustained protest in ancient literature against the "servility" of *proskynesis*, especially when imposed on free men. In addition, it was directed against a king who was supposed to be fighting Persia on behalf of Greece but was instead gradually becoming a Persian himself. Classically educated readers of the *Secret History* may have made this connection. Procopius was the last voice of protest in that tradition, and he wrote at the moment when the most abasing form of the practice was being imposed on the Greek world.

We will return to Alexander below, when we consider the religious overtones of *proskynesis*. For now let us turn to Procopius' second accusation, that concerning the title *despotes*. Under the Principate, it was used on a voluntary basis by those who wished to honor or flatter the emperor. Emperors of the third century, notably Aurelian, seem to have used it officially, but Aurelius Victor claims that Diocletian was the first to "have himself called *dominus* in public," which probably means no more than that he sanctioned its use on formal occasions. The term appears in the panegyrics that honored members of his Tetrarchy[57] and was used widely by emperors of the fourth and fifth centuries.[58] But before we suspect Procopius of misinforming us on this matter as well, let us note that he does not say that Justinian was the first emperor to be called *despotes*, he says only that he was the first to prefer to be called that instead of *basileus*. At least that is what he demanded of his courtiers and magistrates. Besides, it is precisely regarding the new importance of the title *despotes* that Procopius' testimony is corroborated by Lydus. The evidence of inscriptions and papyri also gives depth to the accusations of the *Secret History*. The title *despotes* is included in virtually all official documents from the reign.[59]

Procopius says that Justinian also decided that magistrates should henceforth be referred to as his slaves, and it seems that they accepted this redefinition of their status, as texts from that and later reigns demonstrate.[60] Traces of an opposition can be detected, though it is difficult to gauge its extent and significance. The early seventh-century historian Theophylact evidently approved of the emperor Tiberius II's "hatred for the oppression of tyranny" and "desire to be addressed by his subjects as a father rather than a master (δεσπότης)" (3.16.5). After Justinian these were not idle words. Yet Tiberius does not seem to have taken any measures to change the direction of imperial ideology.[61] The result, as Procopius and Lydus feared, was the destruction of all vestiges of the free state.

Procopius conceptualized the regime of Justinian as an imperial form of oriental despotism. Even some modern scholars regard the demotion of imperial magistrates to the status of imperial slaves as fundamentally "Persian"—in nature if not in origin—though others are probably more correct in seeing it as Christian.[62] In viewing themselves as the slaves of God, Christians had long since transposed the concept of servitude from the social and political sphere to that of religion. Procopius attests this usage in the *Buildings* when he refers to saints as men "enslaved to God" (1.7.14), and countless other examples can be cited from Christian texts. Once the empire adopted Christianity, it was only a matter of time before this new master-slave relationship was transposed back from the religious sphere into that of political ideology. Just as Justinian regarded his subjects as his slaves, he regarded himself as a slave of God. These ideas are very prominent in the hortatory chapters addressed to him by the deacon Agapetus. Justinian is advised there to treat his own "servants" as he would be treated by his own divine "master" (δεσπότης), because all men are "fellow slaves" in the eyes of God.[63]

Whatever all this may have meant to Christians, it was deeply offensive to Procopius. As we will see, he was not blind to the religious dimension of Justinian's reforms. Yet his was not the standpoint of a Christian, who might view the emperor as some kind of representative of God, but that of a classically educated Greek, who condemned the association of monarchy with God as incompatible with political liberty. Many Greeks had early on confused the *proskynesis* offered to the Persian kings with the reverence that they themselves offered to the statues of their gods. As a result, they came to the mistaken conclusion that the Persian kings were regarded as gods by their servile subjects. Hence, many refused to perform the act because, in addition to offending their sense of dignity, it implied to them that the recipient was divine. And gods could not be citizens. Many classical texts declared political freedom to be incompatible with *proskynesis* to men or to any self-proclaimed "masters."[64] The fierce opposition of the Macedonians to Alexander's demand for *proskynesis* makes sense in this context because it was linked to justifiable apprehensions about his intention to be deified and worshipped.[65] As late as the fourth century, the orator and staunch Hellenist Libanius objected to the Cappadocians' habit of greeting each other by saying "I bow before you," because in his eyes it smacked of the Persian custom of granting rulers "a reverence worthy of gods."[66]

That this was exactly the attitude of Procopius is revealed by a fascinating passage in the *Secret History* where he condemns it as "a disgrace upon the state" that the senators accepted Theodora as their empress and then adds, "even though they were made to perform *proskynesis* to her as though she were a god" (10.6). In other words, the senators should have found the courage to oppose her in any case, but certainly when they were made to bow before her. Like any classical Greek, Procopius equates *proskynesis* itself, regardless of whether it was offered to Justinian or Theodora, with divine honors, and *that*, he implies, ought to have offended any self-respecting senator. He makes *no* allowances for the view that the emperor might be honored in that way as a representative of God. This indicates how far he stood from the view of the emperor as God's deputy that most Christians seem to have held. But the passage gets better.

Neither did any priest make it known that he was outraged, and that too, when they all were henceforth to call her "mistress" (δέσποινα). And the populace, who had previously been her spectators upon the stage, straightaway consented, with upturned hands and a total lack of decency, both to be and to be called her slaves. Neither did any soldier become furious at the notion that he was about to experience all the dangers of warfare on behalf of the interests of Theodora, nor did any other person oppose her, but instead I think that all gave way because they thought that matters had been thus ordained (δεδόσθαι). (10.7–9)

This passage is cleverly infused with religious nuances. The stage is set by the claim that by performing *proskynesis* to Theodora, the Senate honored her as a god. This establishes her divine pretensions and, a fortiori, those of her husband. It is worth recalling here Procopius' description in the *Buildings* of the mosaic in the palace that depicted Justinian's triumphs and the Senate standing around him, "granting him honors equal to those of God" (1.10.19). This was the historian's interpretation of what they were doing, for he was describing a picture, not quoting a document. The words are his own, and modern art historians have been unable to identify precisely which features of the mosaic indicated the alleged "divine honors."[67] Irony is thus again created by the interplay between the *Buildings* and the *Secret History*.

Procopius says that in addition to the senators, the priests also were not outraged by Theodora's accession, though they would now have to call her "mistress." Why should the priests care more about this than others? From Procopius' point of view, all free citizens should be offended at having to call anyone "mistress," especially someone such as Theodora. But I believe that there is a special reason why he singles out priests: in the Divine Liturgy and in other devotional contexts, they routinely called God their "master" (*despotes*). So by addressing Theodora in that same way, they would be indirectly granting the empress divine honors and defaming their God. A number of early Christian authors had in fact argued, with an eye on imperial protocol, that the title "master" was appropriate only to God, while others, who could invoke the explicit testimony of *Revelation*, had claimed that *proskynesis* was a divine prerogative. This problem posed great difficulties to the Fathers of the fourth century.[68] Procopius may have had these strains of early Christian thought in mind, though he must have known that they were virtually obsolete by the time Justinian gained the throne.

There are more religious overtones in this passage. Procopius says that the people begged to be Theodora's slaves "with upturned hands," a traditional gesture of prayer and supplication. Finally, he implies that there was no resistance to her accession because everyone simply assumed that it had been "ordained," presumably by providence. That a metaphysical agent of some sort is being implied is indicated by the fact that Procopius immediately digresses on the workings of amoral fortune, or *tyche*, a quasi-divine entity that acts without any concern for what is right (10.9–10). Naturally, those who did not oppose Theodora believed that her accession had been "ordained" not by fortune but probably by God. This implies further that their belief in providence instilled attitudes of passive acceptance, or fatalism. Procopius himself, however, could not have regarded Theodora's accession as the work of a benevolent God, and indeed, the fact that he proceeds to discourse on the power of fortune proves that he did not. This leads to the question of his own beliefs. These will be examined in the final chapter of this book, where it will be argued that the concept of fortune lies at the heart of his historical thought. For now let us note only that Procopius seems to ascribe to fortune what others ascribed to God, a practice that we will encounter often in our analysis of *tyche* in the *Wars*.

In another passage of the *Secret History*, Procopius again represents the new protocol as a mockery of religious ritual. An old patrician whom he discreetly leaves anonymous begged the empress to make one of her servants return a loan to him so that he could pay off his own creditors (15.24–35). Knowing his intentions in advance, the empress instructed her eunuchs to stand around in a circle and reply to anything she said "antiphonally" (ἀντιφθέγγεσθαι), a technical word referring to the way the liturgy was chanted in church. "And when the patrician arrived at the women's quarters, he performed *proskynesis* in the way in which it was customary to perform it before her." He addressed her as "mistress" (δέσποινα) and pleaded for the return of his money in language that again recalls the liturgy: ἀντιβολῶ καὶ ἱκετεύω καὶ δέομαι. But as soon as she addressed him by name, her "chorus" (χορός) "antiphonally" chanted, "What a big hump you have." This occurred repeatedly, until the man gave up and left, though not without again performing *proskynesis* "in the customary manner."

The language used in this passage leaves no doubt that the empress intended her little game as a parody of the liturgy.[69] At least that is how Procopius intended his readers to understand it. This runs against the conventional view that classicizing authors scrupulously avoided Christian allusions in their pursuit of purist diction. It was supposedly not until Theophylact in the seventh century that they felt comfortable enough to, say, include a sermon in their narratives.[70] This view has merit but is based on a failure to recognize that many passages of the *Wars* and *Secret History* are heavily infused with religious language that is not only Christian but specifically liturgical in nature. This, by the way, has nothing to do with so-called unconscious influences intruding through artificial classical barriers. The Christian allusions in Procopius form deliberate rhetorical strategies, deployed precisely for specific effect. The passage describing Theodora's acceptance by the various classes and the scene in the women's quarters that we just examined are deliberately infused with religious and Christian language, though this has nothing to do with the author's religious beliefs, whatever they may have been. His aim in both passages was to comment on the motives of historical agents by revealing the irony of their actions and positing subtle connections between political behavior and religious belief.

Nor did Procopius hesitate to quote Scripture to the same effect. At the peak of Justinian's triumph in the *Vandal Wars*, at the scene in the hippodrome that was mentioned above, right before Procopius recounts the *proskynesis* performed to the emperor by Gelimer and Belisarius he puts into the mouth of the dazed Vandal king the verse "from the Scripture of the Hebrews, 'Vanity of vanities, all is vanity.'" Gelimer was not thinking here of his own failure to resist the emperor's armies. Procopius tells us that the king began to speak this line over and over again "when he reached the hippodrome and saw the emperor sitting upon his lofty seat (βῆμα ὑψηλόν) and the people standing on either side of him" (4.9.11). Nothing could more ironically deflate a Christian ruler's lofty pretensions at the height of his power and glory than this line from Ecclesiastes 1.2. Procopius is possibly looking back to the triumphal processions held in ancient Rome, when a slave rode behind the victorious general and reminded him over and over again that he was only a mortal. Gelimer would then function as the Christian equivalent of this reminder. Be that as it may, we must also wonder about his choice of the word "lofty" to describe Justinian's seat. "Lofty" (ὑψηλός) was a common way of referring to God. Also, the emperor's seat in the hippodrome was commonly called the *kathisma*, not the *bema*, and we happen to know from a contemporary chronicle that in 528 Justinian had it rebuilt, "making it more elevated and brighter than it had been."[71] The *bema* was the area of the church that housed the altar and was regarded by Christians as the "Holy of Holies." So Gelimer's "Vanity of vanities"—itself a line from a sacred text—may refer to more than the emperor's worldly ambitions.

To conclude: again we see that the representation of Justinian in the *Secret History* resonates with the fundamental modes of Persian kingship as portrayed in the *Persian War*. That portrayal was in turn based on the classical image of the oppressive oriental monarchy as despotic on one end and servile on the other and contemptuous of the dignity of political life. Procopius' hostility to the metaphor of slavery as applied to free men was at heart ethical and political, though he did not hesitate to exploit religious language and imagery in order to give his representation of Justinian's tyranny cultural depth and irony. Yet his main concerns were not merely the conceit of courtly protocol or the hollowness of imperial propaganda. Far more was at stake. The demotion of free and potentially heroic men to the status of slaves undermined the entire conception of manly freedom and nobility that was central to the classical tradition. In this respect, the rejection of despotism was fundamentally Hellenic. In his discussion of tyranny in the *Republic*, Socrates imagines men "who won't stand for any man's claiming to be another's master" (579a)—and there are no slaves in the *Republic*. No wonder Procopius admired barbarian rebels such as Totila and Teia!

"The Rule of Women" and the Plan of *Secret History* 1–5

Surprisingly little attention has been paid to the plan of the *Secret History*, probably because of the astonishing nature of its contents. The work seems to consist of a series of amazing and violent denunciations that are loosely organized around three or four targeted personalities. The unrelenting intensity of it all affords the reader little opportunity to pause, reflect, and find the logic that may underlie its bewildering flow. This brings to mind the symptoms that Nietzsche diagnosed for literary decadence: "life no longer dwells in the whole. The word becomes sovereign and leaps out of the sentence, the sentence reaches out and obscures the meaning of the page, the page gains life at the expense of the whole."[72]

Decadent or not, the *Secret History* remains badly misunderstood. Research remains fixated on the juicy details and hysterical denunciations. Various opinions have been expressed on whether the work is complete, but these are often based on subjective criteria or, at most, a loose deconstruction of the work into genres.[73] One intriguing hypothesis has it that Procopius intended to add its contents to the *Wars* after Justinian's death, but as the latter showed no signs of dying after thirty years on the throne, the work remained a loose collection of criticisms out of context.[74] It has been divided plausibly into two or three sections, but the principles underlying the selection and arrangement of material remain opaque. According to a different proposal, the sections of the work were never meant to form a whole and were only assembled later. They were originally separate works following the rules of different genres and so analysis should concentrate on them individually. Other scholars have postulated a combination of genres, some in modified form.[75] There seems to be a consensus that the work lacks structure.[76]

It will be argued here that the *Secret History* possesses a tighter organization than has been suspected so far. But any attempt to deal with this problem must abandon the obsession with genre. Intelligent people write books because they have ideas, not because they are constrained to write in particular genres. Contrary to what is implied in recent scholarship, genres do not write books. Authors do. And each author chooses to adhere to a certain genre only because he believes that its formal characteristics facilitate the exposition of the themes that he has already decided to write about. The search for genres can easily become a surrogate for actually *reading* the work, as some scholars seem to think that once they identify the genre they automatically know what the author is trying to say. In this way, authors and texts are turned into passive vehicles of general cultural values. The literary sophistication of a discipline is inversely proportional to the frequency with which it invokes "genre." The direct and, in my view, only viable approach is to read the work carefully, identify its main themes and the methods by which they are developed, and then try to interpret the author's stance toward his subject. When the genre is known, it can be helpful in providing a literary context, but when it is not, especially when it is in dispute, it is at best a distraction. The *Secret History* adheres to no genre in particular and so adheres to no genre at all.

In this section, I will focus on the first five chapters of the *Secret History*. There is no dispute that they form a unit of some sort. In fact, at first sight the *Secret History* seems to consist of two parts, for at the end of the introduction Procopius says that he will discuss first the wretched deeds of Belisarius and then the wretched deeds of Justinian and Theodora (1.10). The first five chapters seem to focus on the marital history of Belisarius and Antonina. Belisarius is hardly ever mentioned in the text after those chapters; Antonina never.

The trouble begins when we try to understand how those five chapters are organized and what exactly they represent. The material seems jumbled together in no particular order. And despite the programmatic statement that the emphasis will be on Belisarius, the deeds of his wife receive as much if not more attention. To make matters worse, the narrative quickly focuses on the machinations of Theodora to such a degree that she eclipses the miserable couple. How then is this part about Belisarius? And what are we to make of the seemingly irrelevant digressions on the disaffection of Chosroes' troops or the misconduct of Sergius, the governor of Libya? Is there any internal logic behind all this, or is Procopius merely tagging one scurrilous story onto the next through tenuous links? For example, the misconduct of Antonina distracts Belisarius, who, in order to keep an eye on her, fails to invade Mesopotamia, allowing Chosroes to escape, which leads to a discussion of the king's strategy and the disaffection of his army, which is in turn cut short because Antonina has now arrived in the east and our attention must return to the sordid family life of Belisarius, and so on. . . . Is it better to assume that if Procopius had his way all this would have been carved up and the stories distributed to their rightful places in the *Wars*?

This may well have happened had Procopius felt free to publish the material. But just because the opportunity never presented itself does not necessarily mean that he left the *Secret History* in a state of chaos or even that he did not devote as much attention to its literary coherence as he did to that of the *Wars*. What we must do is find the key that unlocks the secrets of its composition by explaining the selection of material, its order, and its peculiarities. I believe that I have found that key.

Simply put, the first five chapters of the *Secret History* develop the theme of "the rule of women"; that is, the subversion of masculine virtues that occurs when feminine vices seize power in the state. The virtues that sustain the welfare of states, for example courage and nobility, were deemed masculine even when they were possessed by women, and allowances were usually made for that possibility. Procopius certainly did, as we saw when we examined his favorable portrayal of Amalasuntha, who was "sagacious, just, and nearer to the masculine" in the way that she ruled the Gothic kingdom.[77]

It is not such women, however, who seize power in the first five chapters of the *Secret History*. What we witness here is the complete subversion of masculinity, exemplified by Belisarius, and the triumph of feminine qualities, particularly vices. Belisarius is presented as a man who could have been a hero and who had many opportunities to perform noble deeds but always failed because his masculinity was sapped by women. This was no excuse: Procopius condemns him utterly for this weakness. This interpretation explains why Belisarius is relatively absent from a narrative that is after all supposed to be about him. His place has been usurped by women, who dominate the narrative because they dominate him. Everything said about them is correspondingly designed to reveal the modes of feminine rule. Procopius did believe in feminine virtues, but he believed that they had little to do with political rule (cf. 10.2). The paradox about Antonina and Theodora is that they ruled over men but lacked both masculine and feminine virtues. They ruled by manipulating sex in all its manifestations, and this is the essence of feminine vice. It is no coincidence that in a later passage Theodora is said to have hated Amalasuntha precisely "because of her magnificence and extraordinary masculinity" (16.1). Theodora aims to destroy all masculine virtues, even when they appear in women. Another passage tells how she destroyed feminine virtues as well by protecting adulteresses from their husbands (17.24–26).

This theme is central to Procopius' representation of the tyranny of Justinian, for the attack on masculinity is closely tied to the "servility" inculcated by the regime in its subjects. An episode in the first section of the *Secret History* establishes a suggestive link between the two themes. After looking at that passage, I will show how the first five chapters of the work are structured around the theme of feminine rule.

When Justinian fell ill with the plague in 542, Belisarius and other officers were suspected of having agreed not to recognize the court's choice in the matter of the succession (4.13–31). Theodora took this a slight against herself and arranged to have them imprisoned, tortured, fined, or disgraced. Belisarius was relieved of command and made to live in the capital in constant fear of assassination. In this the empress was assisted by Antonina, who lost no opportunity to humiliate her husband. The two women conspired to give Belisarius the impression that he would soon be executed or tortured.

In this state of terror he went up to his room and sat down alone on his bed, having no intention of doing anything noble nor even remembering that he had once been a man; he was sweating constantly and feeling dizzy, utterly at a loss and trembling violently, worried to death by servile fears and apprehensions both cowardly and entirely unmanly. (4.22)

The empress then sent a messenger with a note announcing that she had forgiven him for the sake of his wife and informing him that his future behavior toward Antonina would be closely monitored.

Belisarius, wishing to show his gratitude right then and there, stood up and fell on his face before the feet of his wife. And clasping her around her calves with each of his hands he kept moving his tongue from the sole of one foot to that of the other, calling her the cause of his life and salvation, and declared that he would henceforth be her faithful slave and not her husband. (4.29–30; cf. 15.15)

Belisarius' words and strange behavior may allude to contemporary forms of sexual domination. This, unfortunately, we cannot know. But the parallels with the imperial ceremonies described at the end of the work are obvious.

Rather than suffer such indignities, any real man would have destroyed those two monsters or died trying. And this is exactly what Procopius says on the next page, when Belisarius was again given an army and sent off to Italy: "all suspected . . . that as soon as he set foot outside the walls of the city, he would take up arms and resolve to do something brave and befitting a man, against both his wife and those who had violated him (βιασάμενοι)." The word can also mean "those who had *raped* him," one of many double entendres in Procopius' works. But Belisarius did nothing and "meekly followed that woman" (4.40–41).[78]

The humiliation of Belisarius exemplifies the failure of manhood and rise of servility that Procopius associated with Justinian's regime. We may now examine the logic behind the first five chapters of the *Secret History* and show how they develop that theme. The first section, the one ostensibly devoted to Belisarius, begins with the words "Belisarius had a wife . . ." (1.11). She immediately becomes the focal point of the narrative. After mentioning her lewd past, Procopius focuses on her affair with Belisarius' godson Theodosius. She is the protagonist here, not her husband, and the language repeatedly draws our attention to the feminine vices that undermine masculine order: prostitution, adultery, insatiable erotic infatuation, seduction, passion, slander, magic. Next to his wife, Belisarius is a shadow of a man, simple-minded (1.35) and miserable (1.39). Though at first he was blind to her promiscuity, he later became obsessed with it: news of her arrival in the east contributed to his decision to cut short the campaign of 541. As a result, Procopius says, "he was accused by all the Romans of treating the most pressing matters of state as less important than his own domestic affairs" (2.21). This is the first direct statement of what becomes a prominent theme in this section: male enervation and feminine license led to the subordination of public interests to private ones. As one scholar put it, "private comedy has turned into political tragedy."[79]

Procopius elaborates on the consequences of this event by explaining how the inaction of Belisarius allowed Chosroes to depart from Colchis unharmed (2.26–37). This sets the stage for a digression on Persian affairs whose purpose is revealed at the end, when Chosroes reads to his nobles a letter sent by Theodora to a Persian ambassador.[80] To prepare us for this letter, Procopius must first describe the difficulties encountered by the Persian army that year and the disaffection of its officers. It was in response to this that Chosroes read aloud Theodora's letter, in which she declared that her husband did nothing without her consent. The king then reproached the Persian nobility for thinking that "any real state could exist that was governed by a woman." This interpretation of the letter was directed specifically against his nobles' complaint that he had led them to war against "a state that was ancient and most worthy" (2.31). But in the eyes of the Persians, a state ruled by a woman was obviously contemptible. In this way, Procopius says, the king "succeeded in checking the impulse of the men" (2.36). From a historical point of view, this conclusion may sound incredible. But whether Chosroes actually pacified his nobles in this way, or whether he did so at all, is only tangential to the main theme of the work. The real purpose of the digression, located exactly at the middle of the first part of the *Secret History*, is to postulate Theodora as the ruler of the Roman state. From this point onward, she dominates the narrative.

Procopius is not claiming that Theodora actually ruled the empire; after all, that view is ascribed to Chosroes. He is instead unfolding the nuances of a literary theme—the rule of women—by relying on exaggeration and dark humor. Procopius will repeat Chosroes' dictum in his own voice later in the work, when it seems appropriate (cf. 15.9–10; 17.27). We should not mistake the *Secret History* for political science. It is rather a mixture of tragedy and comedy.

There can be little doubt that the sentiment expressed in Theodora's letter is authentic, even if the actual document itself is not. In 535, the Gothic king Theodahad wrote to the empress saying that "you exhort me to bring first to your attention anything I decide to ask from the triumphal prince, your husband." And in the same year the emperor himself declared that before issuing a decree he had discussed it first "with our most august consort whom God has given us."[81] Procopius reveals the effectual truth of Theodora's letter on the next page of the *Secret History*, where he says that she now "recalled Belisarius to the capital" (3.4). This is presented as a decision made by her alone. No mention is made of Justinian, even though her action affected imperial policy. Modern assessments of her power, although judicious in other respects, tend to underestimate or even ignore her influence on the selection and appointment of magistrates and generals.[82] Her motives, moreover, had nothing to do with strategy; in this case, she was "frightened on behalf of Antonina," whom Belisarius had put under guard but was "too weakened" by "white-hot erotic passion" to kill (3.1). Antonina is henceforth subordinated to Theodora in the narrative, at one point even calling the empress her "savior and benefactor and mistress (σώτειρά τε καὶ εὐεργέτις καὶ δέσποινα)" (3.18).

Chosroes' reading of the letter is a turning point in the narrative. The vicious crimes of Theodora now take the rule of women to a new level. So far the story has been merely comical and sordid, a "satirical novel" of sorts.[83] The entry of Theodora transforms it into a nightmare, involving the vindictive imprisonment and murder of magistrates and the ruin of imperial policy.

The focus moves to Italy, specifically to Belisarius' ignominious campaigns of 544–549. Procopius' denigrating remarks about those campaigns, along with his comments on the power of God and Fortune (4.42–5.6), must be read together with what is said about them in the *Gothic War*.[84] The remainder of the first part of the *Secret History* (5.7–33) revolves around the marriages that Theodora arranged or prevented.[85] Her actions in this field, replete with petty vindictiveness and sordid procurements, is the final aspect of the rule of women considered in this part of the text. Though these stories are only tenuously linked to Belisarius, their purpose is again to show the negative consequences of the supremacy of the private over the public (cf. 17.27–37). So Procopius abruptly digresses on the crimes committed by Sergius, the governor of Libya, even though the vilification of Belisarius has explicitly ended at 5.27 and the section on Justinian does not begin until 6.1. It is not until the end of the digression that Procopius explains its inclusion: Theodora kept Sergius in power in spite of his crimes because he was a suitor for one of Antonina's daughters (5.33).[86] He also includes a story that shows the damage done by Theodora's marital intrigues to the Roman cause in Italy (5.7–15). In conjunction with the digressions on Chosroes and the crimes of Sergius in Libya, the theme of the rule of women is thereby extended to all three arenas of the *Wars*. This is a subtle reminder of the way in which the *Secret History* is a supplement to the *Wars* and of how the two texts must be read in tandem.

The final assessment of Belisarius' character in the *Secret History* begins by citing extenuating circumstances: many "suspected that the cause of the man's faithlessness was not the fact that he was ruled by a woman (γυναικοκρατία), but his terror of the empress." Terror of the empress is widely attested outside the *Secret History*; there would have been much sympathy with Belisarius on this point.[87] But when his behavior did not change after her death, he was reviled by everyone "when it became apparent that his wife actually dominated him (δέσποινα)" (5.26–27). Gynecocracy was the problem after all. Once again the "rule of women" is linked to the master-slave relationship fostered by the regime of Justinian and the ideology reflected in its ceremonies and protocol. The true chain of command ran up from Belisarius, though Antonina, to Theodora (cf. 5.13).

The word for "rule of women" is rare in Greek, appearing mostly in comedy or ethnography (e.g., for Amazons). Its most important appearance in a theoretical context is in Aristotle's *Politics*, and it is likely that Procopius had that text in mind when he used the word. It is significant that it appears in Aristotle's discussion of tyranny. Such regimes are characterized by "the rule of women in the household, so that they may report on their husbands, and laxness toward slaves for the same reason. Slaves and women do not conspire against tyrants." Elsewhere in the same work he uses the word in a way that reminds us of Chosroes' reaction to the letter of Theodora: "what difference is there between women ruling and rulers who are ruled by women?"[88]

Therefore, if genre must be involved, I propose that the first part of the *Secret History* be called the Gynecocracy. When the editor of the tenth-century Byzantine dictionary *Souda* listed the works of Procopius, he called the *Secret History* a combination of invective and comedy, possibly the best concise description of the work. One way to achieve this combination is to place vicious accusations in the context of comical or grotesquely exaggerated contexts, and this is what the Gynecocracy does. As it happens, the only works of ancient literature specifically devoted to the rule of women were comic plays, though only those of Aristophanes survive. Curiously, the *Secret History* is full of Aristophanic language, albeit not from the plays on women. Procopius has instead culled lines and terms that refer to the detested Athenian politician Cleon. There are more allusions to Aristophanes in the *Secret History* than to any other author, and some are repeated. One can even speak of a grid of comic language holding the text together.[89]

The choice of source was not accidental. Uncompromising seriousness creates gravity, which lends a measure of dignity even to the accused. Aristophanic language deprives even crimes of their gravity, though not of their seriousness. In a sense, the *Secret History* is itself a kind of stage on which Procopius caricatures Justinian and Theodora and exposes their crimes while portraying them as grotesque creatures. Theodora appears literally on the stage in the work: Procopius graphically recreates the performances of her youth, effectively transforming us into her audience (9.11–26). Comic language is here very dense.[90] Even later, when she was empress, he says that her behavior lacked seriousness "as though she were on the stage in the theater" (15.24). This statement follows his account of the way she parodied the liturgy in order to mock an old patrician. Under Justinian, "the state seemed like the game of 'King' played by children" (14.14).[91]

Laws, Demons, and the Limits of Classicism in the *Secret History*

Oppression has impoverished them to such an extent that they have been reduced to poverty, taxes cannot be collected, and the lawful and customary tribute cannot be obtained without the greatest difficulty; for, when the emperors try to obtain money from magistrates by selling them their offices, the latter, in their turn, indemnify themselves by extortion. . . . If he does not make the payment out of his own property, he must borrow, and in order to do so he will appropriate that of the public, as he must obtain enough from his province to pay his debts. . . . Those who administer the affairs of the provinces, thinking incessantly of what their offices will cost them, discharge many criminals by selling them freedom from prosecution, and convict many who are innocent. . . . Not only do these things occur, but also the sedition in cities, and public disturbances which take place everywhere, go unpunished, in consideration of money paid. . . . The result of this condition of affairs is homicide, adultery, violence, wounds, the rape of virgins, commercial difficulties, contempt of the laws and judges. . . . We are unable to consider or enumerate the evils resulting from thefts committed by the governors of the provinces, and still no one is courageous enough to accuse them of having corruptly purchased their offices.

Oddly enough, this passage is not from the *Secret History*. It is from the preface of Justinian's *Novel* 8 of 535, in which the emperor condemns the sale of offices and vows to terminate it. Yet a passage from the second half of the *Secret History* mirrors this preface (21.9–25; cf. 22.7–9). Procopius explains the cycle of debt and extortion in the same way, and, like Justinian, stresses the misery it inflicted on provincials. The two texts end similarly by stating rhetorically that the evil was too great to be measured.

Procopius and Justinian agreed about the extent and gravity of the problem. In his edict, Justinian presented himself as the solution: "We pass entire days and nights in reflecting upon what may be agreeable to God and beneficial to our subjects." Procopius tells a different story. He specifically refers to *Novel* 8 and its provisions but says that Justinian adhered to them for less than a year (21.16–19). He is as much concerned with the emperor's hypocrisy as he is with the problem itself. The correspondence between the two texts along with the fact that Procopius explicitly cites the *Novel*, make it certain that he wrote this passage of the *Secret History* with an eye on the edict itself.[92]

What is the extent of this correspondence in the *Secret History*? Certainly many passages discuss the emperor's administration, but just how much of the text constitutes a direct response to the rhetoric of his legislation? It is time to look at the second part of the *Secret History*, that devoted to Justinian and Theodora (cf. 1.10), and propose a new explanation for its content and structure.

The second part of the *Secret History* is divided into two sections, which are so different that they have been taken for two originally independent works. Yet there is no significant overlap between them, which suggests a single conception. The sections are (a) chapters 6–18, including the infamous pornography and demonology, and (b) 19–30, a relatively sober if biased attack on Justinian's laws and administration. I will begin with the legal section first, for that will better enable us to examine the chapters that stand between it and Gynecocracy; that is, the heart of the *Secret History*.

After a short introduction (19), Procopius discusses the major magistracies (20–22), taxation and farming (23), soldiers (24), merchants and trade (25), beggars, the poor, and the professions that were abolished (26); finally, he narrates various individual scandals relating to imperial corruption (27–30). The section ends with the account of imperial ceremonies that we examined earlier.

To my knowledge, no other ancient writer approximates modern categories of historical analysis (administrative, economic, and social) more closely than does Procopius here. It is no accident that modern reconstructions of Justinian's policies derive many of their facts, and even their framework of analysis, from this part of the *Secret History*, even though their interpretation may differ. The other major source is the emperor's own legislation, which reflects the imperial point of view. Yet it has not been noticed that the final section of the *Secret History* constitutes a direct and systematic response to those laws. Some of Justinian's edicts have been lost, and not all of his decisions were put into writing. But imperial decrees were purposely made available to the public, and a writer with legal training and access to the court would have had no difficulty obtaining them.[93] It is important to emphasize that Procopius is responding directly to the emperor's propaganda, not, as has been suggested, to a derivative formulation such as we find in the chronicle of John Malalas. This is not to say, however, that we cannot find in Malalas reflections of edicts that are no longer extant but that Procopius did have before his eyes.[94]

In other words, the last section of the *Secret History* is largely a commentary on the edicts of Justinian. Its principle of organization is thematic, though it relies on anecdotes for liveliness and proof. It also discusses the character of the emperor's quaestors and prefects, who were the instigators, recipients, or executors of his laws. Whatever relation Procopius had to the court, he had inside knowledge about the mechanisms of legal activity. In the middle part of the *Secret History*, he says that the emperor insisted on writing many of his own decisions, even though that was the proper task of the quaestor, and that his style was "barbaric" (14.2–4). A modern study of the texts written specifically by Justinian has vindicated this judgment, finding the emperor's Latin "pretentious and vulgar."[95] But it makes no difference to the present argument whether specific edicts were written by Justinian himself or by his quaestors. None could have been promulgated without the emperor's authority.

Most of the topics covered by Procopius in the final section of the *Secret History* can be paired up directly with extant edicts, and, when this cannot be done, it is usually clear that a specific edict is being discussed that has since been lost. This correspondence often extends to rhetorical details. For instance, Justinian complains in *Novel* 122 that merchants were charging triple prices. Procopius uses the same word when he accuses the urban prefects of colluding with merchants to fleece the public (20.1–4). When instituting the offices of quaesitor and praetor of the people, Justinian is anxious to prove that they were not entirely new and that those who would hold them, along with their subordinates, would be honest (*Novels* 13, 80). Procopius begins his account by saying twice that the offices were entirely invented and denounces those who held them, along with their subordinates, for corruption (20.7–12). And so on. The *Secret History* is a distorting mirror of the emperor's own propaganda.

I have laid out this correspondence, to the extent that it can be recovered, in an appendix. Here I will make some general observations on Procopius' project. His primary aim is to show that the law was subverted by the avarice of Justinian and his subordinates. In some cases, the emperor is said not to have implemented his own legislation even when it was good, as, for instance, regarding the sale of offices. In other cases, we are told the secret motive behind the enactment of a specific law. Chapter 28, for instance, discusses the forger Priscus, who bribed Justinian to pass a law allowing churches to enforce century-old claims. Priscus had forged these claims against wealthy families in collusion with the Church of Emessa. The law in question is *Novel* 9 of 535. Though addressed to the Bishop of Rome, it specifically states, no less than three times, that its provisions are equally binding in the east and to cases "presently pending in court." Procopius says that Priscus was exposed as a fraud in Emessa after "the evil spread to most of the notable citizens" (28.12–15). In 541, Justinian repealed the law with *Novel* 111, claiming that "many actions had been brought" and citing vague concerns about the authenticity of documents. Procopius does not mention the repeal.

It is after all to be expected that an author with Procopius' legal background, literary skill, and polemical intent should attempt a systematic deconstruction of the emperor's legislation, which was such a central component of imperial propaganda. Without the *Secret History*, modern reconstructions of the reign would depend to a far greater degree than they do now on those edicts, especially their prefaces. As matters stand now, there is not even an adequate translation of them, and they are used only marginally in modern surveys of the period. This testifies to Procopius' success. Allusions to specific laws can be found in other parts of the *Secret History* as well. We saw in an earlier chapter that Justinian is introduced as a "tyrant" only after he annuls the law that barred him from marrying Theodora. Procopius explains how a more accommodating law was passed, which became part of the *Codex*.[96] The advent of tyranny is therefore linked to a specific edict. Many other passages also have a legal slant of this kind. To be sure, hypocrisy, avarice, and constant innovation are presented as fundamental elements of Justinian's personality. But their primary significance lies in the field of law: hypocrisy, because he did not adhere to the principles stated in his edicts; avarice, because he both enacted and violated his edicts for gain; constant innovation and unsteadiness, because he never let the laws rest. The last point cannot be denied by anyone who actually reads the *Novels*. Even Justinian had to admit, in the preface to *Novel* 22, "On marriage," that "a great number of different laws have been promulgated by us with reference to every branch of legislation; but as many of them appear to us to be imperfect, we desire to open a way to our subjects for better things. . . . We should not blush to amend laws which we have published." A recent study has concluded that it would have been impossible for his subjects to keep pace with the constantly changing provisions on such matters as marriage and inheritance.[97]

Procopius set out to destroy the image of a benevolent Christian emperor ceaselessly laboring on behalf of his subjects, an image powerfully and persuasively projected by the edicts. While the final section of the *Secret History* attacks specific administrative and legal policies, the central section (chapters 6–18) undermines their religious underpinning; namely, the emperor's Christian conception of monarchy and boast of universal benevolence.[98] This section, to which we now turn, includes the pornography and the comparison of Justinian and Theodora to bloodthirsty demons. It is a highly organized work with an almost symmetrical structure. I have set this out in Appendix 2 in order to focus here on the text's polemical aspects.

The demonology (12.14–32) is located in the middle of this section. It is prefigured in the introduction, where we are told that a monstrous being appeared repeatedly in the dreams of a general who had imprisoned and was about to execute Justinian's uncle Justin, ordering him to release the prisoner (6.5–9). This ensured the dynasty's future. There is also no question that chapter 18 forms a conclusion of sorts: Procopius invokes the demonology again after a long silence and surveys the devastation of the world by war and natural catastrophe. The tempo of the prose picks up and reaches a crashing conclusion at the end of the chapter. The demonology therefore both flanks this section and stands at its heart.

It is unfortunate that scholarly discussions of these passages have been haunted by the demon of literalism, a serious failure of the imagination. At the positivist extreme, the demonology is dismissed as an interpolation: "a historian such as Procopius could not have written such nonsense."[99] More recently, a scholar on the historicist side has maintained instead that Procopius "meant these sections to be taken seriously." Yet "seriously" here really means "at face value," and this position has been accepted as insightful and accurate in subsequent scholarship: Procopius *literally* believed that the emperor was a demon. Yet this position is not supported by any arguments other than vague references to the "modes of thought" that allegedly prevailed in his "age."[100] If this interpretation is true it would require a complete rethinking of his works, but this is never undertaken, and the same scholar who would have us take the demonology at face value never uses it elsewhere when discussing Procopius' attitude toward Justinian. But then her stated agenda is to make Procopius look as irrational and nonclassical as possible.[101] There is no need to interpret his thought coherently, given that the resulting incoherence can simply be ascribed to him. This is an evasion of the problem that is linked to the suffocating imperative to read Byzantine texts as literally as possible whenever religion is involved, no matter what the results. The same scholar says about the pornographic passages that "no one was expected to take them literally."[102] No reason is given for this different approach. And no attempt is made to reconcile the literal reading of the demonology with the same author's programmatic warning earlier in her book that "neither here nor anywhere else must Procopius be taken at face value."[103]

Most of my students have no problem making the distinction between reading something "seriously" and taking it "at face value." One could even posit that as the first rule for reading ancient literature. Gregory of Nazianzus did not literally believe that Julian was the Devil, nor Lucifer of Calaris that Constantius was the Antichrist, nor Jerome that the Vandal Gaiseric was the Antichrist.[104] If they did, the study of patristic theology has been off course for centuries. Nor did John Lydus believe that the prefect John the Cappadocian and his minions were really "demons and fiends."[105] Nor, finally, did Procopius literally believe that the Cappadocian was "the most wicked of all demons," yet he calls him just that, in the *Wars* no less (1.25.35). Furthermore, the demonology in the *Secret History* is punctured by disclaimers at a rate unmatched elsewhere in his works, which establishes a critical distance between author and text: "they say that . . ." (12.18, 12.24, 12.28, 12.30, 12.31); "I myself did not see these things, but heard the accounts of those who did" (12.23); "but these things are so according to the opinion of the majority" (13.1; note the change from 12.14); "some say . . . others say . . ." (18.37); "whether Justinian is a man . . . or the lord of the demons . . ." (30.34). The demonology is a function of authorial strategy, not religious belief.

The question is not whether Procopius believed this rhetoric but why he chose to use it. Why does he call Justinian the lord of the demons? More broadly, why does a classicizing author develop a comparison that requires the deployment of strikingly nonclassical images? The answer, I believe, is that the aim of the demonology is to invert Justinian's Christian image. Its function is polemical and not confessional. The conceptual background of Procopius' words is Christian because their target was also overtly Christian.[106] After all, "the lord of the demons" is how the New Testament refers to Satan; the allusion is unmistakable.[107] Procopius is using Justinian's faith to destroy his public image. Yet his seriousness is by no means diminished by his irony.

Let us consider a few examples of this counterpoint. In the *Novels*, Justinian refers to the "purity" of monastic life and the benefits it confers on the empire: "Where these holy persons pray to God for the prosperity of the government with pure hands and souls free from every blemish, there is no doubt that our armies will be victorious and our cities well governed."[108] Well, Procopius cites as witnesses of Justinian's demonic nature "a certain monk, one extremely beloved by God" (12.24), along with some other men who spent the night in Justinian's company, presumably also monks or priests, whom he calls "pure of soul," again echoing the emperor's legislation (12.20; cf. *Wars* 7.32.9). These episodes effect an ideological realignment by turning against the regime the very people on whom it most depended for moral legitimacy. For the sake of his polemic, Procopius accepts Justinian's valuation of monastic life, but only to use it as a weapon against him.

Likewise with Justinian's personal habits. The *Novels* refer often to his vigils and asceticism: "We shall undergo vigils, abstinence, and all the other privations in order to promote the welfare of our subjects." Or, "We pass entire days and nights in reflecting upon what may be agreeable to God and beneficial to our subjects, and it is not in vain that we maintain these vigils."[109] In the panegyrical *Buildings*, these habits are praised as a sign of the emperor's piety (1.7.5–16), and other writers of the reign also commented on them.[110] In the *Secret History*, however, they are presented as proof of the emperor's demonic nature (12.27; cf. 13.28–33) and are described in exactly the same language as in the *Buildings*.

This ideological deconstruction operates on more general levels as well. The macabre stories told by those men with "pure souls" are repeated often in modern studies, with copious citations to religious parallels,[111] but the chief question is never asked: what is their purpose and significance in the context of Procopius' argument? What does it mean that Justinian walked around without his head or that his face transformed into a shapeless mass of flesh? (12.20–23). This is dehumanizing, but in the most striking way possible. The head and face are the most distinctive physical features of humanity: these episodes symbolically validate the charge of inhumanity. Though Procopius is careful to state that he did not witness them himself, he reports them to undercut the emperor's propaganda, for under the influence of Tribonian, Justinian's legislation had given new importance to the imperial quality of *humanitas*, or Greek *philanthropia*. This is invoked in numerous edicts: "We believe that the benevolence of God, and His exceeding clemency toward the human race, should be imitated by us" (*CJ* 5.4.23). The confirmation of the *Digest* refers to God's *divina humanitas*,[112] the inverse of Procopius' demonic inhumanity (12.14). More generally still, where Justinian thanked Christ, his *dominus deus*, for the favor shown to his reign (e.g., *CJ* 1.27.1), according to Procopius some believed that God so hated his wicked deeds that he turned his back on the empire, allowing demons to destroy it (18.37). These must be other demons.

Yet when all is said and done, after we have heard all the movements of the *Secret History's* dark symphony—the Gynecocracy, the demonology, the critique of Justinian's legislation—Procopius' basic question still stands: "how can anyone possibly explain in words the character of Justinian?" (8.27). The shrillness of the text betrays its author's frustration. His subject proved elusive. Classical authors had developed a specialized discourse for the condemnation of tyrants. But Justinian did not fit the mold. He was a tyrant, but he was not a sensualist. He did not rule to gratify his body, as tyrants were supposed to do. Quite the contrary; he was an ascetic. An early *eros* for his future wife was all that could be found. As we saw above, Procopius did develop this event according to the discussion of tyranny in Plato's *Republic*, but charges of continued debauchery would have seriously misrepresented the regime, and Procopius wanted to understand it and expose it on its own terms. The root of his difficulty lay in its nonclassical foundations, which made it more similar in certain interesting respects to modern tyrannies than to anything ancient. The regime of Justinian was founded on ideology, not opportunism, and nothing in classical literature could have prepared Procopius for this. Though he was aware of its ideological dimension and was willing to go beyond classical paradigms in order to attack it, the temptation to reduce it to opportunism simply to make it intelligible was strong. It is this tension that explains the shrill tones, the frustration, and the shortfalls of the *Secret History*.

Procopius and his contemporaries never fully understood the psychological mechanisms that operated beneath Justinian's cold and inscrutable surface. Perhaps only Theodora ever did. A reflection of this is the fact that Justinian never speaks in direct discourse anywhere in the works of Procopius. The *Secret History* depicts a sterile technocrat addicted to secrecy, murder, and greed who has replaced his emotions with doctrines and uses language to conceal rather than speak the truth. His tyranny was modern in that it was founded on ideology; Justinian was incapable of thinking or acting without invoking theological principles. He was not exaggerating when he said that "we are accustomed to consider God in everything that we do" (*Novel* 18, preface). For instance, he invoked Scripture to regulate the price of vegetables. He there revealed the extent of his totalitarian disposition, which he had in common with no other ancient monarch: "there is no part of the administration of either great or small importance which does not demand our attention; we perceive everything with our mind and our eyes, and we do not desire anything to remain neglected, confused, or ambiguous" (*Novel* 64). In many of his constitutions, he stated his desire to reduce the world to a single universal and rational order that was based on infallible principles and marred by no inconsistencies or ambiguities. His compilation of Roman law was motivated by this ambition.[113] It was precisely this aspect of his ideology that Procopius inverted when he accused him in so many passages of the *Secret History* of throwing the whole world into chaos and confusion.

Perhaps the most insightful comment ever made about Justinian's personality is that "his mind was formed by a reading of a Christian and bureaucratic sort." His own writings give "no evidence of classical culture."[114] There is something ineluctably modern about the combination of dogmatism and bureaucracy, and it is no wonder that the same scholar compared Justinian at length to Stalin.[115] We can easily discern Justinian in definitions of modern tyranny that aim to differentiate it from its ancient counterparts: "the Final Tyrant presents himself as a philosopher . . . as the supreme exegete of the only true philosophy, as the executor and hangman authorized by the only true philosophy. He claims therefore that he persecutes not philosophy but false philosophies."[116] He is "a tyrant in command of a party animated by a revolutionary ideology, intent on using propaganda to impose a particular worldview on the populace, and willing to employ terror to snuff out every hint of political and cultural dissent."[117] Wars for glory and plunder Procopius could understand, but a ruler who killed subjects for their religious beliefs while regulating the price of vegetables with his hand on the Bible was not something for which his education had prepared him. Justinian, he realized, "did not consider it to be murder if his victims were of a different faith." Like Stalin, "with a gentle face, lowered brows, and soft voice, he would give orders leading thousands of innocent men to their death."[118]

The tyranny exposed and condemned in the *Secret History* has disturbingly modern qualities, and it is this, perhaps, that explains its popularity with students of Byzantine history. The pornographic sections are ultimately trivial, but religiously motivated murder and the subversion of law by greed speak loudly to our age. The nonclassical aspects of the text are due, as I have argued, to Procopius' attempt to come to grips with the new ideology by reversing its polarities and exposing its fraudulence. This effort took him far from classical paradigms. Nothing indicates this to me more powerfully than the complete absence of genuine humor from the work. Most ancient historians who wrote about tyrannies used humor to expose the absurdities of arbitrary power.[119] A tyrant was after all only a man. He would die and be replaced, perhaps by someone better. His crimes—some seductions and one or two dozen murders—were ultimately petty and could be mocked in retrospect. The *Secret History*, however, may contain sarcasm and tragic comedy but nothing that is even remotely *funny*. The stakes were too high. The modes and orders of civic life that classical authors had taken for granted were under attack, and there could be nothing amusing about this. As Procopius put it in a chapter on the decline of orators, doctors, teachers, and theaters, "there was no laughter in life for anyone" (26.10). Likewise, his fellow traveler Simplicius had lamented in his commentary on Epictetus "the destruction of education and philosophy, of all virtue and friendship and trust in one another" (14.26–27).

Alternatives and Solutions

Does Procopius offer any alternatives or solutions to the problems posed by the regime of Justinian? At first sight, there is little to go on. The *Secret History* is too negative, the *Buildings* too insincere. The latter work, despite occasional irony, reflects the propaganda of Justinian, while the former inverts it. As a result, both approach the regime through its own terms. The emperor is either God's deputy on earth, an imitator of Christ and paragon of virtue (a standard Byzantine view, dubbed "Eusebian" by scholars), or an unholy demon. There is no mention of God in the *Secret History* that is not complicit in the deconstruction of Justinian's ideology. Panegyric and invective are both framed theologically. The question is, did Procopius accept this framework, even if he did not regard Justinian in particular as God's representative? The latest view asserts that he did, though it offers little by way of argument.[120] There are in fact strong reasons to reject this conclusion.

We must work from the *Wars*, which, however, is a descriptive text that does not discuss ideal regimes. Still, Procopius occasionally praises certain rulers in general terms, disclosing the qualities that he deemed necessary. These passages are crucial because they are not fatally compromised by panegyrical or polemical intentions. And we should note at the outset that they are entirely secular.

At the beginning of the *Gothic War*, Procopius strongly praises Theoderic for "possessing those qualities most appropriate to one who is by nature an emperor" (5.1.26–27). In other words, the virtues of Theoderic belong to all good rulers. These are justice, the preservation of the laws, the protection of the land from barbarian neighbors, wisdom, and manliness. There is no hint of piety or God. Even those who view Procopius as a Eusebian admit that this passage reveals his notions about the "ideal monarch."[121] Though I do not believe that there are any "ideal monarchs" in Procopius—even Theoderic sinned against philosophy—it should be noted that this ideal, at least, is entirely secular.

Still, it is curious that Theoderic, a Goth, should be praised for protecting his land from "barbarians." The Goths were supposed to be barbarians themselves (e.g., 5.2.17). Containing barbarian aggression was the proper task of the *Roman* emperor. By his own admission, Procopius has ascribed to Theoderic the virtues appropriate to a Roman emperor. One has to suspect therefore that the ascription of these virtues to Theoderic is an indirect indictment of Justinian, who did not possess a single one of them. It was Justinian who failed to protect his land from barbarians. There is no praise of him in the *Wars* comparable to that of Theoderic, to say nothing of the fact that the founder of the state that gave him so much grief is presented by Procopius as a model emperor.

Be that as it may, it is also for entirely secular virtues that Procopius praises the emperors Theodosius and Anastasius, namely for justice and good generalship in the first case and prudent accounting and foresight in the second. The same is true for his praise of the western emperor Majorian and Justinian's potential successor Germanus. Scholars who try to sacralize Procopius' view of these virtues inevitably draw upon the *Buildings*.[122] The perspective in the *Wars* is entirely secular, which cannot be ascribed to classicizing bias because there was no stylistic restraint against praising a ruler's piety or stating that he was favored by God. The omission reflects the priorities of the author. Conversely, it is also important that Procopius does not say anything about the religious beliefs of Anastasius, who was condemned as a heretic by orthodox writers close to Justinian.[123] As we will see in the next chapter, this was not because Procopius was possibly a Monophysite but because he thought all religious doctrines were foolish. There was little room for religion in his view of the imperial office.

Justice, foresight, wisdom, and courage were conventional virtues, to be sure, and thoroughly classical. Conventionality should not be regarded as a flaw—if only Justinian were so conventional! In any case, ancient authors cannot win this debate: across from the Scylla of conventionality there always lurks the Charybdis of utopian idealism, and modern scholars will find fault with one if not the other. The Byzantines are commonly supposed not to have been able to imagine alternatives to monarchy, though this is an unfair view that reflects a monolithic view of monarchy. The debate in Byzantium was between different kinds of monarchy, which, to those involved, were as different from each another as "democratic" regimes are today. Hardly any modern historians express misgivings about democracy *as such*: are their horizons then as limited as those of the Byzantines? But this debate is best avoided. For better or worse, Procopius chose to uphold the values of an ancient tradition that was secular and tolerant for all its conventionality. This moderation by itself may have been a radical stance, given the extremes to which he was forced in the *Buildings* and the *Secret History* by the nature of the regime itself.

Did Procopius propose remedies for the evil of Justinian? There is only one way to eliminate a tyrant. Yet assassination is a dangerous enterprise. If it is carried out by one man, he will die even if he succeeds, yet if he seeks associates he must form a conspiracy, which may be betrayed. And how do you form a conspiracy? You must know in advance that one shares your feelings so that he will not betray you. On the other hand, you may try to persuade him of the necessity for change before inviting him to join a conspiracy. But this too is a very dangerous strategy. The regime does not tolerate criticism and may punish you for that alone. Your criticism will have to be secret; even more so your conspiracy. But is it possible to incite others to tyrannicide, give them moral legitimacy and even practical advice, without revealing yourself in the act? Would you not then be the ultimate conspirator, an architect of conspiracies?

One of the ways to plan future conspiracies against a tyrant is by discussing past conspiracies against him and noting where they failed. Another way is to discuss conspiracies in general, whether against this tyrant or another, and note why they failed or succeeded. Past conspiracies are a part of history and may be discussed by a historian without arousing much suspicion. A discussion of past conspiracies may be a disguised manual for future ones. But they must be told from the point of view of the conspirators. Such a historian may even suggest that his narrative, though primarily military in nature, will be useful to those who are at war as well as to those "who are engaged in any kind of contest" by demonstrating "what the outcome was for those who planned their actions well" (*Wars* 1.1.2).

Accounts of conspiracies occupy disproportionate space in the *Wars* relative to their military significance and are described in greater detail than any other kind of event. They are also always told from the point of view of the conspirators, even when Procopius was personally attached to their intended victims. In the *Vandal War*, these conspiracies are tangentially linked to the narrative and could have been dealt with far more cursorily. The great conspiracy against Justinian related in the *Gothic War* is completely irrelevant to the main narrative, but is nevertheless told at equally great length. Let us see what we can learn about conspiracies from those passages.

The conquest of Libya was followed by imperial maladministration leading to widespread disaffection. The *Vandal War*, fresh from the celebrations of victory at Constantinople, quickly lapses into mutinies and plots, which lead in turn to civil wars and incursions by the Moors. The final part of the text discusses many conspiracies in detail, while the battles raging around them are gradually relegated to the sidelines. Procopius gives a circumstantial account of a plot to kill the general Solomon, but this is only a prelude to the tour de force that is the conspiracy against the rebel Gontharis. Both are instructive and are told from the point of view of the conspirators.

I will focus here on the actual conspiracies, leaving their political background aside. Procopius recounts the plot against Solomon in 536 dispassionately, even though he was with the general at the time. Disaffection was so widespread that all but a few men were involved (4.14.22–28). The mutineers planned to kill Solomon in church during Easter but twice failed to do so, "either because they felt awe before the mysteries that were then being performed, or because they blushed on account of the general's fame, or even because they were hindered by something divine." Machiavelli noted in his magisterial analysis of conspiracies that if you are prepared to commit murder, you should not hesitate to do it in a church.[124] This is especially true if your victim is known to spend much time in churches or with priests and monks. It also helps if you are not opposed by any "divine things."

Gontharis, who seized control of Carthage in 545, had no religious qualms. He killed the governor Areobindus even though Areobindus had taken refuge in a monastery, had received pledges from the city's bishop sworn on the baptismal rite, had approached Gontharis with the Scriptures in hand and accompanied by a newly baptized child, and had received pledges from the tyrant himself "in the name of all holy things." This is all quite overdone, but none of it mattered to Gontharis, who had the governor killed in his room after dinner (4.26.17–33).[125] Gontharis did not fear God.

The plot to kill Gontharis, with which the *Vandal War* culminates, is recounted in great detail immediately after the murder of Areobindus. A speech is addressed by Gregory to the chief conspirator, his uncle Arta-banes, effusively praising his nobility and arguing that Belisarius' conquest of Libya will appear less glorious than the murder of that one tyrant. This speech "excited the mind of Artabanes to move with even greater resolve against the tyrant" (4.27.11–19).[126] It seems that speeches can incite men to kill tyrants, and we must remember that the speech of Gregory is indirectly the speech of Procopius. As for the praise of nobility, we are reminded of the passage in the *Secret History* that states that "all expected" Belisarius to "do something brave and befitting a man" against those who had abused him (4.40), by killing Theodora perhaps. An entire chapter of the *Vandal War* is devoted to the execution of the plot in the tyrant's "palace" (4.28), as a result of which Artabanes did in fact gain "great fame." And right before the conspirators entered the room, Procopius makes one of them say: "I am unsure whether God, hating the tyrant, will assist me in this daring deed, or whether he will oppose me on account of some past sin of my mine" (4.48.12). God is now a natural ally of tyrannicides.

Procopius' account in the *Gothic War* of the plot against Justinian in 548–549 is again told from the point of view of the conspirators. The narra-tive moves from their grievances to their plans, mistakes, and capture. It is introduced by the promise to "explain how they came to that resolve and, their plans being foiled, the deed failed to materialize" (7.31.1). The chief conspirator is again Artabanes, who has now graduated to greater things. Once again he is incited by the speeches of another, who dares him to prove his bravery, nobility, and manliness (7.32.5–7). This man, Arsaces, delivers one of the most famous lines in the *Wars*: Justinian will be easy to kill, he says, because "he always sits unguarded in some lobby until very late at night, in the company of extremely old priests, intently unrolling the scrip-tures of the Christians" (7.32.9). One scholar has seen this as a "statement of Justinian's vulnerability and valuable information for any would-be as-sassin," but given *by Procopius* through Arsaces to conspirators *other than Artabanes*.[127] Arsaces tells readers of the *Wars* exactly when, where, and in whose company Justinian is most vulnerable. His speech is again also the speech of Procopius and not just because the latter elsewhere says the same thing about Justinian in his own voice.[128] Procopius, the arbiter of all speech in the *Wars* and author of an inflammatory tract against Justinian, sets inflammatory speeches at the heart of both conspiracies led by Artabanes. We may suspect that he had inside information about them; that is, that he knew Artabanes. And the praise of Justinian's mercy and forgiveness in the

Buildings has led some to the conclusion that Procopius may have been involved in a plot himself.[129]

Be that as it may, Procopius describes Artabanes as "tall and handsome, free-spirited (*eleutherios*), and reserved in his speech" (7.31.9). *Eleutherios*, formed from the root of the word for "freedom," means the opposite of "servile."[130] The proximate cause of Artabanes' plot against Justinian was his oppression by two women, namely his own wife and Theodora. Arsaces taunts him to do exactly what "all expected" that Belisarius would do after his oppression by two women, namely his own wife and Theodora. He taunts him to prove his manhood. The conspiracies of Artabanes and his praise by Procopius close the circle that opened with our discussion of the three parts of the *Secret History*.

Chapter 5
God and Tyche in the Wars

Christianity?

In 537, the city of Rome was besieged by the Goths and defended by a small imperial army under Belisarius. Civic life was disrupted and the populace unsure of its loyalties and prospects. Procopius was present throughout the siege, of which he wrote a gripping narrative. Among the omens, intrigues, and wonders that marked that exciting year, he records a peculiar incident. Some Romans tried to open the doors of the temple of Janus, which, the historian explains, their ancestors used to open in times of war until they began "to honor the doctrine of the Christians." Yet during the siege "some who had the old faith in mind" tried to open the doors again "in secret" but managed only to dislodge them slightly from their threshold. The passage ends cryptically: "And those who had attempted this escaped notice. No investigation of the deed was made because it occurred in the midst of a great confusion; also, it did not become known to the commanders, nor did it come to the attention of the multitude, except to very few" (5.25.18–25).

Procopius never says that the doors were shut after the incident, which means that they may have remained slightly ajar indefinitely, for the fact that they had been opened was a closely guarded secret. Is this an anecdotal, that is, a literary way of saying that the war in Italy would simmer on without end? Be that as it may, the passage also raises troubling questions about Procopius himself. It clearly implies that he was one of the few who knew about the incident, if he was not among those who tried to open the doors in the first place. After all, he knows about the "old faith" at least as well as they did. He describes the statue of Janus in detail and gives its dimensions (5.25.21). Assuming, then, that he was not one of them, how did he find out about this incident? Why did *he* not inform the commanders about it? He knows that they would have wanted to "investigate" it. And why does he not tell *us*, the readers of the *Wars*, exactly who was involved? He seems to know more than he says, leaving us with the impression that he could not have known what he does tell us without also knowing more that he does not tell us. His story suggests that non-Christian rites can be attempted in Christian Rome, even with only partial success, if they are veiled in secrecy and the times are right. In a sense, his narrative is an accomplice to that attempt, because it does not reveal enough to compromise its veil of secrecy. Like the event it describes, Procopius' story goes largely unnoticed in the din of the siege that surrounds it. To my knowledge, only one scholar has asked the hard questions that it poses; others dismiss it as a curiosity or impose on it preconceived notions about his religious beliefs, notions that are not at all warranted by this extremely cryptic passage.[1]

Few men's religious beliefs have generated more divergent scholarly opinions than those of Procopius. Seen by Gibbon as a "half pagan" whose "religion betrays occasional conformity, with a secret attachment to paganism and philosophy,"[2] he has since been classified as a possible Jew,[3] a Samaritan,[4] a quasi-Manichaean,[5] a deist-skeptic,[6] a dualist who believed in both God and irrational Fate,[7] "a Christian of the independent and skeptical sort,"[8] an Arian,[9] and a Monophysite sympathizer.[10] One scholar combined the possibilities and produced the world's first free-thinking Jewish Christian (like Spinoza?). Even this position has been interpreted variously, which is only to be expected because it merely reproduces the confusion in the source.[11] The only parallel known to me is the range of opinions that scholars have expressed on the religious beliefs of the militant atheist Paolo Sarpi.[12] Yet a consensus has recently emerged regarding Procopius, namely, that he was "a conventional Christian" whose religious language was only superficially influenced by classical vocabulary. The issue, however, is far from settled, and the fragile foundations of the consensus have never been subjected to scrutiny.[13]

Clearly, there is room for disagreement. The reasons for this quickly become apparent to anyone who approaches the texts with the naive intention of identifying the relevant passages and, after judiciously evaluating their evidence, deciding in favor of one theory or another. Which passages, one asks, ought to be included in such an examination? Certainly Procopius' own digressions on the workings of God and *tyche* and probably also his accounts of omens and miracles, some of which are specifically linked to Christian relics or beliefs. But what about opinions that are expressed in the speeches of generals and ambassadors? And what about the historian's criticism of Justinian's religious policies? How should we treat passages in which concepts such as *tyche* occur, though without strong metaphysical connotations? Is his fatalism to be taken seriously or is it merely a literary device that serves, say, to diffuse suspense or give the aura of inevitability to certain events? Does his apparent superstition count?[14] Or do omens and such serve literary purposes, as we saw earlier with the fall of Antioch?[15] And how are we to deal with the fact that in his digressions, Procopius expresses the most contradictory views, sometimes indicating his belief in a provident and just deity, sometimes not only implying but directly stating that the world is governed by a completely amoral entity called *tyche* who acts utterly capriciously? Not a few scholars have noted "the variety and the seeming confusion of the writer's remarks concerning the divine government of the world,"[16] and some have simply given up on him, concluding that he had no clear conception of man's relation to God.[17] It is amazing that no one has seriously considered that Procopius was writing in an intolerant society that persecuted dissidents. Surely this would have affected his choice of words if his beliefs were not conventional.

In this chapter, I will argue that none of the theories listed above is correct, though some reflect more of the truth than others; for instance, Gibbon's comment on Procopius' "secret attachment to philosophy," for which we found conclusive evidence earlier. Setting aside the utterly speculative suggestions that Procopius belonged to this or that specific sect, the theory that most falls short of the mark is the consensus view that he was a conventional Christian. This theory rests on two lines of argument: first, that the non-Christian elements in his work can be dismissed as "mere affectation" or, in the last resort, as "philosophical confusion"; and second, that numerous passages in his works furnish positive proof that he was a Christian of the ordinary sort. The first line of argument, especially the dismissal of the concept of fortune as frivolous, will be dealt with below. As for the second, the scant sections of the *Wars* on which it is based will be examined more properly in a separate study of that work, where they will be discussed in close connection to the main historical themes of the narrative. It will be shown that those passages are too ambiguous to provide any basis for a secure identification of Procopius' religion. But their use to prove Procopius a conventional Christian faces prior methodological problems that will be dealt with here. These must be resolved before *any* passages can be used to establish his beliefs.

It is commonly assumed that if a Byzantine gives even the slightest hint that he was a Christian then he was and that all indications that he gives to the contrary can be dismissed. This is the pervasive bias of historicism, which wants to make everyone into a "man of his age"—as though we can ever know the age better than the man! In fact the converse is true: if an author living in an age of religious persecution gives even the slightest hint that he is unorthodox then he probably was, despite any declarations that he may make explicitly to the contrary. Conventionality can be ascribed to necessity; heterodoxy cannot. A dissident writer who fears persecution must maintain a façade of orthodoxy. Thus, he will inevitably appear to be confused and inconsistent when he then tries to introduce his own views obliquely. And this is exactly what we find in Procopius and in numerous other Byzantine authors who had a philosophical background. Problems arise when scholars take the confusion at face value and dismiss the anomalies. The exact opposite should be done, provided the author warrants that approach.

Justinian persecuted dissidents with renewed zeal. Pagans, Jews, Samaritans, philosophers, and heretics all experienced his deadly hatred and found that he lent a ready ear to their enemies. The facts are too well known to bear repeating.[18] But the regime's intolerance cannot simply be ascribed to "the times." Its virulence shocked even contemporaries, whether they were Christian or Hellene, Roman or barbarian. Right before his kingdom was invaded by imperial armies, the Gothic king Theodahad pleaded the cause of tolerance to Justinian: "As the Deity allows various religions to exist, I do not dare impose one alone. For I remember reading that we should sacrifice to the Lord of our own will, not at the command of anyone who compels us. He who tries to do otherwise clearly opposes the heavenly decree."[19] The bitterness of pope Agapetus, who faced Justinian personally, reflected western resentment at his high-handed measures: "Sinner that I am, I have long wanted to come to the most Christian emperor Justinian— but now I have encountered Diocletian; yet I am not in the least afraid of your threats."[20] Others, however, were afraid and went into hiding or muted their criticism.[21] Dissidents left their works anonymous or pseudonymous.[22] Far from promoting literary culture, as did the Goth Theoderic and the Persian Chosroes, Justinian burned books for religious reasons.[23] Procopius, on the other hand, the greatest thinker of his age, was perhaps the most principled enemy of religious bigotry the Christian world had yet seen. He decried the persecution of heretics, Samaritans, Hellenes, astrologers, and sexual deviants and claimed that many of the heterodox fled the empire altogether. Among the latter were the Platonists of Athens, who returned only after they had secured the backing of the Persian king and a treaty stipulating their immunity from persecution.[24]

This is the proper context against which to view the problem of dissimulation, both political and religious. No human society is entirely conformist. The universally pious Byzantium of scholarship is a myth. Yet as Polybius noted after arguing that kings should be blamed publicly for their faults, "this is perhaps easy enough to say but extremely difficult to do, on account of the many and varied circumstances and conditions in life that make it impossible for men to speak or write their true opinions" (8.8.8). Similar statements were made in all periods of antiquity, and not only in antiquity. It was as true for the sixteenth century as it was for the sixth that "the presence of irreligion remains elusive and difficult to prove because persecution subjects their expression to the gravest danger. To try to detect them is like trying to recognize the identity of a person wearing a disguise or mask."[25] Yet there is also no doubt that such masks were worn by many ancient writers and that they employed specific rhetorical techniques in order to express guarded dissent.[26] Yet these masks must *mean* something to us; as scholars we are obligated to look behind them. Whereas many studies of Procopius warn that sixth-century thinkers could not speak safely about politics and religion, it is a paradox that none take those warnings seriously. The drift of the argument is lost on those who make it. At one extreme, Procopius has been depicted confidently as a supporter of repressive state violence by a scholar who admits on the very same page that "at any point he may not be writing what he really thinks."[27] The problems of dissimulation have received only lip service. There has been no systematic attempt to study how and about what sixth-century authors veiled their beliefs. Perhaps scholars in modern liberal societies are insufficiently sensitive to the constraints imposed by tyrannies and official churches. Hence, we are presented with a row of interchangeable figures, all orthodox, all conformist. Scratch the surface of any Byzantine political thinker and you will find . . . Eusebius. But Eusebius *is* the surface.

As Montaigne knew, "no quality is so easy to counterfeit as piety."[28] Our first references to insincere converts come from texts written even as Constantine was establishing the groundwork of his official Church.[29] Julian converted to philosophy under the nose of his ecclesiastical tutor. The age of Justinian does not lack examples of its own. The emperor himself referred in one of his edicts to those who pretended to be Christian in order to hold offices.[30] The *Chronicon Paschale* records under the year 530 that certain Samaritans

in fear came to Christianity under compulsion, and were received and baptized, and up to the present day waver between the two: under stringent officials they deceive by appearance and falsely and wickedly manifest themselves as Christians, but under lax and greedy officials, they conduct themselves as Samaritans and haters of Christians.

Procopius also notes the problem of false conversion in the *Secret History*, when he reviews Justinian's persecution of heterodoxy. Some Hellenes accepted "the name of Christians" only to be found later performing sacrifices (11.32). Samaritans, he says, "accepted the name of Christians because of the necessity of the law" (26.27).[31] They found it "prudent" to convert in order to avoid harassment, thinking it "foolish" to suffer for the sake of a "stupid doctrine" (11.25). Which doctrine was stupid? The one renounced by the Samaritans? Or is Procopius implying generally that the notion of fighting over doctrines is stupid, making both the one that is renounced and the one that is embraced stupid? As we will see, for him all doctrines are stupid that divide people into sects, and this includes all doctrines current in the sixth century.

This is the conclusion that we must draw from a famous digression at the beginning of the *Gothic War*, a passage that by itself refutes the notion that Procopius was a conventional Christian, no matter what else he may say in other parts of his work. Discussing relations between Byzantium and Gothic Italy, Procopius mentions two priests who traveled to Rome

on account of an article of faith that the Christians dispute among themselves, holding different opinions. I will by no means mention the points of contention, though I know them well. For I think it is insanely stupid to investigate the nature of God, and ask what sort it is. For I do not believe that human beings have a sufficiently exact understanding of human things, far less of anything that bears on the nature of God. Therefore, I will keep a safe (ἀκινδύνως) silence about these things, with the sole intention of not allowing honored teachings to be disbelieved. For I would say nothing else about God than that he is entirely good and holds everything within his power. But let each say about these things whatever he thinks he knows, both priest and layman. (5.3.5–9)

Under the guise of affirming traditional religious beliefs, Procopius manages to insinuate some startling conclusions. First, all Christian theology, and certainly all theology of the sixth century, is "insanely stupid" because its end is to investigate the nature of God. Thus the "stupid" doctrines of the Samaritans who converted to Christianity were not only those they renounced but also those they embraced, for any creed that affirms more than God's benevolence and power is "insanely stupid." And we now understand better why Procopius accuses Justinian in the *Secret History* of being "too curious about the nature of God" (18.29), using exactly the same words he does at the beginning of the *Gothic War*, thus linking the two passages. But the scope of his complaint goes well beyond one emperor. By rejecting all doctrines that divide men into different sects, and even into different religions, he undercuts any possible justification for religious persecution.

Second, seen as a positive religious credo, Procopius says nothing about God that is specifically Christian. If he were a Christian, even one who stood outside the disputes that divided the community, surely he could have said more about God than that he is benevolent and omnipotent. The ecclesiastical historian Evagrius provides a useful comparison. Taking a self-consciously liberal stance between Chalcedonians and Monophysites, he made the following declaration:

And no one of those who have devised heresies among the Christians originally wanted to blaspheme, or stumbled through wishing to dishonor the divinity, but rather by supposing to speak better than their predecessors if he were to advocate this. And the essential and vital points are commonly agreed by all: for what we worship is a trinity and what we glorify is a unity, and God the Word, though born before the ages, was incarnated in a second birth out of pity for creation. (1.11)

It is of course the differences between Procopius and Evagrius that interest us here. Evagrius is obviously talking about the Christian God; Procopius is not. Evagrius is also not entirely consistent with his principles; he begins his work by reviling some heretics as insane, filthy, wicked, agents of the Devil (1.1–2). Procopius, on the other hand, is probably the only ancient author who argued against religious persecution on behalf of groups to which he did not belong and that, probably, he did not even like. Arguments for toleration in antiquity had so far been produced only by those directly under attack and only on behalf of their own group or by emperors such as Constantine who persecuted heretical groups whenever they did not play along.[32] The author of the *Secret History* does not even mention the group to which he belongs, though he alludes to it. Procopius' statement that "human beings do not have a sufficiently exact understanding of human things, far less of anything that bears on the nature of God" alludes directly to what Plato often makes Socrates say, notably in the *Apology* (e.g., 20d–e). The decision to quote a philosopher accused of impiety in a definitive statement on the nature of God merits reflection: it links him again to the Platonic philosophers persecuted for impiety in the sixth century and it points the search for Procopius' beliefs in an entirely different direction than that taken by current scholarship. Perhaps he was willing to entertain the more skeptical positions expounded by Socrates in Plato's early dialogues.

Those who believe that Procopius was a conventional Christian desperately try to dismiss this passage, stating, for instance, that he was not "obligated to insert a personal credo at this point."[33] But defining the limits of such a credo is precisely what he was doing. Another lame argument is that it reflects "the opinion of the believer, not the skeptic."[34] These are of course relative terms. It is the opinion of the believer only when compared to that of the utter atheist (and not even then, necessarily, if we factor in the need to maintain appearances). This argument is like saying that Marx was a reactionary conservative because he rejected the radical anarchism of Bakunin. It is ironic that those who most wish to integrate Procopius' religious beliefs into his historical context fail to consider here how different were the views of the majority of his contemporaries on this issue. Compared to them, the passage quoted above is the voice of radical skepticism. Be that as it may, it is certainly not the voice of a Christian. Even those who believe otherwise are forced to admit that his tolerance was "unusual" and that he was "exceptional in believing that people should be allowed to believe what they liked."[35] This contradicts the view that he was a "conventional" Christian and seems incompatible with his being one at all. Despite occasional claims to the contrary, no Christian endorsed the view that "people should be allowed to believe what they liked." Nor did any Christian explicitly link an emperor's piety and "firm belief in Christ" to the "destruction of his subjects," as Procopius does in the *Secret History* (13.4 ff.). The very notion of tolerant Christianity seems to have been a myth invented by pagans such as Symmachus, Libanius, and Themistius, pleading to Christian emperors on behalf of pagan traditions. Tolerant Christianity was largely a pagan rhetorical device.

On this point I can see no essential difference between the deism of Procopius and that of the Enlightenment philosophers. Both promoted vague, nonsectarian views of God that were restricted to benevolence and power. Both attacked theological speculation as insanely stupid and the cause of disputes and persecution. Hume wrote that "the nature of God, from the infirmities of human understanding, is altogether incomprehensible and unknown to us. . . . Next to the impiety of denying his existence, is the temerity and prying into his nature and essence."[36] And Voltaire's brief entry on "Theism" in his *Philosophical Dictionary* reads like a loose translation of Procopius' credo, down to the fear that disputes may dishonor ancient teachings about God. Most important, the deism of both Procopius and the Enlightenment was born of disgust at the havoc that theological enthusiasm wreaked in an otherwise civilized world. The sentiments were the same and so too were the motives.

Another similarity is the suspicion that even this rarefied, skeptical deism was itself a veil for even more skeptical views. As one reader of the *Wars* astutely noted, "it must be admitted that we do not hear much about this benevolent God in the rest of the work."[37] It is well known that the deism of the Enlightenment philosophers was a façade for irreligion. They talked much about God but believed in physics. Does the *Wars* testify to the existence of a benevolent deity, or are other forces at work in its world?

Coping with *Tyche*

The remainder of this chapter will reexamine the role of *tyche*, or fortune, in the *Wars*. Despite its prominence and the many digressions that Procopius devotes to it, *tyche* has rarely been regarded as an integral element of his historical thought. Concerted efforts have been made to push it out of the way to make room for Procopius the conventional Christian. Usually it is dismissed as a "purely superficial" and "clumsy evocation" of classical language. We are told that it was merely part of "the inherited language of classicizing writers," and readers of the *Wars* are now encouraged to disregard what once used to be considered a perplexing problem.[38] It is also assumed that Procopius failed to reconcile his notion of *tyche* with the provident Christian God he allegedly worshipped, which resulted in a philosophically incoherent text.[39]

This theory faces a number of prima facie problems. First, its exponents seem to have no difficulty themselves in seeing the incompatibility between amoral *tyche* and a provident Deity. They treat it as an obvious theological contradiction, which indeed it is. Yet the more obvious the contradiction, the less plausible its ascription to Procopius. The conventional view asks us to believe that he was either incredibly confused or indifferent to philosophical coherence. Procopius, however, was by far the most competent Byzantine historian and wrote with greater clarity than almost any Greek historian of any period. He managed to compose and arrange hundreds of pages of detailed information covering a very complex period of history without ever losing narrative coherence or contradicting himself seriously. He also tells us explicitly that he had expert knowledge regarding the theological controversies of his age (*Wars* 5.3.6). Even though that was not a topic he chose to pursue in his works, there is no reason to doubt his boast, which militates strongly against the notion that he did not or could not distinguish between amoral *tyche* and the Christian God. And, as we have seen, he was no ordinary reader of Plato. Nevertheless, the contradiction is undeniable. There are passages where God is described as good, passages where *tyche* is explicitly described as indifferent to good and evil, and passages where God seems to be identified with *tyche*. The vocabulary is identical, therefore deliberate. We seem to be facing an impossible contradiction that exists nonetheless. We cannot just brush it away by ascribing it to incoherence. That would require us to conclude that Procopius could not see a glaring and almost explicit contradiction. As chance has it, we possess the reaction of a frustrated Byzantine scribe, who addressed the following comment to Procopius in the margins of a manuscript: "you are not acting rightly by introducing the *daimonion* and *tyche* and fate into the Christian faith."[40] No analysis of the *Wars* can proceed on the assumption that modern theological intuitions are sharper than those of a highly educated Byzantine.

Second, the notion that *tyche* represents some kind of classical "leftover," mere mental baggage that Procopius picked up from the works of his predecessors, is a nonstarter. There is simply no ancient historian in whose work *tyche* assumes as prominent a role, perhaps not even Polybius. We naturally expect the importance of classical concepts to diminish as the ideological framework of ancient historiography—whatever that was—gave way to Christian modes of thought. But in the *Wars*, the concept of fortune takes the forefront as never before. Procopius invokes it in connection with many accidents and coincidences; he structures many of his speeches around it; and, in the case of every momentous event, such as the sack of Antioch in 540, the plague, or the capture of enemy kings, he digresses on the workings of *tyche* in the world. There is nothing in the tradition like this, although Polybius comes close.[41] In particular, the concept of *tyche* is nowhere near as prominent in the works of the two historians who influenced Procopius most, Herodotus and Thucydides. Whereas *tyche* was part of the classical repertoire, the importance that it attains in the *Wars* and the *Secret History* must be viewed as a deliberate choice on the part of their author. What we must do is try to explain that choice. Vaguely invoking "the tradition" will do us no good.

Finally, we come to what is arguably the greatest flaw in all the discussions of *tyche* in Procopius, regardless of whether they advocate a skeptical or conventional Christian. All discussions so far entirely ignore the narrative in which the concept is at all times embedded. Scholars scan the text for key words such as God and *tyche* and then extract the passages in which they are located, sometimes without bothering to note whether the words are spoken by Procopius himself or by one of his speakers. Passages taken from completely different parts of the same text, or from different works altogether, are then juxtaposed in the hope that they will yield logical sense.[42]

This cut-and-paste approach, which I have criticized in connection with another Byzantine historian,[43] will no longer suffice. This chapter will seek to demonstrate that each individual occurrence of *tyche* or God cannot be understood apart from its surrounding context, which includes the specific events to which it is linked as well as—and this requires particular emphasis—the position of those events in the overall context of the war. In other words, *tyche* and God are likely to function differently, or to have different meanings, depending on their place in the logic of the narrative. They must be carefully contextualized before being used to draw conclusions about what Procopius believed. Conversely, it is impossible to understand the narrative of the *Wars* without also examining the role of *tyche* within it. Against those who would brush it aside, it will be argued here that *tyche*, or "God," is a central component of the overall political aim of the *Wars*. This phenomenological approach will enable us to understand the historian's verdict on the events of his time and on the deeds of Belisarius, whom fortune, in one form or another, follows throughout the *Wars* and *Secret History*.

In short, narrative and *tyche* are interdependent. We cannot fully understand the story of the *Wars* unless we grasp the idea that lies at its core, and, conversely, we cannot understand that idea unless we first examine its dialectical relationship to the developing course of the narrative. The procedure I intend to follow has been described ably in a discussion of Greek tragedy: "We reflect on an incident . . . by burrowing down into the depths of the particular, finding images and connections that will permit us to see it more truly, describe it more richly; by combining this burrowing with a horizontal drawing of connections, so that every horizontal link contributes to the depth of our view of the particular, and every new depth creates new horizontal links."[44]

The theological vocabulary of the *Wars* is minimalist. Procopius uses only a small number of terms such as *tyche*, *theos*, and *daimonion*, thereby enabling us to track their changing fortunes with ease. *Tyche* is the more complex one, for it frequently occurs as a verb, in compounds such as *eutychia* (good fortune), or without having great interpretive weight; for example, when minor events "chance" to happen or occur "by some chance."[45] And yet it is not chance that governs the distribution of these terms in the text. Even though it will not be possible to examine every particular case, sufficient evidence will be presented that Procopius deploys them carefully. I hope the discussion will provide future students of the *Wars* with the tools to appreciate those passages that could not be examined here for reasons of space.

The next two sections will follow closely the narratives of the *Vandal War* and the *Gothic War*, focusing on Procopius' development of key concepts. Through an analysis of the rhetorical techniques by which they are deployed in speeches and the historian's own digressions, we will explicate the relationships among *tyche*, God, and the sixth-century wars. Technical terms will be examined in their immediate narrative context as their cumulative role in the construction of Procopius' metanarratives is gradually revealed. The fifth section of the chapter will look at two important events in the *Persian War*, the sack of Antioch in 540 and the plague of 542, which elicited from Procopius extended meditations on *tyche* and God. A brief section will be devoted to the role of *tyche* in the fall of Totila, told in Book 8 of the *Wars*. Finally, the seventh section will situate Procopius' use of *tyche* within the broader spectrum of ancient thought, looking particularly at other historians, secular and ecclesiastical, as well as at possible philosophical and religious influences.

The Supremacy of *Tyche* in the *Vandal War*

Let me state at the outset my main theses regarding the role of *tyche* in the *Vandal War*. First, Procopius believed that the fall of the Vandals was due to chance and not the virtue of Belisarius. Gelimer's defeat was caused by a series of accidents from which the Romans only happened to benefit. This thesis is stated explicitly, if not helpfully, in the *Secret History*: "*tyche* delivered Gelimer and Vittigis over to Belisarius as captives of war" (4.32). It is also alluded to in the *Gothic War*, where the verbal form of *tyche* is used in connection with Belisarius' victory over the Vandals (5.5.1). This persistent association of *tyche* with the victory in Libya is not accidental and explains why Procopius never praises Belisarius for the reconquest. This, in turn, refutes the pervasive belief that the historian set out to glorify the general in the *Vandal War*.[46] Procopius does occasionally praise Belisarius, but only for events that could be ascribed to his virtue, for example the orderly entry of his troops into Carthage (3.21.8) and the early victories in Italy over the Goths. The defeat of Gelimer was not such an event. Besides, Procopius makes some rather unfavorable remarks about Belisarius in the early stages of the narrative, which he would not have made had he been the general's apologist (3.10.4, 3.14.1–2; cf. 4.4.1–8).

Second, the *Vandal War* establishes a basic opposition between things that men can foresee and control and things that they cannot, and the latter are ascribed alternately to God or to *tyche*. Procopius uses the two terms more or less interchangeably. Naturally, he is aware that most men hold God to be benevolent. Yet in his view, the events that people want to ascribe to God should properly be ascribed to amoral chance, which does not mean that *tyche* is an actual goddess. His ultimate goal is to displace God, not to deify chance. Of course many speakers in the work have a different view of the world, and Procopius allows them to express it. Yet even their choice of words is always subordinated to the imperatives of his metanarrative. For example, in the *Vandal War*, speakers refer to God or fortune frequently, complementing the historian's own ascription of the events in Libya to *tyche*, whereas in the early stages of the *Gothic War*, dominated as they are by the military genius of Belisarius, speakers tend to emphasize instead the power of virtue. Thus we see that the frequency and distribution of concepts such as *tyche* and virtue are carefully controlled by Procopius to reinforce and vary his specific verdict on each war. Analysis reveals that each text is structured by recurring patterns, and patterns are a sure indication of an author's intentions. It is Procopius' seamless fusion of factual reporting, dramatic effect, and abstract conceptualization that places him in the forefront of ancient and Byzantine historians.

The rhetorical techniques that Procopius uses to postulate a polarity between virtue and *tyche*, and to insinuate an equation between *tyche* and God, are presaged in the introduction to the *Vandal War*. These examples are vague and weak, but they build up as the narrative moves closer to contemporary events. Gaizeric is arguably the most important person in the introduction, and despite his well-earned reputation for cruelty and aggression, Procopius often praises his ability and shrewdness, just as elsewhere he acknowledges the "virtue" of the Persian tyrant Cavades.[47] Through his own "providence" (*pronoia*), Gaizeric secured his "good fortune" (*eutychia*). Yet he feared that in time the Vandals would lose both their "strength" and their *tyche*, given that "human things can be overturned by divine things and bodies tend to grow weak." According to the chiasmus, "strength" is naturally undermined by the weakening of "bodies," making bad *tyche* the equivalent to the opposition of "divine things."[48] The correspondence is loose at this point, but it becomes more explicit as the narrative progresses. Procopius frequently attributes events to *tyche* that characters in the work attribute to God, he uses *tyche* and God interchangeably in his own digressions, and he sometimes makes speakers use them interchangeably too. In an anecdote that seems to be a joke on divine providence, Gaizeric sails against his enemies and, when asked by his helmsman against whom he wishes to sail, says, "Clearly, against those with whom God is angry." Procopius straightaway adds that Gaizeric sailed against whomever "it chanced" (3.5.24–25).

Gaizeric's answer is witty on many levels. It hinges upon and hence exposes the circularity of the notion that misfortunes happen only to people with whom God is angry. If providence rules the world, then all suffering must be the effect of God's wrath. The circle is broken when we realize that some events occur by chance or that Gaizeric's victims were not more sinful than others. Also, Gaizeric's cynical view of providence is troubling. Whereas a Christian could believe that the heretical Vandal king was an instrument of God's wrath—Eusebius, after all, had claimed as much for the persecutors of the Church[49]—to ascribe *intention* to God's instrument ruins the desired effect and strains credibility. Any criminal may then claim religious sanction, for the circular logic of providence automatically turns his victims into the targets of God's wrath. That is exactly what Gaizeric's joke does. Christians could endure persecution but not persecutors who joked at the expense of their faith.

There is only one passage in the entire *Vandal War* where Procopius implies in his own voice that God's actions are determined by moral factors, and it has been much touted by scholars interested in his religious views, given the extreme paucity of such passages in the *Wars*.[50] Yet it is questionable whether this tongue-in-cheek comment seriously reflects the historian's views. Its surrounding context, from which scholars carefully excise it, is one of sarcasm and ridicule. It concerns the emperor Honorius, whose reign has already been introduced as a complete disaster: "while he ruled the west, barbarians took possession of his land" (3.2.1). Procopius says that the emperor was such an "idiot" that he was relieved to discover that the Rome that had been destroyed was the city and not his favorite cock, which happened to have the same name (3.2.25–26): "But I just fed him!" In contrast to his father Theodosius, "there was nothing in his mind of a military nature, but he was content, I believe, if he was allowed to rest in his palace" (3.2.8; cf. 3.1.2). According to the very condensed version that Procopius gives of the critical year 410, Honorius was surrounded by usurpers and barbarians and was preparing to flee from Ravenna. "Tossed about on the storms of *tyche*," he fell into "some marvelous pieces of good fortune (εὐτυχήματα). For God likes to help those who are neither clever nor capable of looking after themselves, so long as they are not wicked. . . . And this indeed chanced (τετύχηκεν) to happen to this emperor" (3.2.34–35; cf. 8.14.21). We note the slippage of terms: three references to *tyche* surround the single mention of God. But what is more important is the comical context of Procopius' alleged belief in God's providence. Honorius, "a buffoon whose follies are effortlessly exploited by the barbarians,"[51] received God's help in 410 precisely because he lacked those qualities through which he could have preserved the empire on his own, qualities through which Gaizeric triumphs later in the narrative. The only ruler with whom God is associated in the *Vandal War* is the one who lost the western empire. This mocks the belief in the divine grace enjoyed by the Christian emperors. "So long as they are not wicked." Had Honorius been more wicked, he might have preserved his realm.

Like the introduction to the *Persian War*, the introduction to the *Vandal War* prepares readers for what is to come. The background material on the Vandals is presented by Procopius with an eye to later events and to the attribution of those events to *tyche*. This fact explains not only the sometimes peculiar selection of the material but also the choice of factors that the historian highlights. For example, he says that Gaizeric tore down the walls of all the cities in Libya except Carthage so that no enemy could hold them against him, a policy that seemed wise at the time but was proven foolish later, when Belisarius seized those cities from the Vandals "easily and without any toil" (3.5.8–9).[52] Procopius thereby insinuates that the Roman victory was destined to be easy and adds immediately that men love to change their opinions about past decisions in accordance with later changes in *tyche* (3.5.10). The ease of the reconquest is loosely connected to fluctuations in *tyche* as early as the reign of Gaizeric.

The theme of the "ease" of the reconquest also appears in the account of the expedition of Basiliscus under the emperor Leo in 468, which functions in many ways as a parallel to the later expedition of Belisarius. Before Basiliscus set sail, Leo's generals captured the Libyan Tripolis "easily" and Sardinia "with no difficulty" (3.6.8–9). Likewise, before Belisarius set sail, a local notable seized the Tripolis and wrote to Justinian that he could hold it "with no exertion" (3.10.22–24). At the same time, the Vandal governor of Sardinia simply detached the island from his master's domain and established his own rule (3.10.25–24). These are not the only parallels between the two expeditions. Procopius tells us explicitly that Basiliscus could have captured Carthage and subdued the Vandals "without any trouble or resistance" had he not been venal or cowardly (3.6.10–11, 3.6.14–16). Such statements create expectations and condition readers' responses to later events.[53]

It is in this context that I believe we should view the account of the "amazing" or "miraculous" discovery of water by Belisarius' army when it first disembarked on the arid Libyan coast. Procopius, who was present, relates how he informed the general that this was a sign of an "effortless victory, foretold to them by God" and adds—with hindsight—"and indeed it came to pass in that way" (3.15.34–36). The emphasis here should be placed on the "effortlessness" of the victory, which is confirmed by the historian's later judgment.[54] And, as we will discover when Procopius delivers his verdict on the defeat of the Vandals, "miraculous" or "amazing" events are inherent aspects of "human *tyche*" (cf. 4.7.18–19).

The speeches leading up to the Vandal defeat also set events within Procopius' interpretive schema. The first is delivered by John the Cappadocian, who tries to dissuade Justinian from invading Libya. This is probably the most important speech in the *Vandal War* and merits serious consideration. It has been noted that it is the only occasion on which John is presented somewhat favorably by Procopius, who otherwise detested him,[55] and the prefect's caution is justified by later events. Also, his speech is modeled in content and context on the speech that Herodotus gives to Artabanus, who tried to dissuade Xerxes from invading Greece. John says that if the emperor feels confident of victory he will have to "sacrifice the bodies of men and spend a vast amount of money," though success may compensate for these losses; if, on the other hand, "these things rest on the knees of God," then it is better to stay at home and not run the risk (3.10.12–13). Interestingly, John invokes God as a euphemism for *defeat*, not to justify or predict victory as Justinian would have it.[56] A few lines later he refers again to failure, only this time he attributes it to "the opposition of *tyche*" (3.10.16). This quiet substitution is a persistent Procopian technique. In the corresponding section of his speech in Herodotus, Artabanus claims that even the best plans can be thwarted by *tyche*, which he then immediately equates with God, whose "envy" casts down those whose pride exceeds mortal bounds. Both he and John seem to use *tyche* and God interchangeably and invoke them to explain failure. John could not of course refer to the envy of God, although Procopius does refer elsewhere to the envy of *tyche*.[57]

Belisarius delivers four speeches before defeating the Vandals at Decimum, the second of which is paired with a speech by the prefect Archelaus. Belisarius' first speech is addressed to the troops at Abydos, after the execution of two soldiers for murder (3.12.8–22). He argues that "the fortunes" of war are not won by strength and bravery but through inflexible justice, for God will grant victory to the army that is most just. He does not deny the efficacy of preparation but claims to value it less than having justice and God on his side. An event occurred in Sicily soon afterward that greatly promoted the Roman cause but happened entirely by chance. Belisarius sent Procopius to Syracuse on reconnaissance; in a passage that is elaborated for literary effect, the historian relates how "he unexpectedly chanced upon (παρὰ δόξαν ἐπιτυχών) an old friend of his" whose slave had information about the disposition of the Vandal forces (3.14.7). This event, in which the author becomes a protagonist, occupies a crucial position in the narrative and highlights the role of *tyche* in enabling the Romans to land safely in Libya (3.14.15–17).[58] Yet in his second speech, Belisarius claims that it was God who granted the Romans a safe landing (3.15.20–21).

That second speech is delivered at a council of war, which is attended only by officers. The tone here is different from the muster at Abydos. Archelaus begins by praising the general's "virtue and experience" and claims that "when things go well for men they ascribe events to good judgment or *tyche*" (3.15.2–5)—not, we note, to God. Archelaus never mentions God; when formulating plans for the future, he refers only to "human experience" and "the nature of things" (3.15.11). In his response, Belisarius mentions God briefly, but when formulating plans for the future he claims that "military contests yield to the unexpected" and expects that the war will depend on the relative strength and preparedness of the two armies (3.15.25–26). He concludes by insisting that the Romans will secure provisions through their "bravery" and that victory "lies in your own hands" (3.15.30). The speeches of both Archelaus and Belisarius consist mostly of detailed arguments of a strategic or tactical nature. Yet in his third speech, which is delivered to the troops after some of them had been punished for plundering the locals, Belisarius reverts to his previous position and claims that injustice will do the Roman cause great harm for it will offend God. If, however, the Romans remain just, God will be on their side and the Vandals will lose (3.16.6–8). His argument for justice now has a pragmatic component: injustice will alienate the Libyans, making the struggle with the Vandals more difficult. Belisarius' fourth speech is delivered to the troops before battle is joined with the Vandals (3.19.2–10). He begins by repeating the statement made earlier to the officers that victory "lies in our hands" and ends by exhorting each soldier to recall "his own virtue." Only in the middle of the speech does he refer to God (and only once), and he is naturally on the most just side.[59]

Belisarius develops a clear antithesis between God and virtue but varies his emphasis by audience and circumstance, a tactic that can be viewed cynically. Overall, his speeches in the *Vandal War* make a strong argument for the importance of divine assistance, just as in the *Gothic War* they focus almost exclusively on the power of human judgment and virtue. This pattern is not accidental, for it mirrors the historian's own interpretation of events in the two theaters of war. As we will see, Procopius ascribed great importance to the military virtue of Belisarius in the opening stages of the war in Italy but felt that the victory in Libya was due to the intervention of a higher power, though perhaps not the one invoked in Belisarius' speeches. As the two armies marched across Libya, a series of accidents began to shape the course of events and ultimately determined the outcome. These are at first attributed to both *tyche* and God, though God is quietly forgotten afterward. Procopius' detailed account reveals how the decisive engagements were fought in ways that were neither planned for nor foreseen by the two commanders. Neither side knew exactly what was going on until it was all over. The Roman success was due to events that Belisarius did not control.[60] It is not coincidental therefore that the density of terms such as *tyche* and God becomes high at precisely this point.

Procopius prefaces his account of the battles of Decimum with a digression on

human and divine things, how God, seeing from afar what the future holds, traces out the way in which it seems to him that things should come out, while men, whether they fall into error or plan well, do not know that they have made some mistake, if that should chance (τύχοι) to be the case, or that they have acted wisely, so that in all of this a path is laid down for *tyche*, who brings to completion all that has been ordained beforehand. (3.18.2)

Procopius then lists the accidents that caused the Romans to prevail at Decimum, making it clear that victory was ultimately not due to Belisarius because he knew neither the location nor the plans of the enemy and because certain crucial factors were beyond his control (3.18.3 ff.). The same is true of Gelimer, whose strategy had an equal chance of proving victorious.

It is arbitrary to see in the small digression quoted above a subordination of *tyche* to God; that is, to infer that she carries out his will from the fact that he "lays down a path" for her.[61] It could just as well be that she makes all the major decisions—as Procopius states elsewhere[62]—and that God "lays down a path" for what he "sees" will happen. That God "sees what the future holds" implies that he does not actually ordain it, a task perhaps reserved for some entity such as Fate, which Procopius elsewhere describes in a way that reminds us of *tyche*.[63] The image of a supreme God constrained to obey the dictates of the Fates is not an unfamiliar one to readers of archaic Greek literature. But beyond these textual ambiguities, the subordination of fortune faces serious conceptual difficulties. As Augustine realized, fortune cannot be a capricious and amoral entity if she merely carries out God's will.[64] On the other hand, if her capriciousness is already part of God's plan, the difference between her and God collapses. Thus, if *tyche* is a personal agent who is as capricious and unstoppable as Procopius depicts her in the *Wars*, she must prevail in any association with God, because his agency can only be demonstrated through the inherent goodness of events.[65] The narrative of the *Wars*, however, gives little warrant for such a view, and the digression quoted above says nothing about the goodness of "all that has been ordained beforehand"—a crucial omission. Be that as it may, the language of the digression is too vague for an exact differentiation between God and *tyche*, which was probably exactly what Procopius intended.

Procopius' digression does suggest that the battles of Decimum were in some sense foreordained, and his narrative also possesses an undeniable aura of fatalism. But this is not necessarily superstition. A modern philosopher has argued that "not only does unpredictability not entail inexplicability, but its presence is compatible with the truth of determinism in a strong version."[66] The effect of fatality can be produced by the combination of determinism and unpredictability. Events may be determined by causes beyond our control or by the unpredictable interaction of factors that are under separate human control, for example the movement of two armies. In many ancient historians, fortune designates "an unexpected occurrence produced by the conjuncture of two or more independent chains of historical events."[67] Such events may well seem predetermined to those affected by them, and that would not be an implausible way of describing unexpected events in a world that is nevertheless strictly deterministic. For the Stoics, fate was precisely the inexorable chain of causation responsible for all events.[68] *Tyche* and God in the *Wars* may represent nothing more than uncontrollable or inscrutable causal factors. Let us see whether the narrative bears this out.

Two battles occurred at Decimum in September 533, the first between John the Armenian and Gelimer's brother Ammatas, the second between Belisarius and Gelimer. In both cases, Procopius develops a series of counterfactual propositions designed to show that the Romans did not earn their victory through their virtue—far less through their justice—but rather owed it to a series of contingent accidents, which are specified in detail (cf. 3.18.3ff. with 3.19.25ff.). Gelimer, we are told, had victory "in his own hands" but inexplicably threw it away (3.19.25). Procopius opines that one could ascribe this to God, who clouds the minds of those destined for defeat. It is not surprising that Belisarius soon says the same thing about *tyche* (4.1.18), as does Procopius later (7.13.17). Be that as it may, Procopius states that when Belisarius entered the palace at Carthage and ate the meal that had been prepared for Gelimer,[69] one could then see "*tyche* giving herself airs and making a display of the fact that she controls all things and that nothing really belongs to man" (3.21.7). He uses the same language elsewhere about the *daimonion* (2.30.51) and, once again, *tyche* (8.32.29). Thus, God, who was so prominent in the speeches of Belisarius before the Vandal defeat, is displaced by fortune for the remainder of the *Vandal War*. Beginning with Belisarius' entry into Carthage, fortune emerges as the true mistress of events. This view is faithfully reflected in modern surveys, which, as usual, follow Procopius' lead in vocabulary and interpretation.[70]

The remainder of Book 3 is devoted to the implications for human beings of a world that is dangerously unpredictable. This theme is naturally presented in literary form, through stories that reveal human reactions. Just as Belisarius and Procopius were struck by the power of *tyche* when they entered Gelimer's palace, the Vandals realized that nothing is secure or impossible (3.22.1). An oracle is cited, according to which *G* would drive out *B* (Gaizeric and Boniface), after which *B* would drive out *G* (Belisarius and Gelimer). What could better illustrate the arbitrariness of fortune than mere alphabetical coincidence? (3.21.14–15) The messengers of Gelimer's brother Tzazon, who reclaimed Sardinia, unsuspectingly entered Carthage and were amazed "by the suddenness of the change" (3.24.6). In his letter to Tzazon (3.25.11–18), Gelimer attributes the defeat to "some madness sent from heaven" but then, in accordance with Procopian practice, alters his vocabulary and writes that "it is now possible to know from the outcome what *tyche* had decided beforehand." When he states next that "virtue abandoned the Vandals, taking good fortune with it," we see the fulfillment of Gaizeric's prediction that the "strength" and *tyche* of the Vandals would not last forever (cf. 3.4.12–13). Gelimer's letter ends by contrasting that prior *tyche* to the current "difficulties brought on by the *daimonion*." In the course of this brief letter, Gelimer manages to use heaven, *tyche*, and the *daimonion* repeatedly and more or less interchangeably. Book 3 closes with a pitiful scene, on which Procopius has lavished his literary skill: the two Vandal brothers and their soldiers unite, embracing and weeping silently over their misfortunes (3.25.22–26). There is considerable sympathy for the Vandals here, and Procopius states that their "bad *tyche*" was such that one could feel pity not merely for them but for the whole of "human *tyche*."

Book 4 begins with an account of the battle of Tricamarum, which occurred in December of 533 and ruined the Vandal kingdom. Three speeches are delivered before the battle by Belisarius, Gelimer, and Gelimer's brother Tzazon. They merit attention for both content and literary function. The speeches reaffirm the polarity of virtue and fortune and actually manipulate it in order to enhance the drama of the narrative. They also provide an indirect commentary on events up this point. The two main speakers are the victorious Roman general Belisarius and the defeated Vandal king Gelimer, and we see in their words a reflection of what has happened along with a premonition of what is to come. To test and confirm our hypotheses, Procopius provides us with a control case in the person of the victorious Vandal general Tzazon, who has just returned from conquering Sardinia and does nothing less than formulate the principles of Procopius' method for composing these speeches.

Belisarius' speech consists of two parts. In the first, he claims surprisingly that the Romans prevailed over the Vandals at Decimum through their virtue and that wars are decided by virtue. He then incites his troops to show bravery and daring. In this part of his speech, he mentions virtue and bravery at least four times (4.1.13–17). In the second part, he turns his attention to factors beyond human control (4.1.18–25). He refers first to *tyche*, and specifically to the bad *tyche* of the Vandals, which now oppresses their spirits with the recollection of past misfortunes. Claiming that the Romans "chanced" to win at Decimum with their cavalry alone, he hopes that with the help of God they will be able to capture the enemy camp. Referring once again to the *tyche* of war, which should not be put off, he warns that the *daimonion* punishes those who do not seize opportune moments. Whereas in the first half of his speech Belisarius praises virtue without ever mentioning God or *tyche*, in the second half he refers repeatedly to *tyche*, once to God and the *daimonion*, but never to Roman virtue.

We observe the same neat division in the speech of Gelimer, only in reverse order. Gelimer refers to the bad *tyche* of the Vandals in the first part of his speech (4.2.10) and explicitly attributes the defeat at Decimum to "the opposition of *tyche*, whose stream never flows in the same direction" (4.2.16; cf. 3.10.16). In the second part of his speech, he praises the virtue and bravery of the Vandals. Gelimer never mentions God.

Tzazon then speaks briefly to the Vandals who conquered Sardinia under his command (4.2.23–32). Procopius seems to have thought that these troops deserved separate treatment owing to their past triumphs; he even separates them physically from their compatriots (4.2.24). This confirms our suspicion that the speeches are not "pure rhetoric" unrelated to the factual basis of the narrative.[71] Different words are addressed to different audiences depending on their experiences, and the historian followed definite rules when composing them. In the first part of his speech, Tzazon refers at least three times to his soldiers' virtue, encouraging them to prove its worth in battle against the Romans. The parallel speech of Belisarius, we recall, had proceeded likewise, as it too addressed troops who had been victorious. Tzazon then reveals the principle that underlies the three speeches, namely that "those who have failed in the past are dismayed by their previous *tyche*, whereas those who have not been defeated at all join battle in high spirits" (4.2.29). That is why his speech and that of Belisarius begin with the praise of their soldiers' virtue, while that of Gelimer begins with a meditation on the evils of *tyche*. Referring finally to the defeat of the Vandals under Gelimer as bad *tyche*, Tzazon hopes that his soldiers will earn a better *tyche* in the coming battle. In the end, like Belisarius but unlike Gelimer, he calls upon God for assistance.

The only soldiers who are designated as having fought bravely in the ensuing battle are the Vandals under Tzazon (4.3.14). After the battle, Roman discipline collapsed as soldiers began to plunder without regard for safety. Belisarius failed to control the chaos (4.4.1–8).[72] Procopius again devises a counterfactual argument to show that the Romans could have been destroyed easily at this point had the Vandals rallied and attacked them. Belisarius accordingly receives no praise for this victory, neither here nor anywhere else in Procopius' works.

We need not dwell on the minor appearances of *tyche* in the remainder of the *Vandal War*, however important they may be in their own contexts (e.g., 4.4.32–41, 4.19.24), nor on passages where Procopius ascribes to *tyche* what others attribute to God (e.g., 4.4.32–41, 4.20.5–11). These are by now familiar devices. Yet we must not fail to consider Procopius' final verdict on the fall of the Vandal kingdom, which is located at the end of a series of passages elaborated for literary effect. Once again, the purpose of these passages is to highlight the supremacy of fortune in human affairs. That is the only "meaning" that Procopius was willing to derive from the reconquest. The Roman victory was due to dumb luck. Divine providence was merely the emperor's conceit, superior virtue the general's boast. *Tyche* undermines all ideology. And Procopius does not allow mere success to cloud his historical judgment. The expedition's chances for success seemed as slim to him in retrospect as they had at its outset (cf. 3.10 with 4.7.18–21).

Procopius expounds on the power of *tyche* by focusing on Gelimer, who best exemplifies the bewildering fate of man. In the *Vandal War*, the historian is more attentive to the victims of fortune than to her beneficiaries. Unlike Gaizeric, Theoderic, or Totila, Gelimer was no great statesman or hero, and Procopius readily reveals his negative qualities (3.9.6–9). Yet after the battle of Decimum, he is presented with a considerable degree of sympathy. At the end of Book 3, as we saw, Procopius claims that his sorrowful reunion with Tzazon was so moving that it could arouse pity for human fortune as such. And after the battle of Tricamarum, the historian emphasizes the misery experienced by the Vandal king in the mountain fort of Papua, where he was besieged by the Roman commander Pharas. He begins by contrasting the luxury the Vandals had once enjoyed to the poverty of the Moors, which the king now had to endure at Papua (4.6.4–14). Procopius then quotes, and probably invents, the letters exchanged between Pharas and Gelimer, which revolve around the problem of *tyche*. Pharas encourages Gelimer to surrender and become like Belisarius, the emperor's "slave." He ascribes the king's misfortune directly to *tyche* but claims that *tyche* is likewise responsible for the opportunity to now serve the emperor honorably. In his response, Gelimer hopes that God will punish the emperor for reducing him to such a pitiful *tyche*. Fortune is mentioned five times in these two brief letters (4.6.15–30). Procopius then adds that when Pharas heard of the miserable state of the Vandal king, he "lamented for the *tyche* of men" (4.6.34). This reminds us of the reunion scene at the end of Book 3.

Procopius persists in his depiction of the evil plight of the once happy Vandal king. Along with Gelimer himself, we are forced to watch two children fight over partially chewed food. After this, Gelimer admits to Pharas that he "can no longer resist *tyche* nor struggle with destiny" (4.7.8). Accordingly, the theme of the power of *tyche* over human affairs dominates the account of the king's surrender to Belisarius in Carthage. Gelimer began to laugh so immoderately that some thought he had lost his mind. His friends, however, contended that he was sane but that, having experienced everything from royal dominion to abject despair, "i.e., everything that comes from *tyche*, both good and evil," he laughed because he did not believe that human affairs were worth more than laughter. Procopius adds that the reader, "whether enemy or friend," must decide on his own why Gelimer laughed (4.7.14–15). Regardless of which view Procopius himself held, we have seen that he, along with the king's "friends," was amazed by the extremes of Gelimer's fortune (cf. 4.6.4–14); indeed, that was the main lesson he drew from the war.

Procopius concludes his account of Gelimer's surrender with thoughts on how "many events that seemed beyond expectation in the past have actually occurred, and will always continue to occur, so long as the *tychai* of mankind remain the same" (4.7.18; cf. 8.33.25). This phrase is a slightly modified version of what Thucydides says about the suffering caused by revolutions, "which have happened in the past and will always happen in the future so long as the nature (*physis*) of mankind remains the same" (3.82.2; cf. 1.22.4).[73] The substitution is crucial: *tyche* is in the *Vandal War* what human nature is in Thucydides; that is, virtually supreme. Even so, Procopius claims that he does not know whether any events that "chanced to occur" in the past were as "miraculous" or "amazing" as the fall of the Vandal kingdom to such a pitifully small army (4.7.19–20). That event, he concludes, happened "because of *tyche* or some kind of virtue" (4.7.21). We note that God has long since disappeared from the discussion, the polarity of fortune and virtue is affirmed, and the reader can have no doubt as to which of the two provides the correct explanation for the victory, the salvo to Belisarius' pride notwithstanding. The *Secret History* says openly that it was *tyche* that delivered Gelimer (4.32). And the poet Corippus, who wrote an epic poem on the Libyan campaigns of John Troglita while Procopius was writing the *Wars*, makes his hero refer to Belisarius' victory over the Vandals and wonder at *quae digna virum fortuna secuta est!*[74] A figure of speech, but perhaps one indicative of widespread contemporary perceptions.

Having established Procopius' interpretation of a single campaign, albeit one with far-reaching consequences for Byzantine history, we may now take a few steps back from the domain of fortune. Despite her prominent role in the *Vandal War*, we will see in the *Gothic War* that fortune's supremacy is not unrivaled. There is room in the *Wars* for reason and virtue. *Tyche*, after all, is less a goddess than a hermeneutical device that is deployed when the historian feels that events were beyond control. There are counterexamples to the power of *tyche* in the latter sections of the *Vandal War*. It is worth considering one of them here, for they show Procopius in a more Thucydidean light. Once again, the tight economy of his prose reflects his masterful integration of fact and interpretation. The structure of his account and the speeches of the leading characters are again derived in a strictly logical manner from his view of the overall significance of the event.

A rival paradigm to the supremacy of fortune emerges from the defeat of the Moors by the Roman general Solomon at Mammes in 534. The relevant passages include two speeches and a battle. In his speech, Solomon reminds his troops of their virtue and compares the two armies in terms of equipment, tactics, and "virtue of soul," finding the Romans superior in all respects. He refers frequently to bravery, daring, and virtue but never to God or *tyche* (4.11.22–36). The Moorish commanders also incite their troops to bravery and virtue. Referring to wars in general, and to the defeat of the Vandals in particular, they repeat Procopius' judgment that success was due to either *tyche* or the general's virtue. They also explain why their tactics, equipment, and numbers will ultimately prevail over the Romans (4.11.37–46). As we saw in our analysis of this passage in a previous chapter,[75] the ensuing battle demonstrates that both sides had valid reasons to hope for victory. As with many battles in Thucydides, this one unfolds according to the predictions made by the speakers, demonstrating man's power to discover the truth through reason and implement his plans in the face of adversity. *Tyche* plays no role in this episode, and it is ultimately Solomon's leadership and cleverness that give victory to the Romans. Accordingly, Solomon is the most highly praised person in the *Vandal War* and is even compared, through a direct allusion, to Thucydides' Pericles.[76]

The Struggle Between Virtue and *Tyche* in the *Gothic War*

The war in Italy raged for twenty years and involved numerous armies operating on multiple fronts. It witnessed many, often dramatic, changes of fortune as well as memorable acts of heroism and treachery. As a narrative, the *Gothic War* is a brilliant synthesis of those events. It is lucid, detailed, and exemplary in organization. Procopius omits nothing important, praises and blames Romans and Goths in due proportion to their merits— his heroes are first Belisarius and then Totila—and conveys a powerful sense of how the war was experienced by its victims. His success rests on a combination of meticulous scholarship and literary skill, both of which, in this part of his work, reveal the influence of Thucydides. It is no accident that like Thucydides' account of the Peloponnesian War, Procopius' account of the war in Italy will remain unsurpassed, as even his contemporaries realized.[77]

The original installment of the *Gothic War* carried the narrative down to 550, when Totila had regained near-total control of Italy. No one could have foreseen that two years later he would be dead, the Gothic cause in ruins, and a palace eunuch in control of Italy. Those events would not be told by Procopius until a few years later, when he wrote Book 8 of the *Wars*. The following analysis will focus on the first three books, though its method applies equally to the supplementary account of the war's final years. The fall of Totila in Book 8 develops the themes that shape the account of the rise and fall of Roman fortunes in the first three books.

I will argue that the presentation of events in the *Gothic War* is structured around a second-order narrative about the fluctuating roles of *tyche* and virtue. This is neither independent from, nor crudely imposed upon, the narrative of events. Instead, it expresses the internal mechanisms of the narrative on a higher level of abstraction. Its purpose is to guide us toward an insightful interpretation of the war. It is so seamlessly integrated into the narrative that it shapes the attentive reader's reactions at almost every point. The broad outline of this metanarrative actually corresponds to a neat rhetorical device, a chiasmus, even though it is characterized by complexity on the level of individual episodes. The analysis below will examine its mechanisms in detail for the initial phases of the war (until the major turning point of 540) and will then discuss only the broad sweep of events. I hope that readers will be enabled to interpret for themselves the details passed over in the more general discussion of the later phases of the war. The turning points of the metanarrative are signaled chiefly through the opinions expressed in speeches, the distribution and local function of concepts such as *tyche*, and finally Procopius' own digressions. These techniques are simple enough, and the overall picture they produce will be revealed relatively clearly. One must first, however, be prepared to take seriously such things as speeches and digressions on *tyche* and not dismiss them as superficial affectations of classical devices. This represents a departure from current assumptions.

Belisarius enters the *Gothic War* as the protégé of fortune whom we met in the *Vandal War*. In 535, Justinian ordered him to wrest Sicily from Gothic control, if that could be done "with no trouble" (5.5.7). True enough, the general took Syracuse and other cities "with no trouble" (5.5.12; cf. 4.14.1: the entire island taken "with no trouble").[78] Procopius adds that "a piece of good fortune greater than words can describe" befell him then: it "chanced" that he marched into Syracuse, applauded by all and granting largesse, on the very last day of the year and hence of his consulship. This did not happen intentionally, Procopius emphasizes, but rather through some *tyche* (5.5.18–19).

Yet Belisarius refuses to acknowledge the gifts of his benefactress.[79] In 536, he advises the citizens of Naples to deliberate carefully on their situation and act boldly against the Gothic garrison. He insists that regardless of what fortune has in store, what is important is to fight. Belisarius' speech begins with no less than three references to *boule* and is saturated with verbs of choosing and doing (5.8.12–18). His enemies within, however, believe that he might fail because no one can influence the mind (*gnome*) of fortune (5.8.33). Ironically, Belisarius was about to abandon the siege, having lost many of his most "virtuous" soldiers (5.8.43), when, again, "a piece of good fortune" befell him: an Isaurian discovered a secret entrance through the city's aqueduct (5.9.10 ff.). About to enter by surprise, Belisarius now urges the Neapolitans to surrender and spare themselves the evils of conquest. Suppressing or forgetting the fact that his own imminent victory is due to *tyche*, he tells the Neapolitans that they will have only their own decisions (*boule* and *gnome*) to blame, not *tyche* (5.9.23–28). And yet when he later attempts to stop his troops from looting the city, he begins by saying that it was God who granted victory to the Romans and that they must be just to the vanquished (5.10.30). As we saw in the *Vandal War*, Belisarius mentions God and justice when he needs to discipline his soldiers and ascribes to God what Procopius had previously ascribed to *tyche*.

In the initial phases of the *Gothic War*, Belisarius is favored by fortune but downplays her importance. The Goths, in keeping with the theme of the *Gothic War*, initially underestimate her power as well. Their king Vittigis delivers two speeches before the first siege of Rome that emphasize prudent preparation over rash action and the need to bear initial losses patiently (5.11.12–25, 5.13.17–25). His first speech begins by attributing success directly to *euboulia* and does not mention *tyche*. His second speech begins with another plea for deliberation but grants that "necessity or *tyche*" must be taken into account.[80] Vittigis leaves his men with the impression that proper planning and strategy can guarantee victory.

The siege of Rome in 536–537 marks the apogee of Belisarius' career as a general and his greatest moment in the *Wars*. Procopius devotes disproportionate space to it and through his gripping narrative, mimesis of Thucydides, and strategic distribution of information manages to represent Belisarius as a general of genius whose "daring" and "foresight" reduced his warlike enemies to utter helplessness. To highlight this achievement, Procopius greatly exaggerates the number of soldiers in the Gothic army,[81] a form of distortion that he employs nowhere else. He presages the significance of the siege by making the inhabitants of Rome praise in advance the general's foresight, or *pronoia*, for repairing the walls, and by listing, from their perspective, all the perils and difficulties that the enterprise would entail (5.14.16–17). This naturally serves to magnify the later success.

Yet fortune is never far away. The first building inside the city that the historian mentions is her temple (5.15.11). And it was only "by some *tyche*" that Belisarius was not wounded in a major skirmish with the arriving Gothic army at the Milvian bridge, though he fought in the thick of battle and many Goths tried to kill him (5.18.15). It also "chanced" that he was riding an experienced war horse (5.18.6). On the other hand, the Roman force was saved because of its "virtue," which Procopius mentions many times and emphasizes by recounting the exploits of Valentinus (5.18.12–18; cf. 5.18.29: the valor of Belisarius and a Gothic warrior). When the Romans were then pressed against the city walls, they were saved only by Belisarius' "daring decision" to counterattack (5.18.26). Procopius then does something very interesting from a literary point of view. He states that Belisarius claimed at that moment to know with certainty that he could defeat the Goths but defers explaining the general's claim until it came to pass (5.18.42). The silence created by this postponement makes the general's intelligence seem mysterious, almost superhuman. The people of Rome ridiculed him for making such bold claims after just barely escaping with his life. Yet the tactical realizations that Belisarius made during the battle at the Milvian bridge enabled him later to organize a series of brilliant cavalry sallies that devastated the Gothic forces.[82] It is only then that Procopius reveals the details of what Belisarius had grasped (5.27.24–29). In other words, Procopius discloses Belisarius' thoughts not when they occurred to him, but when they became operative in the war. This arrangement is designed to highlight the efficacy of human understanding. Victory transforms the Romans' earlier incredulity into praise, and Belisarius' intelligence appears to them as "miraculous" or "amazing."[83] Significantly, this was the term used for *tyche* in the *Vandal War*, and to the uncomprehending or proud Goths it appears as the opposition of *tyche* (5.27.24–25).

In the brief negotiations that precede the first assault on the walls, both the Gothic envoys and Belisarius "forget" the role of *tyche*. The envoys distinguish not between virtue and *tyche* but between virtue and rashness—that is, between virtue and excessive virtue—and accuse Belisarius of the latter (5.20.8–11). In his brief response, Belisarius reaffirms the power of independent judgment by again stressing *symboule* and *gnome* (5.20.15–18). And Procopius' account of the assault reveals the efficacy of Belisarian *pronoia* in a way that highlights the difference between the *Vandal* and the *Gothic War*. As the Goths approached the walls, Belisarius began to laugh, causing the city's inhabitants "to abuse him and call him shameless" (5.22.2–3). Procopius again postpones explaining the general's behavior. Belisarius seems rash to the Goths and irrational to the Romans, but only because neither can comprehend his virtue. His confidence initially seems misplaced or enigmatic, but Procopius soon reveals that it stemmed from his exact understanding of the enemy's weakness. With a single shot he "chanced" to kill the point man of the Gothic advance, which the Romans took as "the best omen." But when he repeats the feat twice over, we realize that chance had nothing to do with it and that what the Romans interpreted as supernatural was really the general's skill. By commanding his soldiers to kill the oxen pulling the siege engines, Belisarius halted the Gothic advance. Procopius now looks back and attributes the general's laughter to his *pronoia* (5.22.4–9). It was superior understanding that made the Goths seem laughable to him. This laughter, which Procopius mentions three times, is to the *Gothic War* what the laughter of Gelimer was to the *Vandal War*. The former reflects the virtue of a man who looks down on the world as a playground; the latter expresses the resignation of a man who realizes that fortune controls all.

But pride and confidence are emphatically not what we find in the letter that Belisarius sends to the emperor after defeating the Goths. Belisarius there reverses his stance and depreciates his own role in the victory, attributing it to "some *tyche*" (5.24.4). To be sure, fortune is not entirely absent from Procopius' account of the Gothic assault, but it never significantly affects the fighting (e.g. 5.23.9–12, 5.23.24). It was Belisarius who won the battle, and the soldiers praise him for it at the end of the day's fighting (5.23.27). In his letter to the emperor, however, the general revives the schema and dichotomies of the *Vandal War*: "achievements that transcend the nature of things should not be referred to the virtue of men, but to a higher power (τὸ κρεῖσσον). Those things that have been done by us so far, whether by *tyche* or virtue, are for the best" (5.24.5–6). We note the quiet shift from *tyche* to "a higher power"—a trendy word for God[84]—and then back again to *tyche*. A few lines later, Belisarius reverts once more to God, saying that human affairs follow his will (5.24.7), and then returns again to *tyche*, saying that one should not always trust in her, for she is not accustomed to following the same course forever (5.24.9). This confusing alternation blurs the difference between the various concepts, but it is only an extreme example of a familiar technique. Nevertheless, it is no accident that Belisarius emphasizes God when speaking to his troops, *tyche* when writing to the emperor, and *boule* when addressing adversaries on the field.

One curious detail is that the original version of this letter may have been written by Procopius himself, who was, after all, the general's secretary. The historian would then be embellishing, and attributing to Belisarius, a letter that he himself wrote over a decade earlier as the general's secretary and advisor—"an extraordinary merging of life and art."[85] At the same time, Procopius' account of the siege of Rome is directly modeled on Thucydides' account of the siege of Syracuse. What is significant about this mimesis is less the inevitable verbal parallels than the common points of emphasis and the similarities in the structure, "conceptualization," and "rhythm" of events.[86] More important, Procopius imitates even when he deviates from his models, for by doing so he draws attention to the differences between his subject and that of Thucydides. Belisarius' letter to the emperor is modeled on that of Nicias to Athens, who also wrote under dire conditions and pleaded for reinforcements. But Belisarius' determination is in stark contrast to Nicias' pessimism and resignation. Procopius' hero declares that he will stay and fight to the death (5.24.17); Nicias complains of kidney problems and asks to be relieved of command (7.15). The letter in the *Wars* is "a conscious reversal of the original model"[87] and reflects the very different momentum of the Roman campaign.

That momentum peaked with the surrender of Vittigis in 540, a turning point, as we will see, in both the narrative and the metanarrative of the *Gothic War*. At that point, *tyche* again becomes dominant, her importance increasing gradually after the first siege of Rome. Belisarius, however, continues to recognize only human factors. The severe defeat suffered by the Romans in the spring of 537, when they pressured him into fighting a pitched battle outside the walls of Rome, justified in retrospect the warning that he gave before the battle to the effect that "one should maintain policies that have proven successful, for it is inexpedient to change course when things are going according to plan" (5.28.6–7). In that speech, Belisarius mentioned neither *tyche* nor God and tried to encourage his men by declaring that the most important factor in war is the *gnome* and zeal of the combatants (5.28.8). Later that year, the famished citizens again tried to press him into fighting a decisive battle. Their speech contains numerous references to their miserable *tyche* (6.3.13–22) and fulfills to the letter Belisarius' prediction to the emperor that their loyalty would falter in adversity (cf. 5.24.14–16). Rejecting their demand for another battle, Belisarius repeats that wars are won through *euboulia* and preparation, not rashness (6.3.23–32). Although there are many cognates of *boule* in his speech, which ends with the emphatic words ἐγὼ πϱονοήσω, he never mentions *tyche*. He begins with the same words that Pericles used to pacify the Athenians and gain support for his cautious strategy when, tired of the Spartan siege, they clamored for decisive action. The allusion is again chosen carefully with an eye to its original context.[88]

Fortune makes her first dramatic appearance as a personal agent during the three-month truce of late 537 to early 538. Introducing the ill-omened confrontation between Belisarius and his officer Constantine, Procopius states that *tyche*, "her envy already swelling against the Romans," wanted to mix some evil in with success (6.8.1).[89] Though this episode did not greatly affect the course of the war, it reminds us of fortune's amoral nature and prepares us for the seemingly senseless turns that the war is about to take (cf. 6.12.34–35). Fortune will enable the Romans to capture the Gothic king and conquer almost all of Italy but will then suddenly reverse her favor and help Totila restore the Gothic kingdom. In other words, fortune's behavior in the broad outline of events conforms exactly to the amoral nature that Procopius ascribes to her in his digressions on particular events. This correspondence between the local and the general phenomenology of fortune indicates that the historian did not believe in the intervention of a benevolent God. Whatever scholars have argued about Procopius' religion, his narrative demonstrates only the power of *tyche*.

At a council in mid-538, Belisarius continues to insist that success up to that point was due to "nothing but *pronoia* and *boule*" (6.18.14); that is, his own. But fortune has begun to usurp the place of virtue. Later that summer, as Belisarius was "deliberating" (*bouleuomenos*) on how to attack Urbino, "a piece of good fortune" befell him again: the town's spring dried up and the garrison surrendered (6.19.11–13; cf. 6.19.18). Chance and Roman virtue contributed equally to the early stages of the siege of Auximum in the spring of 539 (6.23.9–22). At this point, references to the virtue and forethought of Belisarius disappear. Vittigis, whose speeches had stressed *euboulia* and "preparation," is the first to yield and acknowledge the power of fortune, even if only to divert attention away from his own negligence.[90]

Replying to the pleas of those in Auximum, he speciously protests that his "preparations" for their relief were thwarted by the unexpected invasion of the Franks: "for whatever is greater than the power of man exculpates even those who have failed, because *tyche* always bears the blame for what happens in those circumstances" (6.26.11). This view of fortune is consistent with Procopius' usage in the *Vandal War*. For the Gothic king, *tyche* signifies the unexpected arrival of the Frankish host, over which he had no control.

Vittigis was soon besieged in Ravenna by Belisarius, after the surrender of Auximum in late 539. Describing the investment of the capital, Procopius states in his own voice that a fortunate thing happened at that time to the Romans, which "proved that *tyche* was directing the course of events for both sides" (6.28.2). The general Vitalius happened to seize a shipment of grain intended for Ravenna, which had run aground because the river Po had become unnavigable, something that had never happened before (6.28.3–4). This *tyche*, the most important factor in the surrender of the capital, is no supernatural entity but an uncontrollable and unpredictable natural event. When the city's granaries were subsequently destroyed by fire, either by arson or lightning, the Goths decided that God was against them (6.28.25–17). Even Belisarius, realizing that he could now win the war "with no trouble" (6.29.4), began his speech to a council of war by referring to the instability and capriciousness of *tyche* and then attributed to her the present opportunity to terminate the Gothic kingdom (6.29.8–14). His belief that victory is sometimes snatched from the jaws of defeat and defeat is something suffered in the midst of almost certain victory nicely presages what is about to happen in the war after his own departure and the rise of Totila. Yet it is unclear whether Belisarius' insistence on *tyche* in this speech stems from conviction or from the presence of the emperor's representatives.[91] Be that as it may, he continues to insist on making right choices and deliberating for the best.

The narrative peaks with the dramatic entry of Belisarius into Ravenna and the surrender of the Gothic king in May 540. At this climactic moment, Procopius intrudes his own thoughts on the significance of the event, just as he had done when Belisarius entered Gelimer's palace in Carthage:

As I watched the entry of the Roman army into Ravenna, it occurred to me that events are by no means brought about by the wisdom of men or by some other virtue, but that there is a certain *daimonion*, which is always twisting the minds of men and leading them to the point where there can be no hindrance to what is happening. (6.29.32; cf. 3.21.7 on fortune)

Given the dichotomy that Procopius habitually draws between fortune and virtue, and what he has already said about the role of fortune in the capture of Ravenna, there can be little doubt that *daimonion* is here merely a synonym for *tyche*. In the *Secret History*, he states directly that "*tyche* delivered Vittigis over to Belisarius as a captive of war" (4.32). References to *tyche* accordingly become very dense in this part of the narrative and are all linked to the capture of Vittigis. The Goths blame him for bad luck and his nephew Uraias attributes his defeat to *tyche*.[92] His successor Ildibad likewise attributes Vittigis' defeat to "the opposition of *tyche*," whose vicissitudes he discusses in his speech in equal measure to the need for good judgment and planning (6.30.18–24). But the tide of the war is about to turn.

Belisarius' campaigns were favored by fortune from the moment he landed in Sicily to his departure for Constantinople with Vittigis and the royal treasure in tow. However, more important than his luck at Naples and Urbino was his good fortune at Ravenna, which he took swiftly and without a fight. The reader may recall the lengthy digression in the introduction to the *Gothic War* on the city's impregnable defenses, which had enabled Odoacer to hold the place for three years against Theoderic.[93] In this way, as in so many others, the first chapters of the text shape our expectations and condition our reaction to later events. The surrender of 540 was a windfall.

At the same time, we must not overlook the crucial difference between the *Vandal War* and the *Gothic War*. Whereas the defeat of the Vandals was conditioned at almost every turn by fortune, Belisarius' spectacular victory at Rome demonstrated the power of virtue. It is no accident that *tyche* is relatively absent from Procopius' account of the siege. For a memorable year it seemed as though the foresight, daring, and tireless energy of one man could determine the outcome of a war. The encomium of Belisarius that prefaces Book 7 is Procopius' tribute to that year. It should be noted that the siege of Rome is the only specific historical event adduced there as a sign of the general's "virtue" (7.1.21). Along with the rise of *tyche* in the account of the fall of Ravenna, the encomium of Belisarius signals a major turning point in the narrative of the *Gothic War* and, viewed from that perspective, can be characterized as an obituary. Through allusions, Procopius compares the general to Thucydides' Pericles.[94] Belisarius will never again attain those heights, and Procopius will castigate his later campaigns in Italy as disgraceful (7.35.1). The encomium at the beginning of Book 7 marks the passing of Roman virtue, an event understood only in retrospect (cf. 7.1.17). It also effects a transition to a different historical paradigm,

signaled by the contrast between the greatness of Belisarius and the mediocrity of his successors (7.1.23 ff.). This passage is modeled on Thucydides'
obituary of Pericles, which contrasts the great general and leader of Athens
to his petty successors. Although there are numerous verbal parallels, the
main function of the mimesis is primarily structural: Procopius exploits a
crucial transitional passage in a classical source to formally inaugurate a
new phase of the Gothic war.[95]

The encomium of Belisarius is placed at the beginning of Book 7 because it plays a pivotal role in the chiastic metanarrative of the *Gothic War*.
The hero of the second part of the work is the Gothic king Totila, and
Procopius gradually ascribes to him all the virtues listed in Belisarius' encomium, particularly those that pertain to personal nobility.[96] The Goths will
also inherit his *tyche*. Thus, the surrender of Vittigis and the recall of Belisarius trigger a complete reversal in the paradigm of virtue and *tyche*. The
encomium looks forward to the rise of Totila as much as it celebrates the
previous *aristeia* of Belisarius.[97] The narrative moves from Roman strength
under Belisarius and Gothic weakness under Vittigis to Gothic strength
under Totila and Roman weakness under Belisarius' successors. And at the
center of it all is fortune, favoring the winning side—who else?—and, in
fact, effecting the transition between Roman and Gothic supremacy.

The possibility that *tyche* could turn against the Romans was considered by Belisarius, as we saw, even before the surrender of Ravenna (cf.
6.29.8–9). In 542, before the battle of Faventia, the able warrior Artabazes
urged Roman commanders to take action against the Goths, "for when
tyche has led to despair and the destruction of all fair hopes, it turns around
and leads to an excess of daring" (7.4.4). His words fell on deaf ears. He
was killed in single combat "by some chance" (7.4.27), after which Totila
routed and slaughtered the Roman army (7.4.30–32).[98] The officers who
escaped held "whatever cities they happened upon by chance" (7.4.32).
Shortly afterward, the armies clashed near Florence. The Roman generals
agreed to draw lots regarding their strategy "and thus await the decision
(*gnome*) of *tyche* in the matter" (7.5.7). Fortune, it seems, had quite literally
replaced the leadership of Belisarius on the Roman side. Later in the engagement, "by some chance," a false rumor led to the disorderly retreat of
the Roman army and a Gothic victory (7.5.14). Again the fleeing troops
"entered such forts as they chanced upon" (7.5.17)—and also the following
year (7.6.8; cf. 8.32.21). Speaking to the Neapolitans in the spring of 543,
Totila ascribed previous Roman successes to *tyche* and confidently predicted
her imminent change of heart (7.7.15).

Yet Totila does not fully understand the nature of *tyche*, even though, unlike Belisarius, he does not ascribe success to skill. Totila propounds a new interpretive paradigm, which, combined with his splendor as a leader and warrior, enhances the nobility of his cause and cuts the feet from under Justinian's imperialist theology and accusations of "tyranny."[99] Yet Totila's noble faith can only seem tragic to a disillusioned disciple of fortune such as Procopius. The seeds of his ruin are sown even in the first edition of the *Wars*, which ends with his seeming victory. Ultimately, there is no reward for nobility in the world, only the twists and turns of *tyche*.

Before the battle of Faventia in 542, Totila encouraged his troops by adverting to the injustice shown by the Romans toward both Goths and Italians and by claiming enigmatically that the wicked are easier to defeat (7.4.15–17). In 543, having captured Naples and nursed its famished inhabitants back to health, he made his meaning clear by punishing one of his warriors who had raped the daughter of a native Calabrian. In his speech to the Gothic nobility, Totila propounds the view that it was God, offended by the injustice of Theodahad, who previously led the Goths to defeat, calling it "the *tyche* that you well know." But now, having punished them sufficiently, God supports their cause, so much so that they have "chanced" to defeat a stronger enemy. "It is not possible for an unjust man to prosper," he asserts (7.8.21–24), taking at face value the noble lie of the Athenian Stranger in Plato's *Laws* (662b ff., 716a). And in his letter to the Roman Senate, Totila claims that the current bad *tyche* of the Roman forces is due to their wickedness and not to Gothic "virtue," because God is punishing the Romans for their injustice (7.9.13–17). Conventional stuff, to be sure, but redeemed by the impressive fact that Totila practiced what he preached. Both the circumstances of his speech and its content remind us of Belisarius in Libya, who also disciplined his soldiers with severity. And in the very next chapter, Procopius confirms the truth of Totila's accusations by denouncing the lawless behavior of the Roman forces in Italy (7.9.1–6; cf. 7.1.23–33). Yet Totila's speech to the Goths ends with a statement that directly contradicts Procopius' view of the war. He claims that "the *tyche* of warfare is regulated in accordance with the conduct of each" (7.8.24). This implies that *tyche* adheres to moral criteria and implements the will of a just God.[100] Wars can therefore be won through justice. We cannot expect that Procopius will allow this opinion to go unchecked. Totila has seriously misunderstood the nature of *tyche*, even though it is this misunderstanding that makes his tragic nobility possible.

Some years will pass before Totila is disabused, and Procopius must first deal with the return of Belisarius to Italy in 544. We note that the general's views have not changed in the meantime: speaking to an assembly at Ravenna, he insists that the previous Roman success had been due to "virtue"—presumably his own—and he blames the wretchedness of his successors for the subsequent defeats (7.11.2–3). Yet his speech at Ravenna was a failure. The Roman army continued to disintegrate, and Belisarius proved incapable of checking the expansion of Totila's power. Procopius soon demolishes the general's pretensions:

Belisarius repented of having come to Ravenna in the first place. . . . It seemed to me either that he had chosen the worse course, because it was fated at that time for things to go badly for the Romans, or that the best course had indeed been chosen (βεβουλεῦσθαι) by him, but that God, having in mind to assist Totila and the Goths, had stood in his way, so that even the best of Belisarius' plans (βουλεύματα) produced thoroughly bad results. For those upon whom the wind of *tyche* blows favorably[101] will suffer no harm even if they have planned (βουλευόμενοι) poorly, because the *daimonion* brings those things around to an entirely favorable conclusion. But there can be no *euboulia*, I believe, for a man with bad *tyche*, because his evil fate deprives him of knowledge and accurate understanding.[102] Even if he should plan (βουλεύσηται) something well, still *tyche* will immediately blow against him who has so planned (βουλεύσας), reversing his *euboulia* and leading to the worst outcome. (7.13.14–18; cf. *Secret History* 4.42–45)

As with the battles at Decimum, it is pointless to attempt to differentiate among the metaphysical concepts that are jumbled together in this convoluted passage.[103] Fate, God, *tyche*, and the *daimonion* are used interchangeably, as a substitution of all by any one would quickly show. And most scholars who hold the conventional view that Procopius was a conventional Christian do just that: they suppress the references to *tyche* and count only the single reference to God.[104] Yet the question remains whether by *tyche* Procopius means God, or vice versa. Whereas it is easy to understand why a sixth-century author who was not a conventional Christian would find it necessary to obfuscate the supremacy of *tyche* by occasionally intruding "God" into his text, it is not clear why a conventional Christian, and a self-proclaimed expert in theology at that, would produce such a convoluted passage. Be that as it may, it is interesting to note that Procopius endorses the view that God was on Totila's side, a slap in the face to Justinianic ideology. It is not clear, however, that Procopius' God is the same as Totila's. Unlike the king, Procopius says *nothing* about justice. And Totila may yet come around to a different view of God. It is also significant that *boule* is persistently subordinated to factors beyond human control; in conjunction with the actual course of the war, this fact signals the end of the Belisarian paradigm.

What exactly does Procopius mean by *tyche* or God? Is it necessary to view them as supernatural causal agents, or would that be taking their personification too literally? Let us look more closely at what the passage is trying to say. The event in need of explanation is the waxing of the Gothic cause in 544–545. Following the dichotomy postulated in the passage above, its proximate cause is either the folly of Belisarius' decision to remain at Ravenna or the unexpected failure of his otherwise well-conceived plan. Is fortune in turn somehow responsible for those proximate causes or is it instead merely a way of characterizing them from a particular point of view? For example, Totila won either because Belisarius made an error or because Belisarius' sound strategy inexplicably failed. The claim that Totila was favored by fortune means precisely that he had little control over the causes of his own success (cf. 7.13.16). That is why Procopius does not ascribe the resurgence of Gothic power entirely to his virtue or to Belisarius' incompetence. Certainly both factors were involved, but ultimately events were beyond the control of either leader. Hence the reference to fortune, or fate, or "God." We saw in the *Vandal War* that fortune can denote unpredictable or uncontrollable contingencies that in retrospect may seem foreordained. In other words, fortune is a dramatic *characterization* of mundane causal relationships, not an independent causal agent. It is how events seem to those who are affected by them but who cannot control or understand them. Procopius' rhetorical personifications certainly confuse the issue, but they are intended for literary effect and not logical analysis. Besides, it is only by depicting fortune as a supernatural agent equivalent to God that Procopius can elevate her to his level and thereby subvert and displace him.

In his account of the clashes at Rome in 546, Procopius clearly demonstrates that fortune is not a metaphysical causal agent but only a literary way of expressing unpredictable or uncontrollable contingencies. With Totila besieging Rome, held by the Roman Bessas, Belisarius left Isaaces in charge of Portus, under orders not to leave it for any reason, and fought his way through the blockade, almost reaching the walls of the city. "However, because that was not the will of *tyche*, some envious *daimon* intervened and contrived to ruin the Roman cause in the following way" (7.19.22): hearing of Belisarius' success, Isaaces impetuously rushed to attack the Goths himself but was captured, leaving Portus, the only Roman stronghold in the region, undefended. Stunned, Belisarius was forced to retreat to save Portus and his wife. "He was so grieved by the opposition of *tyche* that he fell sick" (7.19.32).

The defeat is ascribed twice to *tyche*, but there is no supernatural causation in this passage. The chain of events is perfectly clear, as is the fact that *tyche* is only a characterization of the actual causes: they were unpredictable and uncontrollable, at least from the point of view of Belisarius, who suffered defeat in the midst of almost certain victory (cf. 6.29.9). Isaaces, by contrast, would have no right to invoke *tyche* to explain what happened to him.[105] It was not just fortune that deserted Belisarius. His faith in his own virtue was also affected: "he was rendered speechless, which indeed had never happened to him before" and was "deeply shaken" (7.19.30–32). The reader may recall that according to the encomium at the beginning of Book 7, these were the very weaknesses to which Belisarius never succumbed (7.1.13–15). The alliance of fortune and virtue that shaped the early years of the war has been completely undone, though it is not replaced by a strictly analogous reformulation on the Gothic side.

After finally capturing Rome, Totila speaks to the Goths and reiterates his belief that God enables the just to win, regardless of their virtue, preparation, and numbers. Justice alone guarantees victory, and Totila never mentions *tyche* (7.21.1–11).[106] Yet fate had a temporary setback in store for the king, which would force him to acknowledge the power of Procopius' goddess. In the spring of 547, Belisarius conceived a plan of such "daring" that at first it seemed "insane," though its outcome was "a sublime and *daimonic* achievement of virtue" (7.24.1).[107] He reoccupied Rome and hastily rebuilt the walls demolished by the Goths, repulsing their fierce attack with great determination and courage (7.24.10–15). Having failed to storm the walls, Totila was reproached by the Gothic nobility for *aboulia*, a highly significant term in this context (7.24.27; cf. 8.32.6–8). Procopius now states that man naturally changes his opinions to conform to the fluctuations of *tyche* so that they always match the outcome of events (7.24.28). It is interesting that this is an opinion that recurs throughout the *Vandal War*.[108] Though Totila would eventually retake the capital in 549 (7.36.1–15), the temporary loss of Rome cost him dearly by damaging his reputation and weakening his position in the eyes of both Goths and Franks, with whom he was then seeking an alliance.[109]

Totila now delivers the longest speech in the *Gothic War*, which is also his last before Book 8. He begins by granting that the Goths are understandably upset about the recent "opposition of *tyche*." He wants to prevent them from showing ingratitude to God. "For it is in the nature of human things to falter," owing to "the necessity imposed by *tyche*" (7.25.4–5). Totila's moral ordering of the world is showing signs of strain. He no longer ascribes success to justice, speaking instead of "experience" and *euboulia*, and revives the distinction between courage and rashness (7.25.10–15; cf. 5.20.8–11). He also revives the familiar distinction between virtue and *tyche*, arguing that if the latter is responsible for success, the Goths ought to "revere" her, lest she be forced to teach them gratitude through some reverse (7.25.17). God is mentioned only in a platitude about human fallibility, without reference to the situation at hand, after which the king attributes at least one of his successes to "both *tyche* and *boule*" (7.25.19–21; cf. 7.12.20, and, of course, 7.40.9). Let us add that in his final speech in Book 8 of the *Wars*, before the fatal battle of Busta Gallorum in 552, Totila never mentions God and attributes everything to *tyche* (8.30.12). And it is no coincidence that Procopius concludes his account of that battle with a digression on the amoral and unpredictable dominion of *tyche* without ever mentioning God (8.32.28–34; see below).

In the course of our analysis, we have formulated some tentative conclusions about the philosophical import of *tyche* and its literary function in the *Wars*. What bears special emphasis is the methodical consistency with which it is deployed. Its distribution and fluctuating levels of prominence carefully reflect the character of the participants and Procopius' outlook on events. *Tyche* can no longer be dismissed as a confused attempt by him to embellish his work with classical concepts but must be viewed as a fundamental component of his narrative strategy.

There are implications here about the speeches in the *Wars*. It is true that, following Thucydides, Procopius does not explore the personalities of his subjects in great depth. A few words outline their virtues and vices, abilities and beliefs.[110] Their speeches likewise follow common rhetorical rules and rely upon a narrow range of vocabulary and *sententiae*. Yet it is wrong to conclude from this that they are "little more than formal exercises" expressing only "conventional sentiments."[111] Procopius is an adept minimalist, choosing his words with economy and deploying them with sober skill. Important differences are conveyed through subtle hints, and in this way the *Wars*, unlike the *Secret History*, does not conform to Nietzsche's notion of decadent writing. Reading it requires patience and attention to detail. Distinct personalities emerge from the speeches that are struggling to shape events in different ways. Their ambitions, plans, and beliefs adopt to the twists of fortune. Belisarius and Totila represent different responses to the war, which the reader must evaluate by scrutinizing their speeches, tracking their use of crucial words, and reading them against the narrative in which they are at all times embedded. In this way, alternative paradigms, for example Belisarius' faith in human planning and Totila's faith in a moral order, are set onto the stage of history and contrasted to Procopius' belief in amoral *tyche*. They are not propositions to which we simply grant or withhold belief. They are indissolubly linked to the character and deeds of their proponents, the history that we are trying to understand.[112] As with Plato's dialogues, speech and action must always be examined together.

Catastrophe in the *Persian War*

Tyche is prominent in the *Persian War* as well, though the different contours and discontinuous history of the war on the eastern frontier did not lend themselves to as smooth and progressive a conceptual development as we find in the *Vandal* and *Gothic War*. To be sure, the basic issues and methods underlying those texts are also present in the *Persian War*, though Procopius has adjusted them to suit the eastern context. In particular, numerous episodes, speeches, and digressions in the *Persian War* highlight the uncertain fate of human beings in a world controlled by the chaotic will of fortune. We will focus here on two passages, the destruction of Antioch by the Persians in the summer of 540 and the great plague of 542, arguably the two most important individual events in the text, and, along with the Nika riots, the most sensational. By swiftly exacting a high death toll and causing widespread destruction, these disasters impressed themselves forcefully upon the minds of contemporaries. Procopius set out to ensure that future generations would not miss their significance. He provides an accurate report of the events, allows us to see how contemporaries experienced and interpreted them, and in each case steps back to offer a perspective of his own. Yet scholars have failed to notice the nuances of his own position, preferring to see him as a conventional sixth-century believer, "a man of his times" who had no choice, it seems, but to attribute those events piously to God.

The sack of Antioch was one of the great disasters of Justinian's reign,[113] and it receives extensive treatment in the *Persian War*. As early as 531, Procopius has al-Mundir, the Saracen Lakhmid king, propose an expedition against the Syrian capital to his master Cavades in a speech that presages later events (1.17.29–39). Though that expedition failed, Procopius devotes a substantial portion of Book 2 to the great invasion of Chosroes, which succeeded in capturing Antioch and other Roman cities. The destruction of the great metropolis becomes a focal point for a number of the broader themes developed in the *Persian War,* for example the decrepit condition of the Roman defenses, the misguided foreign policy of the emperor, and the growing religious tension between the two empires. The otherwise discontinuous narrative of the *Persian War* is unified by the gradual development of these themes, which shape the presentation of events, the content of speeches, and the author's digressions. These issues will be dealt with in a separate study. What interests us here are Procopius' digressions on the natures of *tyche* (2.9.13) and God (2.10.4–5), the first such in the *Wars.* That an ancient historian should invoke fortune or God after recounting the greatest military catastrophe of his age is not surprising. But that he should endorse the supremacy of amoral fortune *and* the providence of a just God is perplexing, to say the least. It has been suggested that Procopius never made "a real effort to reconcile" the two and that the role of *tyche* "should not be over-interpreted." In practice, this seems to mean that scholars can ignore *tyche,* attributing to Procopius only "a statement of uncomprehending faith" or of "blind faith."[114] No one wants to over-interpret a text. But ignoring a contradiction will not make it go away, nor will suppressing Procopius' unequivocal affirmation of an omnipotent and amoral *tyche* in order to arbitrarily designate his ambiguous and "uncomprehending" remarks about God as the true content of his allegedly "blind faith."

The contradiction between *tyche* and God in the account of the fall of Antioch is undeniable. The question is whether Procopius produced it unintentionally by clumsily alternating between a classical "decoration" such as *tyche* and his otherwise conventional belief in the Christian God.[115] That would require him to have been either extremely confused, unable to see a problem that every modern reader with no training in theology can spot in a second—even an indignant Byzantine scribe pointed it out in the margin of a manuscript[116]—or so indifferent to the philosophical coherence of his text that he could jumble together concepts from different schools of thought and even religions.[117] But I hope that this chapter has demonstrated that Procopius deploys terms such as *tyche* and God carefully and that *tyche* is grounded in the factual basis of his narrative in a philosophically coherent way. It seems unlikely that he did not or could not see a contradiction as obvious as this. We are entitled therefore at least to "interpret" his text, if not to "over-interpret" it. Even so, the passages under discussion yield hidden truths on their own, without reliance on conclusions drawn elsewhere.

Procopius invokes fortune in connection with both Chosroes' accession to the throne and his sack of Antioch in 540. Even before mentioning fortune by name, Procopius' language indicates the prominent role that she played in the king's rise. Although he was the third son of Cavades, Caoses, the eldest son, was hated by his father "for no particular reason," while Zames, the second, had been blinded in one eye by the *daimonion*. These accidents placed Chosroes in line for the succession. He was subsequently able to suppress a rebellion "with no difficulty" and execute his evil designs against the Romans "with ease" (2.9.12; cf. 1.11.3–5).[118] We have seen this language used elsewhere in the *Wars* in connection with events attributed to fortune, especially in the *Vandal War* and in connection with Belisarius' conquest of Sicily. It is therefore entirely in keeping with this presentation of the king's rise that Procopius inserts in his account of the destruction of Antioch a long digression on *tyche*, in which he states that she has no regard for what is right or fitting, does not care in the least whether people "blaspheme" her for it,[119] and cannot be stopped once her mind is set (2.9.13). Procopius ends this digression with an odd remark: "but let these matters be in whatever way is pleasing to God."[120] Yet arguably nothing could be more displeasing to God than amoral *tyche*, and Procopius could not have been unaware of the incongruity. His *tyche* is the exact antithesis of God, if by God we mean what most Byzantines did. However, Procopius may be deliberately exploiting the word's inherent polysemy. Although *he* may have believed that there is no God but *tyche*, he also knew that most of his readers would interpret his closing statement as conventionally pious.[121] By seeming to subordinate his views to "God," Procopius softens their radical heterodoxy. Readers not wishing to be discomfited will fasten upon his reassuring disclaimer at the end of the digression and not think again of his peculiar goddess. This hypothesis is not conjectural: many modern scholars do just that. As J. B. Bury wrote of Herodotus, "he was doing what a Christian preacher sometimes does, when having delivered an extremely heterodox sermon he winds up with a formal homage to orthodox dogma."[122]

Procopius is not quite finished with God. At the beginning of the next chapter God is made to send a sign to the Antiochenes foretelling their imminent destruction, but they are not allowed to understand its meaning lest any should escape the city's preordained fate (2.10.1–3). This leads Procopius to express bewilderment at God's actions.

But I become dizzy as I write about such great suffering and transmit it to the memory of future times, and simply cannot understand why God would want to exalt on high the affairs of a man or a place, and then cast them down and obliterate them for no cause that we can see. For it is not lawful to say that he does not always do everything with reason, though at that time he endured watching Antioch dragged down to the ground by a most unholy man. (2.10.4–5)

In other words, Procopius cannot understand why God behaved so much like *tyche*. Whereas God is supposed to "do everything with reason," on this occasion he acted "for no cause that we can see," randomly exalting and then overthrowing both people and places, exactly as fortune is said to do elsewhere.[123]

Does this uncomprehending attitude reveal Procopius' "blind faith" or is it a rhetorical strategy for discreetly denying God's benevolence? The former position is untenable. First, it requires the arbitrary suppression of everything that Procopius says about *tyche*. His remarks about her power and amorality are unequivocal. His remarks about God, however, are entirely ambiguous. He never actually endorses the view that God "always does everything with reason" but merely claims that it is not "lawful" (θέμις) to deny it.[124] This statement probably contains another allusion to Socrates' *Apology* (21b), where the philosopher claims that it is not "lawful" for Apollo to speak falsehoods but responds to his oracle by immedietely trying to refute it! In fact, the whole point of Procopius' digression is precisely that God had no apparent reason for destroying Antioch, a city that ironically had once worshipped its Tyche above all other deities, but had been renamed Theoupolis ("City of God") after an earthquake in 528 to avert divine wrath.[125] Though Procopius knew about the Antiochenes' infamous love of luxury, license, and discord,[126] he does not cite it here as a possible ground for divine displeasure. He suggests *no* possible motives for God's decision, not even the "sins of mankind," the conveniently general target of many Christian moralists. As it happens, we are told elsewhere that shortly before the Persian invasion, God in a vision had revealed to St. Symeon the Stylite his intention to destroy Antioch for its "lawless behavior" and pagan practices.[127] Procopius' silence regarding God's motives suggests that the established custom of attributing "reason" to God is misguided, and, if that is the case, then God is no different from *tyche*. Hence Procopius understandably makes no attempt to "reconcile" the two.

Those who attribute blind faith to Procopius ask us to believe that he could discourse on the unrivaled power of amoral *tyche*, produce a narrative that displays that power in action, and imply that even God on this occasion acted like *tyche*, all in order to express his "blind faith" in the Christian God, which he does by claiming *not* to know why God acted so arbitrarily! This stretches the credulity of the reader—and of Procopius— too far. Let us be clear about just how blind this faith would have to be: it entails nothing less than the unconditional surrender of reason to the blind belief in the benevolence of an inscrutable divine will. This does not sound like the author of the *Wars*, and few Christian thinkers went that far. Most were quick to identify the cause of God's displeasure when disaster struck.[128] After all, man must have *some* idea of God's will, otherwise he cannot conform to it.[129] Yet Procopius draws no moral lessons from the fall of Antioch, which is exactly what we expect of a man who believed that the world is governed by amoral fortune.

Procopius' incomprehension operates on two levels. If God is understood as *tyche*, it is perfectly straightforward and sincere, because by definition no one may comprehend her mind. In Book 8 he marks the passing of Totila by digressing again on how *tyche* randomly exalts people only to destroy them later for no reason. This is exactly what "God" did to Antioch. "But these things, I believe, have never been understood by man, nor will they ever be in the future" (8.32.30). On a different level, his incomprehension is part of a rhetorical strategy designed to draw the reader's attention to the contradiction between the traditional belief in God's reason and the apparent randomness and injustice of events in the world. This was not an argument that Procopius could formulate openly, and it was only by a disingenuous pretense of perplexity that he could reveal its premises. Christians were quite open about their intention to "smash to bits" anyone who "makes war against the providence of God" and to "bring him into submission to Christ."[130] So he leaves a pointed question deliberately unresolved, allowing his readers to draw the necessary conclusions. This was a ploy employed by many skeptics: "in these times when we cannot talk about the world except with danger, or falsely," wrote Montaigne, "you must stoop to the level of the people you are with, and sometimes affect ignorance."[131]

The apparent conflict between events such as the destruction of Antioch and the presumed benevolence of an omnipotent God is still debated today in the philosophy of religion as the "problem of evil." It was succinctly stated in antiquity by Epicurus, reformulated by the Skeptic philosopher Sextus Empiricus as an argument against the existence of God, and concisely summarized by David Hume: "Is he willing to prevent evil, but not able? then is he impotent. Is he able, but not willing? then is he malevolent. Is he both able and willing? whence then is evil?"[132] Procopius, of course, did not believe in a malevolent deity, merely an indifferent one. The early Christian writer Lactantius, who attempted to refute Epicurus, raised that possibility when he confessed that "many of the philosophers who defend Providence are often troubled by this argument and are compelled in spite of themselves to admit that God does not care about anything."[133] Ancient theologians produced no satisfactory solution to this problem, which their modern counterparts have tackled with renewed vigor. A careful study of the Greek Fathers has concluded that they failed to "appreciate the contradictions involved" and that their rhetorical attempts to explain the existence of evil in a world created by a benevolent deity were bound to result in philosophical incoherence.[134]

Before examining Procopius' exposition of the problem of evil in connection with the plague, it is worth looking at a speech given by Chosroes to the emperor's representatives after the capture of Antioch (2.9.1–6). This speech, which occurs right before the digression on *tyche*, is interesting because it again illuminates Procopius' methods. The king's words must be read cautiously, because Procopius accuses him immediately afterward of being a skilled liar and adept at feigning piety (2.9.8). This accusation is directed against his closing statement that he had tried to save the city's populace, who had resisted him with suicidal fury, because "it is not holy to trample upon those who have been captured" (2.9.6). The speech is appropriately chauvinistic and self-righteous, but that does not mean that it is entirely false. It so happens that the truth, or Procopius' version of it, is expressed there, though naturally from the king's point of view. Chosroes begins by quoting an "old saying" that God never grants any good without mixing it with evil (2.9.1).[135] This, of course, is exactly what Procopius later says about *tyche* (6.8.1). The king then boasts that Antioch fell "with no difficulty at all, because God contrived at a moment's notice to grant us victory" (2.9.3). This may seem tendentious on the theological side, but it presages Procopius' argument that *tyche* made everything easy for Chosroes (2.9.12–13). In other words, while the speech coats the king's aggression with pious words, it simultaneously hints at the Procopian truth about the deity that really secured his rise and victory. The speech is therefore artfully contrived for ironic effect, because only the reader and Procopius know the true nature of that deity. This speech, like so many others in the *Wars*, preserves the speaker's character while offering a partial version of the truth.

* * *

The problem of evil is also central to Procopius' account of the sixth-century plague, which, as is well known, is modeled on Thucydides' account of the plague in Athens. Crucial differences between the two texts indicate that here too Procopius' mimesis did not alter the facts of his own age.[136] Both authors describe the symptoms of the disease with medical precision while refusing at the outset to speculate on its natural causes.[137] Classifying it among those things sent "by heaven," Procopius denies that anyone understood its scientific, "physiological" causes. Though such "sophistic" explanations were set forth, he does not discuss them, preferring to "refer the whole matter to God" (2.22.1–2; cf. 2.22.18). And that is also where many scholars have left the issue of his beliefs, especially as there is no comparable statement in his classical model.[138] Surely the mention of God reflects the difference between the Christian views of Procopius and those of Thucydides, who adamantly "refused to explain the march of historical events by reference to divine intervention."[139] Perhaps, however, it represents not a different belief but a difference in strategy for dealing with a very different intellectual climate. Unlike the Athenians, the Byzantines had definite views about God and seemed to agree that he was responsible for the plague. In his edicts, Justinian confidently identified the causes of "famine, earthquake, and pestilence" as blasphemy and sodomy, which "incur the just anger of God."[140] Others ascribed plague to the "wrath of God," which sought to punish mankind for its sins.[141] The rationale behind such beliefs was stated clearly by the fifth-century theologian Theodoret of Cyrrhus: "I believe that the God of all is caring for the common salvation when he inflicts misfortunes upon some, in order to acquaint sinners with the medicine that averts evil, to provide an opportunity for champions of virtue to persevere, and to furnish a beneficial example to all observers. For we are such that we fill up with fear when we behold others being punished."[142] Both Thucydides and Procopius were interested in the irrational beliefs and abnormal behavior elicited by plagues, so their discussions of the symptoms are as much sociological as medical.[143] Whereas the credulity that Thucydides witnessed took the form of oracles and ancient prophesies (2.54), Procopius had to confront the implacable logic of punitive theology. Though his account ultimately undermines the foundations of that belief, because he lived in an intolerant theocracy, he could not be as openly critical of it as Thucydides had been of his compatriots' interest in oracles. His account therefore begins piously, by vaguely ascribing the plague to God. But "God" is a notoriously polysemic word. It can make Procopius seem orthodox while simultaneously acting as a surrogate for *tyche*, a device we have seen in the *Wars*. Once again, it is not clear which God Procopius has in mind here. We must carefully follow the sequence of his exposition.

Having ascribed the plague to God, Procopius proceeds to describe how it killed indiscriminately, not only without regard for its victims' location, age, and nature, but also without regard for their character and lifestyle (2.22.3–5). Adapting Thucydides' comments on the inefficacy of religious measures, Procopius adds that even those who invoked divine names and sought refuge in churches were destroyed wholesale.[144] Yet we know that those were precisely the remedies prescribed by the Church and practiced by the populace of the Christian empire in times of distress, including this plague. In the seventh century, for example, Bishop John of Thessaloniki claimed that during the plague of 586, almost all who sought refuge in the church of St. Demetrius were saved, while those who stayed home died.[145] Other examples can be offered, though it should be noted that Procopius' younger contemporary, the ecclesiastical historian Evagrius, avoided making any connection between morality and mortality in his own account of the plague (4.29).

Not only does Procopius reveal the inefficacy of religious responses to the plague, but, following Thucydides, he also discusses its injurious moral effects. He explains that terror caused wicked men to act piously, but only temporarily, for they reverted to even more wicked lives after the danger had passed (2.23.14–16). These men had not been transformed into genuine "lovers of virtue," something impossible in so short a time "unless one is inspired by some divine influence for good." So it seems that the "God" who caused the plague provided no such influence. Procopius thereby tacitly refutes the notion that the plague was sent to correct the moral faults of men. He then exacerbates the contradiction by adding that "the plague, whether by some chance (*tyche*) or providence (*pronoia*), carefully chose the most wicked men and allowed them to live" (2.23.16)—hardly the Christian God! One interesting note is that he says on the next page that Justinian contracted the disease but survived (2.23.20). We also note that, having reached the end of his account, Procopius openly proposes *tyche* as an alternative explanation to *pronoia*,[146] a predictable development to anyone familiar with his bag of tricks.

If Procopius' account of the plague is read without religious preconceptions—and without historicist preconceptions about his religion—its logic and aims are not difficult to discern. The historian begins by paying lip service to the prevailing belief among his contemporaries, but his subsequent account criticizes it thoroughly. He never mentions the "wrath of

God" or attributes the plague to the sins of men, who were its victims, not its cause (cf. 2.9.8). He makes it clear that the plague killed with no regard for justice, even adding rhetorically that it tended to spare the wicked. This amazing and clearly tendentious statement would have no point if Procopius did not intend to reveal the absurdity of ascribing the plague to God, who supposedly wants to make human beings more, not less, moral. And it is no coincidence that he inserts into his text at this very point a rare statement linking divinity to the "love of virtue," which amplifies the incoherence of popular perceptions. Procopius is encouraging his readers to question the basis of punitive theology by providing them with the premises necessary to draw a very different conclusion. The ambiguity of his account is compounded at the end by the inclusion of *tyche* as an alternative explanation to *pronoia*, and careful readers of the *Wars* may notice that in describing the plague's symptoms Procopius uses technical terms that characterize the actions of *tyche* elsewhere.[147] As the ecclesiastical historian Socrates realized, misfortunes that occur because of *tyche* cannot by definition be understood as punishments for sins.[148]

Though Procopius may have disagreed with his contemporaries, and tried to correct them discreetly, he should not necessarily be seen as a lone skeptic in an age of universal faith. Agnosticism was a prominent feature of the Greek philosophical tradition and could infect all who were exposed to it. Thucydides, for instance, "marks the beginning of a tradition of skeptical positivism that limits itself to describing facts and refuses to draw conclusions about causes."[149] Procopius refused to speculate on the natural causes of the plague not because he believed that there were none but because he did not know what they were and did not accept the physiologists' theories. This is a fully scientific stance. He knew and elsewhere stated that the causes of some phenomena may elude even such thinkers as Aristotle (8.6.19–24). It is here, regarding the idea of scientific progress, that Procopius makes his only positive reference to innovation: too many people, he says, are content with ancient accounts and no longer search for the truth through new arguments.[150] Lest anyone assume, however, that by "truth" he means what most of his contemporaries meant, he specifies that "I am not talking about intelligible or intellectual matters or other such invisible things, but about rivers and lands" (8.6.9–10). Metaphysics makes way for scientific progress and skepticism, and this in an age when Anthemius, the architect of Hagia Sophia, was performing experiments with steam power in his basement.[151] This priority complements the nearly complete rejection of theology at the beginning of the *Gothic Wars*. It is no surprise, then, that Procopius' account of the plague contains "the most systematic report of the symptoms."[152]

Procopius was not posing as a classical historian. It was his pietism that was affected. In his attitudes, intellectual aims, and beliefs, he was more distant from the ecclesiastical writers of his own age than even the formal classicism of his language suggests.[153] But the empire's educated classes were probably permeated by attitudes such as his. It is the disproportionate survival of ecclesiastical literature—whether by *tyche* or *pronoia*—that lends an aura of universal pietism to the age of Justinian.

Yet fragments of a dissident tradition survive, and future studies will doubtless expand the circle of Procopius' fellow travelers. Another of Thucydides' most astute sixth-century students was Agathias, who idolized Procopius and called him the most learned man of the age.[154] Agathias desired to imitate Thucydides, but as Procopius had already done so with regard to the plague, he applied the familiar classical model for natural disasters to the earthquakes of the 550s. In doing so, he carefully mixed Thucydidean rationalism with Procopian dissimulation. He is agnostic with respect to causes (2.15.9–13, 5.6–8), notes that those who sought refuge in churches were not spared (2.16.3),[155] and describes the irrational behavior of the populace, noting that conversions proved fleeting and insincere once the terror subsided (5.3–5). Like Procopius, his ascription of events to God is exoteric. He even suggests openly that such beliefs are false and subtly offers alternative, rational explanations based on his view of "nature." He openly invokes the idea of the Noble Lie to explain why he endorses pietism, given that he does not believe in it himself. Agathias is as explicit as can be expected about his intentions.[156] It is only the historicist imperative to view him as a "conventional" Christian that has led scholars to pass over all these fascinating passages in his work with scarcely a glance. This prejudice has robbed us of the intellectual diversity of the sixth century and has reduced Procopius, one of the great historians of antiquity and arguably the most powerful mind of his century, to yet another bland "product of his age."[157]

Tyche and God in Book 8 of the *Wars*

The equation of *tyche* and God is made in an amusing way in Book 8 of the *Wars*, and it is worth looking briefly at this passage because it shows how Procopius used *tyche* to undermine Justinian's propaganda. By speaking out of both sides of his mouth, he managed to treat imperial propaganda ironically and criticize it while simultaneously feigning piety. Concluding his account of the battle of Busta Gallorum of 552, he again digresses on how *tyche*, "giving herself airs and tearing human affairs to shreds,"[158] caused Totila's fall in a manner unworthy of his deeds, after having granted him prosperity for so many years "for no reason whatsoever." He refers to her "irrationality" and "unpredictability," highlighting her capriciousness and indifference to virtue (8.32.28–29). On the next page, he cites an alternative version of the king's death, according to which he was killed by an arrow, "not by the archer's intention" but because "*tyche* directed the shaft toward the man's body" (8.32.34).[159] Yet at the beginning of the next chapter, he states that Narses was so elated by victory that "he would not cease attributing everything to God," a view that Procopius now endorses as "true" (8.33.1)! But the God of Narses cannot be the capricious *tyche* just described on the previous page. The historian's agreement with Narses is ironic, for the general does not know what we do, namely that the "God" responsible for Roman victory was fortune. Far from indicating Procopius' "warm allegiance to Christianity,"[160] Narses' belief illuminates the cryptic remark made by Procopius at the end of his previous digression on the unpredictability of fortune:

But these things, I believe, have never been understood by man, nor will they ever be in the future. Yet there is always talk about them and opinions are endlessly passed around in whispers, in whatever way is pleasing to each, as he comforts his ignorance with whatever explanation seems reasonable to him. (8.32.30)

Writing soon after the event, Procopius preemptively discredits all attempts to make moral sense of the fate of Totila, dismissing them as comforting "whispers" and ignorant rationalizations. In the flush of victory, Narses was the first to venture such an opinion, though he was not to be the last. As Procopius doubtlessly realized, sectarian polemic and imperial propaganda would have their say. In a Pragmatic Sanction of 554, the year Procopius completed Book 8, Justinian remarked that the restoration of Italy and the destruction of the "tyrant" Totila were due to "God, propitious to Our Empire."[161] Toward the end of the century, the ecclesiastical historian Evagrius reported that Narses had triumphed over the Goths by honoring God and receiving detailed military instructions from the Virgin Mary (4.24). Later western writers were certain that it was God who defeated the heretical tyrant.[162] If Procopius did not have precisely such beliefs in mind when he dismissed comforting rationalizations, then what did he have in mind? There is no other reaction in the record. His defense of ignorance makes sense only if he believed that the world was governed by an utterly inscrutable power such as fortune but knew that other views would be expressed. Though the Christian God was considered by many of his worshipers to be inscrutable, they were quite ready to read his mind with certainty whenever enemies such as Totila were destroyed or when plagues carried off thousands. "Truly it has not happened by chance," wrote Alcuin in the late eighth century about a Viking raid, "but is a sign that it was well merited by someone."[163] Apophatic theology was for the books. Procopius knew what he was talking about.

As though to restore the balance, the chapter that begins with Narses' "true belief" ends with yet another digression on the fickleness of fortune. The general's recapture of Rome by the imperial troops leads Procopius to reflect on

> how *tyche* mocks human affairs, not always visiting people in the same manner nor regarding them with uniform glance, but changing along with time and place; and she plays some kind of game with them, changing the value of these miserable wretches in accordance with the times or the place or the circumstance. (8.33.24)[164]

Thus the true belief of Narses is flanked by two forceful declarations on *tyche*, which indicate that the higher power controlling events was of an entirely different nature than Christ. Again, readers who wish to view Procopius as a conventional Christian may disregard his discussions of fortune and seize upon his agreement with Narses as proof. Such tactics merely satisfy—and expose—a priori assumptions. In reality, Procopius viewed the world as governed by no God but *tyche*. He felt so strongly about this that at the close of the same chapter he dared to again revise the verdict of Thucydides, namely that human nature is the chief force in history. Again he uses the exact words of the Athenian historian with one minor, albeit crucial, change: "But this is the way things have been from the beginning and will always be, so long as the *tyche* of mankind remains the same" (8.33.25).[165]

The digression on the death of Totila in Book 8 exemplifies at least two of the techniques by which Procopius insinuates the identity of God and fortune. He often attributes events to fortune in his own voice on one page and then to God on the next (usually through one of his characters); alternately, he describes *tyche* in the same language that he uses elsewhere for God. The latter has been observed by many scholars, though its implications have never been fully appreciated.[166] In two nearly identical passages, placed in two different contexts, Procopius comes close to affirming the equation openly and in his own voice.

Human affairs are governed not according to opinions of men, but by the inclination (ῥοπή) of God, which people are accustomed to call *tyche*, because they do not know the reason why events happen in the way in which they appear to them. For the name of *tyche* tends to attach itself to that which seems to be beyond calculation (παράλογος). But let each believe about these things whatever seems pleasing to him. (8.12.34–35; *Secret History* 4.44–45)[167]

This was the most that could be said safely. Procopius avoids stating the equation directly, first by referring not to God as such but to his ῥοπή and then by ascribing the whole notion vaguely to popular opinion, though, we note, the latter happens to match exactly Procopius' practice throughout the *Wars*. Fortune is then linked to that which people cannot understand. All this is highly tendentious, for it collapses the difference between chance and a God who is completely inscrutable, however benevolent he is presumed to be by others. The possibility is suggested that God, like *tyche*, is nothing more than a name that is used for events that cannot be explained rationally.[168] Even the term that Procopius uses to designate God's inclination—ῥοπή—connotes ambivalence and was used by other writers to refer to *tyche*.[169] We are reminded of Procopius' false amazement that God destroyed Antioch "for no apparent reason" (2.10.4–5). His God *is* fortune—not Christ—and she is the only higher power affecting the course of history.

Precedents and Conclusions

The prominence of fortune in Procopius' work poses complex hermeneutical challenges. The concept itself is at once ambiguous and profound, qualities reflected in its long history in ancient literature and religion. I have attempted to identify its primary ontological meaning in the *Wars* while respecting the wide range of its uses. I also examined the rhetorical mechanisms by which Procopius integrates *tyche* into his narrative. The argument has established the historian's rejection of the dominant Christian modes of thought of his time, which were endorsed by Justinian and a host of ecclesiastical and monastic writers. Yet it has isolated him from the general context of Greek thought. This is not necessarily a flaw in the argument, for the *Wars*, as a carefully written work of literature, must be read and evaluated primarily on its own terms. Yet our understanding of Procopius as an ancient historian would be deficient if we did not locate his usage of *tyche* within the broad spectrum of ancient thought and practice. This enterprise, however, is hampered by the lack of a proper history of fortune in antiquity.[170] Such a work would have to engage a vast and diverse body of evidence, including literary texts, official documents, cultic practices, inscriptions, and figures of speech, each of which has to be evaluated in its historical context as well as with regard to its internal aims and conventions. Up to the 1960s, the philological side of the problem was more popular than it is now, and many articles were published on Fortuna in various authors. Since then, however, scholars have lost interest in such timeless abstract concepts and seek to interpret literature in terms of its concrete political and social background. Fortune is now downplayed or ignored, even in texts like Procopius' where it is obviously important.

The current consensus maintains that in Procopius *tyche* is merely rhetorical, a position required by the belief that he was a conventional Christian. Indeed, many of his contemporaries held religious beliefs that precluded any independent role for such an entity but still used *tyche* for rhetorical effect. If we consider single passages taken out of context from the orators of Gaza, the poet Corippus, or the historian Theophylact, their references to *tyche* seem similar to those in Procopius.[171] Such comparisons, however, occlude the fact that in their works fortune occurs rarely or has little interpretive weight. Only in Procopius does she call for interpretation on all levels: his abstract digressions are faithful to the details of his narrative and highlight important events and transitions; his patterns of thought and literary methods are constant throughout the *Wars*; and, most significant, it can be argued that amoral fortune is fundamental to his view of history. In the Christian classicism of the sixth century, *tyche* never comes as close to usurping the place of God as she does in the *Wars*.

In this respect, Procopius is also different from the pagan historians of late antiquity, for example Ammianus Marcellinus, Olympiodorus, and Zosimus, who recognized *tyche* but did not make her supreme. In them she is one divine being among others (though one scholar argued that Procopius too believed in both *tyche* and God).[172] Ammianus is especially interesting because he refers to fortune often and with the same variety of meanings. But he also refers to a wide range of other divine powers. His religious beliefs have proven very difficult to identify and disentangle from his "elaborate literary gestures."[173] Again, "literary" does not mean superficial.

There is in fact only one Greek historian, Polybius, whose awe for the power of fortune is comparable to that of Procopius. Fortune in the *Histories* has "a variety of meanings operating at different levels of intensity."[174] According to Polybius, historians may legitimately ascribe to "God and *tyche*" only events whose causes are unknown, for example plagues and bad weather, and he criticizes those who refer to *tyche* instead of searching for the causes.[175] It is not entirely clear, however, that he himself adhered to those rules. He ascribes to fortune events such as the rise of Rome (1.4.4–5), which he believed could be explained rationally (1.63.9). Another problem is presented by his references to *tyche* as a conscious divine agent. It is one thing to use the term as a label for inexplicable events and quite another to believe that she was a goddess. Scholars have not yet agreed about whether this language should be taken literally or whether it is a rhetorical convention.[176] There is one more complication. Polybius scarcely veils his lack of belief in other gods, treating God, *tyche*, and *daimonion* as equivalent terms, the last, as in Procopius' *Wars*, designating the higher power in its punitive capacity.[177] In the *Histories*, however, fortune sometimes promotes justice but is more often capricious, which has been called "fundamentally contradictory."[178] Thus, there is a tension in Polybius between moral and amoral instances of fortune, just as there is a prima facie tension in Procopius between fortune and God. In the *Wars* fortune never acts in the interests of justice.

In Procopius, at any rate, personification is not a problem. It was part of what Schopenhauer called "the playful urge of the Greeks to personify everything."[179] The ecclesiastical historian Evagrius described *kairos* ("opportune moment"), a Christian surrogate for *tyche*, as swiftly evading pursuers in flight and laughing at them from above. This was a literary device—"rhetorical self-indulgence," according to one commentator—that was inspired by an artistic image, which Evagrius describes.[180] Statues of Tyche could likewise be seen throughout the Roman world, including in Procopius' own Caesarea.[181] It is highly unlikely that Christian vandals had destroyed them all by the sixth century. The historian Theophylact mentions a Tychaeum still standing in Alexandria in the early seventh century with its statues intact.[182] Such images reinforced the tendency to personify *tyche* in literature. Cicero recognized this explicitly: "Very likely we Romans imagine gods as you say, because from our childhood Jupiter, Juno [et al.], have been known to us with the aspect with which painters and sculptors have chosen to represent them."[183] Procopius no more believed in a playful, capricious *tyche* than Evagrius did in a flying, laughing *kairos*. The trend culminated in Machiavelli's infamous claim that fortune is a woman who allows herself to be beaten and subdued by impetuous young men.[184]

Yet the personification of *tyche* plays an important tactical role in the *Wars* that goes beyond "playful urges" and figures of speech. By casting her as a conscious divine agent, Procopius deliberately elevated her to the level of God, who was, in the sixth century, the dominant contender for the explanatory function that he wanted to ascribe to a different set of causal factors. To displace God, *tyche* had to rival him in standing. That is why the two are so jumbled together in those rambling digressions and described in the same terms. Mystification was as far as Procopius dared to go.

On the other hand, Greek religious practice and thought does not elucidate Procopius' idea of fortune. Granted, in the Hellenistic and Roman periods, her cult was popular and Tyche had even been "the most venerated deity" in his own city of Caesarea.[185] But her worship was hopeful and aimed to secure prosperity in a chaotic world. She was a savior from whom good things were requested, even if, as with all gods, they were not always received. Simplicius observed that "the many say that everything is *tyche* and pray to the gods for good fortune," and other writers viewed fortune as a force for good.[186] In the *Wars*, however, *tyche* is neither good nor just: she destroys hope and confidence, requires no worship, and cannot be thanked or appeased. One has to turn to the Aztecs to find actual gods who were "caprice embodied" and people who felt a "powerless dependence" on forces entirely beyond their control.[187]

When all is said and done, there is nothing supernatural about the way *tyche* operates in the *Wars*. It is a way of characterizing events that seem extraordinary or are not expected by those affected by them but whose causes are otherwise mundane. It was easy to see this even in antiquity, and Christians were eager to do so. Many cited approvingly the verses of the comic poet Philemon: "There does not exist for us any such god as *tyche*; it simply doesn't exist. But spontaneity, that which happens by chance to each, is called *tyche*."[188] For the ontology of *tyche* in Procopius we must look beyond Greek religion and the rhetorical conventions of late antiquity.

That ontology is found in Thucydides. The view that his use of *tyche* reflects a religious outlook has long been abandoned for a more "descriptive and analytical" approach.[189] Thucydides, awed by reason, did not regard *tyche* as the engine of history and felt no urge to personify her. But he could not ignore the unexpected, that which creates a gap between planning and history. That is all that fortune is for him.[190] Philosophers soon produced theoretical discussions. In his *Physics*, Aristotle gave a naturalistic ontology of chance and spontaneity: whereas *tyche* designates the unintentional, "accidental" consequences of otherwise deliberate actions, the *automaton* refers to the unpredictable effects of causal chains beyond deliberation, such as the actions of animals and natural events (2.4–6).[191] Chance is therefore inscrutable by definition. Both Procopius and Aristotle call it *paralogos*. Aristotle's definitions were discussed and excerpted frequently in later times[192] and were happily accepted by some Christians, who liked their philosophy purged of paganism. Nemesius, Bishop of Emesa in the fourth century, defined *tyche* as "the coincidence and concurrence of two causes which have as their original intention something other than what actually comes to be."[193] This definition, which can be accepted even today, represents the ontological core of Procopius' conception of *tyche*, a core preserved relatively intact, I have argued, despite its literary embellishment and the cultural and religious polemic in which it is embedded.

By itself Procopius' notion of *tyche* is neither religious—though it affects religion—nor philosophically profound. No overarching philosophy of history can be based on it. The supremacy of fortune means that people have limited control over the circumstances of their lives and that history has no intrinsic moral significance. The first position in particular is not one that we are inclined to accept today. Bury was right to contrast the ancient fascination with *tyche* to modern notions of progress,[194] which, since the days of Machiavelli and Bacon, explicitly call for the conquest of both nature and chance.

Still, in Procopius' hands, fortune becomes a powerful weapon of cultural polemic and an expression of political dissidence that is inseparable from his overall performance of classicism. This book has argued that in its most sophisticated forms, late antique and Byzantine classicism was not a matter of mere words and phrases, the external veneer of an otherwise typical Christian mentality. By the way in which he set about describing and interpreting his changing world, Procopius declared his belief in the continued relevance of classical modes of thought. This implied a rejection of the cultural trends of his time, which were gradually creating a more biblical and authoritarian culture. On one level, this stance was artistic, yet it did have philosophical and political implications. Christians believed that chance was only apparent, for divine providence, albeit inscrutable, really governed all events in the world, even the cruel and the unjust. For Justinian, this meant divine sanction for imperial aggression. The narrative of the *Wars*, however, toys with these notions and ultimately rejects them.

Fortune also poses moral problems. To be sure, Procopius does not propose a new vision for human life. Yet he neither despairs nor exults in the face of fortune. Virtue is not entirely powerless, as Belisarius demonstrated in the initial phases of the Italian war. And some rulers, for example Theoderic and Gaizeric, maintained their hold on power throughout their long reigns. But Procopius' response to the problem of fortune should not be sought in these exceptional and ambiguous figures. Belisarius' triumph proved fleeting, and the reigns of the barbarian warlords were but preludes to a series of destructive wars from which only fortune emerged victorious. The *Vandal War* concentrates on the fate of the defeated mediocrity Gelimer, and the later books of the *Gothic War* revolve around the tragic career of the noble Totila.

Unlike Machiavelli, Procopius proposes no scheme by which fortune can be mastered. Instead, through his comments on the moral qualities of individuals, which are numerous if laconic, firm and yet full of sympathy, he gently educates his readers about how to behave in a world ruled by fortune. In this way, in the *Wars* he upholds traditional Hellenic virtues: courage in war, justice in politics, moderation in victory, honor and compassion in dealing with others, and dignity in the face of misfortune. And let us not omit Platonic wisdom, a hitherto neglected aspect of his thought. It is piety, to which so much attention has been paid recently, that has little or no place in his list. Chance may undermine ideology but does not change the ethical requirements of political life. In the *Secret History*, Belisarius is ridiculed for not doing what was expected of any honorable man. Justinian is castigated for creating an unjust regime that robbed men of their dignity through both complicity and victimization. As Eunapius had noted, "man is a creature more likely to slip and fall in the face of honor than of misfortune" (fr. 57).

The historian exemplified the virtues he praised and demanded in others. He treated Romans and barbarians impartially, condemning the former as often as he praised the latter. He did not glorify mere success, showing compassion for defeated kings and, especially, for the civilians who suffered in the wars instigated by others. He condemned military aggression, though he was not immune to the charms of military glory. He dared to argue, writing under Justinian, that religion was not worth fighting over. He was the only subject of the Roman empire to write an impartial and even critical history of a reigning emperor; who publicly exposed the crimes, corruption, and incompetence of imperial officials; who glorified the official enemies of the state; and who risked his life to condemn the regime of Justinian and his wife. If anything testifies to the ability of human beings to maintain honor and dignity in a world ruled by chance and tyranny, it is the humanity and the histories of Procopius of Caesarea.

Appendix 1. Secret History *19–30 and the Edicts of Justinian*

This appendix is not a historical commentary on the later chapters of the *Secret History*, although it offers a blueprint for one, by showing that those chapters were written in direct response to Justinian's legislation. Not all can be paired up with extant edicts, but in most cases Procopius is referring to specific laws that have been lost. In particular, few pragmatic sanctions have survived, and many reforms were no doubt effected in that way.

Not all edicts were written by Justinian himself, although of course they were all promulgated under his name, with his approval and authority. In some chapters Procopius discusses in detail the character of his quaestors and prefects, but this too is directly relevant to the legal slant of the work, because they were the magistrates who drafted Justinian's legislation, received it, and enforced it (to the degree that it was enforced).

Unless otherwise noted, all edicts cited below were issued before the *Secret History* was finished.

19.11, 20.9: pretexts for prosecution: heresy, pederasty, sexual relations with nuns. For nuns, see *CJ* 1.3.53, 9.13.1; *Novels* 123.43, 37. For sexual crimes, *Novels* 77, 141 (date 559); cf. Malalas 18.18. For heretics, see esp. *CJ* 1.5.12–22; *Novels* 3.1, 37, 42.3.2, 43, 45, 109, 131.14, 132. Procopius also gives (once each) polytheism, *stasis*, favoring the Greens, and insulting the emperor. For the latter, see Malalas 18.22. For polytheism, see esp. *CJ* 1.5.18.4–5; Malalas 18.42, 18.136 (date 561).

20.1–4: the city prefect relaxed price controls and shared in the profits (this was his initiative, not the emperor's). *Novel* 122 (addressed to the city prefect) caps prices for services and goods, blaming merchants and artisans for charging too much (perhaps a result of the plague). This may have been Justinian's response to the actions of his prefect, but we do not know how vigorously it was enforced. Justinian may have been concerned for the people or may have wanted to placate widespread discontent (see chapter 4, fourth section).

20.5: Justinian established and farmed out monopolies (cf. 26.19). Monopolies are the subject of *CJ* 4.59, but no legislation by Justinian on this topic has survived.

20.7–12: Justinian invented two new offices, the praetor of the people and the quaesitor (cf. 11.37, 16.19, 18.33). Cf. *Novels* 13, 14, and 80 (see chapter 4, fourth section).

20.13–15: Justinian allowed the city prefect, the prefect of the people, and the quaesitor to prosecute all crimes regardless of jurisdiction. No edict specifically mandating this has survived, but provision is made in edicts dealing with the specific crimes Procopius has in mind (e.g., *CJ* 9.13.1).

20.15–23: character and misdeeds of Justinian's quaestors.

21.1–4: *aerikon* tax. The edict has been lost. For the tax, see Haldon (1994).

21.4–8: character and misdeeds of Justinian's praetorian prefects; also 22.1–35 (for the grain supply to the capital, cf. *CJ* 10.27.2).

21.9–25: sale of offices. Cf. *Novel* 8 (see chapter 4, fourth section).

22.36–37: Peter Barsymes discontinues "consolation" gifts (*parapsyche*) from the treasury. There would probably not have been an edict for this. Many edicts refer to *parapsyche* as part of the salaries of governors: *Novel* 24 (end), 25 (end), 26 (preface and end). It is unclear whether it was a specific part of the salary that could be discontinued, as Procopius implies. Elsewhere it seems to refer to the whole salary (*Novels* 28.4.2 and 29.2). The word is also used in the edicts in its usual sense, referring to consolation for the death of a loved one.

22.38: Peter Barsymes debases the gold coinage. There would not have been an edict for this. Bury (1923) v. 1, 427 n. 1, asserted that this was the most dubious of the accusations, but an explanation has been found in coins minted specifically for foreign trade: Adelson (1957) 20 ff., 127–128; but cf. Bellinger (1966) v. 1, 72, 133.

23.1–8: no remission of arrears on taxes. Naturally, this omission was not by edict; but cf. *Novel* 147, preface (date 553), where Justinian admits that he has indeed never granted a general remission.

23.6, 23.16, 23.20: heavy taxes led farmers to desert their lands. This problem is mentioned in identical language in the preface to *Novel* 80, which also notes that they moved to the capital. John Lydus echoes Justinian and the *Secret History* in *On the Magistracies of the Roman State* 3.70.

23.8: Justinian's heavy taxation and refusal to grant remissions made him more onerous to the provincials than the barbarians who attacked them. This echoes the preface of *Novel* 32, which states that some of the abuses of the officials did not cause less damage than the passage of barbarians. John Lydus again echoes both Justinian and the *Secret History* in *On the Magistracies of the Roman State* 3.70.

23.9–10: supplementary fiscal impositions on taxpayers. Procopius does not claim that Justinian invented them, only that he abused them. They are discussed extensively in the edicts. *Novel* 8.10.2 admits that strict enforcement of tax laws was made necessary by the wars. Procopius discusses the following taxes:

> 23.11–14: *synone* (requisitions delivered at the army's convenience). These would have been burdensome due to constant warfare. See *CJ* 10.27.2; *Novel* 130. Cf. Ravegnani (1988) 133–135.
>
> 23.15–17: *epibole* (taxes for abandoned lands imposed on inheritors). See *Novel* 128.7–8 (edict on taxation), an inflexible prescription that must have been onerous after the plague. In 535, Justinian was using it as a punishment (*Novel* 17.14).
>
> 23.17–22: *diagraphe* (a surtax for special needs). See *Novel* 128.16, 128.22. Churches were made exempt with *Novel* 131.5.

23.22–24: billeting of troops. Procopius is here inverting *Novel* 130.9.

24.1–11: abuses of the military *logothetai* (also 18.15). Procopius implies that Justinian instituted them, but edicts have not survived. He also specifically refers to the laws that they violated, thus maintaining the legal bias of his argument. Those violated laws may have been issued by other emperors. Nonmilitary *logothetai* are the subject of *CJ* 10.30.4. See also the similar accusations in Agathias 5.14.2–4.

24.12–14: Justinian failed to pay the eastern *limitanei* and decommissioned them. No edict survives, although *CJ* 4.65.35.1 implies that as early as 530, Justinian did not consider them to be true soldiers. *Wars* 2.7.37 confirms that they were not receiving pay. Treadgold (1995) 59–64, shows that Agathias did not view them as active soldiers either.

24.15–23: reform and exploitation of the *scholai*. Procopius accuses Justinian of exploiting them during the reign of his uncle; this appears to be a malevolent interpretation of *CJ* 1.31.5, issued jointly by Justin and Justinian. Cf. also *CJ* 4.65.35. Later legislation on the *scholai* does not survive.

24.24–29: *domestikoi* and *protiktores* did not receive customary donatives. This omission was certainly not by edict.

24.30–33: pay cuts amounting to loss of pension for civil servants. John Lydus refers to a pragmatic sanction that had the same results (*On the Magistracies of the Roman State* 3.67). Cf. also *CJ* 12.19.13–15.

25.1–6: tolls on the Bosporus and Hellespont, and 25.7–10 at Byzantium. The decrees that established these have been lost, except for a fragment, which may, however, be Anastasius' (Amelotti and Zingale [1985] 115–118). They are perhaps reflected in a later chronicle independent of the *Secret History* that states that Justinian established *kommerkia* exactly where Procopius says he did: see Ahrweiler (1961) 241–242, 246–248; also Külzer (1991) 437 (I owe this last reference to Prof. A. Karpozelos).

25.11–12: reform of the currency exchange. See Adelson (1957) 107 ff.

25.13–26: imperial control over production and sale of silk. Procopius refers to specific edicts, though these have not survived (note the lacuna at 25.19). For a reconstruction of those edicts, see Lopez (1945) 11–13, esp. 11 n. 3 and 13 n.1; for a different view, Oikonomidès (1986) 33–34.

26.1–4: Justinian canceled public support for rhetors, doctors, and teachers and confiscated civic funds (*politika* and *theoretika*) used for entertainment and amenities (theaters, games, etc.; cf. 26.33). A series of edicts reflects the gradual appropriation of the funds (Bury [1923] v. 2, 351–352). Is Procopius giving a hostile interpretation of those measures or referring to lost edicts? For the decline of the rhetors, see Zonaras 14.6.31–32, possibly independent testimony. For the closure of the theater of Antioch, see Malalas 18.41. In *Novel* 105 of 537, Justinian provides for public support of the theater. The reference to teachers may also allude to the prohibition of pagan teachers (*CJ* 1.5.18.4, 1.11.10), especially at Athens (Malalas 18.47).

26.5: poverty of the physicians. Though the edicts are lost, Miller (1997) xxiv has independently argued that Justinian legislated changes in the way they were paid. My argument about the nature of the last section of the *Secret History* and his history of the hospital in the sixth century are mutually supportive.

26.12–15: abolition of the consulship. Cf. *Novel* 105, in which Justinian claims that he tried to save the office and make it "immortal" (105.2.3); Procopius says that no one has seen a consul for a long time, not even in his dreams. Both are primarily concerned with the largesses associated with the office. John Lydus also discusses the end of the consulship from a standpoint similar to that of Procopius: *On the Magistracies of the Roman State* 2.8.

26.18: attacks on beggars, commoners, the poor, and the handicapped (in the capital, presumably). For beggars, see *Novel* 80.4–5. For the ideological importance of the poor in Justinian's legislation, see Patlangean (1974) esp. 70–75.

26.20–22: Justinian increased the price of bread. No edict survives about this.

26.23–25: Justinian failed to repair the aqueduct of Constantinople. This is probably a direct response to the imperial pronouncement reflected in Malalas 18.17 (cf. 18.33 for Alexandria).

At this point, the focus of the text shifts gradually from the poor and the cities to financial reforms initiated by Justinian's agents in the provinces, which were then ratified by the emperor through edicts or pragmatic sanctions. The text then lapses into a series of scandals and anecdotes centering on Justinian. All of these stories are connected to the administration of the empire, and in many cases they reflect directly on extant legislation.

26.26–34: reforms of the *logothetes* Alexander in Rome and Thermopylae (in 540–541), which Justinian ratified. These activities are not mentioned in extant edicts.

26.35–44: reforms in Alexandria by the prefect Hephaestus (in 545–551), which Justinian ratified. These activities are not mentioned in extant edicts. But cf. *Edict* 13: *De urbe Alexandrinorum et aegyptiacis provinciis* (= *Novellae*, pp. 780–795), datable to the late 530s, which defined the position that Hephaestus held.

27.3–25: scandals surrounding the appointment of the bishop of Alexandria. These make a mockery of Justinian's professed respect for ecclesiastical offices and violate specific laws, e.g., those prohibiting their sale: *Novels* 6.1.5, 6.1.9, 123.1–2, 137.2 (date 565). They also show that Justinian did not honor his own instructions to subordinates and confiscated their possessions without warrant and in violation of his own laws (see below).

27.7–10 and 27.26–33: insincere conversions of Samaritans. The conversion of the Samaritans is discussed at length in the *Secret History* (also 11.24–30) because Justinian legislated extensively about it, not because Procopius was himself a crypto- Samaritan (*pace* Adshead 1996). These scandals demonstrate that the emperor did not respect his own laws. Cf. *CJ* 1.5.12, 1.5.17, 1.5.18 (esp. 1.5.18.5 on Samaritans and others who dissimulate); *Novels* 45, 103.2, 129 (date 551).

28.1–15: Priscus the forger. Cf. *Novel* 9 (see chapter 4, fourth section).

28.16–18: Justinian forbade the celebration of Passover before Easter. No edict for this survives, though it may be reflected in other sources. The events in Scott (1987) 217–221, are relevant but not necessarily identical to those described by Procopius.

29.1–38, 30.17–20 (cf. 19.11, 20.17): This series of scandals reveals Justinian's disregard for the law and his own word. The connecting thread of these stories is his contempt for the laws of property and inheritance, which were a major component of his legislative agenda. Procopius refers to specific laws, which have not all survived. Scott ([1985] 102–103) has shown how these stories undermine imperial propaganda (cf. Malalas 18.23).

30.1–16: Justinian cut back on the public post and spies. John Lydus tactfully ascribes the same reform of the post to an administrative enactment of the prefect John the Cappadocian (*On the Magistracies of the Roman State* 3.61). Procopius and Lydus are here not necessarily independent of each other, as their accounts are too similar for coincidence. For spies, see Lee (1989). No relevant edicts have survived.

Appendix 2. The Plan of Secret History 6–18

6 origin and crimes of Justinian (up to 527)
7 circus factions
8 character and appearance of Justinian

9.1–32 origin and character of Theodora
9.33–46 circus factions
9.47–10.23 Theodora's appearance, marriage with Justinian

11 Justinian's foreign policy, persecution of religious groups
12.1–13 Justinian and Theodora's attacks on property
12.14–32 Justinian and Theodora as demons

13–14 lifestyle and crimes of Justinian
15–17 lifestyle and crimes of Theodora
18 destruction of the world by war, natural disasters; demonology

Abbreviations

BZ	*Byzantinische Zeitschrift*
CAG	*Commentaria in Aristotelem Graeca.* Berlin: G. Reimer.
CFHB	*Corpus Fontium Historiae Byzantinae*
CHI	*Cambridge History of Iran.* v. 3.1–2: *The Seleucid, Parthian, and Sasanian Periods.* Ed. E. Yarshater. Cambridge: Cambridge University Press. 1983.
CJ	*Codex Iustinianus*
DOP	*Dumbarton Oaks Papers*
LCL	Loeb Classical Library. Cambridge, Mass., and London: Harvard University Press
LSJ	H. G. Liddell and R. Scott, eds., *A Greek-English Lexicon.* Rev. H. S. Jones. Oxford: Clarendon Press. 1968.
ODB	*The Oxford Dictionary of Byzantium.* ed. A. P. Kazhdan et al. 3 vols. Oxford and New York: Oxford University Press. 1991.
PLRE 2 and 3	J. R. Martindale, *The Prosopography of the Later Roman Empire.* v. 2: *395–526.* Cambridge: Cambridge University Press. 1980; v. 3: *527–641.* 1992.
TTH	Translated Texts for Historians. Liverpool: Liverpool University Press

Notes

Introduction

1. Honoré (1978) 16.

2. Gibbon, *The Decline and Fall of the Roman Empire*, c. 40, 561, and 565. Seneca adulated Claudius in his letter *To Polybius on Consolation* and then ridiculed him in the *Apocolocyntosis* but wrote no history. He seems to have thought that historians are liars anyway (*Natural Inquiries* 4.3, 7.16).

3. Rudich (1993).

4. *Wars* 1.24.12, 7.31.9, for *eleutherios*; 5.3.5–9 for theology, with *Secret History* 18.29; ibid. 26.1–11 for decline of classical culture, and passim for persecutions.

5. *Wars* 6.15.8.

6. *Wars* 8.1.1; cf. Mi. Whitby (1992).

7. Gibbon, *The Decline and Fall of the Roman Empire*, c. 43, 731 n. 1.

8. *Wars* 1.1.4; for examples and an exception, see Kaldellis (1997).

9. Hornblower (1994) 131–134.

10. See Carroll (1990) and Lamarque and Olsen (1994) c. 8–9, and 301–310 for rigorous, lucid, and sane arguments.

11. These were discovered by Cornford (1907). A historicist, Cornford viewed them as influences exerted on Thucydides' unconscious by pre-scientific elements of Greek civilization rather than fully conscious adaptations by the historian himself.

12. Miles (1995) for Livy; Syme (1958) for Tacitus.

13. E.g., Hartog (1988); Arieti (1995); cf. Romm (1998) 6–8, an introductory study. For Herodotus as fabricator, Fehling (1989), which elicited many responses, esp. Pritchett (1993) c. 2. Pritchett's attack on Fehling is devastating, but that on Hartog in c. 4 is unfair and largely irrelevant. Hartog's point is hardly that Herodotus "produced a fancy narrative which has no relation to the facts" (207).

14. *Wars* 1.4.17; see chapter 2, fourth section.

15. Aristotle, *Poetics* 9 (1451a39-b8); for a parallel defense of Herodotus, see Arieti (1995) 3.

16. Lamarque and Olsen (1994) 134: "Interpretation is a process of redescription, generalizing across elements in a work until the maximum number of elements have been subsumed under a higher-order description which articulates the theme of the work." Cf. Nussbaum (1986) 69.

17. Griswold (1996) 9–16, 225.

18. E.g., Saxonhouse (1983) 142–145; Nussbaum (1986) 228–233; Strauss (1989) 99.

19. Lamarque and Olsen (1994) 123; from the perspective of history: 241, 308–310. Auerbach (1953) 50 ff. made famous a passage in Ammianus Marcellinus by showing how he used language and style to create a view of his age in a manner that did not differ from works of literature. For insights into the literary aspect of ancient historiography, coupled, unfortunately, with postmodernist notions about the equivalence of knowledge and belief—which are never applied to the author's own views—see Veyne (1988).

20. Cf. Hobbes' note "To the Readers," 8, prefacing his translation of Thucydides.

21. Benardete (1969) 19: "We must always keep in mind two things in reading Herodotus: what does each story or episode mean in itself and in its context, and how does its meaning fit in with what Herodotus himself does or says."

22. Nietzsche, *Twilight of the Idols*, "What I Owe to the Ancients" 2; cf. Strauss (1989) 75–76, and 89: "The first speech recorded in his work begins with the word justice; the immediately following contradictory speech begins with the word necessity."

23. See esp. Connor (1984).

24. Crossan (1995) 111–112.

25. Plass (1988) 88. Scholars dealing with texts that more obviously inhabit the gray area between fact and fiction confront this problem acutely. See Hansen, introduction to Phlegon's *Book of Marvels*, 10: "a moment that in fact may never have happened . . . ideally captures something characteristic about the protagonist."

26. Cf. Plato, *Republic* 346e (note the omission) with Hesiod, *Works and Days* 106 ff. See Craig (1994) 362–363; Palmer (1995) 148 n. 16. For Plato and democracy, see also chapter 3, first section.

27. Ljubarskij (1993) and Ljubarskij et al. (1998), bravely tackling an incoherent range of new approaches.

28. Frendo (2001).

29. Hobbes, "To the Readers," 7.

30. Hobbes, "Of the Life and History of Thucydides," 18.

Chapter 1. Classicism and Its Discontents

1. Lucian, *How History Should Be Written* 15 for Crepereius; 2, 18–19, 25–26 for other imitators; and 53–54 for advice. For Crepereius, see C. Jones (1986) 161–166; for the history of formulaic introductions, see Marincola (1997) 271–275; for its practical functions, see Earl (1972) 842–846, 855–856.

2. Croke (1990a) 17–25, and (2001). In general, see Croke (1990b) and Karpozelos (1997) 528–533. For the possibility that Procopius knew the work of Malalas and, in at least one instance, corrected it, see Goffart (1980) 66 n. 17. Malalas seems to have reflected imperial propaganda: see Scott (1985), who also discusses his relationship to Procopius.

3. Eusebius, *Ecclesiastical History*, Book 5, preface; for his influence, see, e.g., Victor of Vita, *History of the Vandal Persecution*, prologue 1–2 (cf. 3.61, where Euse-

bius is cited). For Procopius' possible knowledge of Eusebius, see Av. Cameron (1985) 116, though one may perhaps assume it.

4. Socrates, Book 5, preface (a position that alludes to and corrects the programmatic statement of Eusebius); in general, see Croke and Emmett (1983) 6–7. Note the authors cited by Sozomen (1.1), Zachariah (1.1, 2.1), and Evagrius (preface, and 5.24) as their predecessors.

5. There has been no study since Lieberich (1898, 1900). An update is sorely needed.

6. The imbalance is increased decisively later on (*Vandal War* 3.1.1); cf. Agathias 1.6.4.

7. Hornblower (1991) 5.

8. Herodotus 1.1; cf. Agathias, preface 1, 10.

9. See Agathias, preface 5, for a more moralizing view of *euboulia*.

10. E.g., *Wars* 1.17.2–25, 3.11.4, 5.15.4, 5.19.4, 7.8.16–17, 7.27.17–20, 8.1.10, 8.2.13, 8.20.22; *Buildings* 1.8.3, 3.5.5. These passages merit independent study. Cf. Thucydides 3.82–84.

11. Polybius 1.1.1–2, 1.35, 1.57.3, 2.35.4–10, 5.75.2–6, 9.12.1 ff., 11.8.1–2, and passim. For the utility of history in general, see Avenarius (1956) 22–26, who does not, however, recognize Thucydides' intellectual objectives; for those, see Romilly (1956a). The practical use of history was advertised in Diodorus' preface (1.1), which Procopius relied on when writing the preface to the *Buildings*: Lieberich (1898–1900) v. 2, 3–6. But Diodorus is less focused on war than either Procopius or Polybius (for the possibility that he too used Polybius: see Sacks [1990] 10–11). Paschoud (1974) 306, urges caution: Procopius never mentions Polybius by name. But he never mentions Thucydides either, cites Herodotus only in Book 8, and rarely names the authors he read and used.

12. For these qualifications, see Avenarius (1956) 35–40; Marincola (1997) 63–86.

13. Cf. *Secret History* 1.4. For this distinction, see the sources cited by Avenarius (1956) 13–22; for truth as the goal of history, 40–46. Procopius mercifully does not expound upon these tired themes, although there was room for reasonable dissent from the consensus: see Kaldellis (1997).

14. Polybius 1.14.4–8, where praise and blame are balanced, also 2.61, 9.9.9–10, 10.21.4, 23.14.12 (in general, see Eckstein [1995]); and Agathias, preface 1–5, 16–20. Lucian seems to have thought that objectivity consists primarily in blame but grudgingly allowed the inclusion of true praise (*How History Should Be Written* 9, 38–39); for this theme in general, see Avenarius (1956) 157–163 and Marincola (1997) 158–174, who does not, unfortunately, distinguish between the different functions of praise and blame.

15. Haury (1934) 12.

16. See Agathias, preface 18–20, for the difference between writing about the dead and the living (cf. *Secret History* 1.2. In general, see Avenarius [1956] 46–49); and Agathias 5.13.5–15.6 for criticism of Justinian (discussed by Tinnefeld [1971] 37–42).

17. Marincola (1997) 34–43; for the *querelle des anciens et des modernes* in Greek literature, including historiography, see Edelstein (1967) esp. 30–40.

18. Thucydides 1.1–23; Polybius 1.1–4 (discussed by Walbank [1972] 67–68).

19. Reflected in the tripartite division of the *Wars* (8.1.1; cf. *Buildings* 6.1); cf. Plutarch, *Pompey* 45.5; Theophylact 2.14.7; and Cosmas Indicopleustes, *Christian Topography* 2.28.

20. John Lydus, *On the Magistracies of the Roman State* 3.28.

21. *Buildings* 1.1.6–8, 1.1.16, 6.1.5, 6.7.17.

22. *Secret History* 6.19, also 8.29, 13.2, 18.1–45, listing calamities. Agathias used those very disasters as proof of the importance of his *Histories* (preface 10, sensibly without trying to rival Thucydides or other previous historians).

23. For official propaganda in edicts and other writers, as well as the silence of Procopius' preface, see Cesa (1981) 395–397. Cesa concludes rightly that Procopius was opposed to the wars as such, not only to the means by which they were carried out. Av. Cameron prefers the old means-ends distinction but nowhere confronts Cesa's strong arguments. For Procopius' alleged "total support of Byzantine imperialism," see Cameron (1985) 7, 64, 140, 143, 173 n. 15, 181 n. 82, 186, 248; (1982) 32; and (1989) 174–175 and notes. Her position restates that of B. Rubin (1960, 1995) v. 1, 218.

24. See Thornton (1997) 28, for Greek views of archery.

25. *Buildings* 1.2.5–12; see Downey (1940) for this statue. The Renaissance sketch has been ascribed to a lost gold medallion of Theodosius I: see Lehmann (1959) and the debate with Mango (351–358).

26. *Iliad* 11.369–400. For the difference between the opinions expressed by the heroes and the views of the poet, see Edwards (1987) 96, 318. Procopius knew that the words of a character do not necessarily reflect an author's beliefs. For the *Iliad* in Greek education, see Hock (2001).

27. For Paris, see *Iliad* 3.15–75, 6.321–324, 11.369–400 (Procopius cites this passage twice), 11.540 ff. (successful exploits that Procopius does not mention).

28. Warry (1995) 16–17. The relative inferiority of archers is admitted by Pandarus, a bowman (*Iliad* 5.166–216).

29. Apollo: *Iliad* 1.15, 1.21, 1.37, 1.42–53; Artemis: 5.53, 9.538; Philoctetes: 2.716–720; Pandarus: 2.826–827, 4.99–152, 5.95–113; Teucer: 8.266–334, 12.387–403, 15.440–483 (also an able hand-to-hand warrior: 13.313–314, 13.170–187, 14.514–515). Odysseus could also use the bow (10.260), a theme that of course acquires significance in the *Odyssey*.

30. Contingents and widespread use of bows: *Iliad* 2.848–849, 3.79–80, 13.713–722; archers kill or maim enemies or turn battle: 8.266–334, 11.540–520, 580–584, 658–663, 825, 12.387–403, 13.650–655, 660–672, 713–722, 15.312–319, 440–483, 16.23–27; heroes saved from arrows or healed by the gods: 4.127 ff., 5.95–113, 12.400–403, 15.458–465, 16.508–531; even the gods could be wounded by mortal arrows: 5.392–404; cf. Bulanda (1913) 67–70.

31. Scott (1981a) 73; and H. Lieberich (1898, 1900) v. 2, 2. Even scholars who take the comparison at face value criticize its inaccuracies: E. Gray (1973) 24, 37.

32. Ahl (1984); Kaldellis (1999b) c. 20.

33. Lucian, *How History Should Be Written* 62; cf. Strabo 17.1.6.

34. Lucian, *How History Should Be Written* 15; see Braun (1886) 191–195 (plague), 207–211 (sieges of Amida, Edessa, and Rome, modeled on Plataea). Braun

entertained the possibility of factual distortion; cf. Brückner (1896) 7–16 (a very prejudiced work).

35. Haury (1896) 3–10; Moravcsik (1966) 375–376; Hunger (1969–1970) 27. The account of the plague was accepted by Soyter (1951) 541–542; Durliat (1989) 116; Evans (1996) 161; and Meier (1999). In general, Veh (1950–1953) v. 1, 16; Hunger (1978) v. 1, 297; Av. Cameron (1985) 38–42. Other classicizing historians have also found defenders: see, e.g., Blockley (1972) who notes a case of possible carelessness in Procopius arising from imitation (26–27); Blockley (1981, 1983) v. 1, 54–55 for Priscus. Roques (2000b) repeats the accusation but does not advance beyond the arguments of the nineteenth-century view.

36. *Wars* 1.7.22 (a heavily ironic statement in context); Agathias 5.9.30.

37. Al. and Av. Cameron (1964), esp. 320; also Av. Cameron (1965), (1966) 470–471, and (1970) c. 8, entitled "Classicism and Affectation" (also Appendices J and K: "Objective phrases" in Procopius and Theophylact). This view of circumlocutions was first proposed by Krumbacher (1887) 234.

38. E.g., Scott (1981a) 62: the works quoted above "suffice for most of the major questions."

39. Evans (1971) 84, (1972) 113; for classicism as "high" literature, Soyter (1939) 98.

40. E.g., Millar (1964) 40–42; Evans (1972) 40; Howard-Johnston (2000) 24; Blockley, introduction to his edition of Menander the Protector, 6–9.

41. Ma. and Mi. Whitby, introduction to their translation of Theophylact's *History*, xxvii. This negative view will be discussed below.

42. Av. Cameron (1985) 34–37, also 43 "hardly possible to separate the form from the content."

43. Av. Cameron (1985) 3, also xi, and esp. c. 7.

44. Av. Cameron (1985) 113.

45. Av. Cameron (1985) 32 and 39.

46. Av. Cameron (1985) 37–39, quotations from 38 and 45. The problems caused for Cameron's analysis by this contradiction will be discussed below.

47. Thucydides 2.86–90; cf. Romilly (1956b) 138–150; also c. 3 for general principles of composition.

48. Cf. Thucydides 2.86.6 and 2.88.1 with *Wars* 4.11.22 and 4.11.37 (Braun [1886] 182); for Solomon's career, *PLRE* 3, 1167–1177. The battle is also similar to that between the Persians and the Lydians in Herodotus 1.80.

49. Thucydides 2.89.9 (Braun [1886] 190).

50. Romilly (1956b) 139, 144–145, 149–150.

51. B. Liddell Hart, cited as "perhaps the greatest strategist of this century" in Saul (1992) 189.

52. Av. Cameron (1985) 177. B. Rubin (1954) 147, perceived that they had value apart from their rhetoric but avoided fundamental issues of interpretation.

53. E.g., *Wars* 5.27.4–11, and cf. 5.29.13–15 with 5.29.50; see Romilly (1956b) 123–138; and Connor (1984) 233–235.

54. Cf. Thucydides 1.143.5, 2.22.1, 2.62.3. For the reign, see Wolfram (1988) 342–349. His speeches in Procopius are neatly summarized by Agathias 1.6.4–6.

55. *Wars* 6.22.9–13, 6.24, 6.26.2–17, 6.28.27. The concept of military "prepara-

tion" (*paraskeue*), which Procopius uses in the *Wars*, was Thucydidean: Allison (1989).

56. Connor (1984) 110–112, 158, 219–221.

57. Plass (1988) 6.

58. Adshead (1990) 93–104, quotation from 99; also Adshead (1983) and Cresci (1986–1987) 237–239.

59. Cf. *Wars* 7.1.1–24 with Thucydides 2.65; see Cresci (1986). See also chapter 5, fourth section.

60. Scott (1981a) 73–74; Evans (1971) 85–86.

61. Pazdernik (2000) 150–171, and esp. 181–182 on the calculated use of classical paradigms.

62. Hunger (1978) v. 2, 7; and (1969–1970) esp. 29–30.

63. See Mango (1980) c. 13; Agapitos (2002) 200–214.

64. Christidis (1996), esp. 66–69; also Cresci (1986–1987). For examples from Agathias and other late authors, see Kaldellis (1999a), (2003b); Bowie (1995); in letters, Van Dam (2002) 81 ff.; Mullett (1981) esp. 92–93; in an oration, R. Jenkins (1966); also Ševčenko (1954) esp. 51–52. Countless references can be provided.

65. See Finkelpearl (2001) and other essays in the volume of which this essay is a part.

66. Kaldellis (1999a) 226–232, 240.

67. Isocrates, *Panathenaicus* 246; cf. 1–2. See Too (1995) 68–73, 125–127, and 132–138 for one example of what Isocrates might have meant.

68. *Wars* 1.24.32–37; Evans (1984). The parallels were already noted by Baldwin (1982). For Theodora, see chapter 4, sections 2–3.

69. Greatrex (2003), and pers. comm., suggests that "the double edge is far from obvious" and cites Isocrates, who uses the original saying favorably (*Archidamus* 45). But double edges are not obvious—that's the point. Also, it is difficult to accept that the citation in Procopius is neutral, given the bad conscience involved in the deliberate substitution of "kingship" for "tyranny." The parallel of Isocrates proves just this: given his context and audience, Isocrates felt he could use the saying in the original, but Procopius did not. Why not? We must then wonder why he used it at all. Diodorus' account (14.8.5) can help us answer these questions; Isocrates' speech cannot.

70. Colish (1994) 191–192; e.g., Renehan (1976) esp. 97: "an examination of the original context of the borrowed material will reveal a value-judgment of Sallust himself."

71. E.g., Baldwin (1992a), for an excellent discussion of a detail.

72. Gibbon, *The Decline and Fall of the Roman Empire*, c. 53, 420.

73. R. Jenkins (1963).

74. Browning (1977) 1.

75. D. Afinogenov in Ljubarskij et al. (1998) 23.

76. The pitch for postmodernism has been made by Mullett (1990), though she really summarizes a range of mostly positive developments. Byzantine studies are too driven by positivist assumptions to take postmodernism seriously.

77. Mango (1975) esp. 4–8, 17–18.

78. Mango (1981).

79. E.g., Harris (2000), whose argument is not, however, invalidated by the "classical façade" theory (24).

80. Av. Cameron (1985) 7–8, also 36–37, 234–235, in fact passim: 17, 20, 25, 27–29, 31, 130–131, 150, 248; also (1970) vii, 30, 134–135.

81. Av. Cameron (1985) 130.

82. Kaegi (1965) esp. 37.

83. Av. Cameron (1985) 130 and 31 respectively (quoting G. Downey).

84. Av. Cameron (1978) esp. 80, 89. When searching for prior attestations of the cult, she cites . . . Procopius! (87)

85. Av. Cameron (1985) 27–28.

86. Av. Cameron (1982) 50; elsewhere, in (1991) 197–198, the same scholar even accuses Procopius of not mentioning the Council of 553, which occurred *after* the period covered by his narrative! She lamely suggests that it "took place as he was completing" his history ("the real issues . . . they were now what counted." But for whom?). Scott (1981a) 68, criticizes Agathias for not discussing that same Council, in his opinion the most important event of the period discussed by Agathias (more than the abolition of the Gothic kingdom? the war with Persia? Justinian's attack on philosophy?). The Council of 553 was an ineffectual gesture. Scholars who think that Procopius distorts history should look more closely at the religious chronicles that have become fashionable: e.g., Croke (2001) 132.

87. Cf. Tacitus, *Annals* 13.49.

88. Cf. C. Jenkins (1947). Soyter (1939) 102, says that we should be thankful to Procopius for the information he preserves. Some scholars now prefer Malalas: e.g., Croke (1990b) 38.

89. Beck (1984).

90. Matthews (1989) x; also 20, 228.

91. E.g., Av. Cameron (1985) x–xi, 17, 19, and c. 2.

92. For a weaker version of this argument, see Av. Cameron (1985) 11–12. For the latest round of arguments regarding dates, see Greatrex (1994), (1995b), (2003); Evans (1996).

93. Fatouros (1980) 517. Attempts to connect him to circles in Gaza and discover his ancestry (most recently by Greatrex [1996a]) remain entirely conjectural, and, in any case, prove little.

94. For his travels, see Av. Cameron (1985) 13–15.

95. Hegel, *Lectures on the Philosophy of World History*, 154.

96. B. Rubin (1954) 28–31; (1960, 1995) v. 1, esp. 200–202, and 197–244 passim, for the "Opposition." Also Irmscher (1976) 137–138; Tinnefeld (1971) c. 1; and Evans (1972) 95, for Procopius the class-conscious senator (though he is called a bureaucrat on 147 n. 44).

97. So too Greatrex (2000) 223–228 (esp. 227 n. 53: "Procopius' criticisms . . . seem more individual than conventional").

98. Av. Cameron (1985) 7, 23, 64, 144–145, 245.

99. For a concise justification of ancient political conservatism and its philosophical roots, see Behnegar (1995) 260. Cf. Plato, *Republic* 422a.

100. For *Kaiserkritik*, see B. Rubin (1960, 1995) v. 1, 234–244; Tinnefeld (1971)

c. 1, which spawned a large secondary literature. *Contra*: Greatrex (2000) 220–222. For genre, see also chapter 4, third section.

101. Fornara (1983) 142.

102. For this speech, see chapter 1, second section; chapter 4, first and second sections.

103. Greatrex (2000) 216–220.

104. Av. Cameron (1985) 3, 46, 134, reads the *Buildings* and the *Secret History* independently of the *Wars*. Yet she admits elsewhere that "at every point the *Secret History* proclaims its relation to the *Wars*" (16, 50, 54). Therefore, her argument is backward in principle; yet its purpose is to show Procopius as a "less classical" author, the a priori goal of her book (x-xi, 56).

105. The phrase is repeated, with variation, at *Secret History* 13.33; cf. 6.21, 11.2, 21.24, 26.11 for innovation. For the passages cited above, see Teuffel (1871) 213 n. 1 and Braun (1886) 179, 219–220.

106. For classical tyranny, see McGlew (1993) 24–34; for various meanings of tyranny in antiquity, see Courcelle (1980) 202–208.

107. E.g., *Wars* 3.3.5–13: the usurper John, contrasted favorably to Valentinian III, who destroyed him as well as the empire; 5.1.26–31: Theoderic, about whom we will have more to say later.

108. Lieberich (1898, 1900) v. 2, 3–6; this has led to a search for Hellenistic antecedents: Pühlhorn (1977) 382.

109. Ma. Whitby (2000) esp. 46.

110. E.g., Eusebius, *Tricennial Oration in Praise of Constantine* 9; see Ma. Whitby (2000).

111. Teuffel (1871) 208–209; Haury (1890–1891) 31–34; Bury (1923) v. 2, 428; Gantar (1962a) 10, (1962b); Downey (1947) 171; Evans (1968) 137, (1971) 87; Beck (1986) 22.

112. Angold (1996) 24. For conspiracies, see chapter 4, fifth section.

113. Downey (1953) suggested that Book 1 was "a literary show-piece designed to be presented orally before the Emperor and the Court" but that the text as a whole shows signs of incompleteness (1947); *contra*: Mi. Whitby (1988) 73.

114. For the context, see Crow (1995) 121, who notes that there is no evidence for the restorations of the walls that the panegyrist attributes to Justinian.

115. See Cherf (1992) and Gregory (2000) for Thermopylae. For parallels, see Haury (1890–1891) 31–34, to which more can be added: cf. *Secret History* 21.9–25 with *Buildings* 1.1.25–26 (choice of officials); 13.28–33 with 1.7.6–10 (Justinian's fasting and insomnia); 17.5 with 1.9.2–10 (treatment of prostitutes); 10.11 with 1.11.8 (Theodora's appearance). For Alexander, *PLRE* 3, 43–44: Alexander 5. The guards of Thermopylae fought bravely against the "Huns" in 540, though the enemy outflanked them (*Wars* 2.4.10). The garrison installed by Alexander proved its worth in 559 (Agathias 5.23.6).

116. Toland, "Clidophorus, or of the Exoteric and Esoteric Philosophy," in *Tetradymus*, 95–96.

117. Centaurs: Evans (1971) 91, (1972) 126–127; Agathias: Kaldellis (1999a) 232, 245–248.

118. Jullien (2000) 62 on ancient Chinese writing.

119. Star: Gantar (1962a) citing texts on this star's baneful influence; the allusion is accepted by MacCormack (1981) 307–308 n. 304. Krumbacher (1887) 233 also suspected that the *Buildings* was ironic in a way that allowed readers to uncover the truth for themselves. For other possible instances of subversion, see Rousseau (1998). Though sympathetic to Rousseau's aims, I am not convinced by his argument here. For Homer in classical education, see Hock (2001), esp. 69 for sleeping Diogenes. For drunken recognition of Euripides, see Plutarch, *Alexander* 51.5–6, and 53.2–5 for another occasion. Cf. Psellos, *Chronographia* 6.61.

120. Plutarch, *Themistocles* 1.1–2, 2.3; cf. *Cimon* 9.1. The opposite is implied in Plato, *Republic* 329e-330a. *Pace* Mi. Whitby (2000) 66, Procopius was not referring to Thucydides, who mentions neither Neocles nor the boast.

121. *Secret History* 6.1–3, 6.11–17; for Justin's illiteracy, see Vasiliev (1950) 82–84, who rejects the tradition. Baldwin (1989) accepts it, with the provision that it may refer to "lack of formal education."

122. Justiniana: Grabar (1948).

123. See chapter 4, first section; cf. Plutarch, *Themistocles* 27–31.

124. Cf. *Wars* 2.2.15.

125. See Croke and Crow (1983) for various misrepresentations (not limited to Daras), and 147, 157–158 for discrepancies with the *Wars* (*contra*: Mi. Whitby [1986], who argues for exaggeration rather than fabrication); for other distortions, more often than not deliberate, see Downey (1939), who first saw Procopius' physical descriptions as panegyrical; Av. Cameron (1985) 100, 106–108, (1989) 176; Adshead (1990) 108–109; E. K. Fowden (1999) 93–94; Gregory (2000). For general notes on this work, see Pühlhorn (1977). For useful summaries of Justinian's building program, see Maffei (1988) and Evans (1996) 215–225.

126. Av. Cameron (1985) 101; cf. Roques (2000a) 37.

127. For Xenophon in the *Buildings*, see Gantar (1962b).

128. "Sincerity," etc., in Av. Cameron (1985) 11, 31, 57, 84 (thrice in a paragraph), 88, 242; "truth," "true," "real": xii, 31 n. 83, 25, 34, 45, 150, 151. Apparently the concept of "greed" is also off limits, being too classical for the sixth century (7; yet it was used by the ecclesiastical historian Evagrius: 4.30, 5.1). Cameron sometimes uses this device reflexively: what, for example, is wrong with calling ethnographic digressions "classical" (34)? On the other hand, she has no problem calling the Three Chapters one of "the real issues of the day" (27), calls the views that *she* ascribes to Procopius his real views and real opinions in (1966) 481 (but note the title), and questions the sincerity of the panegyrist Corippus in (1983) 176.

129. Av. Cameron (1986) 54.

130. Augustine, *Confessions* 6.6.9.

131. Av. Cameron (1985) 11. Nor is it really helpful to say, so long as we actually want to *understand* our authors, that the question of sincerity is "not particularly helpful," as does Mi. Whitby (2000) 59. Both scholars want the text to be sincere but cannot get around the *Secret History*.

132. Kaldellis (1999b) 136–137 n. 285, and below.

133. Herodotus 3.80.5 (Otanes notes that they also find flattery repulsive); Xenophon, *Hiero* 1.14–15, 7.5–9; Plato, *Republic* 575e; Maximus of Tyre, *Or.* 14.7–8.

134. Strauss (1991) 30.

135. Agapetus 12, 22, 31, 32, 56.

136. John Lydus, *On the Magistracies of the Roman State* 3.76; for the emperor's requests, 3.28.

137. Av. Cameron (1985) 103 n. 144, also 35 (citations to both Aristophanes and the *Secret History* here are mistaken), 87 n. 21, 245 n. 27.

138. Av. Cameron (1985) 106–108 (and n. 182).

139. Av. Cameron (1985) 88–89. But note that if "there is no reason to believe that he could not have accepted the standard view of God and emperor," the *Buildings* also offers no persuasive evidence that he did.

140. Av. Cameron (1985) 245–246.

141. Av. Cameron (1985) 247, 252 n. 76, 260.

142. Aristophanes, *Clouds* 225–228; cf. Plato, *Apology* 19c. For Aristophanes in the *Secret History*, see also chapter 4, third section.

143. Note the unnecessary comparison to Semiramis in *Buildings* 1.1.53 (cf. *Secret History* 1.9).

144. Honoré (1978) 64–67, does not deem it impossible. Tribonian may have been alluding to Cicero's ambiguous quip about Octavian: "laudandum adulescentem, ornandum, tollendum" (*Letters to His Friends* 11.20.1, "lifted up," i.e., "done away with." See also Cicero's *On Friendship* 99). For more possible sarcasm on the quaestor's part, see Honoré (1975) 117. For Tribonian and philosophy, see chapter 3, fourth section.

145. Ahl (1984) 198–199.

146. Respectively, Rousseau (1996) 19 and Moorhead (1994) 87. For this passage of the *Buildings*, see also chapter 4, second section. Cf. the periegete Pausanias 8.2.5 (Arcadia): "For now that evil has attained such magnitude and has covered the entire earth and all the cities, no longer does any human being become a god, except in the speeches and flattery given to those in power."

147. For Mermeroes, see *PLRE* 3, 884–885; for Goubazes, see 559–560.

148. Seneca, *Letter to Lucilius* 79.6; for his views on authorship, see Finkelpearl (2001) 83 ff.

149. Powell (1991) 167.

150. Choerilus of Samos fr. 1.

Chapter 2. *Tales Not Unworthy of Trust: Anecdotes and the* Persian War

1. Agathias, preface 4–5; see Kaldellis (1999a) esp. 207–211, and (1997).

2. Plutarch, *Theseus* 1.1–5.

3. Drake (2000) 163.

4. Mango (1980) 243; for an incredulous survey, see Brückner (1896) 19–24.

5. Av. Cameron (1985) 153–156.

6. Scott (1981a) 73.

7. Greatrex (1998) 74. The either/or contrast employed here rests on positivist assumptions about "historical accuracy" that impel British scholarship especially. Goffart (1980) 58–70 recognized that the introduction of each *War* is different in

nature and intention from the rest of its narrative and should be treated differently. Yet the examples that he gives of distorted material are not entirely convincing (65), and his solutions are vague and not always helpful (classifying the introductions with the ethnographic digressions or treating them as political propaganda).

8. The ecclesiastical historians of the mid-fifth century also realized that the dynasty was weak: Sozomen 9.6; Theodoret 5.36.

9. Both sides cited and discussed by Av. Cameron (1969–1970) 149; Holum (1982a) 83 favors the story; Blockley (1992) 51–52 doubts the details, but sees fire behind the smoke.

10. Bury (1923) v. 2, 1–3; Blockley (1992) 53–55.

11. Av. Cameron (1985) 153.

12. John Lydus, *On the Magistracies of the Roman State* 2.11, 3.41, noted this transition and ascribed it to a law by Theodosius I. The policy inaugurated by Arcadius was immediately criticized by Synesius, *On Kingship* 13 (cf. 3.3b-c); for its repercussions, see Kaegi (1981) 20–24; McCormick (1986) 47.

13. Holum (1982a) 50–51, 79 (quotation), and 90–95 for the regime of Theodosius II. Cf. Machiavelli, *Florentine Histories* 1.1.

14. *Wars* 1.2.6; confirmed by Synesius, *On Kingship*, esp. 13–15; Philostorgius 11.3; Zosimus 5.12.1.

15. For the influential *logioi* of Arcadius' reign, see Al. Cameron and Long (1993) 72 ff.

16. Cf. Mi. Whitby (1994), who discusses kings after Chosroes who preferred not to campaign, perhaps in imitation of their Roman counterparts: 256–257.

17. Isdigerdes was praised by Christian authors for his toleration and reviled in Persian sources (see Av. Cameron [1969–1970] 150, for texts and studies).

18. Av. Cameron (1969–1970) 151–152, citing previous scholarship; and *PLRE* 2, 84–86: Flavius Anatolius 10.

19. Holum (1977) esp. 169, and (1982a) 101, argues for (an) Anatolius in 420–422; *contra*: Synelli (1986) 59–61, 67–69. Blockley accepts Anatolius, but still thinks that Procopius has conflated the wars: (1992) 57, 61, and 200 n. 31, 201 n. 39.

20. *PLRE* 2, 920: Procopius 2.

21. For Perozes' campaigns, see Drouin (1895) 232–238; Ghirshman (1948) 87–92. Briefer treatments by Christensen (1944) 289–294; and R. N. Frye in *CHI*, 147–148. Procopius' account tallies on the whole with the eastern sources.

22. Otherwise unknown: *PLRE* 2, 431: Eusebius 19.

23. Cf. 2 Samuel 12.1–15. For this fable, see Dijk (1994).

24. The stratagem of the Ephthalites during Perozes' second invasion is suspiciously similar to that used by the Phocaeans against the Thessalian cavalry in Herodotus 8.28. But eastern sources support Procopius: Haury (1896) 6–7; Moravcsik (1966) 375–376; Hunger (1969–1970) 27. It is also reported in Agathias 4.27.4; and Maurice, *Strategikon* 4.3.1–20.

25. See the curious archaeological discoveries of Ghirshman (1948) 4–6; for such customs, see Matthews (1989) 61–62.

26. Hartog (1988) 256; for the effect on readers, see Arieti (1995) 140. For burying alive among the Persians, see Herodotus 7.114 (though not a funeral custom).

27. For cities as "the barrier between 'Roman' and 'non-Roman,' between the 'civilized' and the 'barbarian,' " see Matthews (1989) 392–397, from the point of view of defense. Cf. Peter the Patrician fr. 9.2.

28. *LSJ*, s.v. γοργός, Γοργώ; *Secret History* 16.1. It can probably be identified with Gurgan (classical Hyrcania), near the Caspian Sea, which seems to have been on the border of Ephthalite territory (A. D. H. Bivar in *CHI*, 214). The fifth-century historian Priscus of Panium (fr. 41.3) records that the Roman ambassador Constantius (actually Constantine) met Perozes in 464–465 at "Gorga" on the border between Persia and the Kidarite Huns, i.e., in this instance, the Ephthalites. Procopius either had faulty information or changed the name to suit his characterization. Their main city was probably Balkh (Hellenistic Bactra), possibly the "Balaam" mentioned later by Priscus (fr. 51.1; cf. Hannestad [1955–1957] 435). A Turkish envoy to Constantinople in 568–569 claimed that the Ephthalites lived in cities rather than villages (Menander the Protector fr. 10.1).

29. Cf. Menander the Protector fr. 15.3 for the notion of Scythian invincibility. Note that Perozes is the third Persian king in Procopius' account.

30. Moravcsik (1958) v. 2, 279; for this and other names, see King (1987) 83–85.

31. Ghirshman (1948) 127–128; Chinese sources consistently depict them as nomadic: Miyakawa and Kollautz (1989) 92–99.

32. Jullien (2000) 62.

33. Güterbock (1906) esp. 4 ff.; in diplomatic exchanges: Chrysos (1976) and (1978) 35–36.

34. E.g., *Wars* 1.16.1, 2.10.13–14; Peter the Patrician fr. 13; Theophylact 4.11.2 (in a letter of Chosroes II to Maurice); and Mi. Whitby (1994) 245 and n. 54. For other expressions, see G. Fowden (1993) 18 n. 21.

35. See the excellent survey by N. Garsoïan in *CHI*, 568–592; for interactions across the frontier, see Lee (1993) 49–66.

36. See Alföldi (1970) 9–25; and Hartog (1988) 322–339, for the portrayal that proved decisive, even if its empathy was rarely emulated. The view of Achaemenid Persia as a servile tyranny was promoted by many classical writers (e.g., Hippocrates, *On Airs, Waters, and Places* 16, 23; Isocrates, *Or.* 4.150–152; Aristotle, *Politics* 3.14, 5.11, 7.7; for the tragedians, see Hall [1989] 190–200), even those who idealized its founder (Xenophon, *Cyropaedia* 8.8, *Agesilaus*, passim; Plato, *Laws* 694a-696a). This view of the Achaemenids was upheld by writers of the Roman period (e.g., Aelius Aristides, *On Rome* 15–23; Heliodorus, *Aethiopica* 6.13, 7.2; Agathias 2.10.1–4).

37. For Parthians as Achaemenids, see Lucian, *How History Should Be Written* 18; cf. Spawforth (1994). For the depiction of Sasanid Persia, see Carratelli (1971), which only alludes to the importance of the classics. Absent an adequate discussion, I mention some of the more interesting texts. Herodian's account of contemporary Persian education (i.e., bows and horses: 6.5.4) is taken from Herodotus (1.136). For the orator Libanius, the wars against the Sasanids reenacted or continued the Persian Wars of antiquity (*Or.* 11.158, 15.16, 59.65–70; *Letter* 1402). Themistius flat-out called the Persians of his time "Achaemenids" (*Or.* 4.57b), while the Latin writers called Ardashir, the founder of the Sasanid empire, "Xerxes" (Dodgeon and Lieu [1991] 26–28). It is interesting that the method by which Gibbon composed his account of the Sasanids is similar to that of the writers of late antiquity: "From

Herodotus, Xenophon, Herodian, Ammianus, Chardin &c. I have extracted such *probable* accounts of the Persian nobility, as seem either common to every age, or particular to that of the Sassanides" (*The Decline and Fall of the Roman Empire*, c. 8, 229 n. 58; Gibbon's italics).

38. E.g., Priscus of Panium (fr. 41.3), who modeled his account of the relations between the Sasanids and the Ephthalites on Herodotus' account (3.1) of the relations between the Egyptian Amasis and Cambyses; for this and other examples, see Moravcsik (1966) esp. 369–371, 374–376; Hunger (1969–1970) 22, 26–28, 31; and Blockley (1972), to which can be added, with reference to Persian history, Gregory of Nazianzus, *Or.* 5.11; and John Lydus, *On the Months* 4.118. For examples from Procopius, see Av. Cameron (1985) 40–42.

39. Cassius Dio 80.4.1; Herodian 6.2.1–2, 6.2.6–7, 6.4.5; Ammianus Marcellinus 17.5.5; Julian, *Or.* 2.63a-b; cf. Tacitus, *Annals* 6.31. For the Greek writers, see Potter (1999) 99–100, citing previous treatments; for the Sasanids' knowledge of their ancestors, see Yarshater (1971) and, for Sasanid ideology in general, Wiesehöfer (1996) 165–169. However, some conscious Sasanid evocation of the Achaemenids has been postulated by Mi. Whitby (1994) 234–235 and G. Fowden (1993) 27–30.

40. Questa (1989). Cf. Agathias 4.29.6, where Chosroes is compared to Cyrus, Darius, and Xerxes. For his limited use of Herodotus, see Av. Cameron (1969–1970) 75, 90, 96, and passim. Cameron's article on "Herodotus and Thucydides in Agathias" (1964) is, however, unconvincing: the possibility of a correspondence of ideas without verbal parallel is rejected out of hand, whereas numerous verbal parallels are laboriously explained away.

41. Cesa (1981) 404; for "barbarian" as an insult, see Belisarius in *Wars* 4.15.20.

42. Chrysos (1976) 12–16.

43. According to Av. Cameron (1985) 219, Procopius claims that the Ephthalites "are as good as the Romans or the Persians, that is, that they have transcended the quality of barbarism." But the Persians are the barbarians in the two first books of the *Wars*. Unlike Procopius, Cameron perhaps does not consider the Persians to have been barbarians (152; Cesa's article is relegated to a footnote with no discussion: 169 n. 140).

44. For Chosroes and Justinian, see chapter 4, first section; for the *Vandal War*, see Scott (1981a) 73–74.

45. For tyranny as antithetical to *politeia*, see Aristotle, *Politics* 1293b29.

46. Strauss (1991) 69; cf. Aristotle, *Politics* 1279b6–7, 1295a19–22, 1311a2–4.

47. Priscus of Panium fr. 11.2.406–510; Blockley (1981, 1983) v. 1, 57–59. It is possible that the Greek and his views were invented by Priscus, or at least greatly elaborated, in order to make those points. For Procopius' knowledge of Priscus, see Av. Cameron (1985) 208–209 (esp. Priscus fr. 22, 53, 66).

48. See various instances in A. H. M. Jones (1986) 148, 503–504, 559, 629–632, 703–704, 811, 819. For Priscus and other defectors, see Goffart (1989) 105–106 (and n. 104).

49. For Pliny and Tacitus, see Drake (2000) 49–50.

50. Av. Cameron (1985) 154–155, four times in one paragraph.

51. Not the first shark to taste Persian flesh: Herodotus 6.44. For sharks, see Aelian, *On the Nature of Animals* 1.55, 9.65; for pearls in the Persian Gulf, see the

Greek writers quoted by Potts (1990) 138, 142, 148–149, esp. Isidore of Charax; to these should be added Aelian, *On the Nature of Animals* 10.13, 15.8; see Philostratus, *Life of Apollonius of Tyana* 3.57, for the dangers posed to pearl fishers by sharks. For Persian love of anecdotes, see Howard-Johnston (1995) 170–171.

52. Christidis (1996) 100–101.

53. Kustas (1970) 62.

54. Benardete (1969) 4–5; Arieti (1995) 89–90, 119; Plato also tells a false story to reveal a truth about *eros*: see Nussbaum (1986) 212–213.

55. For *eros* as a beast, see Thornton (1997) 38.

56. Montgomery (1965) 191–217, citing other occurrences of the word.

57. Cf. *Wars* 1.4.17: ὅσα . . . λέγουσιν εἰπεῖν ἄξιον· ἴσως γὰρ ἄν τῳ καὶ οὐ παντάπασιν ἄπιστος ὁ λόγος δόξειεν εἶναι with *Anabasis*, preface 3: ὅτι καὶ αὐτὰ ἀξιαφήγητά τέ μοι ἔδοξε καὶ οὐ πάντη ἄπιστα. Procopius knew the *Anabasis* and used it as a model (cf. *Wars* 4.16.12–25 with *Anabasis* 7.9–10). He consulted Arrian's geographical treatises and cited another now-lost text: see Roos (1926) 116; Av. Cameron (1985) 216–218. For Arrian in the sixth century, see Hunger (1978) v. 1, 528; v. 2, 326. A large number of his fragments are preserved in a range of sixth-century texts: see Roos (1967) v. 2, 315–320. For the use of Arrian by Malalas, see Jeffreys (1990) 173–174, 196; by John Lydus and Stephanus of Byzantium, see Bosworth (1983).

58. Herodotus 7.44, 7.54, 7.128; cf. Mardonius' "longing" to seize Athens for the second time (9.3). Any similarities between Alexander and Xerxes are naturally ironic, given the ideological dimension of the Macedonian expedition.

59. Thornton (1997) 13; cf. 14 for instances from the world of politics.

60. Thucydides 6.24; for his use of *eros*, see Forde (1989) esp. 31–50; for this episode from a Platonic perspective, see Saxonhouse (1983) 150–151; for the Athenian empire as a tyranny, see Croix (1954) 2–3.

61. Benardete (1969) 136.

62. Thornton (1997) 45–46, 128.

63. Plato, *Republic* 572d–579b; for tyrannical and philosophical *eros* in Plato, see Rosen (1988). For the same distinction (exoterically), see Xenophon, *Symposium* 8 (quoted by Procopius in the *Secret History*; see below); for philosophical *eros* in the *Wars*, see 2.12.9, 5.6.16, 7.32.24. For the erotic drives of the tyrant, see also Aristotle, *Politics* 5.11.

64. For minor instances of tyrannical *eros* in the *Wars*, see 3.3.11, 3.6.1 (= 3.7.18), 4.22.2.

65. *Secret History* 8.1–28, also 12.28, 17.16.

66. *Secret History* 16.11–12: no one was allowed to speak of him. The empress, it seems, covered her tracks well (the man is known only from this passage: *PLRE* 3, 107: Areobindus 1). Yet her chastity after her marriage is assured by Procopius' silence: Honoré (1978) 10.

67. *Secret History* 9.30–32; note the spin put on this *eros* in *Wars* 1.25.4.

68. For the *eros* of Belisarius for Antonina, see *Secret History* 1.20, 3.2, 4.41; for Antonina, 1.17–18, 1.35. For a full discussion, see chapter 4, third section.

69. *Secret History* 9.47–51. The law is *CJ* 5.4.23; see Vasiliev (1950) 392–397. For

a legal examination, upholding Procopius' accuracy, see Daube (1966); cf. Honoré (1978) 9–11.

70. ἠράσθη, ἐρωμένη, and συνοικίζω are used by both Herodotus and Procopius; cf. also οὔτε τὸν νόμον ἔλυσαν δείσαντες Καμβύσεα . . . παρεξεῦρον ἄλλον νόμον, with Ἰουστινιανὸν δὲ ξὺν δέει πολλῷ ἐθεράπευον . . . λῦσαί τε τοὺς νόμους τὸν βασιλέα [Justin] νόμῳ ἑτέρῳ ἠνάγκασε [Justinian]. For Cambyses in Herodotus, see Hartog (1988) 330–332, 336–339.

71. Connor (1984) 156.

72. Plato, *Republic* 574e. Cf. McGlew (1993) 30 n. 32: "Herodotus' portrait of Cambyses offers a perfect complement to Plato's theoretical account of tyranny." Browning (1987) 40, captured the essence of Procopius' account: "Justinian was by now too powerful to care for convention." See Angold (1996) 26 for further thoughts on Procopius' view of this marriage.

73. Grumel (1958) 270 gives 4 April for Easter 527. Most sources give 1 April for the coronation: Marcellinus Comes and the *Chronicon Paschale* under 527; Justinian, *Novel* 47.1; Evagrius 4.9; and Procopius. Only Peter the Patrician gives 4 April (in Constantine VII Porphyrogennetus, *Book of Ceremonies* 1.95).

74. Cf. *Secret History* 9.31–32: ἐγίνετό τε ἡ πολιτεία τοῦ ἔρωτος τοῦδε ὑπέκκαυμα, with Xenophon, *Symposium* 4.25: . . . οὗ ἔρωτος οὐδέν ἐστι δεινότερον ὑπέκκαυμα (cf. Achilles Tatius, *Leucippe and Cleitophon* 1.5.6). It is believed that Procopius knew only the *Cyropaedia* (Greatrex [1996a] 132 n. 12, citing previous bibliography), but this is unlikely.

75. Justinian, *Novel* 74.4; Moorhead (1994) 36, cites Plato, *Laws* 839b.

76. Xenophon, *Cyropaedia* 1.4.5; cf. Nadon (2001) 160.

77. Cf. Polybius 15.20.3.

78. E.g., Av. Cameron (1985) 155.

79. *Wars* 1.23.1, 2.5.1, 2.5.27, 2.10.10, 2.17.2, 2.20.1, 2.26; *Secret History* 2.26.

80. Benardete (1963) 12–13. Homer's use of patronymics is not determined solely by constraints of meter. Plato used them also to make esoteric arguments: e.g., in *Republic* 427c.

81. For the early years of Cavades, see Christensen (1925) 91–115, following a lengthy analysis of the sources; also (1944) 296–297, 335–352. For summaries, see Ghirshman (1948) 88, 92; R. N. Frye in *CHI*, 149–150.

82. See the excellent article of Crone (1991); for a discussion of previous views, see E. Yarshater in *CHI*, 991–1024, esp. 991–1001, 1018–1024.

83. See the versions in Christensen (1925) 112–113, (1944) 349 n. 4; Av. Cameron (1969–1970) 157–158; E. Yarshater in *CHI*, 994.

84. See the versions in Christensen (1925) 114, (1944) 350–351.

85. Christensen (1925) 93–94 n. 5, (1944) 297 n. 2; Ghirshman (1948) 18, 93; cf. *Wars* 1.7.1. For relations between Persians and Ephthalites after Perozes, see Hannestad (1955–1957) 441–442.

86. Z. Rubin (1995) uses this statement as a springboard for an analysis of the Persian and Arabic sources on the king's policies.

87. *Secret History* 8.26, also 6.21, 11.2, 21.24, 26.11, and, prudently placed in the mouth of enemies, *Wars* 2.2.6. See also chapter 1, fourth section. Cf. John Lydus, *On the Magistracies of the Roman State* 2.19 for tyrants and innovation (for this

passage, see also chapter 4, second section). For Justinian's own view of innovation, see Honoré (1978) 27–28, based on the emperor's laws.

88. Cf. Otanes in Herodotus 3.80.5.

89. Strabo 7.3.7: τὰς γυναῖκας Πλατωνικῶς ἔχοντας κοινάς (reading Herodotus 1.216.1); cf. Benardete (1969) 99.

90. Av. Cameron (1969–1970) 101.

91. For Agathias' use of Procopius here, see Av. Cameron (1969–1970) 154–157; in general, 69, 74, 114, 149–151.

92. Cf. Saxonhouse (1994); Craig (1994) c. 6. Plato meant something quite different from Cavades.

93. For whom see Christensen (1925) 9, 92–93, 111–115, (1944) 295, 347–351.

94. Christensen (1925) 115 n. 2, (1944) 351 n. 2.

95. Again Agathias imitated Procopius in producing his own parallel history of Rome and Persia: 4.29.1–4. For Hypatius' prestigious but inglorious career, see Greatrex (1996b).

96. Cf. *Wars* 1.2.1–4 with 1.11.2; but note that 1.2.5 has no correlate: Cavades did not fear the Romans.

97. See chapter 5, fifth section.

98. *Secret History*, chapters 6 (20, 24, 26, 28), 8 (29, 31), 11 (4, 5, 6, 12, 23), 13 (7, 13); also 18.29, 19.6, 19.11, 22.13, 22.30, 24.13, 26.23; applied to Theodora: 16.11, 17.3, 17.31.

99. Av. Cameron (1969–1970) 156; Christensen (1925) 90, (1944) 345.

100. Note the significant usage in *Wars* 1.7.31 (though not in the voice of Procopius himself).

101. Cf. *Wars* 7.21.6–7, where virtue is dissociated from justice. See Thucydides 8.68 (on which, see Forde [1989] 143–147); and Machiavelli, *The Prince* c. 8 (on which, see Mansfield [1996] c. 1).

102. Herodotus 7.2–4; Xenophon, *Anabasis* 1.1.1–3; *Cyropaedia* 8.7.9–11: "in accordance with tradition, custom, and law." For succession in Sasanid Persia, see Christensen (1944) 64–65, 98 n. 3, 263, 353–356 (the alternatives seem to have been nomination by the previous king or election by the nobility; in this respect, *Wars* 1.21.20 is more accurate than 1.11.3); cf. the approaches to this complex problem by R. N. Frye in *CHI*, 133–134; Mi. Whitby (1994) 250–251; and Wiesehöfer (1996) 169–170. Whatever the details, there was no "law of primogeniture" (Blockley [1992] 104).

103. See, e.g., Herodotus 5.39–42: despite his ἀνδραγαθίη, Dorieus had to submit by law to his older (but mad) brother Cleomenes; cf. Zames' ἀνδρεία (ἦν γὰρ ἀγαθὸς τὰ πολέμια) in *Wars* 1.11.5. For the tension among virtue, law, and heredity in kingdoms, see Aristotle, *Politics* 3.15–18. Xenophon also implied that in monarchies law follows the royal will: *Cyropaedia* 8.1.22, 8.8.1.

104. The same argument, mutatis mutandis, has been made about much of Herodotus; see Hartog (1988); Fehling (1989) 28–30, 49–57, 62–63, though it need not be that the information is entirely invented.

105. For the office and the man, see *Wars* 1.6.18; Christensen (1944) 131–132, 348–352, 355–356. For the negotiations, see *Wars* 1.11, and the narrative of Vasiliev (1950) 265–268, who follows Procopius.

106. Cf. *Wars* 2.9.8 with *Secret History* 8.24–25.

107. Mentioned also in *Buildings* 3.1.6.

108. For date, title, and authorship, see Garsoïan's "Introduction" to the *Epic Histories*, 6–16; Garsoïan supposes that Procopius drew upon a wider tradition and not upon a version (perhaps Greek) of this specific text (10, 20). However possible, such a conclusion does not seem necessary. Note that Procopius suppresses all references to religious discord between the Persians and the Armenians (a prominent theme of the *Epic Histories*) in accordance with his suppression of religious differences between Romans and Persians in the introduction to the *Persian War*. The possibility of a Greek source, as well as the authorship of "Faustus," is tentatively defended by Traina (2001), who also promises a "complete commentary" on these passages of Procopius: 407 n. 17.

109. *Wars* 1.5.8; *Epic Histories* 5.7; for the fortress, northwest of the Persian Gulf, see Garsoïan's "Appendix on Toponymy," 443–445; from an administrative point of view, see Wiesehöfer (1996) 188. Ammianus Marcellinus calls it "Agabana" (27.12.3).

110. For various possibilities, see Traina (2001) 410 n. 35.

111. Cf. Herodotus 3.133 ff., 3.139 ff., 7.38 ff.; Esther 5 ff.; Mark 6.17–28 = Matthew 14.3–11. The king's role can just as well be played by a god, as in the legend of Midas (Ovid, *Metamorphoses* 11.90–193; Maximus of Tyre, *Or.* 5.1). This is a universal literary device: see, for example, the first story of the *Mabinogion*.

112. For Arsak II, see Garsoïan (1967).

113. *Wars* 1.5.19–28, following *Epic Histories* 4.54. In her "Commentary" (302 n. 8), Garsoïan notes the story's similarity to the myth of Hercules and Antaeus (see Apollodorus, *Bibliotheca* 2.5.11). Cf. *Wars* 2.12.8–30.

114. Cf. *Wars* 4.10.13–22.

115. For the hostility of the *Epic Histories* to Persia, see Garsoïan's "Introduction," 51.

116. *Wars* 1.1.5, and see chapter 1, first section.

117. Teuffel (1871) 202; examples in B. Rubin (1960, 1995) v. 1, 178–197; Bury (1897) 93, (1923) v. 2, 303 n. 2, 424–425; Evans (1972) 17, 93–94, 140 n. 15, n. 17, 141 n. 30.

118. The Latin tradition offers excellent examples; see, e.g., Strauss (1958) 42, 138–142 (Livy); Syme (1958) 528–529; and Rudich (1993) 47 (Tacitus); also Sacks (1990) 127 ff. (Diodorus); Blockley (1981, 1983) v. 1, 57–59 (Priscus). In this respect, as in so many others, Agathias followed Procopius (e.g., 1.5.3–10, at the beginning of the work, and unchallenged).

119. Cited in Mansfield (1996) 134.

120. *Epic Histories* 4.20; it is irrelevant here whether Procopius used this text or another version in the same tradition. The event itself was, of course, unhistorical (see Garsoïan's "Commentary," 290 n. 8, 291 n. 18).

121. *Secret History* 14.2 (see esp. chapter 2, third section, and chapter 4, first section); cf. Cassiodorus, *Variae* 10.31.2.

122. E.g., Av. Cameron (1985) 239–241; Alonso-Núñez (1987) 11, 13.

123. Schopenhauer, *Parerga and Paralipomena*, v. 1, 361.

124. Soyter (1939) 102.

125. Benardete (1969) c. 1; see esp. Herodotus 2.158.5.

126. Menander the Protector fr. 6.1.405–407. For Christians identified by Persians on the basis of burial practices, see Brock (1982) 9. I have yet found no reference in modern works to Seoses as a Christian martyr, although I would not be surprised if one turned up.

127. Agathias 2.22.6–23.10, 2.31.5–9; see the discussion by Av. Cameron (1969–1970) 90–91; for Agathias' view of Persian culture, see Questa (1989), and 381–386 for funeral customs.

128. Kaldellis (1999a) 240–242, 247–248.

129. Agathias 2.30.3, alluding to Pindar, *Isthmian Ode* 7.25.

Chapter 3. The Secret History of Philosophy

1. Benardete (1969) 6.

2. Cassiodorus, *Variae* 11.1.19.

3. Polybius 6.3–18; see Walbank (1972) c. 5, for sources and discussion; for theories on the transformation of regimes, see Ryffel (1949) focusing on historians and philosophers. Aristotle objected that there was no reason to cast the sequence in a particular order (*Politics* 5.12) but did so himself nonetheless (3.15).

4. Plato, *Republic* 375a–376a. Aristotle saw these as the chief qualities of Plato's guardians (*Politics* 1327b38 ff.).

5. Synesius, *On Kingship* 19. For the context, see Al. Cameron and Long (1993) c. 4, who conclude that it was never delivered before the emperor. For another interesting parallel, see Amory (1997) 54–55.

6. Craig (1994) 28.

7. Scott (1985) 102–103.

8. Socrates follows Hesiod's sequence of the races of man in *Works and Days*: golden, silver, bronze, heroes, iron. Democracy thus corresponds in some sense to the race of heroes (see my Introduction). Besides, if Plato evaluated regimes on the basis of their tendency to produce philosophers and their tolerance and acceptance of philosophy, he must have concluded that democracy was the best of the regimes known to the Greeks. That is why he has Socrates state explicitly that precisely because democracies produce all kinds of men, a philosophical legislator should choose "to go to a city under a democracy" (557d). Without using these arguments, Monoson (2000) explores Plato's positive engagement with democratic theory and practice.

9. Crone (1991) 26.

10. *Secret History* 19.4–7, 23.7; *Wars* 1.7.35, 1.10.11.

11. *Pace* Av. Cameron (1985) 45, 205; and Howard-Johnston (2000) 24 (a hostile treatment). Procopius uses this phrase often, but always in order to highlight through contrast an individual's or city's preparedness for war (e.g., *Wars* 5.25.22, 7.40.9; *Buildings* 2.2.17, based on Thucydides 3.82.2). For a different example, see the clever variations on Thucydides 2.65.9 in *Wars* 5.1.29 and 5.12.51. Procopius' style

was in this matter directly influenced by Thucydides (for whom, see Romilly [1956b] c. 1, esp. 36, 47–48, 83).

12. Procopius' praise for Anastasius has often been exaggerated since Brückner (1896) 44–49. The prosperity of his reign was celebrated in Latin by Priscian, *In Praise of the Emperor Anastasius* 149 ff., and in Greek by Procopius of Gaza, *Panegyric on the Emperor Anastasius* 28–30. For the perils of peace, see *Buildings* 2.9.16; Vegetius 1.7–8, 1.28, 3.10; John Lydus, *On the Magistracies of the Roman State* 3.51 (under Anastasius); Theophylact 1.4.1 (on the capture of Singidunum by the Avars). For the bad state of defenses at the beginning of the sixth century, see Kaegi (1995) 94–95, 99, based almost entirely on Procopius.

13. *Secret History* 6.11–12, 6.18, 8.2–3; *Wars* 3.9.5; Justin's illiteracy is attested elsewhere: Vasiliev (1950) 82–84 rejects the tradition. Baldwin (1989) accepts it, with the provision that it may refer to "lack of formal education."

14. *Secret History* 6.19; also 8.30, and passim.

15. Blockley (1981, 1983) v. 1, 55–57; cf. Av. Cameron (1985) 208–209 (esp. Priscus fr. 22, 53, 66).

16. For the author's Platonism, see below.

17. For *diabole* and *phthonos*, see Plato, *Apology* 18d, 28a; *Euthyphro* 3c-d; Xenophon, *Apology* 14, 32; Diogenes Laertius 2.38. For envy and slander against the wise, see Xenophon, *Memorabilia* 1.2.31, 4.2.33; Philostratus, *Life of Apollonius of Tyana* 1.2, 4.36, 6.13; Themistius, *Or.* 21.256–257, 23.285a. For envy and justice, *Wars* 2.2.15.

18. Justice: Plato, *Phaedo* 118a (the last word), *Letter* 7.324e; Xenophon, *Memorabilia* 1.1.18, 4.8.11 (the last chapter), *Apology* 14, 16: "most just." Arrogance: Diogenes Laertius 2.28; Xenophon, *Apology* 1–2, 32; note the defensiveness in *Memorabilia* 1.1.5, 1.2.5, 1.7.1, 1.7.5.

19. Plato, *Apology* 24b; Xenophon, *Memorabilia* 1.1.1; *Apology* 10, 12, 24; Diogenes Laertius 2.40. In general, see Hansen (1995).

20. Aristophanes, *Clouds* 1400; Xenophon, *Memorabilia* 1.2.9. The formulation in *Wars* 1.11.34 also contains an allusion to Thucydides 1.130 (the Spartan king Pausanias' adoption of Persian habits), a phrase used by Procopius on a number of occasions (Braun [1886] 175). In the case of Seoses it is playful, as the charge of Medism is reversed to signify the adoption of *Roman* customs such as burial by a Persian (see chapter 2, fifth section).

21. For such speculation, see Christensen (1944) 355–356; B. Rubin (1960, 1995) v. 1, 260. Vasiliev (1950) 268, though unaware of the problems of this passage, limited his account to what can be said safely: Seoses was "executed for exceeding his power and frustrating the peace."

22. Agathias vainly tried to rival his audacity: 4.1.8.

23. Agathias 2.30–31; note the pun in ἡ κρατοῦσα ἐπὶ τῷ κρείττονι δόξα. For Agathias, the Platonists, and their code words for Christianity, see Kaldellis (1999a) 240–242.

24. See Al. Cameron (1969) 18–19; Av. Cameron (1969–1970) 175; Athanassiadi (1993) 25. "Without pushing skepticism too far," Al. Cameron wonders whether Chosroes would have been so devoted to the Platonists as to insist on the clause. But devotion is probably less an issue than the desire to meddle in the internal affairs of the empire by posturing as the protector of its persecuted minorities (a

tactic regularly used by modern states). Later events showed that it pleased the ostentatious Chosroes immensely to act as the champion of Justinian's enemies or victims: cf. his support of the Greens at Apamea (*Wars* 2.11.32 ff.) and treatment of the pagans of Carrhae (Harran) as though they were natural allies of Persia (2.13.7). As a patron of learning and acclaimed philosopher-king (in Persia at least: Wieseh-öfer [1996] 216–221), insisting on the protection of the empire's greatest minds had an irresistible ideological appeal. Independent evidence supports Agathias' account, in the form of a treatise written by one of the philosophers named by him, Priscian of Lydia, which addresses questions raised by Chosroes and survives in Latin trans-lation: Tardieu (1986) 23–24 n. 105; Walker (2002) 62–63. For other possibly related testimony, see Topping (1976) 13–15. Justinian intervened in Gothic Italy on behalf of converts to Catholicism (Cassiodorus, *Variae* 10.26), as Theoderic seems to have done on behalf of the empire's Arians (Moorhead [1992] 235 ff.). Roman emperors also showed an interest in Persia's Christian minority (Brock [1982] 9), and Justin-ian added clauses of protection for them in later treaties with Chosroes (Guillau-mont [1969–1970] 49–50). It is not clear that the philosophers' journey to Persia was caused by Justinian's "closure of the Academy": Hällström (1994), whose own suggestion, however, is as conjectural as those he criticizes.

25. E.g., Bury (1923) v. 2, 88 (treaty), 370 ("The Suppression of Paganism"); B. Rubin (1960, 1995) v. 1, 295–297 (the philosophers illustrate Chosroes' reputation for learning but are not mentioned in the discussion of the treaty); Av. Cameron (1969–1970) 175, (1970) 101–102, accepts the story, but fails to mention it in her discussion of Procopius' account of the treaty: (1985) 158. For ideological uses of the story, Walker (2002) 56–59. A recent monograph on the early sixth-century war, which carefully examines all the available sources, fails to mention Agathias' testi-mony in the chapter which discusses the treaty: Greatrex (1998) c. 10. This oversight was later brought to the author's attention: in an addendum to his preface, he dismisses it as unimportant (xiv). But to whom?

26. Cf. *Secret History* 11.23.

27. Chadwick (1981), for Symmachus, 6–10, 15–16. See also Moorhead (1992) 158–161.

28. Bornmann (1974) 144–147. For Theoderic's reign, see Moorhead (1992), esp. 106 for his *sapientia*, which is mentioned by contemporary sources. For more praise, see *Wars* 5.12.21–54.

29. *Wars* 1.11.33; cf. Agathias 2.30.5.

30. Cf. Strauss (1991) 205–206.

31. Boethius claimed that his devotion to philosophical ideals while in office offended powerful men and that his involvement with philosophy, probably mis-construed as magic, was among the charges leveled against him (*The Consolation of Philosophy* 1.4.5–9, 37–43). See Chadwick (1981) 48–56 (esp. 83: "one thirteenth-century manuscript claims that he was unable to complete the work 'because of the envy of the Italians' bringing about his death"); and Moorhead (1992) 219–222 (who forgets that Procopius supports Boethius' claim that philosophy was one of the charges). The role of philosophy in these events is sometimes completely invisible to scholars despite its centrality in the sources: e.g., Garzya (1995) 346.

32. Herodotus 3.64; cf. Bornmann (1974) 147.

33. See chapter 2, fourth section.

34. Arguments for various dates in Moorhead (1992) 224–226.

35. Al. Cameron (1966–1967) 669–670, (1969) 8–11; for the archaeological evidence, which reinforces the conclusion, see Frantz (1975).

36. For the dates of Simplicius, see Al. Cameron (1966–1967) 664–665, (1969) 24.

37. Athanassiadi (1993) 17–24: "The strategies of survival." Damascius offers numerous examples of high-placed Hellenes and philosophers. For the political activities of pagans in the fifth century, see Kaegi (1968) c. 2.

38. Damascius, *The Philosophical History* fr. 124; cf. fr. 26B.

39. For general accounts, see Constantelos (1968) 372–380; Harl (1990) 21–27.

40. Simplicius, *Commentary on the* Manual *of Epictetus*, epilogue (a clear reference to Justinian, according to Hadot, "Introduction," 20). The text was certainly written after 529 and probably after 532: ibid. 8–19. I would place it after 550.

41. Reading ἐκπυρώσεις for ἐκπτώσεις (cf. 14.89–90).

42. Earthquakes, floods, plagues, and famine: *Secret History* 2.27, 4.1, 6.22, 18.19, 23.20, 24.11, 25.10, 25.25, 26.22; for nature amplifying human depravity, 12.16–17, 18.36–45; cf. the conjunction in *Wars* 4.14.5–6.

43. Cf. Simplicius 14.21–23 σεισμοὺς καὶ κατακλυσμοὺς καὶ ἐκπτώσεις (ἐκπυρώσεις?) . . . πόλεων ἁλώσεις, with *Secret History* 7.6 (in a metaphor about the factions) ὥσπερ σεισμοῦ ἢ κατακλυσμοῦ ἐπιπεσόντος ἢ πόλεως ἑκάστης πρὸς τῶν πολεμίων ἁλούσης.

44. Cf. Simplicius 14.24 φόνους ἀδίκους καὶ λῃστείας καὶ ἁρπαγὰς with *Secret History* 6.20 ἄδικον φόνον καὶ χρημάτων ἁρπαγὴν (cf. also 11.3) and 21.14 τὸ γὰρ τοῦ φονέως τε καὶ τοῦ λῃστοῦ ὄνομα; for more λῃστείας see 21.3, ἁρπαγὰς 7.16

45. *Secret History* 9.15, 9.17, 9.24, 9.28.

46. *Secret History* 2.6, 3.30, 5.20, 7.36, 13.33, 17.26, 22.7, 25.20, 27.27.

47. Cf. Simplicius 14.31 ἰατρικῆς καὶ οἰκοδομικῆς καὶ τεκτονικῆς, and 14.26 for education with *Secret History* 26.7 οὔτε ἰατρῶν τις ἢ διδασκάλων τὸ λοιπὸν ἐγίγνετο λόγος οὔτε δημοσίας τις ἔτι οἰκοδομίας προνοεῖν. Cf. also 26.24, 26.33. For the attack on education (including teachers and rhetors), see also 26.1–2, 26.5–7. For the charge of useless constructions (οἰκοδομία), see *Secret History* 8.7, 11.3, 19.6, 26.23.

48. Simplicius, *Commentary on the* Manual *of Epictetus* 32.186 ff.; for many who left the empire, see *Secret History* 11.38. Cf. Strauss (1991) 98: "If [a philosopher] has to choose between a fatherland which is corrupt and a foreign city which is well ordered, he may be justified in preferring the foreign city to his fatherland" (cf. 211). For Simplicius and philosophers in corrupt states, see the analysis of Al. Cameron (1969) 14–21, and the remarks in the "Introduction" of Hadot's edition, 16–19 (though I disagree that the exposition of traditional themes precludes autobiographical or contemporary references).

49. Simplicius, *Commentary on the* Manual *of Epictetus* 30.11–25, 32.211–215; cf. Craig (1994) 108.

50. Olympiodorus, *Commentaries on Plato's* Gorgias 26.18; for wild beasts, see 32.4, 41.2.7. For the date of this work, see Tarrant (1998) 417 n. 3.

51. See Westerink's "Introduction" to the *Anonymous Prolegomena to Platonic Philosophy*, xiii–xx.

52. See chapter 1, first section.

53. For religious dissimulation, see chapter 5, first section.

54. Al. Cameron argued for Athens (1969); *contra*: Blumenthal (1978). The current favorite is Carrhae (Harran), following the impressive research of Tardieu (1986), (1987); for elaboration on his thesis, see Hadot (1990) and the "Introduction" to her edition of Simplicius, 24–50; also Athanassiadi (1993) 24–29. Harran is attractive, but there is no direct evidence: Foulkes (1992). For the state of the question, Thiel (1999); Walker (2002) 63–65.

55. Agathias 2.31.3; also suspected by Hadot (1990) 280.

56. Av. Cameron (1970) 9–10.

57. Agathias 4.29.1; Av. Cameron (1969–1970) 158.

58. Agathias, preface 9: Plato; 2.30.3: Neoplatonists (Pindar, *Isthmian Ode* 7.25, supplies the missing word). The "wise men of old" are mentioned in 3.1.4 and 5.20.7 (both may refer to Procopius). Emulous of his awesome superiority, Agathias pedantically tried to correct Procopius on matters of detail (e.g., 4.26.4–7).

59. Wolfram (1988) 262–263, 330; Moorhead (1992) 13–14, 87, 104–106. The mention of his illiteracy in another source has been ascribed to confusion with the emperor Justin: Baldwin (1989).

60. Cf. Amory (1997) 157: Procopius "has inserted the allegation to strengthen his explanatory opposition . . . between classical education and barbarian soldierly virtue." Amory's analysis of the episode is astute, but his discussion of its significance relies on the false premise that the historian was a propagandist for Justinian. Amory's contention that in Procopius' view "barbarians" were not fit to rule (156) falters before his praise of Theoderic and Amalasuntha and his outright heroization of Totila—in the *Wars*, no less! Procopius has no comparable praise for any Roman emperor.

61. Amory (1997) 156; but *Wars* 5.2.2, 5.4.4 establish a precise chronology *in spite* of the narrative. Note Athalaric's solicitude for grammarians as late as 533: Cassiodorus, *Variae* 9.21.

62. Wolfram (1988) 336, and 334–337 for the reign.

63. Diabetes: Frye (1995).

64. *Wars* 5.2.3–6, 5.4.29. Cassiodorus praised her education in Greek, Latin, and Gothic culture (*Variae* 11.1).

65. *Wars* 5.2.24, 5.3.4, 5.3.12, 5.3.28, 5.6.2–5, 5.6.11, 5.6.19; cf. *Secret History* 16.1.

66. The opposite view was taken in 507 by Ennodius, Theoderic's panegyrist, who boasted that the Gothic king had united classical learning and military virtue: Amory (1997) 114–117.

67. *Wars* 5.2.3, 5.2.21; *Secret History* 16.1.

68. E.g., Herodotus 1.60, in equally strange circumstances.

69. Cf. *Wars* 5.2.30 with 5.1.27.

70. Ἀνδρεία does not occur in Book 5 of the *Republic*, although it appears most frequently in Books 4 and 6. The reader should note the concentration and distribution of cognates of ἀνήρ in the section of the *Wars* dealing with Amalasuntha.

71. Barnish (1990) 28–31, esp. 29; and Cassiodorus, *Variae* 10.3.

72. *Wars* 5.3.1–4, 5.4.1–3, 5.11.1, 5.11.8, 7.8.21; Theodahad unlawfully seized the property of others and even "considered it a great misfortune to have neighbors."

Cf. Cassiodorus, *Variae* 4.39, 5.12, 10.3.6; in ibid. 10.5.2 the king states (through Cassiodorus) that "I have changed my conduct with my station" but also declares "that whatever, by God's help, I rule, that thing is peculiarly my own." For his properties, see Wolfram (1988) 298–299; for the reign, see 332–342. Cf. Plato, *Republic* 485e; for no private property, see 416d ff., 464b-d, 543b-c; also 390d-391c, 486b, and 521a. For Socrates' poverty, see 337d, 338b; *Apology* 19d-20a, 38b.

73. *Wars* 5.3.1. Cf. 5.6.15–16; Plato, *Republic* 521d, 525b, 543a.

74. *Wars* 5.6.1–2, 5.6.6, 5.7.11, 5.9.1–2, 5.9.6; Plato, *Republic* 486a-b, 503c-d; cf. 537c-d.

75. *Wars* 5.3.30; cf. 5.6.26, simply "the orator." Peter was one of Justinian's most important officials and diplomats, later holding the rank of *magister officiorum* for an unprecedented term of twenty-five years (539–565). He wrote historical and political works. See in general Antonopoulos (1990); for his career, see *PLRE* 3, 994–998: Petrus 6; for his works, see Karpozelos (1997) 420–431.

76. For a legal and historical analysis of this agreement, see Chrysos (1981).

77. Cf. *Wars* 5.7.19–20.

78. Craig (1994), esp. c. 1.

79. Saxonhouse (1983).

80. Plato, *Republic* 423d (ἐπιτηδεύων), 433a ff. (ἐπιτηδεύειν, ἐπιτηδειοτάτη). The verb φυλάσσω is pervasive in the dialogue. For the epistemic status of this view of justice in the *Republic*, cf. 432c-e with 479d and 515a.

81. Procopius has introduced another dialogue into the *Wars*, which also shows equally the influence of Plato's Socrates and Thucydides' Melian Dialogue: it is that between the Gothic envoys and Belisarius, which leads to a temporary truce (6.6). This passage will be examined in a separate study.

82. So too Antonopoulos (1990) 79. Cf. the Goths in Agathias 1.5.

83. Cf. *Wars* 5.3.30 with *Republic* 336b and 354a (which comes after 350d); one may choose between two views of gentleness to understand this discrepancy: 375c-e or 566e. In the *Republic*, at any rate, Thrasymachus is converted (358b, 498c-d).

84. Similar arguments in Plato's *Theaetetus* 172c-176a (cf. *Republic* 496d-e and 620c-d, which should be contrasted to 433a-434b and 443c-444b). If the view of the philosophical life in the *Theaetetus* and the *Gorgias* is not entirely accurate, that found in the *Republic* is downright fantastic. For a more active political role for philosophers, see Damascius, *The Philosophical History* fr. 124. Olympiodorus was less hopeful (*Commentary on Plato's* Gorgias 45.2). For the irony in Socrates' view of philosophers in the *Gorgias*—considering his own fate—see Clay (2000) 36–37.

85. Bury (1923) v. 2, 164–167; Foss (2002) 162–163, 171–172; Evans (2002) 63–66. Peter's innocence is not established by the arguments of Antonopoulos (1990) 62–69, who relies on a priori assumptions about his high moral character. Others do not believe Theodora capable of such a crime, e.g., Comparetti (1925) 74.

86. *Wars* 5.4.25; cf. Bury (1923) v. 2, 164–165 n. 3: Procopius "designedly made his statement ambiguous." In the *Secret History* (16.3) he says that fear of Theodora prevented him from divulging the truth in the *Wars*.

87. So too Teuffel (1871) 201.

88. Plato, *Gorgias* 466b-c ff. For Peter's greed and thefts, see *Secret History*

24.22–23; for his wealth, which is independently attested, Antonopoulos (1990) 30–32.

89. Saxonhouse (1983) 145.

90. Cicero, *Republic* 2.52.

91. Saxonhouse (1994) 67 and 75. For Aristotle's criticisms (*Politics* 2.1–5), see Strauss (1991) 277: "he understands perfectly what Plato is doing, but he refuses to treat as ironical what is meant ironically."

92. Saxonhouse (1982) 203.

93. In Cassiodorus, *Variae* 9.24.8. For the ubiquity of this Platonic theme in antiquity and beyond, see Praechter (1905) 482–484.

94. Boethius, *The Consolation of Philosophy* 1.4.5.

95. Barnish (1990) 29.

96. Agapetus 17; see Letsios (1985), esp. 182; also Henry (1967) 295–296: "Agapetus implies that the Bible provides the definition of a key term in Plato's prescription, so that a Christian emperor becomes the concrete expression of what Plato had in mind."

97. For the author's Platonism, see Valdenberg (1925) 56–58, 62–64, whose arguments suffice but do not go as far as they might. The author's conceptual framework is thoroughly Platonic, despite the fact that he criticizes some of Socrates' specific proposals, which his reviewer Photius mistook for a total rejection of the *Republic* (*Bibliotheca* 37). See Fotiou (1985) and O'Meara (2002).

98. Wiesehöfer (1996) 216–221; Walker (2002) 59–67.

99. Kaldellis (2003b).

100. Starnes (1990) 4.

101. Kaldellis (2003a).

102. Lanata (1984), esp. pt. 2., c. 4, and (1989).

103. Kaldellis (1999a).

104. Av. Cameron (1985) 7, 199; Downey (1949) 98; also Veh (1950–1953) v. 1, 5, and Evans (1972) 113: "he was no philosopher."

105. For Agathias, see above. For Ammianus, see Libanius, *Letter* 233.4: "to judge from his dress he is enlisted in the army, but in fact he is enrolled among philosophers; he has imitated Socrates despite having gainful employment" (tr. Barnes [1998] 61–62; cf. 76–78, 166–167). Theophylact prefaced his *History* with a dialogue between "queen" Philosophy and her "daughter" History. For later authors, see Kaldellis (1999b); and Anna Komnene, *Alexiad*, preface 1.2, and 10.2.1 (Browning [1977]). Cf. Syme's denials that Sallust was influenced by Plato's "doctrines" in (2002) 241, 244, with MacQueen (1981). In a new foreword to Syme's book, R. Mellor more or less admits MacQueen's thesis (xliv–xlv), though he still tries to minimize the seriousness of Sallust's philosophical aims.

Chapter 4. The Representation of Tyranny

1. See chapter 2, third section.

2. *Wars* 1.16.1, 2.10.13–14; Chrysos (1976) 17–20.

3. For Chosroes, see *Wars* 1.23.1, 2.9.8; for Justinian, see *Secret History* esp. 8.22 ff., also 6.28, 13.10, 22.31–32, 29.1, 29.12 (for avarice, passim); for love of innovation, see chapter 1, fourth section, and chapter 2, fifth section.

4. Av. Cameron (1985) 66, also 143, 162–163. *Pace* Cameron, Procopius nowhere accuses Chosroes of "preoccupation with theology" (143); also Evans (1972) 60 for the parallel. Howard-Johnston (1995) 177 suggests that the portrait of Chosroes is unreliable precisely because it "bears a suspiciously close resemblance to Procopius' own view of Justinian."

5. Romm (1998) 24.

6. See chapter 5, fifth section.

7. Roux (1992) 189–190, 289.

8. See chapter 2, fourth section.

9. Cf. Agathias 2.28–32; for a more balanced assessment, see Wiesehöfer (1996) 216–221.

10. The attractions of Daphne are described by Libanius, *Or.* 11 (on Antioch), and others.

11. Al. Cameron (1976) 180, also 104.

12. Evans (1996) 18, and 37; more fully, Al. Cameron (1976) c. 7.

13. For paganism at Harran, see Segal (1955) 124–126. Contrariwise, when Belisarius captured the Persian fort of Sisauranon the following year, he found that the inhabitants were all Christian and let them go (*Wars* 2.19.24).

14. See chapter 2, second section.

15. On which see Crone (1991) 31–34.

16. For Origenes, see *PLRE* 3, 957. For the riots, see Bury (1897), (1923) v. 2, 39–48; Stein (1949) v. 2, 449–456; Greatrex (1997).

17. See chapter 2, fifth section.

18. Procopius implies that this was a Persian custom, applicable even to foreign kings (cf. *Wars* 1.5.29, in another passage that mirrors the imprisonment of Cavades). It is unclear whether there was such a custom: Christensen (1925) 114, (1944) 351; Mi. Whitby (1994) 251–252.

19. Evans (1984) 381. Also in Homer, *Iliad* 10.173, but the context suggests Herodotus.

20. See chapter 1, second section.

21. Cf. *Wars* 5.6.22–25 with Thucydides 1.129; see Carolla (1999) 165–168.

22. For John, see Stein (1949) v. 2, 433–449, 463–483; for the faults of Tribonian, Honoré (1978) 64.

23. Jullien (2000) 49.

24. Bury (1897) 93: his "sympathy is not with Justinian."

25. For Marcellinus, see Bury (1897) 92–93; for Malalas, Scott (1981b) esp. 17–18, 23. Av. Cameron (1985) 159, unfairly paints Procopius' account of the riots with the brush of fascism, claiming that he "sympathized totally with the interests of law and order." (A sinister statement, for who doesn't? Apparently anyone who knows that "order" is merely "repression": 166 n. 120). Cameron's arguments are weak and contradictory. She accuses Procopius of "blaming the affair entirely on the Blues and the Greens" without explaining their grievances (166) but on the next page concedes that he did differentiate between the people and the factions and

admitted the responsibility of Justinian's ministers. So which is it? Her claim that as a true loyalist he "condemns the senators who followed Hypatius for behaving 'as a crowd usually does' " totally misrepresents his criticism (1.24.31), which is that they lost the chance to eliminate Justinian. To support her contention that he whitewashed the massacre from sheer enthusiasm for "state violence" and "repression," she cites the number of dead *from Malalas* (30,000), implying that Procopius suppressed it. In fact it is he who gives that figure (1.24.54; cf. *Secret History* 18.32); Malalas gives 35,000 (18.71). It is Cameron who cannot keep her figures straight: elsewhere she cites 50,000 (23). Her carelessness with the text is revealed when she says that the "only specific reference" to the senators "places them on the side of the emperor" (64), wrongly citing 1.24.6 instead of 1.24.10, and forgetting the speech of Origenes. Finally, her admission that "at any point he may not be writing what he really thinks" undermines her entire position. That Procopius' view of state violence was the exact opposite of what she alleges is demonstrated by Scott (1985).

26. Cf. *Secret History* 11.12 with *Wars* 2.1.12–15.

27. For a genuinely astrological treatment of the omens that signaled the fall of Antioch, see John Lydus, *On Celestial Signs,* preface 1. Lydus seems to have been inspired by that event to write his treatise.

28. Crone (1991) 30, citing other examples; for an additional possibility, see Mi. Whitby (1994) 256–257; for the foundation, see Christensen (1944) 386–387; for Persia's need for skilled Romans, Blockley (1980).

29. Theophanes the Confessor 301. For Sasanid solar adoration, see Christensen (1944) 143–145.

30. For Goubazes, see *PLRE* 3, 559–560. For Sasanid royal protocol and ceremony, especially under Chosroes, Christensen (1944) 397 ff.; in Persian royal literature, Sundermann (1964).

31. Avery (1940) 79, interprets this to mean that senators kissed the emperor's right breast.

32. Garland (1999) 13; also Foss (2002) 159–164, who highlights the inferior nature of other sources: 142 ff.

33. I cannot accept Fisher's argument that the testimony of the *Secret History* is suspect because it would have offended sixth-century readers: (1978) 255, 268. The truth is not always agreeable. If only Fisher's argument were true of the warlords of the twentieth and twenty-first centuries! For misogyny, see also Av. Cameron (1985) 75, and c. 5 passim.

34. Isidore of Seville, *Etymologiae* 2.29.14.

35. For Moschopoulos, whose work is still unpublished (if it is his), as for the relative strength of these words, see Dickey (2001) 9. For a similar definition of *despotes*, see Aelius Aristides, *On Rome* 23.

36. Chrysos (1978) 35.

37. Herodotus 8.102; see Mi. Whitby (1994) 243.

38. For Pharas and Gelimer, see also chapter 5, third section. Cf. Boudicca in Cassius Dio 62.3.1.

39. MacCormack (1981) 76; for the treatment of defeated kings before Justinian, see McCormick (1986) 97 (esp. n. 79); cf. 125–129 for the celebrations of 534. For a lively picture of the court, see Ravegnani (1989).

40. Pazdernik (1997) 40–47, also 175; summary in (2000) 154–158.

41. The topic deserves extensive study; see Scott (1985) for preliminary remarks.

42. Fotiou (1981). For Zosimus, see Paschoud (1975).

43. Honoré (1975) 123 and n. 306.

44. Lanata (1984), esp. pt. 2., c. 4, and (1989).

45. John Lydus, *On the Magistracies of the Roman State* 1.6; for Agapius, 3.26. My examination of Lydus' politics has been accepted provisionally for publication in the 2004 volume of *Byzantine and Modern Greek Studies*.

46. I intend to argue this elsewhere.

47. Suetonius, *Domitian* 13; Pliny, *Panegyric* 2.3. But Pliny calls Trajan *dominus* in his letters. The term seems to have been weaker than its Greek equivalent: see Dickey (2001). Cf. Pompeianus and Commodus in Herodian 1.6.4; for other examples, see Bréhier (1905) 163–164.

48. See Comparetti (1925) 68–72, for an imaginative explanation. I do not accept B. Rubin's view that the story evokes Domitian's reputation as the Antichrist, thus linking it to the later comparison of Justinian to a demon (see fourth section, below). It is told from a senatorial standpoint and its significance is political, not religious. A butchered emperor makes a lame Antichrist. Besides, Rubin finds that almost all the 'bad' emperors had reputations for being the Antichrist, which means that Procopius cannot make any negative comparison without confirming Rubin's thesis!

49. John Lydus, *On the Magistracies of the Roman State* 1.49, 2.19.

50. Matthews (1989) 245, a useful discussion of the fourth-century debate (citing previous bibliography).

51. Procopius' accusations are treated as rhetorical by Alföldi (1970) 24–25.

52. Eusebius, *Life of Constantine* 4.67; see Avery (1940) esp. 72–73 (Eusebius), and 79–80 (Procopius). For the history of Roman *proskynesis*, see Treitinger (1956) 81–90.

53. Constantine VII Porphyrogennetus, *Book of Ceremonies* 1.84, 86–87, 89; for Peter's work, see Al. Cameron (1976) 249–250, though no detailed study exists; for the book in general, see Av. Cameron (1987). The accounts preserved by Peter of the accessions of Anastasius (1.92) and Justin I (1.93) do not mention *proskynesis*. But the account of Leo's accession refers once to *proskynesis* involving the kissing of the emperor's feet (1.91, p. 415 Bonn ed.), and this must be explained. As Bury noted in (1923) v. 1, 316 n. 2, the actual narrative of the accession reaches only to p. 412, line 18, of the Bonn edition, everything after that being "generalized (in the present tense) so as to apply to any emperor who is crowned in the Hebdomon palace." In other words, it is a later addition, possibly by Peter himself or Constantine VII (Treitinger [1956] 10 n. 9). Note that *proskynesis* is qualified there (as well as on p. 414, line 3) as taking place "only if it is not Sunday." A factual account of a historical event would not contain such conditions.

54. Corippus, *Iohannis* 1.118–121, 1.155–158, and, less elaborately, to the general himself: 4.310–311; cf. Corippus, *In Praise of the Emperor Justin the Younger* 1.156–158 (including kissing the imperial feet); other references in this poem to *adoratio* are general: 2.275–277, 2.410–414, 3.258–259 (an Avar ambassador), 4.130–131.

55. Lane Fox (1986) 320–325 makes sense.

56. Quintus Curtius 8.5.22; the Greek accounts are Arrian, *Anabasis* 4.10–12; Plutarch, *Alexander* 51, 54–55.

57. Aurelius Victor, *On the Caesars* 39.2–4; cf. *Panegyrici Latini* 8.13.3 (*Caesar Constantius*), 9.6.1 (Eumenius, *For the Restoration of the Schools*); for earlier uses, see Bréhier (1906) 168; and Hagedorn and Worp (1980) 166–167. The shift to the exclusive use of *despotes* in official documents occurred in the early fourth century.

58. Rösch (1978) 39–40, examples on 94–95, 144, 148; also Worp (1982).

59. Bréhier (1906) 171; Rösch (1978) 139.

60. Guilland (1967) v. 2, 1; for later *proskynesis*, v. 1, 144–150.

61. Worp (1982) 212.

62. Persian: Treitinger (1956) 88–89, 228; Christian: Pazdernik (1997) 231–233.

63. Agapetus 23, 68; see Letsios (1985) 187, 191. The origins of this Christian metaphor lay in St. Paul.

64. E.g., Aeschylus, *Persians* 584–590; Herodotus 7.136.1; Xenophon, *Anabasis* 3.2.13; *Agesilaus* 1.34; Isocrates, *Panegyricus* 151; Plutarch, *Artaxerxes* 22.4.

65. Lane Fox (1986) 320–325.

66. Cited and discussed in Van Dam (2002) 65.

67. Mango (1959) 32–33; MacCormack (1981) 75. See also chapter 1, fourth section.

68. *Revelation* 19.10, 22.8–9; Justin Martyr, *Apology* 1.17; Theophilus, *To Autolycus* 1.11; Tertullian, *Apology* 34.1–2; (= Orosius, *History against the Pagans* 6.22); for the fourth century, Setton (1941) c. 8. Procopius mentions *proskynesis* in a Christian context in *Wars* 2.11.15–16.

69. Cf. *Secret History* 3.25; for a later example, see Michael III in Theophanes Continuatus 4.38 (pp. 200–201).

70. Av. Cameron (1970) c. 8–9, (1985) 115 n. 16, 259; and Frendo (2001) 130 (two different approaches to reading Procopius).

71. Marcellinus Comes, *Chronicle*, s.a. 527. Paul the Silentiary reversed the comparison between church and hippodrome: Macrides and Magdalino (1988) 55–56.

72. Nietzsche, *The Case of Wagner* 7. Nietzsche knew that this applies primarily to his own writings.

73. Unfinished: B. Rubin (1960, 1995) v. 1, 224; Av. Cameron (1985) 50, 53–55; *contra*: Evans (1975) 109. For genres, see below.

74. Greatrex (2000) 218–220, (1995a) 9–13.

75. Adshead (1993) breaks it into three works based on genre (Milesian Tale, Aetiology, and Financial Pamphlet). She excludes the preface and transitions as interpolations. Though she offers insightful comments about specific aspects of the work, she ignores its unifying threads, and her genres do not always fit. Besides, Thucydides 3.82–83 is not a genre, and it is circular to ascribe the putative coherence of the work to the cleverness of the compiler (28). Also, her thesis tends to collapse on itself when she suggests that the compiler was none other than Procopius himself (19). The suggestion that it is the only extant example of the genre of *anecdota* devised by Theopompus of Chios has little to recommend it (B. Rubin

[1960, 1995] v. 1, 470; Angold [1996] 21–22). For the nonexistent genre of *Kaiserkritik*, see chapter 1, fourth section. Combination: Evans (1975) 107–108.

76. Bury (1923) v. 1, 423 n. 2; Tinnefeld (1971) 18; Av. Cameron (1985) 66; Lozza (2000) 81.

77. *Wars* 5.2.30; see chapter 3, third section.

78. Cf. Corbulo in Cassius Dio 62.19.4, and the comment of Tiridates in 62/63.6.4.

79. B. Rubin (1960, 1995) v. 1, 199.

80. Zaberganes, otherwise unknown: *PLRE* 3, 1410.

81. Cassiodorus, *Variae* 10.20.2; Justinian, *Novel* 8.1.

82. James (2001) esp. 69, 90; Moorhead (1994) 38–40; Angold (1996) 27–29.

83. Adshead (1993) 7–10, a good analysis of the first part, whose focus on genre, however, cannot explain the role of Theodora and is therefore silent about it.

84. See chapter 5, fourth section.

85. See Evans (2002) c. 5.

86. For Sergius, see *PLRE* 3, 1124–1128.

87. Pazdernik (1994) 280.

88. Aristotle, *Politics* 5.11 (1313b32–38), 2.9 (1269b33–34). Aristotle's view of women was more nuanced than is implied by these passages and many scholars: see Swanson (1992). Plutarch cites Aristotle when he uses the word: *Lycurgus* 14.1. For the "rule of women" in myth, Vidal-Naquet (1986) c. 10. For women and tyranny in Herodotus, Lateiner (1989).

89. Specific allusions: *Secret History* 1.14 and 13.3 (*Peace* 620); 9.50 (*Peace* 320; *Knights* 692); 13.11, 18.29, and 20.22 (*Clouds* 225–228); 14.11 (*Knights* 632); 14.11 (*Clouds* 889 ff.); 17.31 (*Knights* 41); and 18.21 (*Acharnians* 704). Language: Lozza (2000). For Aristophanes in the *Buildings*, see chapter 1, fourth section.

90. Bornmann (1978) 30–37; Baldwin (1987) 152 n. 10; Lozza (2000) 91–93.

91. For the game, see also chapter 1, fourth section; for the patrician, see chapter 4, second section.

92. For the edict, see Bonini (1980), and 97–105 for Procopius. The accusation is also made by Evagrius (4.30), who may have known the *Secret History*, though this is doubted today (Allen [1981] 190).

93. For the professional background, see Greatrex (2001). The lawyer Agathias directly cites the *Novels* (5.2.4). For John Lydus, Caimi (1981).

94. Scott (1985) admits not looking at the *Novels* too closely (102 n. 38).

95. Honoré (1975), (1978) 24.

96. *CJ* 5.4.23; for a discussion, see chapter 2, fourth section.

97. Honoré (1978) 54.

98. For Justinian's notion of monarchy, see the works cited by Maas (1986) 25 n. 46.

99. Rühl (1914) esp. 290.

100. Av. Cameron (1985) 56–61, and n. 48 (with misquotations and wrong citations). Her evidence for pervasive belief is slim, especially considering the bulk of sixth-century literature. B. Rubin (1951) 477–479, admitted that there is *less* evidence from that century than others. Other scholars invoke the same platitudes to

explain the demonology, e.g., Evans (1972) 92; Mango (1980) 244. Cameron notes the *Souda's* characterization of the *Secret History* as part invective part comedy, but dismisses the latter component as too "simple"—as though serious comedy is simpler than invective! Not all modern readers take the demonology at face value: Beck (1986) 20, 106.

101. Av. Cameron (1987) 108, esp. n. 9.

102. Av. Cameron (1985) 59–60, 68.

103. Av. Cameron (1985) 44.

104. Examples in B. Rubin (1951) 478–479, (1960) 60–61.

105. John Lydus, *On the Magistracies of the Roman State* 3.58–59.

106. B. Rubin (1951), (1960), (1960, 1995) v. 1, 204, 206–209, 442–457. Despite its volume, Rubin's work has remarkably little to say about Procopius as an author, dissolving every aspect of his text into nebulous "backgrounds," whether religious, political, or literary. Also, Procopius' demonology has no clear apocalyptic component (*pace* Scott [1985] 108–109). In fact, the beginning of the *Secret History* looks ahead to better times.

107. Cf. *Secret History* 12.26, 12.32, with Mark 3.22; Matthew 9.34, 12.24.

108. Justinian, *Novels* 133.5 (and preface), 5 (preface).

109. Justinian, *Novels* 30.11, 8 (preface).

110. Av. Cameron (1985) 246–247, 256.

111. Gantar (1961).

112. Honoré (1978) 65, 85–86, 126–127, 241. The words in *Tanta* may have been Justinian's: 42.

113. See the constitutions that introduce and confirm the *Digest*; also the prefaces of *Novels* 7, 18, 46, 49, 84, and 107.1.

114. Honoré (1975) 122–123.

115. Honoré (1978) 28–30; Hitler: Mango (1980) 135.

116. Strauss (1991) 211.

117. Rahe (1994) v. 1, 5.

118. *Secret History* 8.29, 13.2, 13.8, *Wars* 8.21.7. See Shukman (1999) 78, 84, for Stalin.

119. Plass (1988) 37.

120. Av. Cameron (1985) 88–90; also 56–57, 65–66, 242, for taking the *Buildings* and *Secret History* "at face value."

121. Av. Cameron (1985) 57 n. 53; for the panegyrical aspect, see Garzya (1995) 342–343, who notes that it was copied into the *Souda*. For more praise of Theoderic, see *Wars* 5.12.21–54.

122. *Wars* 1.10.11, 3.1.2, 3.7.4 ff., 7.40.9; *Secret History* 19.5. Cf. Veh (1950–1953) v. 2, 5–7.

123. Croke (2001) 96, 98, 107, 128–133, 176–177.

124. Machiavelli, *Discourses on Livy* 3.6.13.

125. For these men, *PLRE* 3, 107–109, 574–576.

126. For these men, *PLRE* 3, 125–130, 547–548.

127. Frendo (2001) 126 n. 11. We may wonder why this conspiracy is recounted in the *Gothic War*, where it has no place, rather than in the *Persian War* (given the

Armenian origin and grievances of the conspirators). For a good discussion of the account, see Av. Cameron (1985) 141.

128. *Secret History* 12.20, 18.29; *Wars* 7.35.9–11, 7.36.4–6.

129. See chapter 1, fourth section. For Procopius' praise of usurpers and rebels, see Brückner (1896) 34.

130. Cf. Xenophon, *Memorabilia* 2.8.4.

Chapter 5. God and Tyche *in the* Wars

1. Exception: Kaegi (1990) 78. Av. Cameron (1986) 57 sees it as opposition to paganism. Adshead (1990) 100 suggests an imitation of Thucydides (mutilation of the Herms).

2. Gibbon, *The Decline and Fall of the Roman Empire*, c. 32, 261 n. 64, and c. 40, 561 n. 12.

3. Dahn (1865) 193.

4. A thesis revived by Adshead (1996).

5. Browning (1987) 170, 178, perhaps only reflective of his attitude toward power.

6. Teuffel (1871) 222, among other German scholars.

7. Elferink (1967).

8. Downey (1949) 102.

9. Bonfante (1933) 285, rightly rejected by Kaegi (1965) 31 n. 38 and Evans (1968) 137.

10. Evans (1971) 91; Honoré (1978) 3 n. 12.

11. B. Rubin (1954) 65, (1963) 641: "a Syrian, if not Jew." Kaegi (1968) 217 n. 125 called Rubin's Procopius "fundamentally Christian," whereas Evans (1971) 82 n. 6 viewed him as a skeptic. The same confusion exists in the position of Stein (1949) v. 2, 715–716.

12. Wootton (1983) 120–123.

13. Evans (1976) 357: "Gibbon's doubts . . . thoroughly refuted. Procopius and his contemporaries were children of their own time." Also Av. Cameron in numerous publications, esp. (1966), (1985) c. 7. Her position is now widely accepted; for example, by Hunger (1978) v. 1, 298–299; Kaegi (1990) 55; Croke and Emmett (1983) 5, as well as in all studies of later historiography and subsequent surveys of the age. Not everyone is convinced: Mango (1980) 243–244; cf. the silence of B. Baldwin in the *ODB*.

14. Downey (1960) 33: Procopius as superstitious as his contemporaries.

15. See chapter 4, first section.

16. Downey (1949) 89.

17. Haury (1896) 13; also those cited in Av. Cameron (1966) 467.

18. The bibliography is extensive; in general, see Bury (1923) v. 2, 366–394. For pagans, Constantelos (1968); Irmscher (1981); Trombley (1985). For heretics, Cront (1982). For Palestine, Holum (1982b); P. Gray (1993).

19. In Cassiodorus, *Variae* 10.26.

20. *The Book of Pontiffs* 59.

21. One example in Av. Cameron (1982) 47.

22. Fotiou (1981) 547; Fiaccadori (1979) 130 n. 12.

23. Cavallo (1978). For Chosroes, Wiesehöfer (1996) 216–221.

24. *Secret History* 11.14–33, 11.39; Agathias 2.30–31; see chapter 3, second section.

25. Zagorin (1990) 292 (c. 12 in general).

26. Ahl (1984). The literature is growing. Cf. *Wars* 2.6.3–7, 2.7.23, and 8.16.23–24.

27. Av. Cameron (1985) 161, also 17, 21–23, 43, 243–245, 253; (1966) 481 (could give no suspicion of paganism). For similar warnings, Teuffel (1871) 201; Soyter (1939) 100, 105; Hunger (1978) v. 1, 296; Evans (1971) 81: "it is virtually necessary to believe that Procopius maintained a successful façade of orthodoxy."

28. Montaigne, *Essays* 3.2.

29. Eusebius, *Life of Constantine* 4.54. For a spectrum of practices and beliefs, see Guignebert (1923).

30. *CJ* 1.5.18.5. For religious dissimulation in the sixth century, see Kaldellis (2003a).

31. Cf. *Secret History* 27.6 ff., and, from a different view, *Buildings* 5.7.16.

32. See the lucid survey of Garnsey (1984), who notes that "toleration implies a degree of acceptance as well as a degree of disapproval," otherwise it is indifference. Drake (2000) has recently argued that Constantine's declarations were principled and not just rhetorical, but he downplays his persecution of heretics and almost completely ignores the measures he took against pagan cults. He also fails to consider the apologists' interested motives. Other scholars state that Procopius opposed persecution not on principle, but *only* because it disturbed order, violated rights, and caused untold devastation to so many people! (This is essentially the view of Evans [1972] 115, 118.)

33. Av. Cameron (1966) 469, avoiding all the problems of this passage.

34. Av. Cameron (1985) 119; also 6, 66, citing Agathias, who was, however, not a Christian either; also Baldwin (1992b). For the passage as skeptical, see Teuffel (1871) 221; Westerink, introduction to the *Anonymous Prolegomena to Platonic Philosophy*, xxiii.

35. Av. Cameron (1991) 208. For a liberal, tolerant Procopius, see Scott (1985); Greatrex (2000) 221.

36. David Hume, *Dialogues Concerning Natural Religion*, parts 2 and 12.

37. Soyter (1939) 106–107, but he finds the historian's position ultimately contradictory.

38. Quotations from Av. Cameron (1985) 30, 36, 119. True to her argument, Cameron devotes scarcely two pages to the whole matter (yet in [1966] 467, she remarks that "it is wrong to concentrate on some passages to the exclusion of others"). This view of *tyche* is not new; it was outlined by Krumbacher (1887) 233–234 and B. Rubin (1954) 58, though they rarely receive credit for it now.

39. Av. Cameron (1966) 479.

40. Cited in Teuffel (1871) 229.

41. See seventh section below.

42. For particularly egregious examples, see Veh (1950–1953) v. 2, 20–30; Downey (1949) 91, though they are not untypical.

43. Kaldellis (1999b), introduction.

44. Nussbaum (1986) 69.

45. Cf. Teuffel (1871) 205. *Tyche* will be referred to as feminine when considered as a personal agent and as neuter when considered as a concept.

46. For example, Pflugk-Harttung (1889) 74; Hannestad (1960) 181; Av. Cameron (1985) 171.

47. Gaizeric: *Wars* 3.3.24, 3.4.6, 3.4.14; for Cavades, see chapter 2, fifth section.

48. *Wars* 3.4.12–13. For the antithesis of "force" and *tyche*, see Attila in 3.4.29–35 (for Gaizeric and Attila, cf. 3.3.24 and 3.4.6 with 3.4.34).

49. Eusebius, *Ecclesiastical History* 8.1.

50. E.g., Teuffel (1871) 229; B. Rubin (1954) 62; Kaegi (1968) 215–216; Elferink (1967) 120–121; Evans (1971) 94, (1972) 124–125.

51. Moorhead (1994) 77 n. 12.

52. Cf. *Buildings* 6.5.1 ff., 6.6.2.

53. Cf. *Wars* 3.3.14–36 with 4.8.1–2. Procopius' account of Basiliscus is probably based on Priscus of Panium (cf. fr. 53).

54. Av. Cameron (1985) 173 finds proof here that Procopius saw the reconquest as divinely ordained (probably following the version given in *Buildings* 6.6.8–16). She omits *all* references to *tyche* (which are bountiful in the passages she cites) and does not contrast the favorable signs that marked the beginning of the expedition with its disastrous net results. Furthermore, some of the statements she attributes to Procopius do not exist in the text (e.g., 3.17.6 on 173–174), a not-uncommon problem in her book and many articles. Also Knaepen (2001) 392–393, who thinks that by *tyche* Procopius means the Christian God, citing Gelimer's letter as proof (394–395 n. 49)!

55. Scott (1981a) 73–74.

56. Cf. *Wars* 3.10.18–21 and the later official interpretation of events: *Buildings* 6.5.6; cf. Pazdernik (2000) 153–159.

57. *Wars* 6.8.1. Evans (1971) 85–86 notes the allusions and changes but tries to differentiate between *tyche* and God. For exceeding mortal bounds, *Wars* 2.3.42–43; for divine envy, see Dodds (1951) 29–32; in Herodotus, Arieti (1995) 50–51; for the envy of *tyche*, see Polybius 39.8.2.

58. Austin (1983) 58–60; for the journey and fleet, see Casson (1982).

59. An interesting parallel to the fluctuating prominence of God in these four speeches is Cicero's four *Catilinarian Orations* (two before the Senate, two before the people); cf. the speech of Xenophon in *Anabasis* 3.1.15–25 with that in 3.1.35–44. For a good analysis of the problems Belisarius tried to solve with these speeches, see Pazdernik (2000) 160 on the Thucydidean background. Pazdernik does not note that the council of war is based on Thucydides 6.47–50 and therefore indirectly suggests that Belisarius' leadership was a unifying force such as was absent from the Athenian expedition.

60. Romanelli (1935) 129, recognizes that the campaign was a series of accidents and concludes that this reflects Procopius' superstition!

61. So, e.g., Downey (1949) 92–93, 95, who places too much weight on this

ambiguous statement; cf. Wolfram (1990) 181: "God and his rod Tyche ('fate')."
Knaepen (2001) 391–392 simply ignores the references to *tyche*.

62. E.g., *Wars* 2.9.13, 3.21.7; Gelimer in 3.25.13; *Secret History* 10.9–10.

63. E.g., *Wars* 4.7.8; cf. Teuffel (1871) 227 and n. 2.

64. Augustine, *City of God* 4.18: "Why do people worship her, if she is blind?
. . . . Or does Jupiter send her too, where he pleases? Then let him alone be worshipped, because Fortuna cannot oppose him when he gives orders and sends her
where he pleases."

65. As Augustine seems to have realized, though his argument smacks of his
usual sarcasm: *City of God* 7.3. Both Augustine and Boethius tried to subordinate
fortune to God by eliminating her autonomy and seeing a plan behind her apparent
indifference to justice, for which plan, of course, only faith could furnish proof (cf.
Boethius, *The Consolation of Philosophy* 4.5.7: "you must not doubt that all things
happen as they should"). They also subtly substituted fate for fortune, because
fate—defined conveniently as "the order imposed on things that change" (ibid.
4.6.9)—is neutral and lacks precisely those qualities they wanted to avoid. In short,
what they subordinated to God was nothing like Procopius' notion of *tyche* (cf.
Augustine, *City of God* 5.1: fate is either the will of God or astral determinism). For
general treatments, see Haefele (1954) 51–58; Chadwick (1981) 242–244, 250. Cf. the
Souda s.v. τύχη: "According to the Hellenes *tyche* is the improvident governance of
the world . . . whereas we Christians confess that God governs all." The difficulties
faced by Christians were foreshadowed in Josephus, who was not averse to Hellenic
notions but also wished to preserve the supremacy of God: Lindner (1972) 42–48,
85–94. Josephus sacrificed both the independence and the capriciousness of *tyche*.
For the ecclesiastical historians, see below.

66. MacIntyre (1984) 100.

67. Chesnut (1986) 39, also 9–13, an excellent discussion of *tyche*; cf. Walbank
(1957) v. 1, 17.

68. E.g., Cicero, *On the Nature of the Gods* 1.20.55.

69. Cf. Herodotus 9.82; Cassius Dio 74.13.1; *Wars* 1.13.17, 1.14.12.

70. Pflugk-Harttung (1889) 90, referring to "Belisarius' luck." Browning
(1987) 79–80: "They were lucky with the weather. . . . Procopius had a stroke of
luck. . . . Belisarius, scarcely able to believe his luck. . . . This was Gelimer's chance,
and he missed it . . . it had been a close-run thing." Wolfram (1990) 179: "The battle
was winnable for the Vandals, had Gelimer not been abandoned by fortune and
good sense." Evans (1996) 127–129: "before departure, the Byzantines had two
strokes of luck. . . . The army disembarked and chanced upon a stroke of luck. . . .
Gelimer threw away his one chance for victory," 132: Justinian "had grasped the
chance to invade," and 139: "the Vandal conquest had been easy." The city's traditional appellation was actually Felix Karthago: Clover (1986) 2–5, 9–10.

71. *Pace* B. Rubin (1954) 143.

72. The *Strategikon* of Maurice warns against this behavior after a victory,
which "can be disastrous" (7A.14; cf. 7B.17.38–39, 8.2.44); cf. Plato, *Republic* 469d.

73. The same passage was cited, to different effect, by Agathias: Kaldellis
(1999a) 222; also Cassius Dio 36.20.1, and, with variation, Menander the Protector
fr. 7.6.

74. Corippus, *Iohannis* 3.22; for the value of this text, see Moderan (1986), who shows that it is a propagandistic and unreliable text that should never be preferred over the *Vandal War*; cf. Av. Cameron (1983).

75. Chapter 1, second section.

76. Cf. *Wars* 4.19.3–4, 4.20.33 with Thucydides 2.65.5 (Braun [1886] 177).

77. Evagrius 4.19: "which Procopius the *rhetor* has elaborated exceedingly clearly."

78. For this ease, cf. Thucydides 3.86.4 with *Wars* 5.5.7.

79. Cf. Plutarch, *On Praising Oneself Inoffensively* 11 (= *Moralia* 542e-543a).

80. In defeat or hardship, and particularly during sieges, necessity is often associated with *tyche* (cf. *Wars* 4.6.23–24, 6.3.16, 6.21.35, 7.17.2, 7.25.5, 8.12.4–5). For the reign of Vittigis, see Wolfram (1988) 342–349. For the speeches and deeds of Vittigis, see also chapter 1, second section.

81. Hannestad (1960) esp. 157 ff., who concludes that the narrative is reliable in other respects.

82. For the military details, see Wolfram (1988) 302–304.

83. See *Wars* 6.9.23 for the inevitable reformulation. Cf. Democritus fr. D29; Plutarch, *On Praising Oneself Inoffensively* 11 (= *Moralia* 542f). For postponement in the *Wars*, see chapter 1, second section.

84. Av. Cameron (1966) 472.

85. Adshead (1990) 98.

86. See Adshead (1990) 95–104, who treats Procopius as "an experienced Thucydidean," but discards all of Belisarius' references to *tyche*. For the parallels, Braun (1886) 209–211.

87. Adshead (1990) 99; Carolla (1999) 171–176.

88. Thucydides 2.60.1; cf. Braun (1886) 184.

89. For the reason for Constantine's execution, see *Secret History* 1.24–30. Perhaps by *tyche* Procopius means Antonina; the language he uses in the *Gothic War* fits her as well as fortune.

90. Cf. *Wars* 5.11.11–14 and 5.13.17–18 with 6.3.23–27 and 6.18.14, as well as 5.11.25 with 6.3.32 and 6.7.2 on *pronoia*.

91. Cf. *Wars* 6.29.7, 6.29.11, and the letter from Rome.

92. *Wars* 6.29.17, 6.30.5, 6.30.12. These expressions are bound to be misunderstood if they are taken out of the context of Procopius' use of *tyche*; e.g., Wolfram (1964) 14, (1988) 350.

93. *Wars* 5.1.15–24. The parallel between Theoderic's strategy against Odoacer and Belisarius' against Vittigis is noted by Wolfram (1988) 347, who relies on Procopius throughout. The defenses of Ravenna were legendary: it was only by the guidance of an angel that Aspar penetrated them in 425 against the usurper John (Socrates 7.23). Procopius notes that Honorius fled to Ravenna chiefly because of its defenses (3.2.9; additional reasons have been postulated: Neri [1990] 535–539).

94. Thucydides 2.65.6–8, and 4.126.6 for Brasidas; cf. Braun (1886) 177–178, 180.

95. Thucydides 2.65; cf. Cresci (1986) 451–456, who recognizes that *Wars* 7.1 is a "key" passage. For the contrast in Thucydides as "especially important," Connor (1984) 60–63.

96. Cf. *Wars* 7.2.7 with 7.1.13–14 (ability); 7.6.4 (*philophrosyne, synesis,* and *philanthropia*: abstains from offending women) and 7.8.1–9 (*philanthropia*) with 7.1.11 (abstinence from women) and 7.10.17 (Belisarius' *philophrosyne*); 7.20.31 (*sophrosyne* toward women) with 7.1.11 (Belisarius' *sophrosyne*); 7.8.15 (*praos,* etc.) with 7.1.7 and 7.1.15; for behavior toward farmers, cf. 7.13.1 with 7.1.8–10; cf. 7.8.12–13 punished his own soldiers who offended Italians. For the reign, Wolfram (1988) 353–361.

97. For the conventional view of this passage as a diversionary tactic to mitigate Belisarius' failures or clear him of suspicion, see Av. Cameron (1985) 160, 188 n. 7.

98. Cf. Artabazes in *Wars* 7.4.4 with Totila in 7.4.15–17.

99. See the emperor's Pragmatic Sanction regarding Italy (App. 7 in the Schoell and Kroll ed. of the *Novels* [pp. 799–802]). For an analysis, Archi (1978), esp. 22–24 for designating Totila a tyrant.

100. For a similar view of *tyche,* see Dio Chrysostom, *Or.* 65.5 ("On Fortune").

101. For *tyche* and the wind, see *Wars* 1.14.36, 1.17.10, 3.6.15–17, 3.24.11, 4.4.32–36, 4.15.40 ff., 6.4.26, 7.7.5, 7.8.9, 7.10.7, 7.15.12, 7.18.4–8, 7.28.3, 7.28.18, 7.30.11, 7.40.15–16, 8.11.60, 8.26.2; for the metaphor itself, cf. *Secret History* 30.18. The comparison came naturally: pseudo-Dio Chrysostom, *Or.* 63.1 ("On Fortune"), and Favorinus, *On Fortune* (= Dio Chrysostom, *Or.* 64.7).

102. Cf. Polybius 29.22.2.

103. Attempted by Elferink (1967) 116–122.

104. E.g., Evans (1971) 89–90; Av. Cameron (1985) 138 (cf. 117–118).

105. For this "subjective" ontology of *tyche,* possibly Stoic, see Alexander of Aphrodisias, *On the Soul (Supplement)* 179. Totila claims that those who make the same mistake twice cannot blame *tyche* (7.16.23). The determining criterion here is the "knowledge" gained from the "experience" of the first mistake. Ignorance is a precondition of *tyche,* and the fourth-century B.C. historian Anaximenes of Lampsacus even identified them (John of Stobi 2.8.17).

106. Consistent, however, with his view that *tyche* is subordinate to God, he does say that the Goths have "chanced" to defeat the Romans (*Wars* 7.21.5).

107. For *tolma* in Thucydides, see Forde (1989) 17–26, 37.

108. *Wars* 3.5.10, 3.25.22–26, 4.16.19; for example, cf. 3.12.13–14 with 4.1.16 and 4.15.29.

109. Wolfram (1988) 306, 357, speaks of "irreparable damage."

110. Av. Cameron (1985) 44–45, 143, 240, views this as a defect; also Howard-Johnston (2000) 24. One wonders what their verdict would be on Thucydides (cf. Romilly [1956b] 50–52; Westlake [1986] c. 2); cf. a scholiast on Homer: he "has the art of revealing the whole character of a man by one word" (cited in Griffin [1980] 50). For Procopius' characterizations, see B. Rubin (1954) 70–75. For the Thucydidean background, see Braun (1886) 174–181: "Thucydides vitas et mores hominum excellentium . . . paucis quidem sed perspicuis verbis depinxit; iisdem saepe verbis Procopius usus est."

111. Av. Cameron (1985) 148–149, and 45: "empty of real content." Also Stein (1949) v. 2, 718; Howard-Johnston (2000) 24 (a hostile treatment).

112. So too the speeches in Sallust: Syme (2002) 198, 255, and most ancient historians.

113. Downey (1961) 533–546; Kennedy and Liebeschuetz (1988) 65–66.

114. Av. Cameron (1985) 117, (1966) 468; and Evans (1971) 88–89, who does not cite the digression on *tyche* in *Wars* 2.9.

115. Av. Cameron (1985) 117–119; for the word, 145.

116. See second section above.

117. Downey (1949) 95, suggested that Procopius "felt constrained for literary reasons" to produce a balance between God and *tyche*. But this constraint is reflected in the work of no other historian of late antiquity, nor is *tyche* as prominent in the work of any other. Procopius' successor Agathias, who was no Christian, hardly ever mentions *tyche*, whereas the Christian Theophylact does (e.g., 2.5.2, 2.5.5, 2.15.5, 2.17.13, 3.6.13). For the flexibility of classicizing history, see Mi. Whitby (1988) 41, 354.

118. See chapter 2, fifth section.

119. Cf. the view of *tyche* attributed to Rome's enemies by Dionysius of Halicarnassus in the preface of his *Roman Antiquities* (1.4.2), though he uses stronger language to characterize her amorality. For the pagan gods' indifference to the abuse of mortals, see Libanius, *Or.* 19.12, 20.12.

120. For the sequence of amoral *tyche* followed by a deferment to God, see *Secret History* 10.10.

121. When the governor ordered Polycarp to say "Away with the atheists" (meaning the Christians), the saint looked at the crowd and said "Away with the atheists" (meaning the unbelievers): *The Martyrdom of Polycarp* 9.2 (= Eusebius, *Ecclesiastical History* 4.15.18–19). The governor seems not to have noticed the double entendre. Cassius Dio records that the populace of Rome rejected Macrinus' elevation of his son Diadumenian, but, when pressured by the senators to praise the two rulers, "raised their hands to heaven and cried out 'He is the Augustus of the Romans; having him, we have everything,'" referring to Jupiter (79.20.2). Cf. Perozes and the king of Ephthalites: chapter 2, third section. Av. Cameron (1966) 478 claimed that in the passage under discussion Procopius did "confuse, or identify, God and Fortune" but draws no conclusions from this.

122. Bury (1909) 49.

123. E.g., *Wars* 8.32.29 (discussed below); *Secret History* 10.10.

124. *Pace* Av. Cameron (1966) 468, 478, who omits the crucial words (in [1991] 200, the entire context of professed—or feigned—bewilderment is suppressed, and the statement is taken as a straightforward confession of religious belief); Evans (1971) 89 at least recognizes the ambiguity.

125. *Buildings* 2.10.2, 5.5.1, 5.29.9; see Downey (1961) 529–530, and 73–75 for Tyche.

126. *Wars* 1.17.37, 2.8.6. The city was notorious: cf. Julian's *Misopogon*; Ammianus Marcellinus 22.10.1. The decadence of Syrians was a commonplace. In a playful paradox, Cavafy contrasted the sensual Christians of Antioch to the prudish pagan emperor ("Julian and the Antiochenes").

127. *Life of St. Symeon the Stylite the Younger* 57, with references to God's "wrath" and "anger." Cf. Peter the Patrician in Menander the Protector fr. 6.1.36–

40, attributing the capture of Antioch to God's punishment of "the excessive good fortune of the Romans." This is more Herodotean than Christian, but not necessarily un-Christian. Elferink (1967) 132 n. 54 supposes that Procopius *was* implying a cause for God's anger: Justinian's iniquity. But this has no basis in the text, and the argument depends on a clear distinction between God and *tyche*.

128. For examples, see Kaegi (1968) c. 4–5. See below for the plague.

129. For an instructive formulation, see Lactantius, *On the Anger of God* 1.

130. E.g., Theodoret, *On Divine Providence* 1.11.

131. Montaigne, *Essays* 3.3 (pp. 623–624); see Schaefer (1900) 16–18, 79–87, and 144–150 for Pyrrhonism as "rhetorical window-dressing, designed to mitigate the shocking effect of the attack on Christianity." Cf. the complaints against Socrates' cynical professions of ignorance, which undermined the beliefs of others: Plato, *Republic* 336e-337a, *Symposium* 216e; Augustine, *City of God* 8.3–4; and Clay (2000) 94: "In the view of those he annoyed, Socrates knew the answers to his questions, and his questions were designed to expose the pretensions and ignorance of his unwilling victims," and 179–180. Also Cicero, *On the Nature of the Gods* 2.1.2–3, 3.1.4, 3.3.7, 3.39.93. For a modern example, Popkin (1979) 226.

132. Epicurus in Lactantius, *On the Anger of God* 13.20–21; Sextus Empiricus, *Outlines of Pyrrhonism* 3.9–12; cf. Cicero, *On the Nature of the Gods* 3.32–38. David Hume, *Dialogues Concerning Natural Religion*, parts 10–11, remains the most succinct exposition, though the reader must pay attention to the shifting alliances between the speakers and their tendentious arguments. Like Procopius, Hume was not entirely free to speak his mind. The problem of evil was at the core of a number of dualist heresies, both in antiquity and throughout the medieval period: see, in general, Runciman (1947), although this work is outdated in many respects.

133. Lactantius, *On the Anger of God* 13.22. Augustine devoted a wide-ranging though inconclusive treatise to this subject (the *De Ordine*), in which he upholds various vague solutions; cf. 2.15: "These and other things in human life drive many men to the impious belief that we are not governed by any order of divine Providence. Others, however, upright and good . . . are so confused by the great obscurity and maze of affairs, so to speak, that they cannot see any order." See Chadwick (1981) 239–241, for a post-Augustinian, albeit still inconclusive, treatment.

134. Young (1973).

135. Possibly Homer, *Iliad* 24.525–533.

136. See chapter 1, second section.

137. Jouanna (1999) 209: Thucydides, "though implicitly he challenges religious causality, shows himself to be openly skeptical of the rational explanations advanced by the physician."

138. E.g., Croke (1981) 123; Meier (1999) 185–186, 189–190 (though recocgnizing his differences from the ecclesiastical tradition); and esp. Av. Cameron (1985) 40, 168, 234–235, who again cites statements that do not exist in the text: e.g., 29: "coupled with his conviction that all must be for the best." It seems that Cameron has transposed a comment made in connection with the fall of Antioch to the account of the plague. Neither passage is examined critically and everything is taken entirely at face value, except, of course, for *tyche* and related terms, which are strictly excluded. It is also unclear what it means when she says that Procopius

differs from Thucydides in that "he can find no human explanation" for the plague (40). For the plague, see Evans (1996) 160–165; Allen (1979) (correctly identifying Procopius as "agnostic" but omitting the testimony of Corippus, *Iohannis* 3.343–400, possibly the earliest source). For a medical diagnosis, see Leven (1987) 140–144. Modern discussions have possibly exaggerated its effect: Durliat (1989).

139. Jouanna (1999) 181; for Thucydides' rationalist view of nature, see Edmunds (1975) 169–172.

140. Justinian, *Novels* 77.1 (before the plague) and 141.

141. According to Malalas, God, "in his mercy," punished mankind for its "lawlessness" (18.92; cf. Croke [1990a] 23). According to Agathias, many believed that the plague represented the "wrath of God," punishing man's injustice (5.10.6, the historian himself did not subscribe to such beliefs; cf. Kaldellis [1999a] 223–226, and below). Among those mentioned by Agathias was to be the Syriac ecclesiastical historian John of Ephesus (cf. Allen [1979] 20), and the author of the *Life of St. Symeon the Stylite the Younger* 69. The Syriac continuator of Zachariah claimed that the plague was "a scourge from Satan, who was ordered by God to destroy men" (10.9; cf. Allen [1980] 472–473). Evagrius, influenced by both Thucydides and Procopius, blandly claimed that only God, who directed the plague, knew its causes (4.29; cf. Allen [1981] 190–194). He did not refer to his wrath (*pace* Av. Cameron [1985] 42 and n. 60). Corippus, possibly the earliest source, offers a different interpretation: God punished the inhabitants of Libya for the sins they committed *during* the plague by sending the Moors against them afterward (*Iohannis* 3.343–400). The Christian historian Theophylact reports that Jesus visited the Avars with plague to punish their ruler's impiety (7.15.1–3). See in general Meier (1999) 197–204.

142. Theodoret, *Letter* 52. For instances of "divine wrath" in early Christian writers, see Young (1973), and, regarding events of the fifth century, Kaegi (1968) c. 4–5. For a treatise, see Lactantius, *On the Anger of God*, esp. 16 ff.

143. Traces of this interest, though from a Christian viewpoint, can be found in Corippus: *Iohannis* 3.343–400. Cf. Bury (1909) 129: "Thucydides occasionally refers to oracles, but their sole significance for him lies in the psychical effect they produce on those who believe them."

144. Cf. *Wars* 2.22.11 with Thucydides 2.47.4, 2.53.4.

145. Skedros (1999) 124. See also the *Life of St. Symeon the Stylite the Younger* 78. For the ways in which the Byzantines reconciled their faith with disasters, in practice and theory, see Dagron (1981) and Vercleyen (1988).

146. This is the only passage in the *Wars* where *pronoia* is ascribed to divinity; elsewhere it is a human quality (cf. the ironic usage of 2.10.6–9).

147. *Aprophasiston* and *automaton* occur twice in the account of the plague (*Wars* 2.22.23, 2.22.31, 2.22.33–34); cf. 6.19.11–12, 8.14.34 (which must be taken with 8.14.38), and 8.32.28–34 (multiple occurrences). For *automaton* and *tyche*, see below. For *aprophasiston* and plague, see Thucydides 2.49.2.

148. Socrates, Book 5, preface.

149. Jouanna (1999) 209: "One unexpected consequence of this refusal to speculate about causes is that the historian saw things more clearly than the physicians of his time."

150. For innovation, see chapter 1, fourth section, and chapter 2, fifth section.

151. Agathias 5.6–8.

152. Allen (1979) 6.

153. *Pace* Av. Cameron (1985) 234–235.

154. Agathias 4.26.4; for his knowledge of Thucydides, see Adshead (1983).

155. The Christian historian Theophylact, discussing the earthquake of 583, differs from the classical model here (1.12.11).

156. Kaldellis (1999a).

157. Av. Cameron (1985) 3, also xi.

158. Cf. *Wars* 2.30.51, 3.21.7.

159. Roisl (1981) 44–50 unconvincingly impugns Procopius' account of Totila's death by relying on a priori assumptions about the king's psychology and fussing about the details of his attire.

160. Av. Cameron (1966) 473–474, (1985) 114, 237. Again, the digressions on *tyche* are ignored.

161. App. 7 to the Schoell and Kroll ed. of the *Novels* (pp. 799–802).

162. Gregory the Great, *Dialogues* 2.15.2 and the seventh-century continuator of *The Book of Pontiffs* 61 (on pope Vigilius).

163. Alcuin, *Letter* on the sack of Lindisfarne, in Loyn and Percival (1975) 110.

164. Cf. Belisarius in *Wars* 5.24.9. For *tyche* playing with men, see Herzog-Hauser (1943) 1668–1669.

165. See third section above, on *Wars* 4.7.18.

166. E.g., Teuffel (1871) 228–229; Av. Cameron (1966) 477–478.

167. The context of both passages repays study. Cf. Thucydides 1.140.1; Plutarch, *How to Read Poems* 6 (= *Moralia* 23c ff.).

168. For the *paralogos* and *tyche*, cf. *Wars* 1.9.12–13, 8.32.29; Totila in 7.7.15; cf. Polybius 2.7.1–2.

169. E.g., Demosthenes, *Or.* 2.22; Polybius 15.6.8, 29.22.2; Herodian 1.13.6; Julian, *Letter to Themistius* 255d, 257a; cf. *Wars* 7.14.23 (fate).

170. See the encyclopedic entries of Herzog-Hauser (1943) and Ruhl (1915). See Chesnut (1986) c. 2, for *tyche* in historical and philosophical texts; see Haefele (1954) 49–86 and Wolfram (1964), esp. 1–15, in Latin literature of late antiquity.

171. Gaza: Haury (1896) 13–14; Corippus, *Iohannis* 3.234–235, 3.413–425; Theophylact: see n. 117. Christians were at first reluctant to use such pagan terms. Eusebius deliberately used other words to designate accidents (Chesnut [1986] 39–50). His successors used surrogate terms such as *kairos*, though were not averse to *tyche* (ibid. 188–192, 206, 212–214). By the sixth century it was acceptable in Christian circles because theologians had cleared the ground and a heavily providential view was taken for granted (ibid. 216–223).

172. Olympiodorus: Matthews (1970) 95–97; Zosimus: Paschoud (1974) 328. Elferink (1967) sees a contradiction between God and fortune in Procopius while recognizing that he sometimes uses them interchangeably. He argues that they are distinct but can find no clear principle for why either term is used in any particular instance (132). Elferink deserves credit for trying to discover the principles of Procopius' composition, even though the two entities cannot, in my view, be differentiated.

173. See Matthews (1989) 427–428, 544–545 n. 9, and 424–435 for his religios-

ity; Naudé (1964) for Fortuna. *Tyche* made its historiographical debut in the work of Duris, the early third-century B.C. tyrant of Samos, whose usage has also been understood in terms of literary aims: Fornara (1983) 126 ff.

174. Walbank (1972) 61; in general: 60–65.

175. Polybius 36.17.1–2; cf. Walbank (1957) v. 1, 22.

176. Walbank (1972) 60, 64–65, (1957) v. 1, 25. Various compromises have been proposed (e.g., Green [1989] 170–171), and theories that postulate a development in his thought have rightly been rejected. For *tyche* in the Hellenistic period, see Green (1990) 55, 74, 400–401.

177. Walbank (1972) 61–62; Pédech (1965) esp. 54–57. For *daimonion* in the *Wars*, see 2.30.51, 3.11.30, 3.25.18, 4.1.24, 4.14.16, 6.29.32, 7.13.16, 7.19.22. The *Secret History* needs separate treatment (see chapter 4, fourth section). B. Rubin (1954) 59 saw a similarity between Procopius' *daimonion* and the Christian Devil.

178. Walbank (1957) v. 1, 23, (1972) 63–64. Unfortunately fortune in the *Histories* has not been studied with attention to the broader aims of each episode in which it occurs. As with Procopius, scholars are content to excerpt statements and discuss them analytically, which occludes the role played by particular instances of *tyche* in promoting Polybius' philosophical objectives, his "moral vision," which has only recently been identified: Eckstein (1995) esp. 262–271, who places *tyche* in the context of his pessimism.

179. Schopenhauer, *Parerga and Paralipomena*, v. 2, 408. For personification, see Deubner (1902–1909), esp. 2075–2076, 2142–2145 for *tyche*; in general, see Stafford (2000). It was discussed by Cicero, *On the Nature of the Gods* 3.16–25, esp. 3.24.61 regarding Fortuna: "obviously an abstraction" and "nobody will dissociate fortune from inconstancy and haphazard action, which are certainly unworthy of a deity." Also Pliny, *Natural History* 2.5.14–15.

180. Evagrius 3.26; Allen (1991) 139; cf. Chesnut (1986) 191, 219–220.

181. Herzog-Hauser (1943) 1648, 1653, 1678–1689; Ruhl (1915) 1344–1357 (geographically); Waser (1915).

182. Theophylact 8.13.10; for pagan statues in early Byzantium, see Mango (1963).

183. Cicero, *On the Nature of the Gods* 1.27.77–30.85; cf. Dio Chrysostom, *Or.* 65.12 ("On Fortune").

184. Machiavelli, *The Prince*, c. 25.

185. Fischer (1996) 258, 260.

186. Simplicius, *On Aristotle's Physics* 328; cf. 333, 360–361 for worship. For moralizing views of fortune, see Dio Chrysostom, *Or.* 65 ("On Fortune"); pseudo-Dio Chrysostom, *Or.* 63.7 ("On Fortune"): "Let us then not call any fortune evil. For neither does anyone say that virtue is evil, nor that goodness is evil." Cassius Dio professed his devotion to Tyche (73.23), but she seems to have been quite unlike the *tyche* of Procopius. For less positive views, see Pliny, *Natural History* 2.5.22, though his intention is to ridicule her followers and so probably does not represent their beliefs faithfully. Also the first-century A.D. *Tabula of Cebes* 7–9, 30–31, though it is not clear that personification here represents divination. Historians tended to present a negative image: Herzog-Hauser (1943) 1663, influenced perhaps by the uncaring deity of New Comedy: Ruhl (1915) 1320–1321.

187. See Clendinnen (1991) 67–83, 122, 141–152, and passim for a fascinating reconstruction.

188. In Clement of Alexandria, *Stromata* 5.14.128; Eusebius, *Evangelical Preparation* 13.13.687d; Theodoret, *Therapy for Greek Maladies* 6.16.

189. Edmunds (1975) 3, 174, against the pioneer F. M. Cornford.

190. Romilly (1956b) 175–176; see Edmunds (1975) 187 for a definition; cf. 174: "that Tyche ruled history is out of the question." So too Sallust: Syme (2002) 246.

191. For *tyche* and the *automaton* in the *Wars*, cf. 8.14.34 with 8.14.38; also 8.32.29. Procopius does not differentiate between them, but he uses the *automaton* rarely.

192. Anthologies: Aetius, *On the Teachings of the Philosophers Regarding Physical Doctrines* 1.29 (= Plutarch, *Moralia* 885c); John of Stobi 1.6.17. Discussions: Alexander of Aphrodisias, *On the Soul (Supplement)* 176–179; Themistius, *Paraphrase of Aristotle's Physics* 47–57; John Philoponus, *Commentary on Aristotle's Physics* 259–296; Simplicius, *On Aristotle's Physics* 327–361. Simplicius realized that Aristotle did not view chance theologically (359.25), so, as a dutiful Neoplatonist, he transformed *tyche* into a benevolent divine principle in his cosmology (360–361). For an anthology of mostly Neoplatonic views, see John Lydus, *On the Months* 4.7, 4.46, 4.100 (cf. Kaldellis [2003a]).

193. Nemesius, *On the Nature of Man* 39.313; cf. 31.272.

194. Bury (1909) 257–258.

Bibliography

Ancient Authors and Texts

Translations of ancient texts are my own unless otherwise noted below.

Agapetus the Deacon. *Ekthesis*. Ed. and tr. R. Riedinger, *Der Fürstenspeigel für Kaiser Iustinianos*. Athens: Hetaireia Philon tou Laou, 1995.

Agathias. *The Histories*. Ed. R. Keydell, *Agathiae Myrinaei Historiarum Libri Quinque*. Berlin: W. de Gruyter, 1967. (= *CFHB* v. 2)

———. *The Histories*. Tr. J. D. Frendo. Berlin and New York: W. de Gruyter, 1976. (= *CFHB* v. 2A)

Alexander of Aphrodisias. *On the Soul (Supplement)*. Ed. I. Bruns, *Alexandri de anima cum mantissa*. In *Alexandri Aphrodisiensis Praeter Commentaria: Scripta Minora* (= *Supplementum Aristotelicum* v. 2, pt. 1, to *CAG*). 1887.

Ammianus Marcellinus. *Res Gestae*. Ed. and tr. J. C. Rofle. LCL. 3 vols. 1950–1952.

Anonymous. *On Politics*. Ed. and tr. C. M. Mazzucchi, *Menae patricii cum Thoma referendario de scientia politica dialogus*. Milan: Vita e pensiero, 1982.

Anonymous Prolegomena to Platonic Philosophy. Ed. and tr. L. G. Westerink. Amster-
• dam: North-Holland, 1962.

Aristotle. *Poetics*. Ed. and tr. S. Halliwell. LCL. 1995.

———. *The Politics*. Tr. C. Lord. Chicago: University of Chicago Press, 1984.

Augustine. *The City of God Against the Pagans*. Ed. and tr. G. E. McCracken, W. M. Green, D. S. Wiesen, P. Levine, F. M. Sanford, and W. C. Greene. LCL. 1956–1972.

———. *Confessions*. Tr. H. Chadwick. Oxford: Oxford University Press. 1991.

———. *De Ordine*. Ed. and tr. R. P. Russell, *Divine Providence and the Problem of Evil: A Translation of St. Augustine's* De Ordine. New York: Cosmopolitan Science & Art Service, 1942.

Boethius. *The Consolation of Philosophy*. Tr. P. G. Walsh. Oxford: Oxford University Press, 1999.

The Book of Pontiffs (Liber Pontificalis). Tr. R. Davis. TTH. 1989.

Cassiodorus. *Variae*. Tr. S. J. B. Barnish. TTH. 1992.

Choerilus of Samos. Fragments. Ed. P. Radici Colace, *Choerili Samii Reliquiae*. Rome: L'Erma di Bretschneider, 1979.

Chronicon Paschale 284–628 AD. Tr. M. and M. Whitby. TTH. 1989.

Cicero. *On the Nature of the Gods*. Ed. and tr. H. Rackhan, *Cicero: De Natura Deorum*. LCL. 1933.

————. *Republic*. Ed. and tr. C. W. Keyes, *Cicero: De Re Publica*. LCL. 1928.

Constantine VII Porphyrogennetus. *Book of Ceremonies*. Ed. J. J. Reiske, *Constantini Porphyrogeniti imperatoris De cerimoniis aulae byzantinae*. Bonn, 1839.

Corippus. *Iohannis*. Ed. J. Diggle and F. D. R. Goodyear, *Flavii Cresconii Corippi Iohannidos seu de bellis Libycis libri VIII*. Cambridge: Cambridge University Press, 1970.

————. *In Praise of the Emperor Justin the Younger*. Ed. and tr. Av. Cameron, *Corippus: In laudem Iustini Augusti minoris libri IV*. London: Athlone Press, 1976.

Cosmas Indicopleustes. *Christian Topography*. Ed. and tr. W. Wolska-Conus, *Cosmas Indicopleustès: Topographie chrétienne*. Paris: Éditions du Cerf. 1968–1970. (= *Sources chrétiennes* v. 141, 159)

Damascius. *The Philosophical History*. Ed. and tr. P. Athanassiadi. Athens: Apameia, 1999.

Democritus. Fragments. Ed. and tr. C. C. W. Taylor, *The Atomists, Leucippus and Democritus: Fragments*. Toronto: University of Toronto Press, 1999.

Diodorus of Sicily. *The Library of History*. Ed. and tr. Russel M. Geer. LCL. v. 10. 1953.

The Epic Histories Attributed to P'awstos Buzand (Buzandaran Patmut'iwnk'). Tr. N. G. Garsoïan. Cambridge, Mass.: Harvard University Press. 1989.

Eunapius. *History*. Ed. and tr. R. C. Blockley (1981, 1983) v. 2, 1–150.

Evagrius Scholasticus. *Ecclesiastical History*. Ed. J. Bidez and L. Parmentier, *The Ecclesiastical History of Evagrius, with the scholia*. London: Methuen, 1898.

————. *The Ecclesiastical History of Evagrius Scholasticus*. Tr. M. Whitby. TTH. 2000.

Gregory the Great. *Dialogues*. Ed. A. de Vogüé and tr. P. Antin, *Grégoire le Grand: Dialogues*. Paris: Éditions du Cerf. 1978–1980. (= *Sources chrétiennes* v. 251, 260, 265)

Herodotus. *The Histories*. Tr. D. Grene. Chicago: University of Chicago Press, 1987.

Homer. *Iliad*. Tr. R. Lattimore. Chicago: University of Chicago Press, 1951.

————. *Odyssey*. Tr. R. Fitzgerald. New York: Vintage Books, 1990.

John Lydus. *On Celestial Signs*. Ed. C. Wachsmuth, *Ioannis Laurentii Lydi Liber de ostentis*. Leipzig: Teubner, 1897.

————. *On the Months*. Ed. R. Wuensch, *Ioannis Laurentii Lydi Liber de mensibus*. Leipzig: Teubner, 1898.

————. *On Powers or The Magistracies of the Roman State*. Ed. and tr. A. C. Bandy. Philadelphia: American Philosophical Society, 1983.

John Philoponus. *Commentary on Aristotle's Physics*. Ed. H. Vitelli, *Ioannis Philoponi in Aristotelis Physicorum Commentaria* (= *CAG* v. 16–17). 1887–1888.

Justinian. *Codex Iustinianus*. Ed. P. Krueger. In *Corpus Iuris Civilis*. v. 2. Berlin: Apud Weidmannos. 1967. (reprint)

————. *Novellae*. Ed. R. Schoell and G. Kroll. In *Corpus Iuris Civilis*. v. 3. Berlin: Apud Weidmannos, 1959. (reprint)

————. *Novels*. Tr. S. P. Scott, *The Civil Law*. v. 16–17. Cincinnati: Central Trust Company, 1932.

Lactantius. *On the Anger of God*. Ed. and tr. C. Ingremeau, *Lactance: La colère de Dieu*. Paris: Éditions du Cerf. 1982. (= *Sources chrétiennes* v. 289)

Life of St. Symeon the Stylite the Younger. Ed. and tr. P. van den Ven, *La vie ancienne de S. Syméon Stylite le Jeune (521–592).* 2 vols. Brussels, 1962–1970. (= *Subsidia Hagiographica* v. 32)

Malalas, John. *Chronographia.* Ed. I. Thurn. Berlin and New York: W. de Gruyter, 2000. (= *CFHB* v. 35)

Marcellinus Comes. *Chronicle.* Ed. and tr. B. Croke. Sydney: Australian Association for Byzantine Studies. 1995. (= *Byzantina Australiensia* v. 7)

Maurice. *Strategikon.* Ed. G. T. Dennis and tr. E. Gamillscheg, *Das Strategikon des Maurikios.* Vienna: Verlag der österreichischen Akademie der Wissenschaften, 1981. (= *CFHB* v. 17)

Menander the Protector. *History.* Ed. and tr. R. C. Blockley, *The History of Menander the Guardsman.* Liverpool: Francis Cairns, 1985.

Nemesius of Emesa. *On the Nature of Man.* Ed. M. Marani, *Nemesii Emeseni de natura hominis.* Leipzig: Teubner, 1987.

Olympiodorus. *Commentaries on Plato's* Gorgias. Ed. L. G. Westerink, *Olympiodori in Platonis Gorgiam Commentaria.* Leipzig: Teubner, 1970.

Peter the Patrician. *History.* Ed. K. Müller, *Fragmenta historicorum graecorum.* v. 4, 181–191. Paris: A Firmin-Didot, 1885.

Philostorgius. *Ecclesiastical History.* Ed. J. Bidez, *Philostorgius: Kirchengeschichte. Mit dem Leben des Lucian von Antiochien und den Fragmenten eines arianischen Historiographen.* Leipzig: Teubner. 1913. (= *Griechischen christlichen Schriftsteller der ersten drei Jahrhunderte* v. 21)

Phlegon of Tralles. *The Book of Marvels.* Tr. W. Hansen. Exeter: University of Exeter Press, 1996.

Photius. *The Bibliotheca.* Tr. N. G. Wilson. London: Duckworth, 1994.

Plato. *Phaedrus.* Tr. J H. Nichols, Jr. Ithaca, N.Y.: Cornell University Press, 1998.

———. *Republic.* Tr. A. Bloom. 2nd ed. New York: Basic Books, 1991.

Priscian of Caesarea. *In Praise of the Emperor Anastasius.* Tr. P. Coyne, *Priscian of Caesarea's De laude Anastasii imperatoris.* Lewiston, N.Y.: Edwin Mellen Press, 1991.

Priscus of Panium. *History.* Ed. and tr. R. C. Blockley (1981, 1983) v. 2, 221–400.

Procopius of Caesarea. Ed. J. Haury, *Procopii Caesariensis Opera Omnia.* Rev. G. Wirth. 4 vols. Leipzig: Teubner, 1963–1964.

Procopius of Gaza. *Panegyric on the Emperor Anastasios.* Ed. and tr. A. Chauvot, *Procope de Gaza, Priscien de Césarée: Panégyriques de l'empereur Anastase Ier.* Bonn: Habelt, 1986.

Seneca. *Letters to Lucilius.* Ed. and tr. R. M. Gummere, *Seneca: Ad Lucilium Epistulae Morales.* LCL. v. 2. 1920.

Simplicius. *Commentary on the* Manual *of Epictetus.* Ed. I. Hadot, *Simplicius: Commentaire sur le* Manuel *d'Épictète.* Leiden and New York: E. J. Brill, 1996.

———. *On Aristotle's* Physics. Ed. H. Diels, *Simplicii in Aristotelis Physicorum* (= *CAG* v. 9–10). 1882–1895.

Suidae Lexicon. Ed. A. Adler. Leipzig: Teubner, 1971.

Synesius. *De regno.* Ed. N. Terzaghi, *Synesii Cyrenensis Opuscula.* 5–62. Rome: Typis R. Officinae polygraphicae, 1944.

————. *On Kingship.* Tr. A. Fitzgerald, *The Essays and Hymns of Synesius of Cyrene.* v. 1, 108–147. London: Oxford University Press, 1930.

The Tabula of Cebes. Ed. and tr. J. T. Fitzgerald and L. M. White. Chico, Calif.: Scholars Press, 1983.

Themistius. *Paraphrase of Aristotle's* Physics. Ed. H. Schenkl, *Themistii in Aristotelis Physica Paraphrasis.* (= *CAG* v. 5, pt. 2). 1900

Theodoret of Cyrrhus. *On Divine Providence.* Tr. T. Halton. New York: Newman Press, 1988.

————. *Letters.* Ed. and tr. Y. Azéma, *Théodoret de Cyr: Correspondance.* Paris: Éditions du Cerf. 1955–1965. (= *Sources chrétiennes* v. 40, 98, 111)

Theophanes the Confessor. *Chronographia.* Ed. C. de Boor. Leipzig: Teubner, 1883.

Theophanes Continuatus. Ed. I. Bekker. Bonn, 1838.

Theophylact. *History.* Ed. C. de Boor, *Theophylacti Simocattae Historiae.* Rev. P. Wirth. Stuttgart: Teubner, 1972.

————. *The History of Theophylact Simocatta.* Tr. M. and M. Whitby. Oxford: Clarendon Press, 1986.

Vegetius. *Epitome of Military Science.* Tr. N. P. Milner. TTH. 1993.

Victor of Vita. *History of the Vandal Persecution.* Tr. J. Moorhead. TTH. 1992.

Zachariah Scholasticus. *Ecclesiastical History.* Tr. F. J. Hamilton and E. W. Brooks, *The Syriac Chronicle Known as that of Zachariah of Mitylene.* London: Methuen, 1899.

Zosimus. *New History.* Ed. L. Mendelssohn, *Zosimi comitis et exadvocati fisci Historia nova.* Leipzig: Teubner, 1887.

Modern Scholarship

Adelson, H. L. (1957). *Light Weight Solidi and Byzantine Trade During the Sixth and Seventh Centuries.* New York: American Numismatic Society.

Adshead, K. (1983). "Thucydides and Agathias." In B. Croke and A. M. Emmett, eds., *History and Historians in Late Antiquity.* New York: Pergamon Press. 82–87.

————. (1990). "Procopius' Poliorcetica: Continuities and Discontinuities." In G. Clarke, ed., *Reading the Past in Late Antiquity.* Rushcutters Bay, NSW: Australian National University Press. 93–119.

————. (1993). "The Secret History of Procopius and Its Genesis." *Byzantion* 63: 5–28.

————. (1996). "Procopius and the Samaritans." In P. Allen and E. Jeffreys, eds., *The Sixth Century: End or Beginning?* (= *Byzantina Australiensia* v. 10). Brisbane: Australian Association for Byzantine Studies. 35–41.

Agapitos, P. A. (2002). "Η θέση της αισθητικής αποτίμησης σε μια "νέα" ιστορία της βυζαντινής λογοτεχνίας." In P. Odorico and P. A. Agapitos, eds., *Pour une "nouvelle" histoire de la littérature byzantine: Problèmes, méthodes, approches, propositions.* Paris: Centre d'Études Byzantines, Néohelléniques et Sud-est Européennes, École des Hautes Études en Sciences Sociales.

Ahl, F. (1984). "The Art of Safe Criticism in Greece and Rome." *American Journal of Philology* 105: 174–208.

Ahrweiler, H. (1961). "Fonctionnaires et bureaux maritimes à Byzance." *Revue des études byzantines* 19: 239–252.

Alföldi, A. (1970). *Die monarchische Repräsentation im römischen Kaiserreiche.* Darmstadt: Wissenschaftliche Buches.

Allen, P. (1979). "The "Justinianic" Plague." *Byzantion* 49: 5–20.

———. (1980). "Zachariah Scholasticus and the *Historia Ecclesiastica* of Evagrius Scholasticus." *Journal of Theological Studies* 31: 471–488.

———. (1981). *Evagrius Scholasticus the Church Historian* (= *Spicilegium Sacrum Lovaniense: Études et Documents*, fasc. 41). Louvain.

Allison, J. W. (1989). *Power and Preparedness in Thucydides.* Baltimore: Johns Hopkins University Press.

Alonso-Núñez, J. M. (1987). "Jordanes and Procopius on Northern Europe." *Nottingham Mediaeval Studies* 31: 1–16.

Amelotti, M., and L. M. Zingale. (1985). *Le costituzioni giustinianee nei papiri e nelle epigrafi.* Milan: A. Giuffrè.

Amory, P. (1997). *People and Identity in Ostrogothic Italy, 489–554.* Cambridge: Cambridge University Press.

Angold, M. (1996). "Procopius' Portrait of Theodora." In C. N. Constantinides et al., ed., ΦΙΛΕΛΛΗΝ. Studies in Honour of Robert Browning. Venice: Istituto ellenico di studi bizantini e postbizantini di Venezia. 21–34.

Antonopoulos, P. (1990). *Πέτρος Πατρίκιος. Ο βυζαντινός διπλωμάτης, ἀξιωματοῦχος καί συγγραφέας.* Athens: Historical Publications St. D. Basilopoulos.

Archi, G. G. (1978). "Pragmatica sanctio pro petitione Vigilii." In O. Behrends et al., eds., *Festschrift für Franz Wieacker zum 70. Geburtstag.* Göttingen: Vandenhoeck und Ruprecht. 11–36.

Arieti, J. A. (1995). *Discourses on the First Book of Herodotus.* Lanham, Md.: Littlefield Adams Books.

Athanassiadi, P. (1993). "Persecution and Response in Late Paganism: The Evidence of Damascius." *Journal of Hellenic Studies* 113: 1–29.

Auerbach, E. (1953). *Mimesis: The Representation of Reality in Western Literature.* Tr. W. R. Trask. Princeton, N.J.: Princeton University Press.

Austin, N. J. (1983). "Autobiography and History: Some Later Roman Historians and their Veracity." In B. Croke and A. M Emmett, eds., *History and Historians in Late Antiquity.* New York: Pergamon Press. 54–65.

Avenarius, G. (1956). *Lukians Schrift zur Geschichtsschreibung.* Meisenheim am Glan: Hain.

Avery, W. T. (1940). "The *adoratio purpurae* and the Importance of the Imperial Purple in the Fourth Century of the Christian Era." *Memoirs of the American Academy in Rome* 17: 66–80.

Baldwin, B. (1982). "An Aphorism in Procopius." *Rheinisches Museum für Philologie* 125: 309–311.

———. (1987). "Sexual Rhetoric in Procopius." *Mnemosyne* 40: 150–152.

———. (1989). "Illiterate Emperors." *Historia* 38: 124–126.

———. (1992a). "Three-Obol Girls in Procopius." *Hermes* 120: 255–257.

————. (1992b). "Procopius on Theological Disputation." *Mnemosyne* 45: 227–228.

Barnes, T. D. (1998). *Ammianus Marcellinus and the Representation of Historical Reality.* Ithaca, N.Y.: Cornell University Press.

Barnish, S. J. B. (1990). "Maximian, Cassiodorus, Boethius, Theodahad: Literature, Philosophy and Politics in Ostrogothic Italy." *Nottingham Medieval Studies* 34: 16–32.

Beck, H.-G. (1984). *Byzantinisches Erotikon: Orthodoxie, Literatur, Gesellschaft.* Munich: Verlag der Bayerischen Akademie der Wissenschaften: In Kommission bei C. H. Beck.

————. (1986). *Kaiserin Theodora und Prokop: Der Historiker und sein Opfer.* Munich: Piper.

Behnegar, N. (1995). "The Liberal Politics of Leo Strauss." In M. Palmer and T. L. Pangle, eds., *Political Philosophy and the Human Soul: Essays in Memory of Allan Bloom.* Lanham, Md.: Rowman and Littlefield. 251–267.

Bellinger, A. R. (1966). *Catalogue of the Byzantine Coins in the Dumbarton Oaks Collection and in the Whittemore Collection.* Vol. 1: *Anastasius I to Maurice, 491–602.* Washington, D.C.: Dumbarton Oaks.

Benardete, S. (1963). "Achilles and the Iliad." *Hermes* 91: 1–16.

————. (1969). *Herodotean Inquiries.* The Hague: Nijhoff; reprint, South Bend, Ind.: St. Augustine's Press, 1999.

Blockley, R. C. (1972). "Dexippus and Priscus and the Thucydidean Account of the Siege of Plataea." *Phoenix* 26: 18–27.

————. (1980). "Doctors as Diplomats in the Sixth Century A.D." *Florilegium* 2: 89–100.

————. (1981, 1983). *The Fragmentary Classicising Historians of the Later Roman Empire: Eunapius, Olympiodorus, Priscus and Malchus.* Liverpool: Francis Cairns.

————. (1992). *East Roman Foreign Policy. Formation and Conduct from Diocletian to Anastasius.* Leeds: Francis Cairns.

Blumenthal, H. J. (1978). "529 and Its Sequel: What Happened to the Academy?" *Byzantion* 48: 369- 385.

Bonfante, P. (1933). "Il movente della Storia Arcana di Procopio." *Bullettino dell' Istituto di Diritto Romano* 41: 283–287.

Bonini, R. (1980). *Ricerche sulla legislazione giustinianea dell'anno 535.* Nov. Iustiniani 8: *Venalità delle cariche e riforme dell'amministrazione periferica.* 2nd ed. Bologna: Pàtron.

Bornmann, F. (1974). "Motivi Tucididei in Procopio." *Atene e Roma* 19: 138–150.

————. (1978). "Su alcuni passi di Procopio." *Studi Italiani di Filologia Classica* 50: 27–37.

Bosworth, A. B. (1983). "Arrian at the Caspian Gates: A Study in Methodology." *Classical Quarterly* 33: 265–276.

Bowie, E. (1995). "Names and a Gem: Aspects of Allusion in Heliodorus' *Aethiopica*." In D. Innes, H. Hine, and C. Pelling, eds., *Ethics and Rhetoric: Classical Essays for Donald Russell on His Seventy-Fifth Birthday.* Oxford: Clarendon Press and New York: Oxford University Press. 269–280.

Braun, H. (1886). *Procopius Caesariensis quatenus imitatus sit Thucydidem.* In I. Müller and A. Luchs, eds., *Acta seminarii philologici Erlangensis* 4: 161–221.

Bréhier, L. (1905). "L'origine des titres impériaux à Byzance. Βασιλεὺς et δεσπότης." *BZ* 15: 161–178.

Brock, S. P. (1982). "Christians in the Sasanian Empire: A Case of Divided Loyalties." *Studies in Church History* 18: 1–19.

Browning, R. (1977). "An Unpublished Funeral Oration on Anna Comnena." In Browning, *Studies on Byzantine History, Literature and Education.* London: Variorum Reprints. vii.

———. (1987). *Justinian and Theodora.* 2nd ed. London: Thames and Hudson.

Brückner, M. (1896). *Zur Beurteilung des Geschichtschreibers Procopius von Cäsarea.* Ansbach: C. Brügle & Sohn.

Bulanda, E. (1913). *Bogen und Pfeil bei den Völkern des Altertums.* Vienna: Hölder.

Bury, J. B. (1897). "The Nika Riot." *Journal of Hellenic Studies* 17: 92–119.

———. (1909). *The Ancient Greek Historians.* London: Macmillan; reprint, New York: Dover, 1958.

———. (1923). *History of the Later Roman Empire from the Death of Theodosius I to the Death of Justinian.* London: Macmillan; reprint, New York: Dover, 1958.

Caimi, J. (1981). "Ioannis Lydo *de magistratibus* III 70. Note esegetiche e spunti in tema di fiscalità e legislazione protobizantine." *Rivista di studi bizantini e slavi* 1: 317–361.

Cameron, Al. (1966–1967). "The End of the Ancient Universities." *Cahiers d'histoire mondiale* 10: 653–673.

———. (1969). "The Last Days of the Academy at Athens." *Proceedings of the Cambridge Philological Society* 195: 14–30.

———. (1976). *Circus Factions: Blues and Greens at Rome and Byzantium.* Oxford: Clarendon Press.

Cameron, Al. and Av. Cameron (1964). "Christianity and Tradition in the Historiography of the Late Empire." *Classical Quarterly* 14: 316–328.

Cameron, Al., and J. Long, with L. Sherry (1993). *Barbarians and Politics at the Court of Arcadius.* Berkeley: University of California Press.

Cameron, Av. (1964). "Herodotus and Thucydides in Agathias." *BZ* 57: 33–52.

———. (1965). "Procopius and the Church of St. Sophia." *Harvard Theological Review* 58: 161–163.

———. (1966). "The "Scepticism" of Procopius." *Historia* 15: 466–482.

———. (1969–1970). "Agathias on the Sassanians." *DOP* 23–24: 67–183.

———. (1970). *Agathias.* Oxford: Clarendon Press.

———. (1978). "The Theotokos in Sixth-Century Constantinople." *Journal of Theological Studies* 29: 79–108.

———. (1982). "Byzantine Africa—The Literary Evidence." In J. H. Humphrey, ed., *Excavations at Carthage, 1978, Conducted by the University of Michigan.* v. 7. Ann Arbor, Mich.: Kelsey Museum. 29–62.

———. (1983). "Corippus' *Iohannis*: Epic of Byzantine Africa." *Papers of the Liverpool Latin Seminar* 4: 167–180.

———. (1985). *Procopius and the Sixth Century.* London: Duckworth; reprint, London: Routledge, 1996.

————. (1986). "History as Text: Coping with Procopius." In C. Holdsworth and T. P. Wiseman, eds., *The Inheritance of Historiography 350–900*. Exeter: University of Exeter Press. 53–66.

————. (1987). "The Constructions of Court Ritual: The Byzantine *Book of Ceremonies*." In D. Cannadine and S. Price, eds., *Rituals of Royalty: Power and Ceremonial in Traditional Societies*. Cambridge: Cambridge University Press. 106–136.

————. (1989). "Gelimer's Laughter: The Case of Byzantine Africa." In F. M. Clover and R. S. Humphreys, eds., *Tradition and Innovation in Late Antiquity*. Madison: University of Wisconsin Press. 171–190.

————. (1991). *Christianity and the Rhetoric of Empire: The Development of Christian Discourse*. Berkeley: University of California Press.

Carolla, P. (1999). "Spunti tucididei nelle epistole di Procopio." *Atene e Roma* 42: 157–176.

Carratelli, G. P. (1971). "La Persia dei Sasanidi nella Storiografia Romana da Ammiano a Procopio." In *Accademia Nazionale dei Lincei: Problemi Attuali di Scienza e di Cultura* 160: *La Persia nel Medioevo*. Rome. 597–604.

Carroll, N. (1990). "Interpretation, History and Narrative." *The Monist* 73: 134–166.

Casson, L. (1982). "Belisarius' Expedition against Carthage." In J. H. Humphrey, ed., *Excavations at Carthage 1978, Conducted by the University of Michigan*. v. 7. Ann Arbor, Mich.: Kelsey Museum. 23–28.

Cavallo, G. (1978). "La circolazione libraria nell'età di Giustiniano." In G. G. Archi, ed., *L'imperatore Giustiniano: Storia e Mito*. Milan: A. Giuffrè. 201–236.

Cesa, M. (1981). "La politica di Guistiniano verso l'occidente nel guidizio di Procopio." *Athenaeum* 59: 389–409.

Chadwick, H. (1981). *Boethius: The Consolations of Music, Logic, Theology, and Philosophy*. New York: Oxford University Press.

Cherf, W. J. (1992). "Carbon-14 Chronology for the Late-Roman Fortifications of the Thermopylai Frontier." *Journal of Roman Archaeology* 5: 261–264.

Chesnut, G. F. (1986). *The First Christian Histories: Eusebius, Socrates, Sozomen, Theodoret, and Evagrius*. 2nd ed. Macon, Ga.: Mercer University Press.

Christensen, A. (1925). *Le règne du roi Kawadh I et le communisme mazdakite* (= *Det Kongelige Danske Videnskabernes Selskab. Historisk-filologiske Meddelelser 9.6*). Copenhagen.

————. (1944). *L'Iran sous les Sassanides*. 2nd ed. Copenhagen and Paris: E. Munskgaard.

Christidis, D. A. (1996). Παραθεμάτων Παρανοήσεις και Κατανοήσεις. Thessaloniki: Aigeiros.

Chrysos, E. K. (1976). "Some Aspects of Roman-Persian Legal Relations." Κληρονομία 8: 1–52.

————. (1978). "The Title ΒΑΣΙΛΕΥΣ in Early Byzantine International Relations." *DOP* 32: 31–75.

————. (1981). "Die Amaler-Herrschaft in Italien und das Imperium Romanum. Der Vertragsentwurf des Jahres 535." *Byzantion* 51: 430–474.

Clay, D. (2000). *Platonic Questions: Dialogues with the Silent Philosopher*. University Park: Pennsylvania State University Press.

Clendinnen, I. (1991). *Aztecs: An Interpretation*. Cambridge: Cambridge University Press.

Clover, F. M. (1986). "Felix Karthago." *DOP* 40: 1–15.

Colish, M. L. (1994). "Intellectual History." In J. V. Engen, ed., *The Past and Future of Medieval Studies*. Notre Dame, Ind.: University of Notre Dame Press. 190–203.

Comparetti, D. (1925). "Maldicenze procopiane." *Raccolta di Scritti in Onore di Giacomo Lumbroso (1844–1925)*. Milan: Aegyptus.

Connor, W. R. (1984). *Thucydides*. Princeton, N.J.: Princeton University Press.

Constantelos, D. J. (1968). "Paganism and the State in the Age of Justinian." *Catholic Historical Review* 50: 372–380.

Cornford, F. M. (1907). *Thucydides Mythistoricus*. London: E. Arnold.

Courcelle, P. (1980). "Le tyran et le philosophe d'après la 'Consolation' de Boèce." In *Passaggio dal Mondo Antico al Medio Evo da Teodosio a San Gregorio Magno* (= *Atti dei Convegni Lincei* v. 45). Rome. 195–224.

Craig, L. H. (1994). *The War Lover. A Study of Plato's* Republic. Toronto: University of Toronto Press.

Cresci, L. R. (1986–1987). "Aspetti della μίμησις in Procopio." Δίπτυχα Ἑταιρείας Βυζαντινῶν καὶ Μεταβυζαντινῶν Μελετῶν 4: 232–249.

———. (1986). "Ancora sulla μίμησις in Procopio." *Rivista di filologia e di istruzione classica* 114: 448–457.

Croix, G. E. M. de Ste. (1954). "The Character of the Athenian Empire." *Historia* 3: 1–41.

Croke, B. (1981). "Two Early Byzantine Earthquakes and Their Liturgical Commemoration." *Byzantion* 51: 122–147.

———. (1990a). "Malalas, the Man and His Work." In E. Jeffreys, ed., with B. Croke and R. Scott, *Studies in John Malalas* (= *Byzantina Australiensia* v. 6). Sydney: Australian Association for Byzantine Studies. 1–25.

———. (1990b). "The Early Development of Byzantine Chronicles." E. Jeffreys, ed., with B. Croke and R. Scott, *Studies in John Malalas* (= *Byzantina Australiensia* v. 6). Sydney: Australian Association for Byzantine Studies. 1–25. 27–38.

———. (2001). *Count Marcellinus and His Chronicle*. Oxford: Oxford University Press.

Croke, B., and J. Crow. (1983). "Procopius and Dara." *Journal of Roman Studies* 73: 143–159.

Croke, B., and A. M. Emmett. (1983). "Historiography in Late Antiquity: An Overview." In Croke and Emmett, eds., *History and Historians in Late Antiquity*. New York: Pergamon Press. 1–12.

Crone, P. (1991). "Kavad's Heresy and Mazdak's Revolt." *Iran* 29: 21–42.

Cront, G. (1982). "La répression de l'hérésie au bas-empire pendant le règne de Justinien 1er (527–565)." Βυζαντιακά 2: 37–51.

Crossan, J. D. (1995). *Who Killed Jesus? Exposing the Roots of Anti-Semitism in the Gospel Story of the Death of Jesus*. New York: HarperCollins.

Crow, J. G. (1995). "The Long Walls of Thrace." In C. Mango and G. Dagron, ed., *Constantinople and Its Hinterland*. Brookfield, Vt.: Variorum. 109–124.

Dagron, G. (1981). "Quand la terre tremble . . ." *Travaux et Mémoires* 8: 87–103.

Dahn, F. (1865). *Procopius von Caesarea: Ein Beitrage zur Historiographie der Völker-wanderung und des sinkenden Römertums*. Berlin: E. S. Mittler.

Daube, D. (1966). "The Marriage of Justinian and Theodora: Legal and Theological Reflections." *Catholic University of America Law Review* 16: 380–399.

Deubner, L. (1902–1909). "Personifikationen abstrakter Begriffe." In W. H. Roscher, ed., *Ausführliches Lexikon der griechischen und römischen Mythologie*. Leipzig: Teubner. v. 3, pt. 2, cols. 2068–2169.

Dickey, E. (2001). "κύριε, δέσποτα, *domine*: Greek Politeness in the Roman Empire." *Journal of Hellenic Studies* 121: 1–11.

van Dijk, G.-J. (1994). "The Lion and the He-Goat: A New Fable in Procopius." *Hermes* 122: 376–379.

Dodds, E. R. (1951). *The Greeks and the Irrational*. Berkeley: University of California Press.

Dodgeon, M. H., and S. N. C. Lieu. (1991). *The Roman Eastern Frontier and the Persian Wars, AD 226–363: A Documentary History*. London: Routledge.

Downey, G. (1939). "Procopius on Antioch: A Study of Method in the 'De aedificiis.'" *Byzantion* 14: 361–378.

———. (1940). "Justinian as Achilles." *Transactions and Proceedings of the American Philological Association* 71: 68–77.

———. (1947). "The Composition of Procopius, *De aedificiis*." *Transactions of the American Philological Association* 78: 171–183.

———. (1949). "Paganism and Christianity in Procopius." *Church History* 18: 89–102.

———. (1953). "Notes on Procopius, *De aedificiis*, Book 1." In G. E. Mylonas and D. Raymond, ed., *Studies Presented to David Moore Robinson*. Saint Louis: Washington University. v. 2, 719–725.

———. (1960). *Constantinople in the Age of Justinian*. Norman: University of Oklahoma Press.

———. (1961). *A History of Antioch in Syria from Seleucus to the Arab Conquest*. Princeton, N.J.: Princeton University Press.

Drake, H. A. (2000). *Constantine and the Bishops: The Politics of Intolerance*. Baltimore: Johns Hopkins University Press.

Drouin, E. (1895). "Mémoire sur les Huns Ephthalites dans leurs rapports avec les rois Perses Sassanides." *Le Muséon. Revue internationale* 14: 73–84, 141–161, 232–247, 277–288.

Durliat, J. (1989). "La peste du VIᵉ siècle: pour un nouvel examen des sources byzantines." In G. Dagron, ed., *Hommes et richesses dans l'Empire Byzantine*. v. 1: *IVᵉ–VIIᵉ siècle*. Paris: P. Lethielleux. 107–119.

Earl, D. (1972). "Prologue-form in Ancient Historiography." *Aufstieg und Niedergang der römischen Welt* v. 1, 2: 842–856.

Eckstein, A. M. (1995). *Moral Vision in the Histories of Polybius*. Berkeley: University of California Press.

Edelstein, L. (1967). *The Idea of Progress in Classical Antiquity*. Baltimore: Johns Hopkins University Press.

Edmunds, L. (1975). *Chance and Intelligence in Thucydides*. Cambridge, Mass.: Harvard University Press.

Edwards, M. W. (1987). *Homer: Poet of the* Iliad. Baltimore: Johns Hopkins University Press.

Elferink, M. A. (1967). "Τύχη et Dieu chez Procope de Césarée." *Acta Classica* 10: 111–134.

Evans, J. A. S. (1968). "Procopius of Caesarea and the Emperor Justinian." *Canadian Historical Association: Historical Papers*, 126–139.

———. (1971). "Christianity and Paganism in Procopius of Caesarea." *Greek, Roman, and Byzantine Studies* 12: 81–100.

———. (1972). *Procopius*. New York: Twayne Publishers.

———. (1975). "The Secret History and the Art of Procopius." *Prudentia* 7: 105–109.

———. (1976). "The Attitudes of the Secular Historians of the Age of Justinian Toward the Classical Past." *Traditio* 32: 353–358.

———. (1984). "The "Nika" Rebellion and the Empress Theodora." *Byzantion* 54: 380–382.

———. (1996). "The Dates of Procopius' Works: A Recapitulation of the Evidence." *Greek, Roman, and Byzantine Studies* 37: 301–313.

———. (1996). *The Age of Justinian: The Circumstances of Imperial Power*. London: Routledge.

———. (2002). *The Empress Theodora: Partner of Justinian*. Austin: University of Texas Press.

Fatouros, G. (1980). "Zur Prokop-Biographie." *Klio* 62: 517–523.

Fehling, D. (1989). *Herodotus and His "Sources": Citation, Invention and Narrative Art*. Tr. J. G. Howie. Leeds: Francis Cairns.

Fiaccadori, G. (1979). "Intorno all'anonimo vaticano Περὶ πολιτικῆς ἐπιστήμης." *La Parola del Passato* 185: 127–147.

Finkelpearl, E. (2001). "Pagan Traditions of Intertextuality in the Roman World." In D. R. MacDonald, ed., *Mimesis and Intertextuality in Antiquity and Christianity*. Harrisburg, Pa.: Trinity Press International. 78–90.

Fischer, M. (1996). "Marble, Urbanism, and Ideology in Roman Palestine: The Caesarea Example." In A. Raban and K. G. Holum, eds., *Caesarea Maritima: A Retrospective After Two Millennia*. Leiden and New York: E.J. Brill. 251–261.

Fisher, E. A. (1978). "Theodora and Antonina in the Historia Arcana: History and/or Fiction." *Arethusa* 11: 253–279.

Forde, S. (1989). *The Ambition to Rule: Alcibiades and the Politics of Imperialism in Thucydides*. Ithaca, N.Y.: Cornell University Press.

Fornara, C. W. (1983). *The Nature of History in Ancient Greece and Rome*. Berkeley: University of California Press.

Foss, C. (2002). "The Empress Theodora." *Byzantion* 72: 141–176.

Fotiou, A. S. (1981). "Dicaearchus and the Mixed Constitution in Sixth-Century Byzantium: New Evidence from a Treatise on 'Political Science.'" *Byzantion* 51: 533–547.

———. (1985). "Plato's Philosopher King in the Political Thought of Sixth-Century Byzantium." *Florilegium* 7: 17–29.

Foulkes, P. (1992). "Where Was Simplicius?" *Journal of Hellenic Studies* 112: 143.

Fowden, E. K. (1999). *The Barbarian Plain: Saint Sergius between Rome and Iran.* Berkeley: University of California Press.

Fowden, G. (1993). *Empire to Commonwealth: Consequences of Monotheism in Late Antiquity.* Princeton, N.J.: Princeton University Press.

Frantz, A. (1975). "Pagan Philosophers in Christian Athens." *Proceedings of the American Philosophical Society* 119: 29–38.

Frendo, J. D. (2001). "Three Authors in Search of a Reader: An Approach to the Analysis of Direct Discourse in Procopius, Agathias and Theophylact Simocatta." In C. Sode and S. Takacs, eds., *Novum Millennium: Studies on Byzantine History and Culture Dedicated to Paul Speck.* Burlington, Vt.: Ashgate. 123–135.

Frye, D. (1995). "Athalaric's Health and the Ostrogothic Character." *Byzantium* 65: 249–251.

Gantar, K. (1961). "Kaiser Justinian als kopfloser Dämon." *BZ* 54: 1–3.

———. (1962a): "Kaiser Iustinian "jenem Herbststern gleich." Bemerkung zu Prokops Aed. I 2, 10." *Museum Helveticum* 19: 194–196.

———. (1962b). "Prokops 'Schaustellung der Tapferkeit.'" *Ziva Antika* 11: 283–286.

Garland, L. (1999). *Byzantine Empresses: Women and Power in Byzantium, AD 527–1204.* London and New York: Routledge.

Garnsey, P. (1984). "Religious Toleration in Classical Antiquity." In W. J. Sheils, ed., *Persecution and Toleration* (= *Studies in Church History* v. 21). Oxford: B. Blackwell. 1–27.

Garsoïan, N. G. (1967). "Politique ou Orthodoxie? L'Arménie au quatrième siècle." *Revue des études arméniennes* n.s. 4: 297–320.

Garzya, A. (1995). "Teodrico a Bisanzio." In A. Carile, ed., *Teoderico e i Goti tra Oriente e Occidente.* Ravenna: Longo editore. 341–351.

Ghirshman, R. (1948). *Les Chionites-Hephthalites* (= *Mémoires de l'Institut français d'achéologie orientale du Caire* v. 80 = *Mémoires de la délégation archéologique français en Afghanistan* v. 13). Cairo.

Gibbon, Edward. (1994). *The History of the Decline and Fall of the Roman Empire.* Ed. D. Womersley. London and New York: Penguin Classics.

Goffart, W. (1980). *Barbarians and Romans, A.D. 418–584: The Techniques of Accommodation.* Princeton, N.J.: Princeton University Press.

———. (1989). "Zosimus, The First Historian of Rome's Fall." In Goffart, *Rome's Fall and After.* London and Ronceverte, WV: Hambledon Press. 81–110.

Grabar, A. (1948). "Les monuments de Tsaritchin Grad et Justiniana Prima." *Cahiers archéologiques* 3: 49–63.

Gray, E. W. (1973). "The Roman Eastern *Limes* from Constantine to Justinian—Perspectives and Problems." *Proceedings of the African Classical Association* 12: 24–40.

Gray, P. T. R. (1993). "Palestine and Justinian's Legislation on Non-Christian Religions." In B. Halpern and D. W. Hobson, eds., *Law, Politics and Society in the Ancient Mediterranean World.* Sheffield: Sheffield Academic Press. 241–270.

Greatrex, G. (1994). "The dates of Procopius' works." *Byzantine and Modern Greek Studies* 18: 101–114.

————. (1995a). "The Composition of Procopius' *Persian Wars* and John the Cappadocian." *Prudentia* 27: 1–13.

————. (1995b). "Procopius and Agathias on the Defences of the Thracian Cheronese." In C. Mango and G. Dagron, eds., *Constantinople and Its Hinterland*. Burlington, Vt: Ashgate. 125–129.

————. (1996a). "Stephanus, the Father of Procopius of Caesarea?" *Medieval Prosopography* 17: 125–145.

————. (1996b). "Flavius Hypatius, *quem vidit validum Parthus sensitque timendum*. An Investigation of His Career." *Byzantion* 66: 120–142.

————. (1997). "The Nika Riot: A Reappraisal." *Journal of Hellenic Studies* 117: 60–86.

————. (1998). *Rome and Persia at War, 502–532*. Leeds: Francis Cairns.

————. (2000). "Procopius the Outsider?" In D. C. Smythe, ed., *Strangers to Themselves: The Byzantine Outsider*. Burlington, Vt.: Ashgate. 215–228.

————. (2001). "Lawyers and Historians in Late Antiquity." In R. W. Mathisen, ed., *Law, Society, and Authority in Late Antiquity*. Oxford: Oxford University Press. 148–161.

————. (2003). "Recent Work on Procopius and the Composition of Wars VIII." *Byzantine and Modern Greek Studies* 27 (2003) forthcoming.

Green, P. (1989). *Classical Bearings: Interpreting Ancient History and Culture*. New York: Thames and Hudson; reprint, Berkeley: University of California Press, 1998.

————. (1990). *Alexander to Actium: The Historical Evolution of the Hellenistic Age*. Berkeley: University of California Press.

Gregory, T. E. (2000). "Procopius on Greece." *Antiquité tardive* 8: 105–114.

Griffin, J. (1980). *Homer on Life and Death*. Oxford: Clarendon Press.

Griswold, C. L., Jr. (1996). *Self-Knowledge in Plato's* Phaedrus. University Park, Pa.: Pennsylvania State University Press.

Grumel, V. (1958). *La chronologie* (= *Traité d'études byzantines* v. 1). Paris: Presses Universitaires de France.

Guignebert, C. (1923). "Les demi-chrétiens et leur place dans l'église antique." *Revue de l'histoire des religions* 88: 65–102.

Guilland, R. (1967). *Recherches sur les institutions byzantines*. Berlin: A. M. Hakkert.

Guillaumont, A. (1969–1970). "Justinien et l'église de Perse." *DOP* 23–24: 39–66.

Güterbock, K. (1906). *Byzanz und Persien in ihren diplomatisch-völkerrechtlichen Beziehungen im Zeitalter Justinians. Ein Beitrag zur Geschichte des Völkerechts*. Berlin: J. Guttentag.

Hadot, I. (1990). "The Life and Work of Simplicius in Greek and Arabic Sources." Tr. V. Caston, with rev. by author, in R. Sorabji, ed., *Aristotle Transformed: The Ancient Commentators and Their Influence*. London: Duckworth, 275–303.

Haefele, H. F. (1954). *Fortuna Heinrici IV. Imperatoris: Untersuchungen zur Lebensbeschreibung des dritten Saliers*. Graz: H. Böhlaus Nachf.

Hagedorn, D., and K. A. Worp. (1980). "Von κύριος zu δεσπότης. Eine Bemerkung zur Kaisertitulatur im 3./4. Jhdt." *Zeitschrift für Papyrologie und Epigraphik* 39: 165–177.

Haldon, J. (1994). "*Aerikon/aerika*: A Re-Interpretation." *Jahrbuch der österreichischen Byzantinistik* 44: 135–142.

Hall, E. (1989). *Inventing the Barbarian: Greek Self-Definition Through Tragedy*. Oxford: Clarendon Press; New York: Oxford University Press.

Hällström, G. af (1994). "The Closing of the Neoplatonic School in A.D. 529: An Additional Aspect." In P. Castrén, ed., *Post-Herulian Athens: Aspects of Life and Culture in Athens A.D. 267–529*. Helsinki: Suomen Ateenan-instituutin säätiö. 141–160.

Hannestad, K. (1955–1957). "Les relations de Byzance avec la Transcaucasie et l'Asie centrale aux 5ᵉ et 6ᵉ siècles." *Byzantion* 25–27: 421–456.

———. (1960). "Les forces militaires d'après la *Guerre gothique* de Procope." *Classica et Mediaevalia* 21: 136–183.

Hansen, M. H. (1995). *The Trial of Sokrates—from the Athenian Point of View* (= *Det Kongelige Danske Videnskabernes Selskab. Historisk-filologiske Meddelelser* 71). Copenhagen.

Harl, K. W. (1990). "Sacrifice and Pagan Belief in Fifth- and Sixth-Century Byzantium." *Past and Present* 128: 7–27.

Harris, J. (2000). "Distortion, Divine Providence and Genre in Nicetas Choniates's Account of the Collapse of Byzantium 1180–1204." *Journal of Medieval History* 26: 19–31.

Harrison, T. (2000). *Divinity and History: The Religion of Herodotus*. Oxford: Clarendon Press.

Hartog, F. (1988). *The Mirror of Herodotus: The Representation of the Other in the Writing of History*. Tr. J. Lloyd. Berkeley: University of California Press.

Haury, J. (1890–1891). *Procopiana*. Augsburg: Hass & Grabherr.

———. (1896). *Zur Beurteilung des Geschichtschreibers Procopius von Cäsarea*. Munich: H. Kutzner.

———. (1934). "Zu Prokops Geheimgeschichte." *BZ* 34: 10–14.

Hegel, G. W. F. (1975). *Lectures on the Philosophy of World History: Introduction*. Tr. H. B. Nisbet. Cambridge: Cambridge University Press.

Henry, P., III (1967). "A Mirror for Justinian: The *Ekthesis* of Agapetus Diaconus." *Greek, Roman, and Byzantine Studies* 8: 281–308.

Herzog-Hauser, G. (1943). "Tyche." In *Paulys Real-Encyclopädie der classischen Altertumswissenschaft*. 2nd series 7A: 1643–1689.

Hobbes, Thomas. (1975). "To the Readers" and "Of the Life and History of Thucydides." In R. Schlatter, ed., *Hobbes's Thucydides*. New Brunswick, N.J.: Rutgers University Press. 6–27.

Hock, R. F. (2001). "Homer in Greco-Roman Education." In D. R. MacDonald, ed., *Mimesis and Intertextuality in Antiquity and Christianity*. Harrisburg, Pa.: Trinity Press International. 56–78.

Holum, K. G. (1977). "Pulcheria's Crusade A.D. 421–22 and the Ideology of Imperial Victory." *Greek, Roman, and Byzantine Studies* 18: 153–172.

———. (1982a). *Theodosian Empresses: Women and Imperial Dominion in Late Antiquity*. Berkeley: University of California Press.

———. (1982b). "Caesarea and the Samaritans." In R. L. Hohlfelder, ed., *City*,

Town and Countryside in the Early Byzantine Era. New York: Columbia University Press. 65–73.

Honoré, T. (1975). "Some Constitutions of Justinian." *Journal of Roman Studies* 65: 108–123.

———. (1978). *Tribonian.* Ithaca, N.Y.: Cornell University Press.

Hornblower, S. (1991). *A Commentary on Thucydides.* v. 1: *Books I–III.* Oxford: Clarendon Press; New York: Oxford University Press.

———. (1994). "Narratology and Narrative Techniques in Thucydides." In Hornblower, ed., *Greek Historiography.* New York: Clarendon Press. 131–166.

Howard-Johnston, J. (1995). "The Two Great Powers in Late Antiquity: A Comparison." In Av. Cameron, ed., *The Byzantine and Early Islamic Near East.* v. 3: *States, Resources and Armies.* Princeton, N.J.: Darwin Press. 157–226.

———. (2000). "The Education and Expertise of Procopius." *Antiquité tardive* 8: 19–30.

Hunger, H. (1969–1970). "On the Imitation (ΜΙΜΗΣΙΣ) of Antiquity in Byzantine Literature." *DOP* 23–24: 17–38.

———. (1978). *Die hochsprachliche profane Literatur der Byzantiner.* Munich: C. H. Beck.

Irmscher, J. (1976). "Justinianbild und Justiniankritik in frühen Byzanz." In H. Köpstein and F. Winkelmann, eds., *Studien zum 7. Jahrhundert in Byzanz.* Berlin: Akademie-Verlag. 131–142.

———. (1981). "Paganismus im justinianischen Reich." *Klio* 63: 683–688.

James, L. (2001). *Empresses and Power in Early Byzantium.* London: Leicester University Press.

Jeffreys, E. (1990). "Malalas' Sources." In E. Jeffreys, ed., with B. Croke and R. Scott, *Studies in John Malalas* (= *Byzantina Australiensia* v. 6). Sydney: Australian Association for Byzantine Studies. 167–216.

Jenkins, C. (1947). "Procopiana." *Journal of Roman Studies* 37: 74–81.

Jenkins, R. J. H. (1963). "The Hellenistic Origins of Byzantine Literature." *DOP* 17: 37–52.

———. (1966). "The Peace with Bulgaria (927) Celebrated by Theodore Daphnopates." In P. Wirth, ed., *Polychronion. Festschrift Franz Dölger zum 75. Geburtstag.* Heidelberg: C. Winter. 287–303.

Jones, A. H. M. (1986). *The Later Roman Empire, 284–602: A Social, Economic, and Administrative Survey.* Baltimore: Johns Hopkins University Press; reprint.

Jones, C. P. (1986). *Culture and Society in Lucian.* Cambridge, Mass.: Harvard University Press.

Jouanna, J. (1999). *Hippocrates.* Tr. M. B. DeBevoise. Baltimore: Johns Hopkins University Press.

Jullien, F. (2000). *Detour and Access: Strategies of Meaning in China and Greece.* Tr. S. Hawkes. New York: Zone Books.

Kaegi, W. E. (1965). "Arianism and the Byzantine Army in Africa 533–546." *Traditio* 21: 23–53.

———. (1968). *Byzantium and the Decline of Rome.* Princeton, N.J.: Princeton University Press.

————. (1981). *Byzantine Military Unrest, 471–843: An Interpretation.* Amsterdam: A.M. Hakkert.

————. (1990). "Procopius the Military Historian." *Byzantinische Forschungen* 15: 53–85.

————. (1995). "The Capability of the Byzantine Army for Military Operations in Italy." In A. Carile, ed., *Teoderico e i Goti tra Oriente e Occidente.* Ravenna: Longo editore. 79–99.

Kaldellis, A. (1997). "Agathias on History and Poetry." *Greek, Roman, and Byzantine Studies* 38: 295–305.

————. (1999a). "The Historical and Religious Views of Agathias: A Reinterpretation." *Byzantion* 69: 206–252.

————. (1999b). *The Argument of Psellos' Chronographia.* Leiden: E.J. Brill.

————. (2003a). "The Religion of Ioannes Lydos." *Phoenix* 57 (2003) forthcoming.

————. (2003b). "Things Are Not What They Are: Agathias Mythistoricus and the Last Laugh of Classical Culture." *Classical Quarterly* 53 (2003) 295–300.

Karpozelos, A. (1997). Βυζαντινοί Ἱστορικοί καί Χρονογράφοι. v. 1 (4ος–7ος αἰ). Athens: Kanaki.

Kennedy, H., and J. H. W. G. Liebeschuetz. (1988). "Antioch and the Villages of Northern Syria in the Fifth and Sixth Centuries A.D.: Trends and Problems." *Nottingham Medieval Studies* 32: 65–90.

King, C. (1987). "The Veracity of Ammianus Marcellinus' Description of the Huns." *American Journal of Ancient History* 12: 77–95.

Knaepen, A. (2001). "L'image du roi vandale Gélimer chez Procope de Césarée." *Byzantion* 71: 383–403.

Krumbacher, K. (1887). *Geschichte der byzantinischen Litteratur von Justinian bis zum Ende des oströmischen Reiches (527–1453).* Munich: C. H. Beck.

Külzer, A. (1991). "Studien zum Chronicon Bruxellense." *Byzantion* 61: 413–447.

Kustas, G. L. (1970). "The Function and Evolution of Byzantine Rhetoric." *Viator* 1: 55–73.

Lamarque, P., and S. H. Olsen. (1994). *Truth, Fiction, and Literature: A Philosophical Perspective.* Oxford: Clarendon Press.

Lanata, G. (1984). *Legislazione e natura nelle Novelle giustinianee.* Naples: Edizioni scientifische italiane.

————. (1989). "L'immortalità artificiale. Appunti sul proemio della Novella 22 di Giustiniano." *Serta Historica Antiqua* II. Roma. 259–263.

Lane Fox, R. (1986). *Alexander the Great.* New York: Penguin.

Lateiner, D. (1989). *The Historical Method of Herodotus.* Toronto: University of Toronto Press.

Lee, A. D. (1989). "Procopius, Justinian and the *kataskopoi.*" *Classical Quarterly* 39: 569–572.

————. (1993). *Information and Frontiers: Roman Foreign Relations in Late Antiquity.* Cambridge: Cambridge University Press.

Lehmann, P. W. (1959). "Theodosius or Justinian? A Renaissance Drawing of a Byzantine Rider." *Art Bulletin* 41: 39–57, with an exchange of letters with C. Mango on 351–358.

Letsios, D. G. (1985). "Η "Ἔκθεσις Κεφαλαίων Παραινετικῶν" τοῦ διακόνου

Αγαπητού. Μια σύνοψη της ιδεολογίας της εποχής του Ιουστινιανού για το αυτοκρατορικό αξίωμα." *Δωδώνη* 14: 175–210.

Leven, K.-H. (1987). "Die "Justinianische" Pest." *Jahrbuch des Instituts für Geschichte der Medizin der Robert Bosch Stiftung* 6: 137–161.

Lieberich, H. (1898, 1900). *Studien zu den Proömien in der griechischen und byzantinischen Geschichtsschreibung.* Munich: J. G. Weiss'sche Buchdruckerei.

Lindner, H. (1972). *Die Geschichtsauffasung des Flavius Josephus im Bellum Judaicum: Gleichzeitig ein Beitrag zur Quellenfrage.* Leiden: E.J. Brill.

Ljubarskij, J. N. (1993). "New Trends in the Study of Byzantine Historiography." *DOP* 47: 131–138.

Ljubarskij, J. N., et al. (1998). "*Quellenforschung* and/or Literary Criticism: Narrative Structures in Byzantine Historical Writings." *Symbolae Osloenses* 73: 5–73.

Lopez, R. S. (1945). "The Silk Industry in the Byzantine Empire." *Speculum* 20: 1–42.

Loyn, H. R., and J. Percival. (1975). *The Reign of Charlemagne: Documents on Carolingian Government and Administration.* London: E. Arnold.

Lozza, G. (2000). "Tracce di linguaggio comico negli *Anecdota* di Procopio." In U. Criscuolo and R. Maisano, eds., *Categorie linguistiche e concettuali della storiografia bizantina.* Naples: M. D'Auria. 81–97.

Maas, M. (1986). "Roman History and Christian Ideology in Justinianic Reform Legislation." *DOP* 40: 17–31.

MacCormack, S. G. (1981). *Art and Ceremony in Late Antiquity.* Berkeley: University of California Press.

Machiavelli, Niccolo. (1985). *The Prince.* Tr. H. C. Mansfield. Chicago: University of Chicago Press.

———. (1988). *Florentine Histories.* Tr. L. F. Banfield and H. C. Mansfield. Princeton, N.J.: Princeton University Press.

———. (1996). *Discourses on Livy.* Tr. H. C. Mansfield and N. Tarcov. Chicago: University of Chicago Press.

MacIntyre, A. (1984). *After Virtue: A Study in Moral Theory.* 2nd ed. Notre Dame: University of Notre Dame Press.

MacQueen, B. D. (1981). *Plato's Republic in the Monographs of Sallust.* Chicago: Bolchazy-Carducci.

Macrides, R., and P. Magdalino. (1988). "The Architecture of Ekphrasis: Construction and Context of Paul the Silentiary's Poem on Hagia Sophia." *Byzantine and Modern Greek Studies* 12: 47–82.

de' Maffei, F. (1988). *Edifici di Giustiniano nell'ambito dell'impero* (= *Centro Italiano di Studi sull'Alto Medioevo* v. 10). Spoleto.

Mango, C. (1959). *The Brazen House: A Study of the Vestibule of the Imperial Palace of Constantinople.* Copenhagen: I kommission hos Munksgaard.

———. (1963). "Antique Statuary and the Byzantine Beholder." *DOP* 17: 53–75.

———. (1975). *Byzantine Literature as a Distorting Mirror.* Oxford: Clarendon Press.

———. (1980). *Byzantium: The Empire of New Rome.* New York: Scribner.

———. (1981). "Discontinuity with the Classical Past in Byzantium." In M. Mullett and R. Scott, ed., *Byzantium and the Classical Tradition*. Birmingham: Center for Byzantine Studies, University of Birmingham. 48–57.

Mansfield, H. C. (1996). *Machiavelli's Virtue*. Chicago: University of Chicago Press.

Marincola, J. (1997). *Authority and Tradition in Ancient Historiography*. Cambridge: Cambridge University Press.

Matthews, J. F. (1970). "Olympiodorus of Thebes and the History of the West (A.D. 407–425)." *Journal of Roman Studies* 60: 79–97.

———. (1989). *The Roman Empire of Ammianus*. London: Duckworth.

McCormick, M. (1986). *Eternal Victory: Triumphal Rulership in Late Antiquity, Byzantium and the Early Medieval West*. Cambridge: Cambridge University Press.

McGlew, J. F. (1993). *Tyranny and Political Culture in Ancient Greece*. Ithaca, N.Y.: Cornell University Press.

Meier, M. (1999). "Beobachtungen zu den sogennaten Pestschilderung bei Thukydides II 47–54 und bei Prokop, *Bell. Pers.* II 22–23." *Tyche* 14: 177–210.

Miles, G. B. (1995). *Livy: Reconstructing Early Rome*. Ithaca, N.Y.: Cornell University Press.

Millar, F. (1964). *A Study of Cassius Dio*. Oxford: Oxford University Press.

Miller, T. S. (1997). *The Birth of the Hospital in the Byzantine Empire*. Baltimore: Johns Hopkins University Press.

Miyakawa, H., and A. Kollautz. (1989). "Die Hephthaliten, ihr Volkstum und Geschichte nach den chinesischen, orientalischen und byzantinischen Berichten." *Βυζαντιακά* 9: 89–118.

Moderan, Y. (1986). "Corippe et l'occupation byzantine de l'Afrique: Pour une nouvelle lecture de la *Johannide*." *Antiquités africaines* 22: 195–212.

Monoson, S. S. (2000). *Plato's Democratic Entanglements: Athenian Politics and the Practice of Philosophy*. Princeton, N.J.: Princeton University Press.

Montaigne. (1965). *The Complete Essays*. Tr. D. M. Frame. Stanford, Calif.: Stanford University Press.

Montgomery, H. (1965). *Gedanke und Tat. Zur Erzählungstechnik bei Herodot, Thukydides, Xenophon und Arrian*. Lund: C. W. K. Gleerup.

Moorhead, J. (1992). *Theoderic in Italy*. Oxford: Clarendon Press.

———. (1994). *Justinian*. London: Longman.

Moravcsik, G. (1958). *Byzantinoturcica*. Berlin: Akademie-Verlag.

———. (1966). "Klassizismus in der byzantinischen Geschichtsschreibung." In P. Wirth, ed., *Polychronion: Festschrift Franz Dölger zum 75. Geburtstag*. Heidelberg: C. Winter. v. 1, 366–377.

Mullett, M. (1981). "The Classical Tradition in the Byzantine Letter." In M. Mullett and R. Scott, eds., *Byzantium and the Classical Tradition*. Birmingham: Center for Byzantine Studies, University of Birmingham. 75–93.

———. (1990). "Dancing with Deconstructionists in the Gardens of the Muses: New Literary History vs ?" *Byzantine and Modern Greek Studies* 14: 258–275.

Nadon, C. (2001). *Xenophon's Prince: Republic and Empire in the* Cyropaidia. Berkeley: University of California Press.

Naudé, C. P. T. (1964). "Fortuna in Ammianus Marcellinus." *Acta Classica* 7: 70–88.

Neri, V. (1990). "Verso Ravenna Capitale: Roma, Ravenna e le residenze imperiali tardo-antiche." In G. Susini, ed., *Storia di Ravenna*. v. 1: *L'evo antico*. Ravenna: Comune di Ravenna. 535–584.

Nietzsche, Friedrich. (1976). *Twilight of the Idols*. In *The Portable Nietzsche*. Tr. W. Kaufmann. New York: Penguin.

———. (1967). *The Birth of Tragedy* and *The Case of Wagner*. Tr. W. Kaufmann. New York: Random House.

Nussbaum, M. C. (1986). *The Fragility of Goodness: Luck and Ethics in Greek Tragedy and Philosophy*. Cambridge: Cambridge University Press.

Oikonomidès, N. (1986). "Silk Trade and Production in Byzantium from the Sixth to the Ninth Century: The Seals of the Kommerkiarioi." *DOP* 40: 33–53.

O'Meara, D. (2002). "The Justinianic Dialogue *On Political Science* and Its Neoplatonic Sources." In K. Ierodiakonou, ed., *Byzantine Philosophy and Its Ancient Sources*. Oxford: Clarendon Press. 49–62

Palmer, M. (1995). "Kings, Philosophers, and Tyrants in Plato's *Republic*." In M. Palmer and T. L. Pangle, eds., *Political Philosophy and the Human Soul: Essays in Memory of Allan Bloom*. Lanham, Md.: Rowman and Littlefield. 121–148.

Paschoud, F. (1974). "Influences et échos des conceptions historiographiques de Polybe dans l'antiquité tardive." *Fondation Hardt pour l'étude de l'antiquité classique, Entretiens*. v. 20: *Polybe*. 305–344.

———. (1975). "La digression antimonarchique du préambule de l'*Histoire nouvelle*." In Paschoud, *Cinq études sur Zosime*. Paris: Belles Lettres. 1–23.

Patlangean, E. (1974). "La pauvreté byzantine au VIᵉ siècle au temps de Justinien: aux origines d'un modèle politique." In M. Mollat, ed., *Études sur l'histoire de la pauvreté*. Paris: Publications de la Sorbonne. 59–81.

Pazdernik, C. F. (1994). "'Our Most Pious Consort Given Us by God': Dissident Reactions to the Partnership of Justinian and Theodora, A.D. 525–548." *Classical Antiquity* 13: 256–281.

———. (1997). "A Dangerous Liberty and a Servitude Free from Care: Political 'Eleutheria' and 'Douleia' in Procopius of Caesarea and Thucydides of Athens." Dissertation, Princeton University.

———. (2000). "Procopius and Thucydides on the Labors of War: Belisarius and Brasidas in the Field." *Transactions of the American Philological Association* 130: 149–187.

Pédech, P. (1965). "Les idées religieuses de Polybe: Étude sur la religion de l'élite gréco-romaine au IIᵉ siècle av. J.-C." *Revue de l'histoire des religions* 167: 35–68.

Pflugk-Harttung, J. v. (1889). "Belisar's Vandalenkrieg." *Historische Zeitschrift* 61: 69–96.

Plass, P. (1988). *Wit and the Writing of History: The Rhetoric of Historiography in Imperial Rome*. Madison: University of Wisconsin Press.

Popkin, R. H. (1979). *The History of Scepticism from Erasmus to Spinoza*. Berkeley: University of California Press.

Potter, D. S. (1999). *Literary Texts and the Roman Historian*. London: Routledge.

Potts, D. T. (1990). *The Arabian Gulf in Antiquity*. v. 2: *From Alexander the Great to the Coming of Islam*. New York: Oxford University Press.

Powell, B. B. (1991). *Homer and the Origin of the Greek Alphabet*. Cambridge: Cambridge University Press.

Praechter, K. (1905). "Antikes in der Grabrede des Georgios Akropolites auf Johannes Dukas." *BZ* 14: 479–491.

Pritchett, W. K. (1993). *The Liar School of Herodotos*. Amsterdam: J. C. Gieben.

Pühlhorn, W. (1977). "Archäologischer Kommentar zu den "Bauten" des Prokop." In Prokop, *Bauten*. Ed. and tr. O. Veh. Munich: E. Heimeran. 381–474.

Questa, C. (1989). "Il morto e la madre: Romei e Persiani nelle 'Storie' de Agatia." *Lares* 55: 375–405.

Rahe, P. (1994). *Republics Ancient and Modern*. v. 1: *The Ancien Régime in Classical Greece*. Chapel Hill: University of North Carolina Press.

Ravegnani, G. (1988). *Soldati di Bisanzio in età giustinianea*. Rome: Jouvence.

——. (1989). *La corte di Giustiniano*. Rome: Jouvence.

Renehan, R. (1976). "A Traditional Pattern of Imitation in Sallust and His Sources." *Classical Philology* 71: 97–105.

Roisl, H. N. (1981). "Totila und die Schlacht dei den Busta Gallorum, Ende Juni/Anfang Juli 552." *Jahrbuch der österreichischen Byzantinistik* 30: 25–50.

Romanelli, P. (1935). "La riconquista africana di Guistiniano." In *Africa Romana* (*Istituto di Studi Romani*). Milan: U. Hoepli. 123–140.

de Romilly, J. (1951). *Thucydide et l'impérialisme athénien: la pensée de l'historien et la genèse de l'oeuvre*. Paris: Belles Lettres.

——. (1956a). "L'utilité de l'histoire selon Thucydide." *Entretiens sur l'antiquité classique*. v. 4: *Histoire et historiens dans l'antiquité*. 41–66.

——. (1956b). *Histoire et raison chez Thucydide*. Paris: Belles Lettres.

Romm, J. (1998). *Herodotus*. New Haven, Conn.: Yale University Press.

Roos, A. G. (1926). "Ad Ursulum Philippum Boissevain septuagenarium epistula de Arriani Periplo Ponti Euxini." *Mnemosyne* 54: 101–117.

——. (1967). *Flavii Arriani quae extant omnia*. Rev. G. Wirth. Leipzig: Teubner. 1967.

Roques, D. (2000a). "Les *Constructions de Justinien* de Procope de Césarée." *Antiquité tardive* 8: 31–43.

——. (2000b). "Histoire et rhetorique dans l'œuvre de Procope de Césarée: Procope est-il un historien?" In U. Criscuolo and R. Maisano, eds., *Categorie linguistiche e concettuali della storiografia bizantina*. Naples: M. D'Auria. 9–39.

Rösch, G. (1978). *Onoma Basileias. Studien sum offiziellen Gebrauch der Kaisertitel in spätantiker und frühbyzantinischer Zeit* (= *Byzantina Vindobonensia* v. 10). Vienna: Verlag der österreichischen Akademie der Wissenschaften.

Rosen, S. (1988). "The Role of Eros in Plato's *Republic*." In Rosen, *The Quarrel Between Philosophy and Poetry: Studies in Ancient Thought*. New York: Routledge. 102–118.

Rousseau, P. (1996). "Inheriting the Fifth Century: Who Bequeathed What?" In P. Allen and E. Jeffreys, eds., *The Sixth Century: End or Beginning?* (= *Byzantina Australiensia* v. 10). Brisbane: Australian Association for Byzantine Studies. 1–19.

——. (1998). "Procopius's *Buildings* and Justinian's Pride." *Byzantion* 68: 121–130.

Roux, G. (1992). *Ancient Iraq*. 3rd ed. New York: Penguin.

Rubin, B. (1951). "Der Fürst der Dämonen. Ein Beitrag zur Interpretation von Prokops Anekdota." *BZ* 44: 469–481.

————. (1954). *Prokopios von Kaisareia.* Stuttgart: A. Druckenmüller = *Paulys Real-Encyclopädie der classischen Altertumswissenschaft* v. 23 (1957): 273–599.

————. (1960). "Der Antichrist und die "Apokalypse" des Prokopios von Kaisareia." *Zeitschrift der deutschen Morgenländischen Gessellschaft* 110: 55–63.

————. (1960, 1995). *Das Zeitalter Iustinians.* Berlin: W. de Gruyter.

————. (1963). "Das römische Reich im Osten Byzanz." In G. Mann and A. Heuss, eds., *Propyläen Weltgeschichte: Eine Universalgeschichte.* v. 4. Berlin: Propyläen-Verlag. 605–658.

Rubin, Z. (1995). "The Reforms of Khusro Anushirwan." In Av. Cameron, ed., *The Byzantine and Early Islamic Near East.* v. 3: *States, Resources and Armies.* Princeton, N.J.: The Darwin Press. 227–297.

Rudich, V. (1993). *Political Dissidence under Nero: The Price of Dissimulation.* London: Routledge.

Rühl, F. (1914). "Die Interpolationen in Prokops Anekdota." *Rheinisches Museum für Philologie* 69: 284–298.

Ruhl, L. (1915). "Tyche." In W. H. Roscher, ed., *Ausführliches Lexikon der griechischen und römischen Mythologie.* Leipzig: Teubner. v. 5, cols. 1309–1357.

Runciman, S. (1947). *The Medieval Manichee: A Study of the Christian Dualist Heresy.* Cambridge: Cambridge University Press.

Ryffel, H. (1949). Μεταβολὴ Πολιτειῶν. *Der Wandel der Staatsverfassungen: Untersuchungen zu einem Problem der griechischen Staatstheorie.* Bern: P. Haupt.

Sacks, K. S. (1990). *Diodorus Siculus and the First Century.* Princeton, N.J.: Princeton University Press.

Saul, J. R. (1992). *Voltaire's Bastards: The Dictatorship of Reason in the West.* New York: Vintage Books.

Saxonhouse, A. W. (1982). "Family, Polity, and Unity: Aristotle on Socrates' Community of Wives." *Polity* 15: 202–219.

————. (1983). "An Unspoken Theme in Plato's *Gorgias*: War." *Interpretation* 11: 139–169.

————. (1994). "The Philosopher and the Female in the Political Thought of Plato." In N. Tuana, ed., *Feminist Interpretations of Plato.* University Park: Pennsylvania State University Press. 67–85.

Schaefer, D. L. (1990). *The Political Philosophy of Montaigne.* Ithaca, N.Y.: Cornell University Press.

Schopenhauer, Arthur. (1974). *Parerga and Paralipomena: Short Philosophical Essays.* Tr. E. F. J. Payne. New York: Clarendon Press. 1974.

Scott, R. (1981a). "The Classical Tradition in Byzantine Historiography." In M. Mullett and R. Scott, ed., *Byzantium and the Classical Tradition.* Birmingham: Center for Byzantine Studies, University of Birmingham. 61–73.

————. (1981b). "Malalas and Justinian's Codification." In E. and M. Jeffreys and Ann Moffatt, ed., *Byzantine Papers: Proceedings of the First Australian Byzantine Studies Conference* (= *Byzantina Australiensia* v. 1). Canberra: Australian Association for Byzantine Studies. 12–31.

————. (1985). "Malalas, *The Secret History*, and Justinian's Propaganda." *DOP* 39: 99–109.

———. (1987). "Justinian's Coinage and Easter Reforms and the Date of the *Secret History*." *Byzantine and Modern Greek Studies* 11: 215–221.

Segal, J. B. (1955). "Mesopotamian Communities from Julian to the Rise of Islam." *Proceedings of the British Academy* 41: 109–139.

Setton, K. M. (1941). *Christian Attitude Toward the Emperor in the Fourth Century, Especially as Shown in Addresses to the Emperor*. New York: Columbia University Press.

Ševčenko, I. (1954). "Nicolaus Cabasilas' Correspondence and the Treatment of Late Byzantine Literary Texts." *Byzantinsche Zeitschrift* 47: 49–59.

Shukman, H. (1999). *Stalin*. Stroud: Sutton.

Skedros, J. C. (1999). *Saint Demetrios of Thessaloniki: Civic Patron and Divine Protector, 4th-7th Centuries CE*. Harrisburg, Pa.: Trinity Press International.

Soyter, G. (1939). "Prokop als Geschichtschreiber des Vandalen- und Gotenkrieges." *Neue Jahrbücher für Antike und deutsche Bildung* 2: 97–108.

———. (1951). "Die Glaubwürdigkeit des Geschichtschreibers Prokopios von Kaisareia." *BZ* 44: 541–545.

Spawforth, A. (1994). "Symbol of Unity? The Persian-Wars Tradition in the Roman Empire." In S. Hornblower, ed., *Greek Historiography*. New York: Clarendon Press. 233–247.

Stafford, E. (2000). *Worshipping Virtues: Personification and the Divine in Ancient Greece*. London: Duckworth.

Starnes, C. (1990). *The New Republic: A Commentary on Book I of More's* Utopia *Showing Its Relation to Plato's* Republic. Waterloo, Ont.: Wilfrid Laurier University Press.

Stein, E. (1949). *Histoire du Bas-Empire*. v. 2: *De la disparition de l'empire d'occident à la mort de Justinien (476–565)*. Paris: Desclée de Brouwer.

Strauss, L. (1958). *Thoughts on Machiavelli*. Glencoe, Ill.: Free Press.

———. (1989). "Thucydides: The Meaning of Political History." In Strauss, *The Rebirth of Classical Political Rationalism: An Introduction to the Thought of Leo Strauss*. Ed. T. L. Pangle. Chicago: University of Chicago Press. 72–102.

———. (1991). *On Tyranny, Including the Strauss-Kojève Correspondence*. Ed. V. Gourevitch and M. S. Roth. 2nd ed. New York: Free Press.

Sundermann, W. (1964). "Zur Proskynesis im sasanidischen Iran." *Mitteilungen des Instituts für Orientforschung*. 275–286.

Swanson, J. A. (1992). *The Public and the Private in Aristotle's Political Philosophy*. Ithaca, N.Y.: Cornell University Press.

Syme, R. (1958). *Tacitus*. Oxford: Clarendon Press.

———. (2002). *Sallust*. 2nd ed. Berkeley: University of California Press.

Synelli, K. (1986). *Οἱ διπλωματικὲς σχέσεις Βυζαντίου καὶ Περσίας ἕως τὸν ΣΤ' αἰώνα*. Athens: Historical Publications St. D. Basilopoulos.

Tardieu, M. (1986). "Sabiens coraniques et "Sabiens" de Harran." *Journal asiatique* 274: 1–44.

———. (1987). "Les calendriers en usage a Harran d'après les sources arabes et le Commentaire de Simplicius a la Physique d'Aristote." In I. Hadot, ed., *Simplicius—Sa vie, son oeuvre, sa survie*. Berlin: W. de Gruyter. 40–57.

Tarrant, H. A. S. (1998). "Olympiodorus and History." In T. W. Hillard, R. A.

Kearsley, C. E. V. Nixon, and A. M. Nobbs, eds., *Ancient History in a Modern University*. v. 2: *Early Christianity, Late Antiquity and Beyond*. NSW, Australia: Macquarie University. 417–425.

Teuffel, W. S. (1871). "Der Geschichtschreiber Prokopius." In Teuffel, *Studien und Charakteristiken zur griechischen und römischen sowie zur deutschen Literaturgeschichte*. Leipzig: Teubner. 191–236.

Thiel, R. (1999). *Simplikios und das Ende der neuplatonischen Schule in Athen*. Stuttgart: Akademie der Wissenschaften und der Literatur.

Thornton, B. S. (1997). *Eros: The Myth of Ancient Greek Sexuality*. Boulder, Colo.: Westview Press.

Tinnefeld, F. H. (1971). *Kategorien der Kaiserkritik in der byzantinischen Historiographie von Prokop bis Niketas Choniates*. Munich: W. Fink.

Toland, John. (1720). *Tetradymus*. London: J. Brotherton and W. Meadows.

Too, Y. L. (1995). *The Rhetoric of Identity in Isocrates: Text, Power, Pedagogy*. Cambridge: Cambridge University Press.

Topping, E. C. (1976). "The Apostle Peter, Justinian and Romanos the Melodos." *Byzantine and Modern Greek Studies* 2: 1–15.

Traina, G. (2001). "Faustus "of Byzantium," Procopius, and the *Armenian History* (Jacoby, *FGrHist* 679, 3–4)." In C. Sode and S. Takacs, eds., *Novum Millennium: Studies on Byzantine History and Culture Dedicated to Paul Speck*. Burlington, Vt.: Ashgate. 405–413.

Treadgold, W. (1995). *Byzantium and Its Army, 284–1081*. Stanford, Calif.: Stanford University Press.

Treitinger, O. (1956). *Die oströmische Kaiser- und Reichsidee nach ihrer Gestaltung im höfischen Zeremoniell. Vom oströmischen Staats- und Reichsgedanken*. Darmstadt: H. Genter.

Trombley, F. R. (1985). "Paganism in the Greek World at the End of Antiquity: The Case of Rural Anatolia and Greece." *Harvard Theological Review* 78: 327–352.

Valdenberg, V. (1925). "Les idées politiques dans les fragments attribués à Pierre le Patrice." *Byzantion* 2: 55–76.

Van Dam, R. (2002). *Kingdom of Snow: Roman Rule and Greek Culture in Cappadocia*. Philadelphia: University of Pennsylvania Press.

Vasiliev, A. A. (1950). *Justin the First: An Introduction to the Epoch of Justianian the Great*. Cambridge, Mass.: Harvard University Press.

Veh, O. (1950–1953). *Zur Geschichtsschreibung und Weltauffassung des Prokop von Caesarea* (= *Wissenschaftliche Beilage zum Jahresbericht* [1950/51, 1951/52, and 1952/53] *des Gymnasiums Bayreuth*). Bayreuth: Vorwort.

Vercleyen, F. (1988). "Tremblements de terre à Constantinople: l'impact sur la population." *Byzantion* 58: 155–173.

Veyne, P. (1988). *Did the Greek Believe in Their Myths? An Essay on the Constitutive Imagination*. Tr. P. Wissing. Chicago: University of Chicago Press.

Vidal-Naquet, P. (1986). *The Black Hunter: Forms of Thought and Forms of Society in the Greek World*. Tr. A. Szegedy-Maszak. Baltimore: Johns Hopkins University Press.

Walbank, F. W. (1957). *A Historical Commentary on Polybius*. v. 1: *Commentary on Books I–VI*. Oxford: Clarendon Press.

————. (1972). *Polybius*. Berkeley: University of California Press.

Walker, J. T. (2002). "The Limits of Late Antiquity: Philosophy Between Rome and Iran." *The Ancient World* 33 (2002): 45–69.

Warry, J. (1995). *Warfare in the Classical World: An Illustrated Encyclopedia of Weapons, Warriors and Warfare in the Ancient Civilizations of Greece and Rome*. Norman: University of Oklahoma Press.

Waser, O. (1915). "Tyche in bildlicher Darstellung." In W. H. Roscher, ed., *Ausführliches Lexikon der griechischen und römischen Mythologie*. Leipzig: Teubner. v. 5, cols. 1357–1380.

Westlake, H. D. (1968). *Individuals in Thucydides*. London: Cambridge University Press.

Whitby, Ma. (2000). "Procopius' *Buildings*, Book I: A Panegyrical Perspective." *Antiquité tardive* 8: 45–47.

Whitby, Mi. (1986). "Procopius' Description of Dara (*Buildings* II.1–3)." In P. Freeman and D. Kennedy, eds., *The Defence of the Roman and Byzantine East* (= *BAR International Series* v. 297). Oxford: B.A.R. 737–783.

————. (1988). *The Emperor Maurice and His Historian: Theophylact Simocatta on Persian and Balkan Warfare*. Oxford: Clarendon Press.

————. (1992). "Greek Historical Writing After Procopius: Variety and Vitality." In Av. Cameron and L. I. Conrad, eds., *The Byzantine and Early Islamic Near East*. v. 1: *Problems in the Literary Source Material*. Princeton, N.J.: Darwin Press. 25–80

————. (1994). "The Persian King at War." In E. Dabrowa, ed., *The Roman and Byzantine Army in the East*. Krakow: Drukarnia Uniwersytetu Jagiellonskiego. 227–263.

————. (2000). "Pride and Prejudice in Procopius' Buildings: Imperial Images in Constantinople." *Antiquité tardive* 8: 59–66.

Wiesehöfer, J. (1996). *Ancient Persia from 550 BC to 650 AD*. Tr. A. Azodi. London and New York: I. B. Taurus.

Wolfram, H. (1964). "Fortune in mittelalterlichen Stammesgeschichten." *Mitteilungen des Instituts für österreichische Geschichtsforschung* 72: 1–33.

————. (1988). *History of the Goths*. Tr. T. J. Dunlap. 2nd ed. Berkeley, Los Angeles, and London: University of California Press.

————. (1990). *The Roman Empire and Its Germanic Peoples*. Tr. T. Dunlap. Berkeley, Los Angeles, and London: University of California Press.

Wootton, D. (1983). *Paolo Sarpi: Between Renaissance and Enlightenment*. Cambridge and New York: Cambridge University Press.

Worp, K. A. (1982). "Byzantine Imperial Titulature in the Greek Documentary Papyri: The Oath Formulas." *Zeitschrift für Papyrologie und Epigraphik* 45: 199–226.

Yarshater, E. (1971). "Were the Sasanians Heirs to the Achaemenids?" In *Accademia Nazionale dei Lincei: Problemi Attuali di Scienza e di Cultura* 160: *La Persia nel Medioevo*. Rome. 517–531.

Young, F. M. (1973). "Insight or Incoherence? The Greek Fathers on God and Evil." *Journal of Ecclesiastical History* 24: 113–126.

Zagorin, P. (1990). *Ways of Lying: Dissimulation, Persecution, and Conformity in Early Modern Europe*, Cambridge, Mass.: Harvard University Press.

Index

People mentioned throughout the book (Procopius, Justinian, Romans, Greeks, Byzantines, Persians, barbarians, pagans, Christians, and heretics) are not included, nor are broad geographical names (Europe, Italy, Syria, etc.). References to modern scholars are not comprehensive and focus on discussions of Procopius as a writer.